Backwards Game

BaKeGyAMON

Quiet in the library!

How to Deceive

Lie And Succeed

Buns Are Scary

The Easy Life

Win By Lying

TACTICS OF

Easy Targets

VOL. 3

MITSUHISA TAMURA

Original concept by
Kazuhiro Fujita

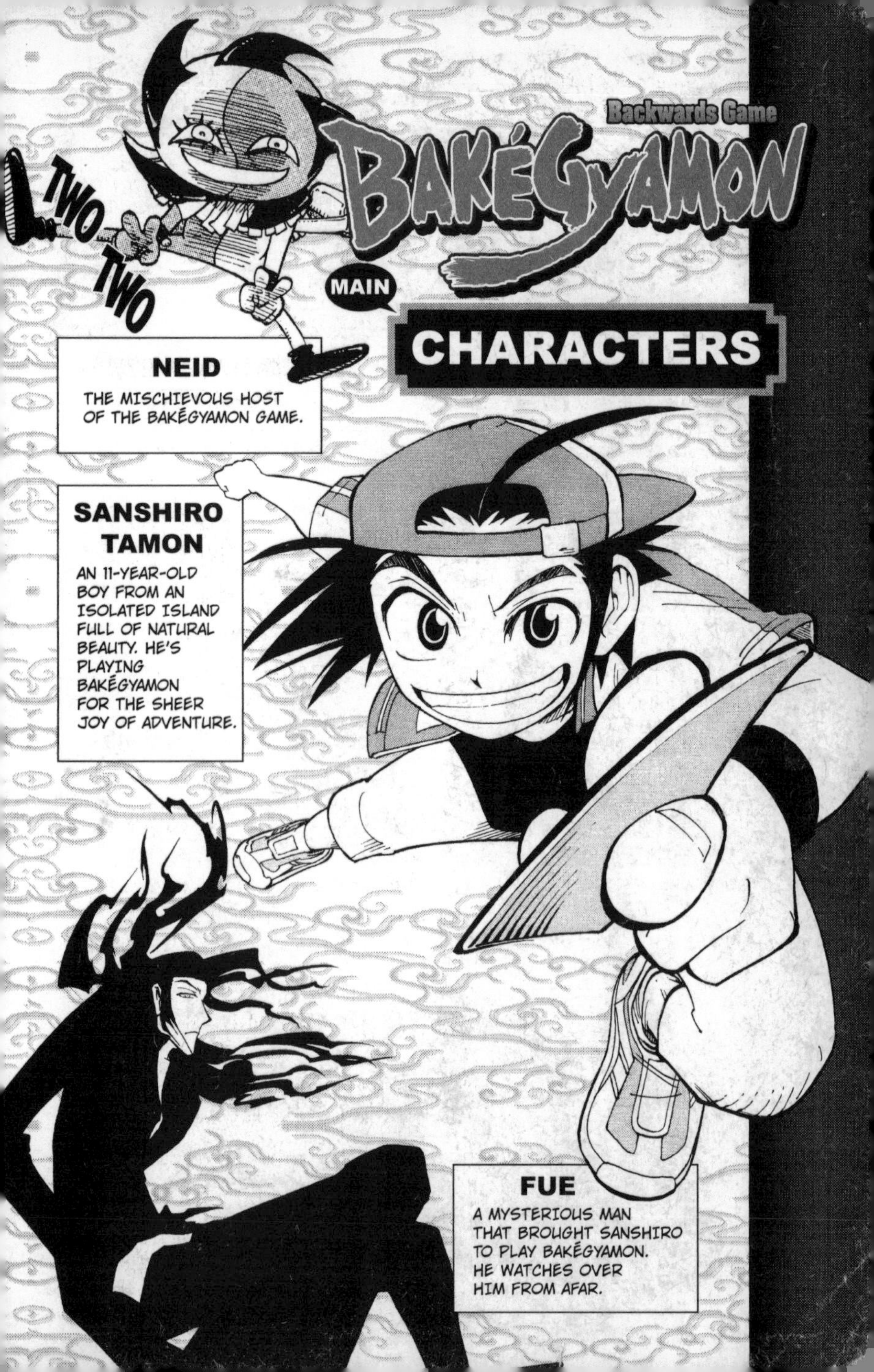
Backwards Game
BAKÉGYAMON
MAIN
CHARACTERS
TWO TWO
NEID
THE MISCHIEVOUS HOST OF THE BAKÉGYAMON GAME.
SANSHIRO TAMON
AN 11-YEAR-OLD BOY FROM AN ISOLATED ISLAND FULL OF NATURAL BEAUTY. HE'S PLAYING BAKÉGYAMON FOR THE SHEER JOY OF ADVENTURE.
FUE
A MYSTERIOUS MAN THAT BROUGHT SANSHIRO TO PLAY BAKÉGYAMON. HE WATCHES OVER HIM FROM AFAR.

SHIORI FUMIZUKI

A BRAINY BAKÉGYAMON PLAYER. SHE CONSIDERS YUKINOSHIN HER BIGGEST RIVAL.

LONDON

HIS REAL NAME IS TOSHIO SAEGUSA. HE WANTS TO BECOME A MUSICIAN BUT HE'S TONE DEAF. HIS MANTRA IN LIFE IS TO BE *COOL*.

MOHAWK

A TROUBLEMAKER WHO'S QUICK TO PICK FIGHTS. HE PUTS A LOT OF EFFORT INTO HIS HAIRSTYLE.

YUKINOSHIN KABURAGI

AN UNASSUMING LAID-BACK PLAYER, HE HAS THE SKILL TO BE ONE OF THE BEST.

MICK

HIS REAL NAME IS MIKIHARU KAWAGUCHI. A SMOOTH TALKER AND A CHEAT, HE'S TURNING PEOPLE AGAINST HIM.

"BAKÉGYAMON" IS A GAME FOR CHILDREN CREATED BY MONSTERS. PLAYED ONCE EVERY 44 YEARS IN "BACKWARDS JAPAN," WHOEVER WINS THE GAME WILL BE GRANTED ONE WISH. ELEVEN-YEAR-OLD SANSHIRO TAMON IS EAGER TO FOLLOW IN HIS ADVENTURER FATHER'S FOOTSTEPS AND JUMPS AT THE CHANCE TO PARTICIPATE. IF SANSHIRO WINS, HIS WISH WILL BE TO FREE ALL OF THE MONSTERS FROM THE GEKI FU CARDS. BUT FIRST, HE'LL HAVE TO BATTLE AGAINST ANOTHER PLAYER IN THE PUSHING BUNS CONTEST!

Contents

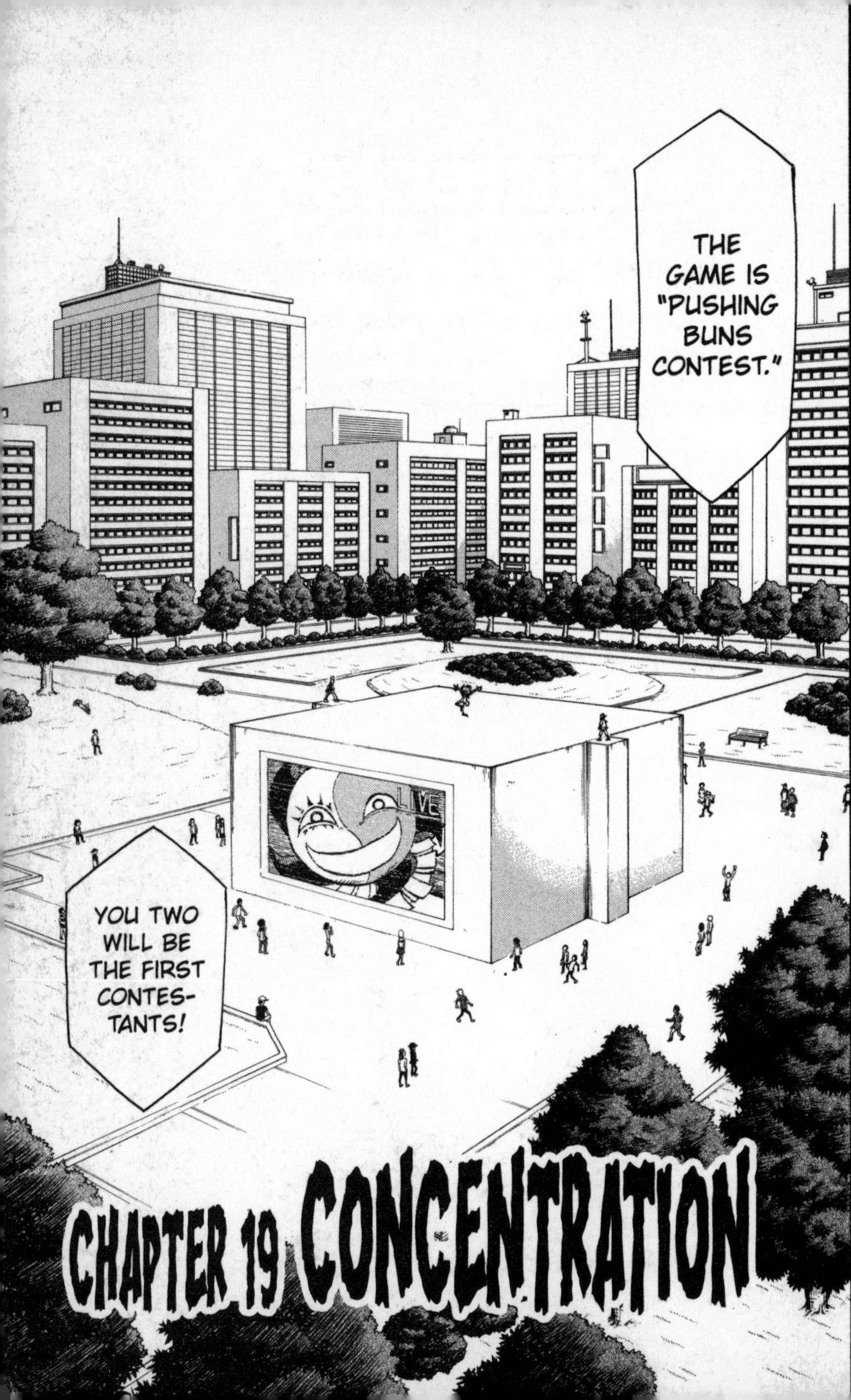
THE GAME IS "PUSHING BUNS CONTEST."
LIVE
YOU TWO WILL BE THE FIRST CONTES-TANTS!
CHAPTER 19 CONCENTRATION

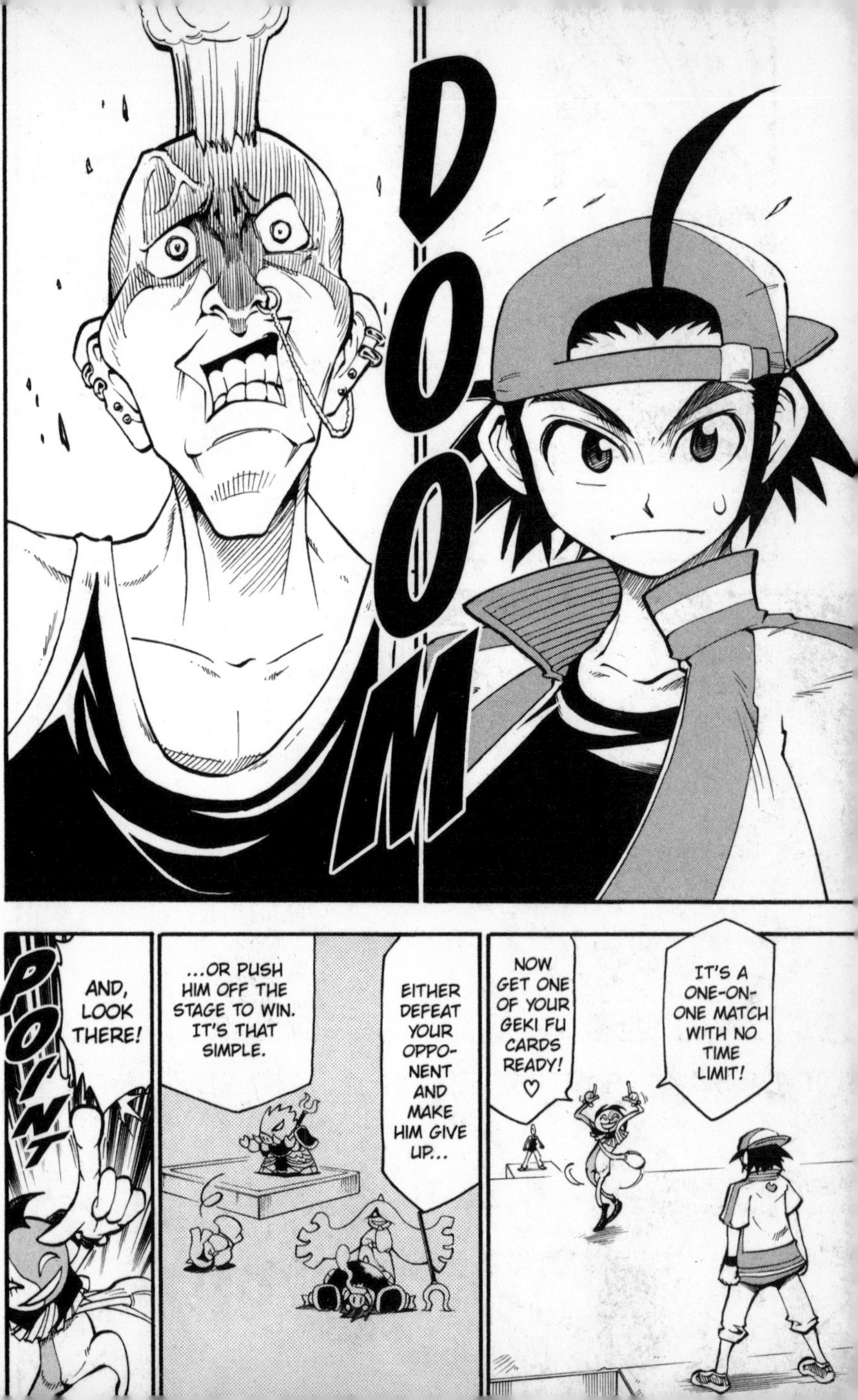
DOOOM
IT'S A ONE-ON-ONE MATCH WITH NO TIME LIMIT!
NOW GET ONE OF YOUR GEKI FU CARDS READY! ♡
EITHER DEFEAT YOUR OPPONENT AND MAKE HIM GIVE UP...
...OR PUSH HIM OFF THE STAGE TO WIN. IT'S THAT SIMPLE.
AND, LOOK THERE!
POINT

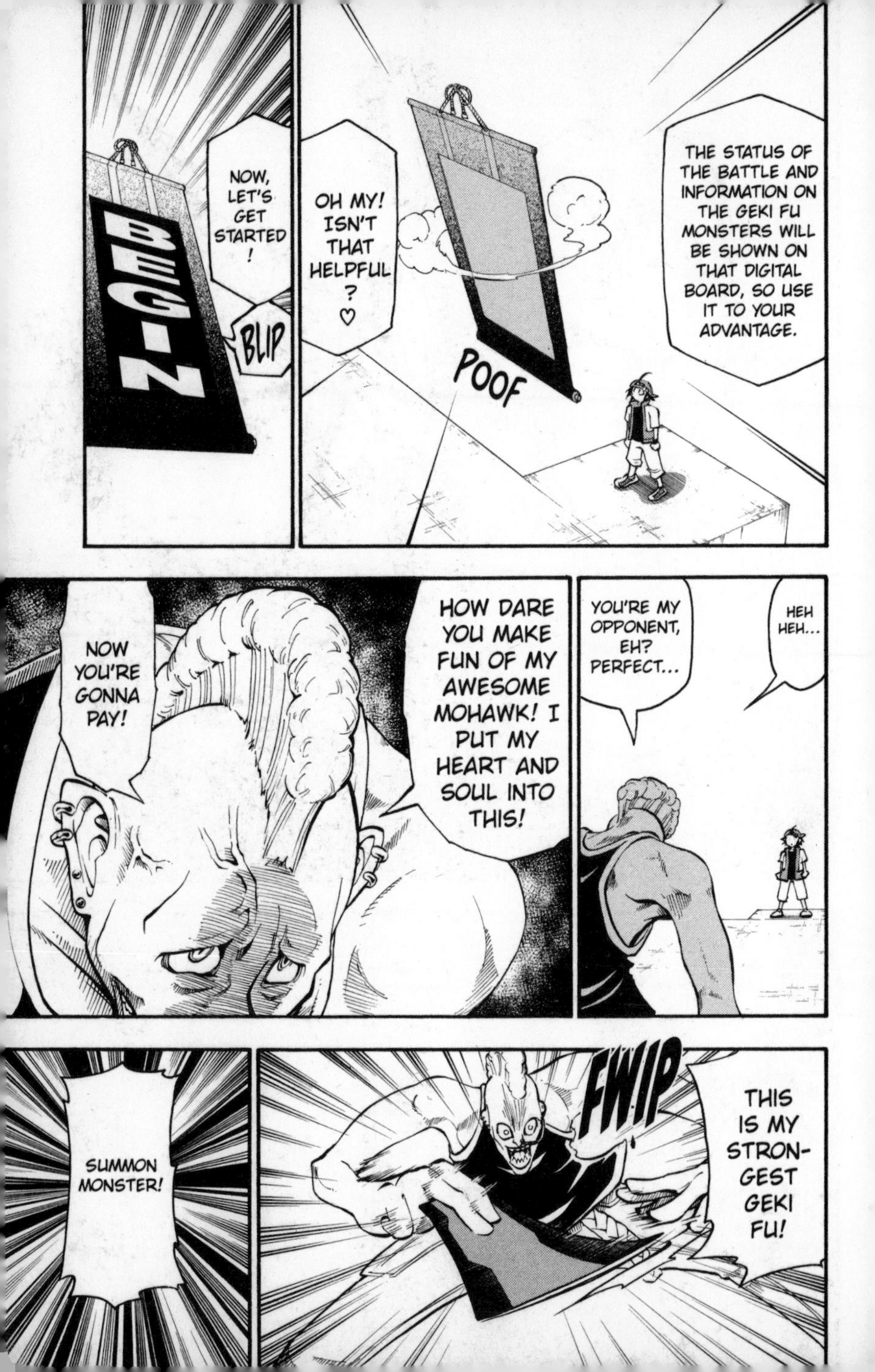
THE STATUS OF THE BATTLE AND INFORMATION ON THE GEKI FU MONSTERS WILL BE SHOWN ON THAT DIGITAL BOARD, SO USE IT TO YOUR ADVANTAGE.
OH MY! ISN'T THAT HELPFUL? ♡
POOF
NOW, LET'S GET STARTED!
BLIP
BEGIN
HEH HEH...
YOU'RE MY OPPONENT, EH? PERFECT...
HOW DARE YOU MAKE FUN OF MY AWESOME MOHAWK! I PUT MY HEART AND SOUL INTO THIS!
NOW YOU'RE GONNA PAY!
THIS IS MY STRONGEST GEKI FU!
FWIP
SUMMON MONSTER!

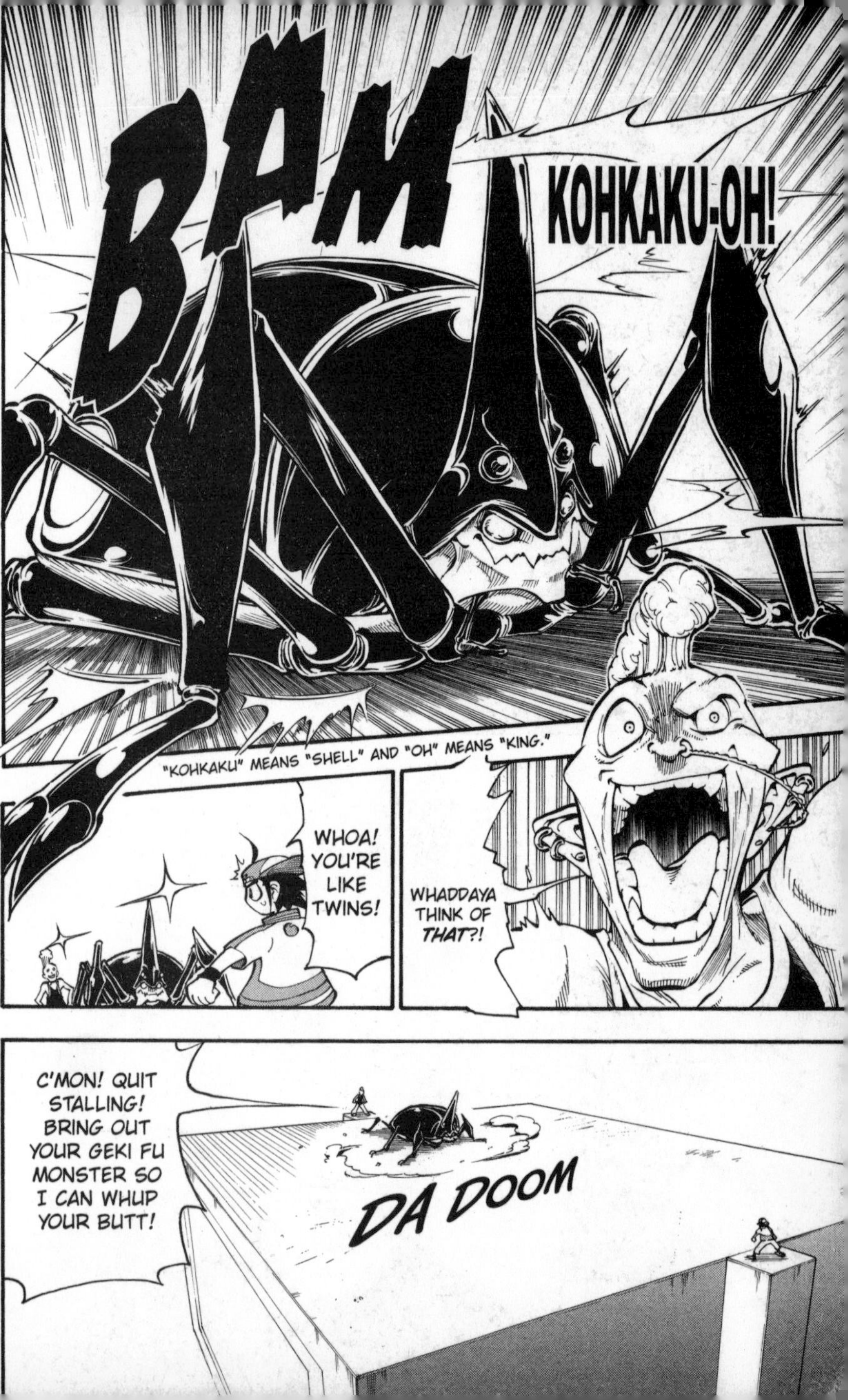
BAM
KOHKAKU-OH!
"KOHKAKU" MEANS "SHELL" AND "OH" MEANS "KING."
WHADDAYA THINK OF *THAT*?!
WHOA! YOU'RE LIKE TWINS!
C'MON! QUIT STALLING! BRING OUT YOUR GEKI FU MONSTER SO I CAN WHUP YOUR BUTT!
DA DOOM

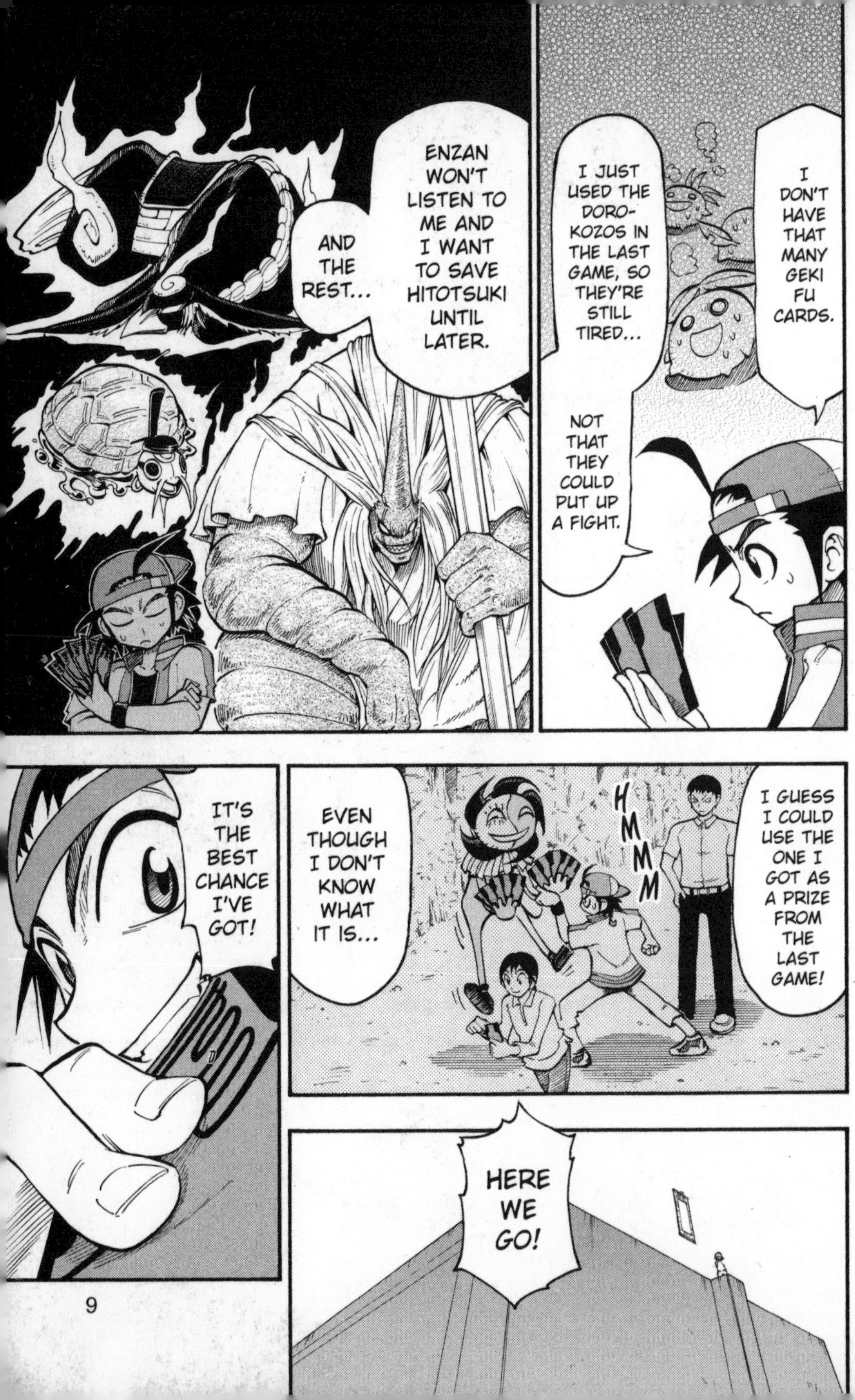
I DON'T HAVE THAT MANY GEKI FU CARDS.
I JUST USED THE DORO-KOZOS IN THE LAST GAME, SO THEY'RE STILL TIRED...
NOT THAT THEY COULD PUT UP A FIGHT.
ENZAN WON'T LISTEN TO ME AND I WANT TO SAVE HITOTSUKI UNTIL LATER.
AND THE REST...
I GUESS I COULD USE THE ONE I GOT AS A PRIZE FROM THE LAST GAME!
HMMMM
EVEN THOUGH I DON'T KNOW WHAT IT IS...
HERE WE GO!
IT'S THE BEST CHANCE I'VE GOT!

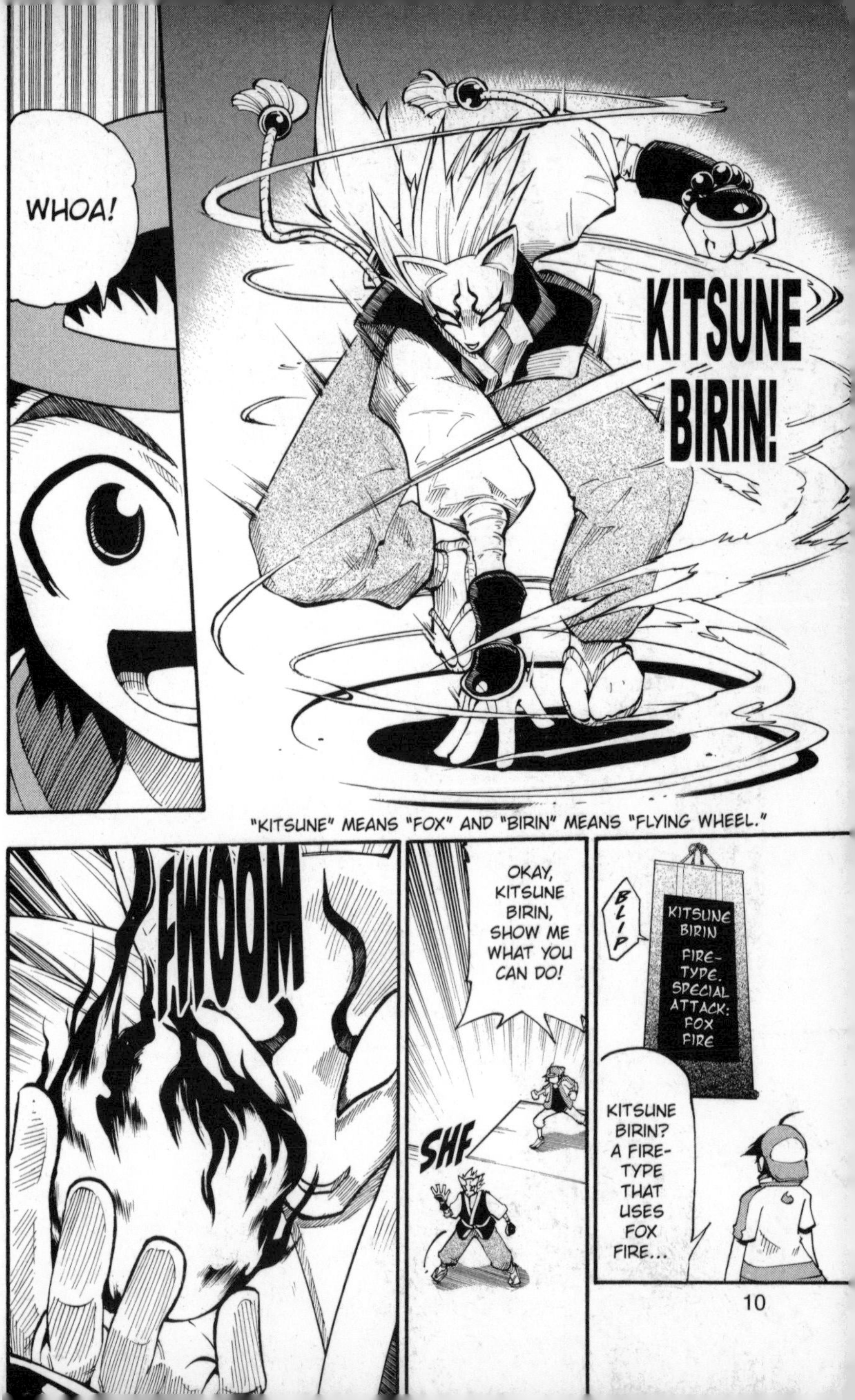
KITSUNE BIRIN!
WHOA!
"KITSUNE" MEANS "FOX" AND "BIRIN" MEANS "FLYING WHEEL."
KITSUNE BIRIN FIRE-TYPE. SPECIAL ATTACK: FOX FIRE
BLIP
KITSUNE BIRIN? A FIRE-TYPE THAT USES FOX FIRE...
OKAY, KITSUNE BIRIN, SHOW ME WHAT YOU CAN DO!
SHF
FWOOM

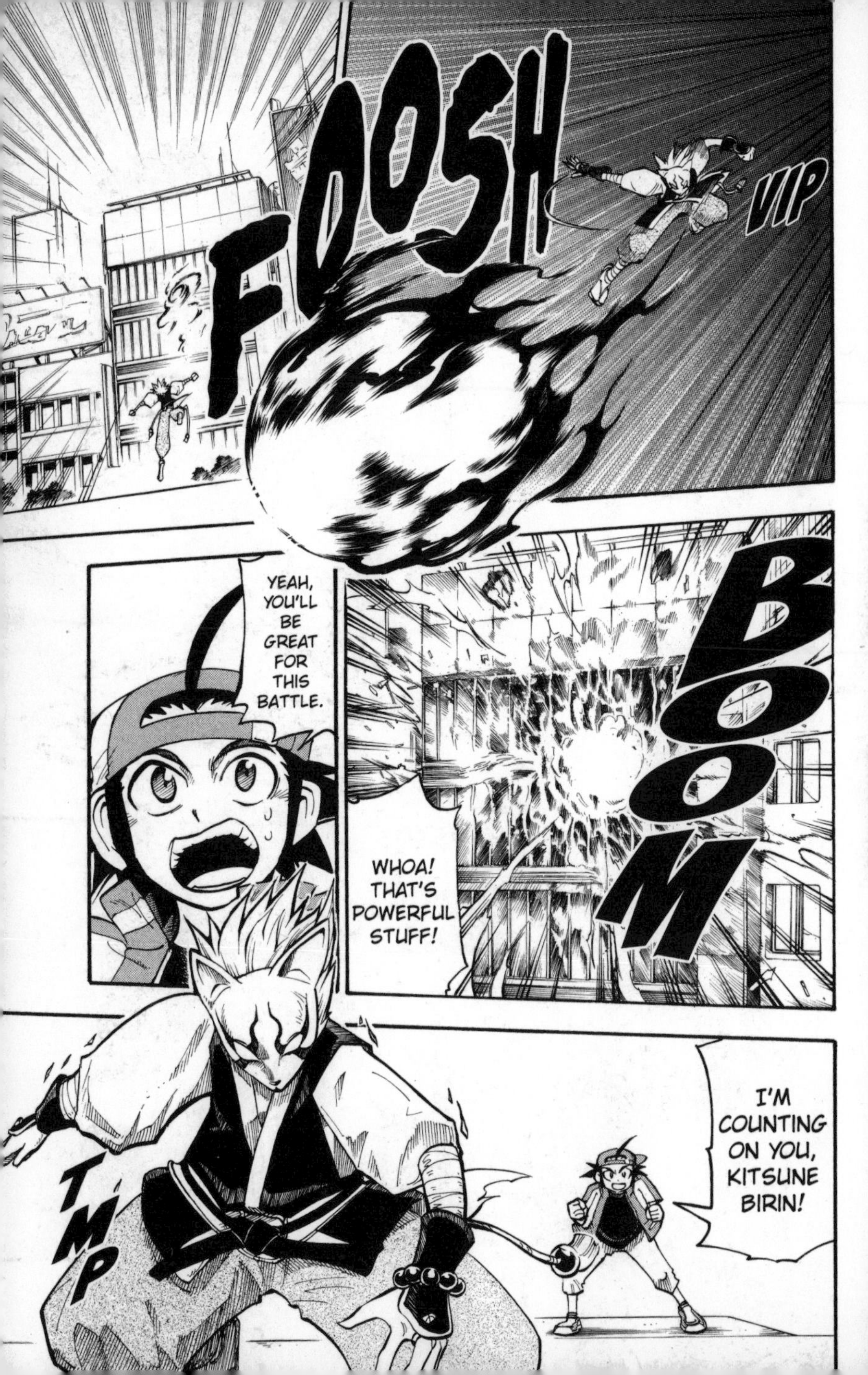
FOOSH
VIP
BOOM
WHOA! THAT'S POWERFUL STUFF!
YEAH, YOU'LL BE GREAT FOR THIS BATTLE.
I'M COUNTING ON YOU, KITSUNE BIRIN!
TMP

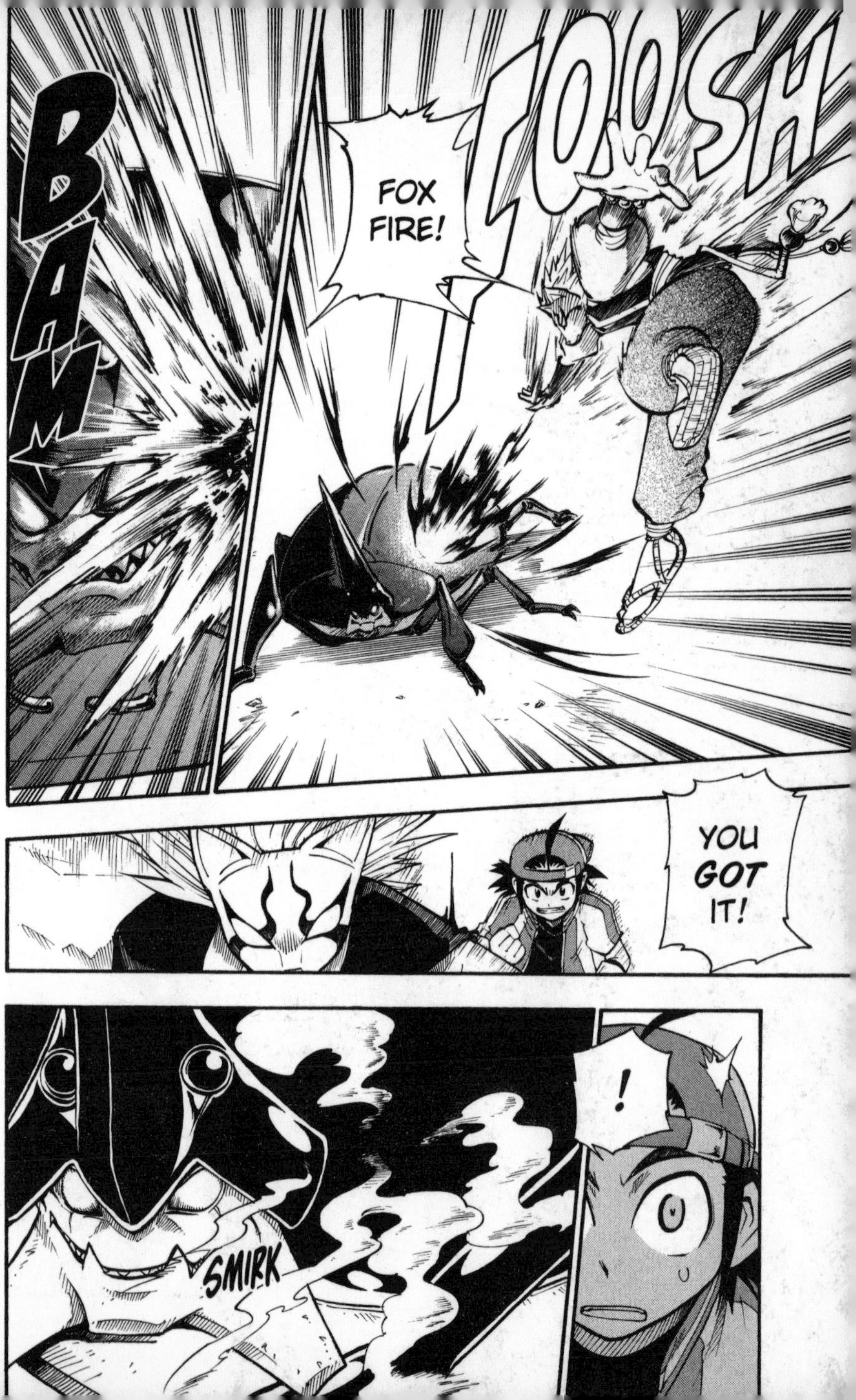
FWOOSH
FOX FIRE!
BAM
YOU GOT IT!
!
SMIRK

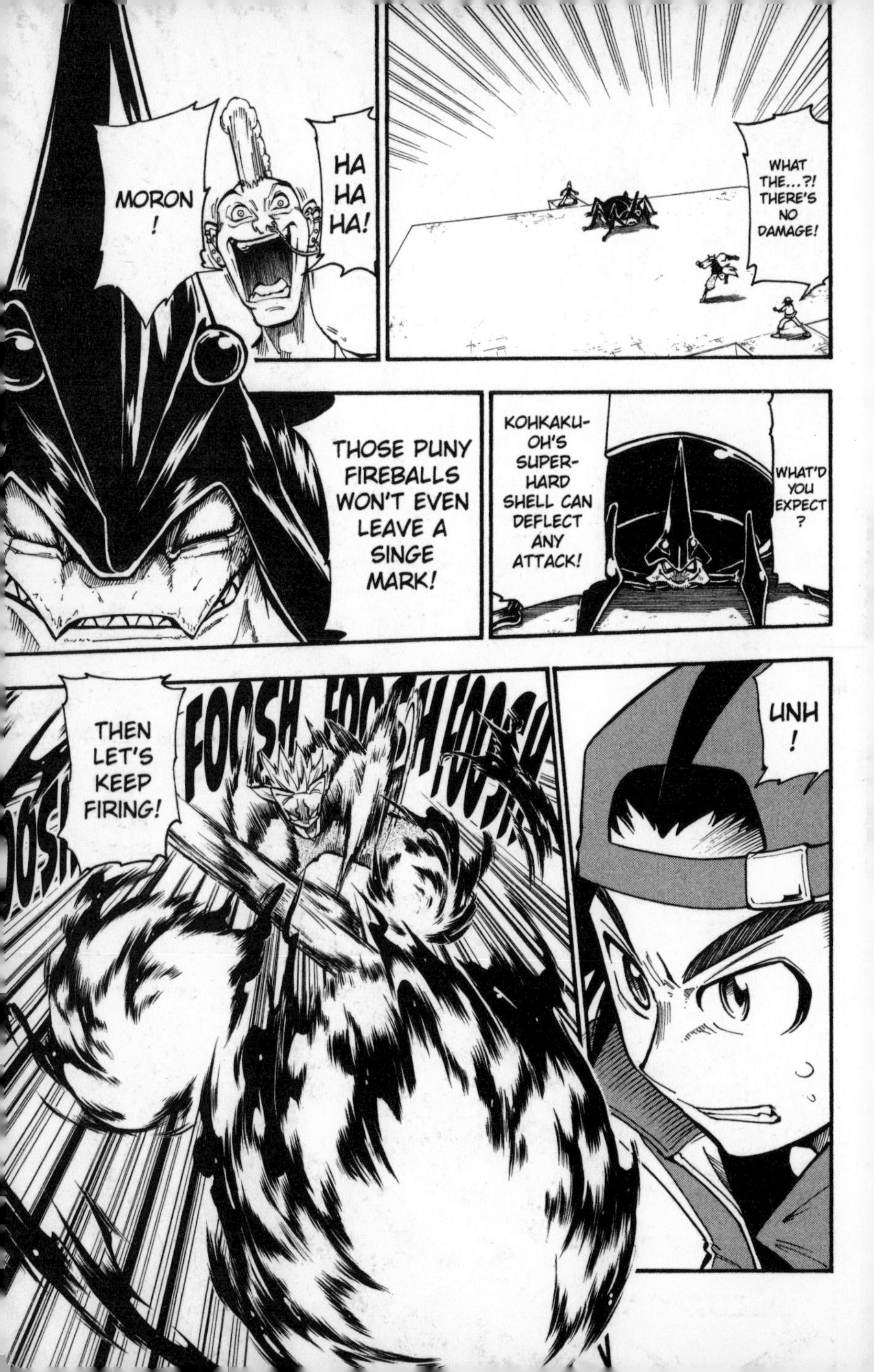
WHAT THE...?! THERE'S NO DAMAGE!
HA HA HA!
MORON!
WHAT'D YOU EXPECT?
KOHKAKU-OH'S SUPER-HARD SHELL CAN DEFLECT ANY ATTACK!
THOSE PUNY FIREBALLS WON'T EVEN LEAVE A SINGE MARK!
UNH!
THEN LET'S KEEP FIRING!
FOOSH FOOSH FOOSH

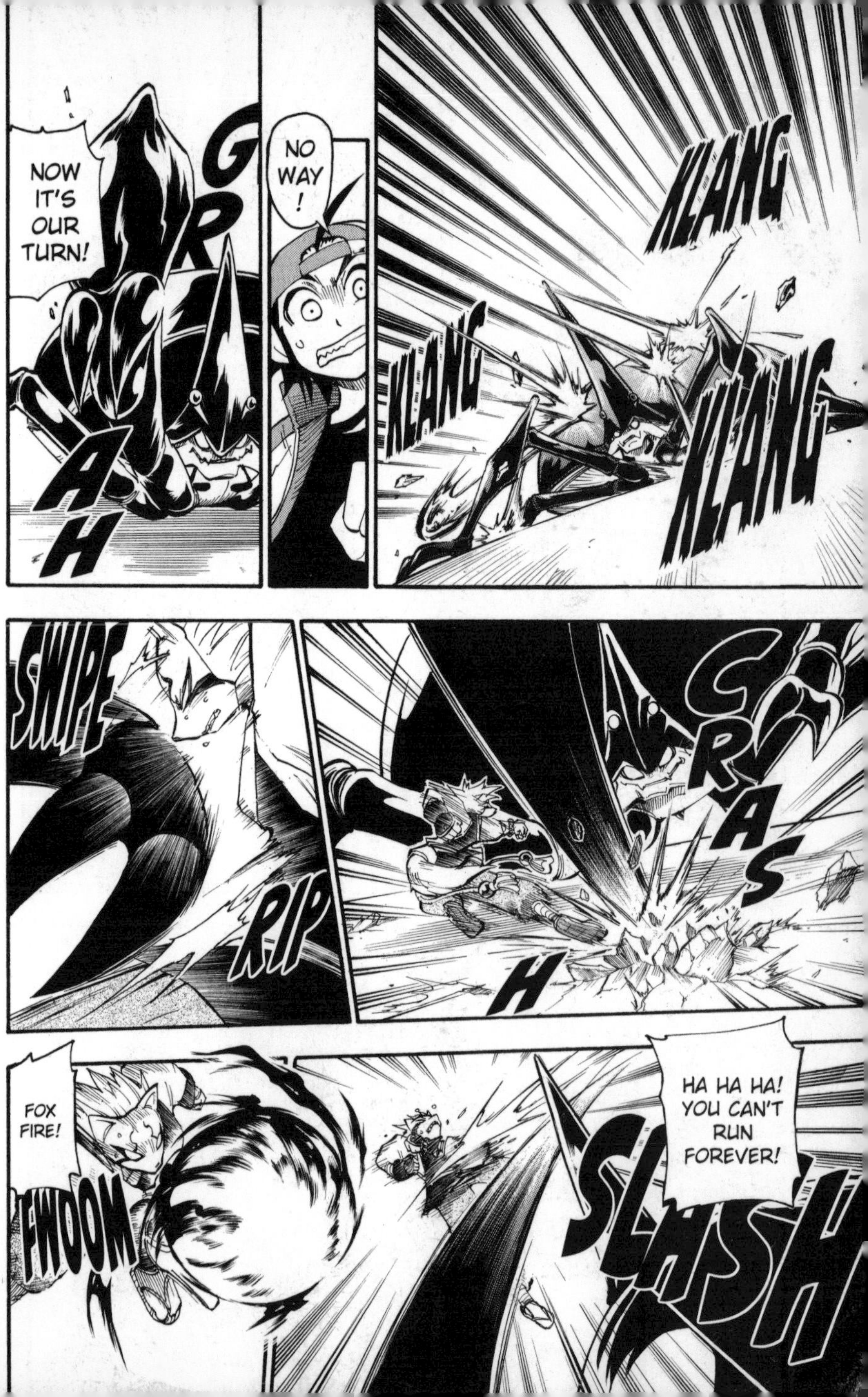
KLANG
KLANG
KLANG
KLANG
NO WAY!
NOW IT'S OUR TURN!
CRASH
SWIPE
RIP
HA HA HA! YOU CAN'T RUN FOREVER!
SLASH
FOX FIRE!
FWOOM

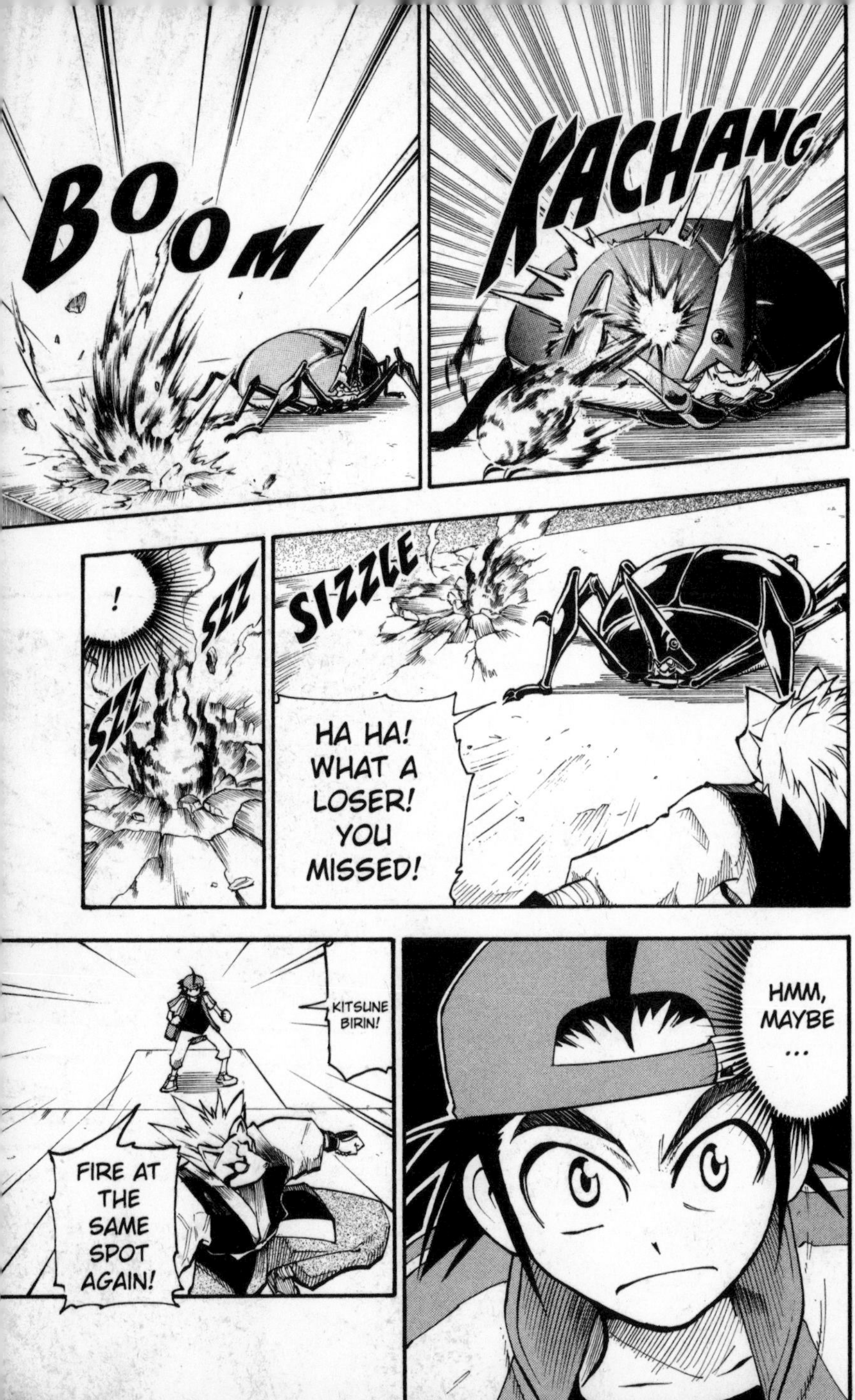
KACHANG
BOOOM
SIZZLE
HA HA! WHAT A LOSER! YOU MISSED!
SZZ SZZ
!
HMM, MAYBE ...
KITSUNE BIRIN!
FIRE AT THE SAME SPOT AGAIN!

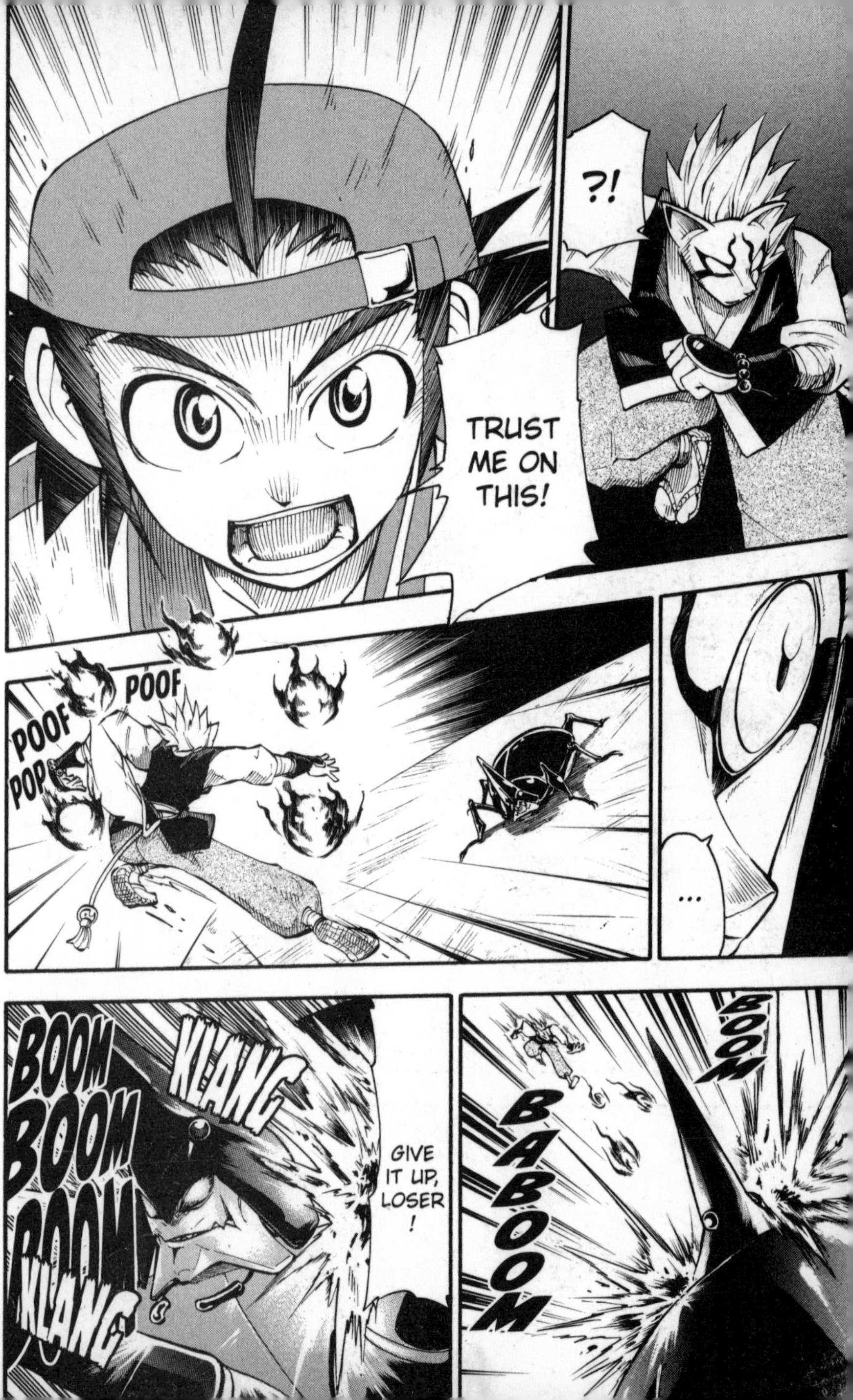
?!
TRUST ME ON THIS!
...
POOF
POOF
POP
BOOM
BABOOM
KLANG
BOOM
BOOM
BOOM
KLANG
GIVE IT UP, LOSER!

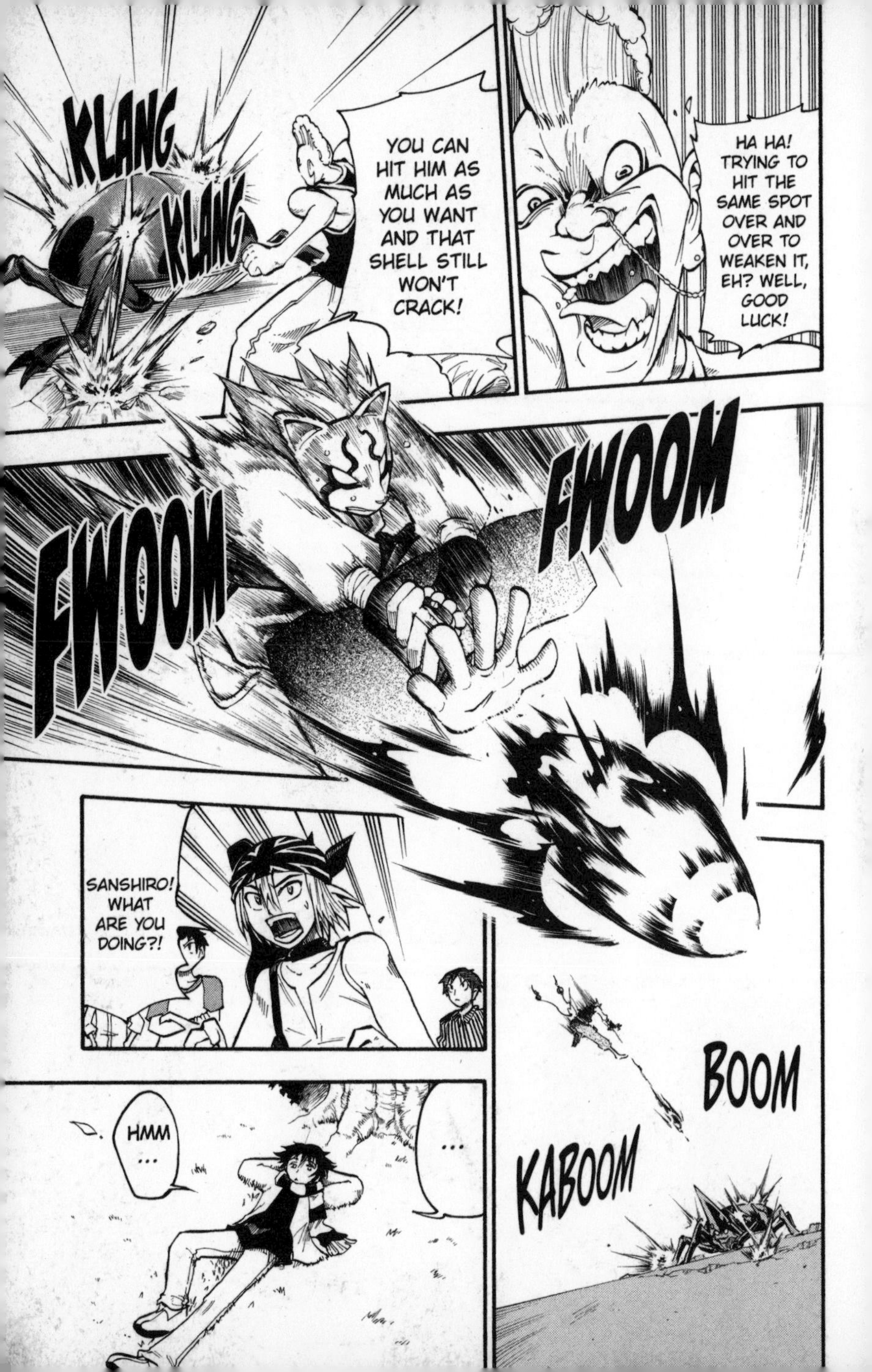
HA HA! TRYING TO HIT THE SAME SPOT OVER AND OVER TO WEAKEN IT, EH? WELL, GOOD LUCK!
YOU CAN HIT HIM AS MUCH AS YOU WANT AND THAT SHELL STILL WON'T CRACK!
KLANG
KLANG
FWOOM
FWOOM
BOOM
KABOOM
SANSHIRO! WHAT ARE YOU DOING?!
...
HMM ...

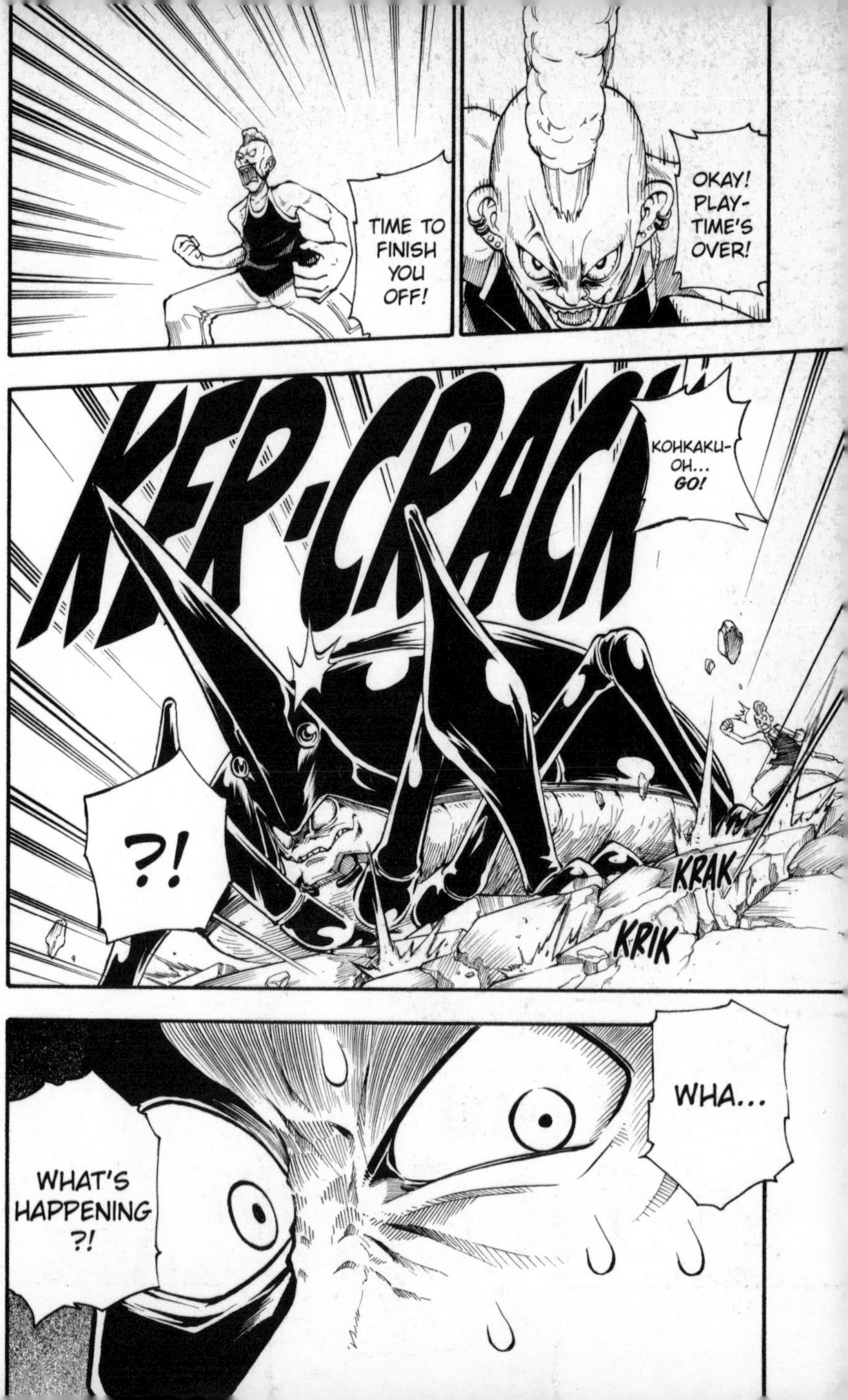
OKAY! PLAY-TIME'S OVER!
TIME TO FINISH YOU OFF!
KOHKAKU-OH... GO!
KER-CRACK
?!
KRAK
KRIK
WHA...
WHAT'S HAPPENING ?!

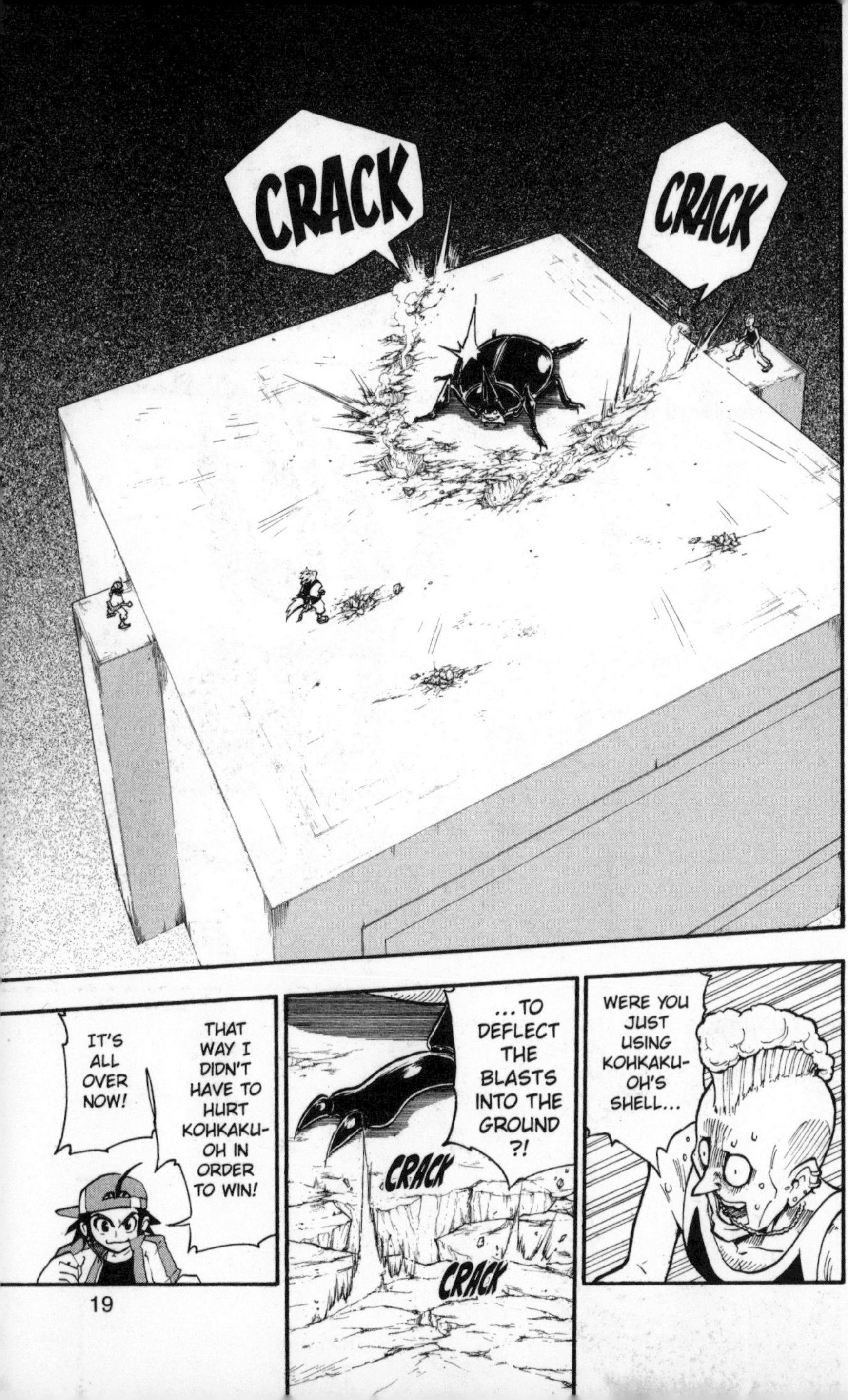
CRACK
CRACK
WERE YOU JUST USING KOHKAKU-OH'S SHELL...
...TO DEFLECT THE BLASTS INTO THE GROUND ?!
CRACK
CRACK
THAT WAY I DIDN'T HAVE TO HURT KOHKAKU-OH IN ORDER TO WIN!
IT'S ALL OVER NOW!

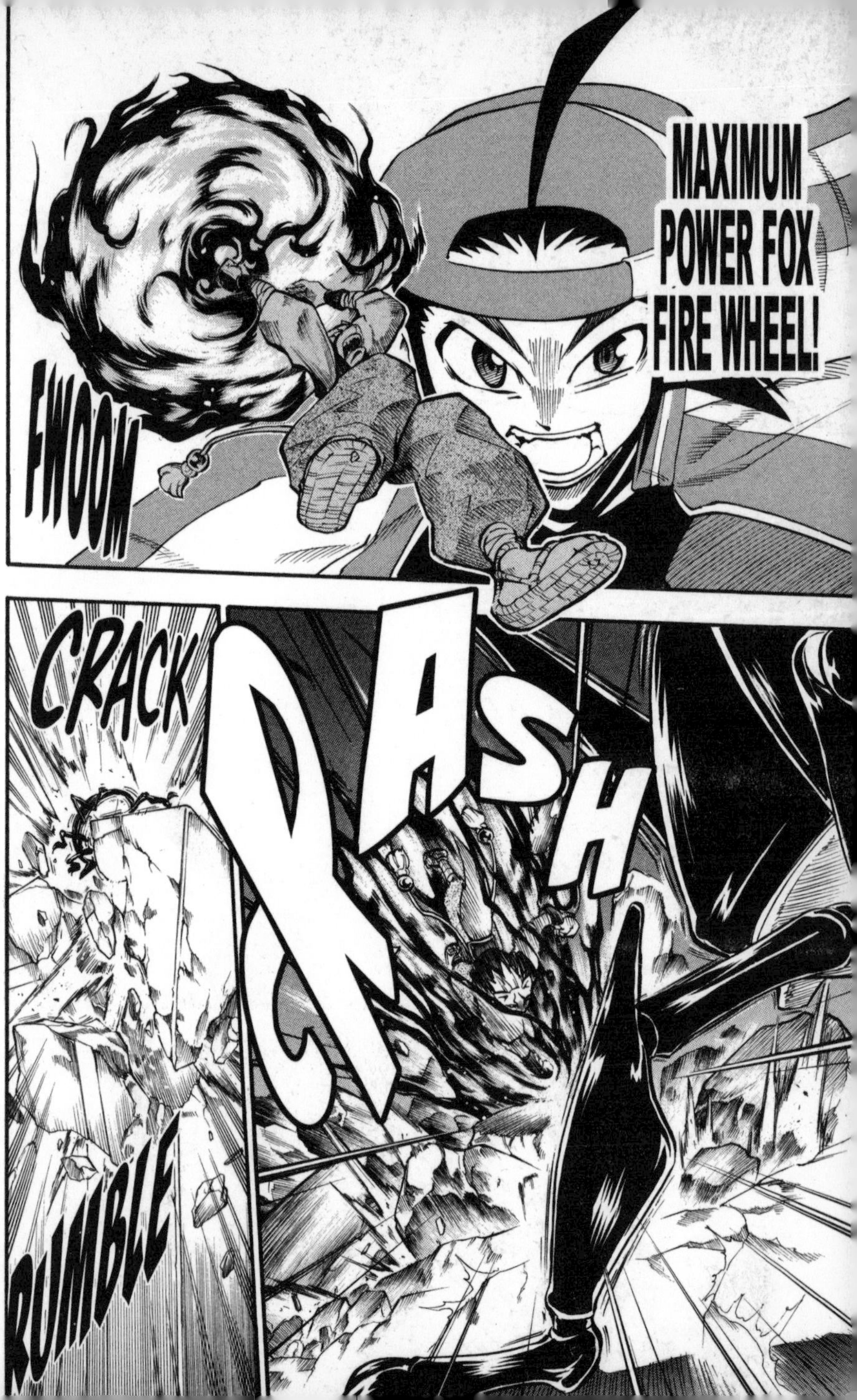
MAXIMUM POWER FOX FIRE WHEEL!
FWOOM
CRASH
CRACK
RUMBLE

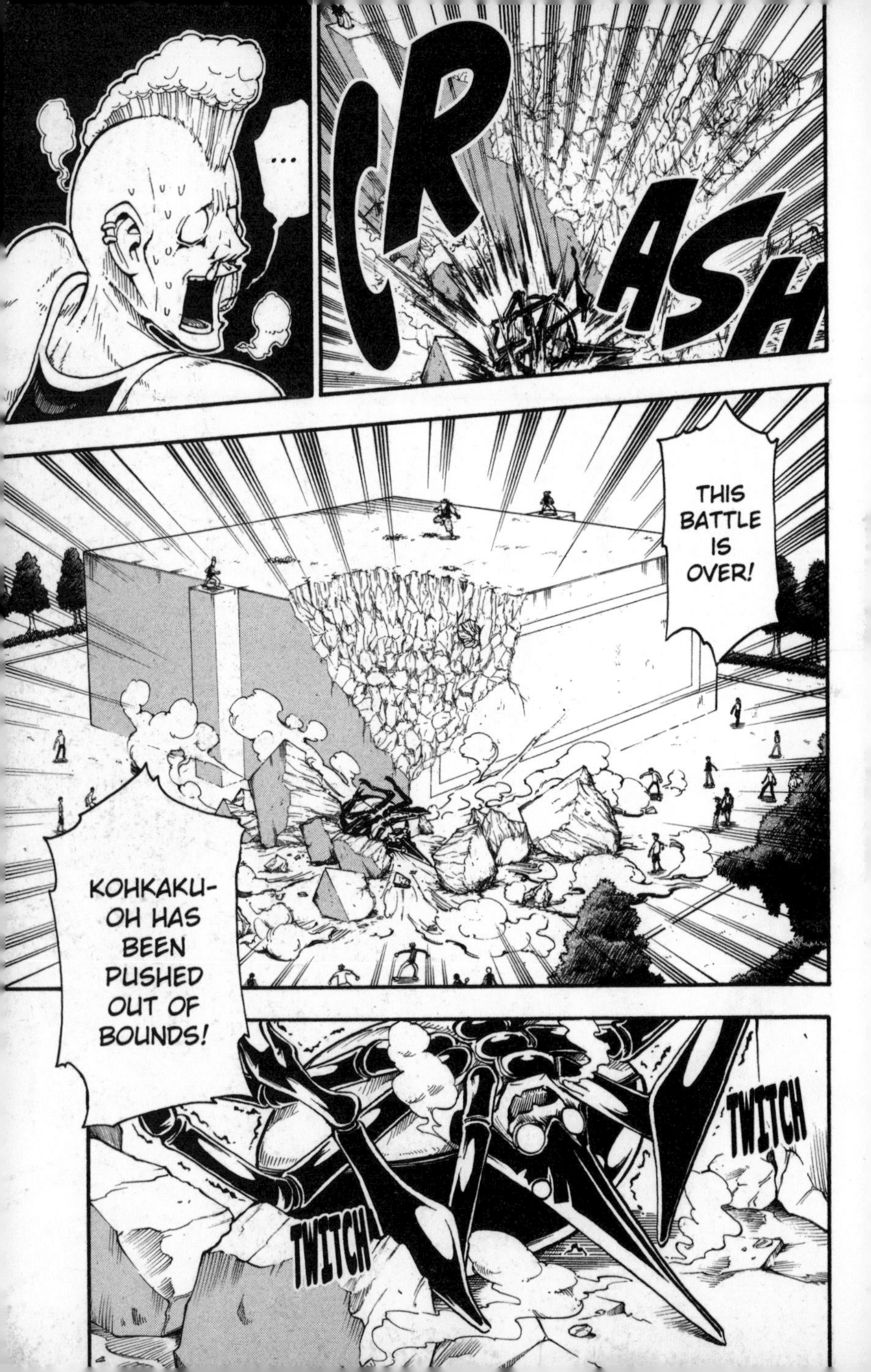
CRASH
...
THIS BATTLE IS OVER!
KOHKAKU-OH HAS BEEN PUSHED OUT OF BOUNDS!
TWITCH
TWITCH

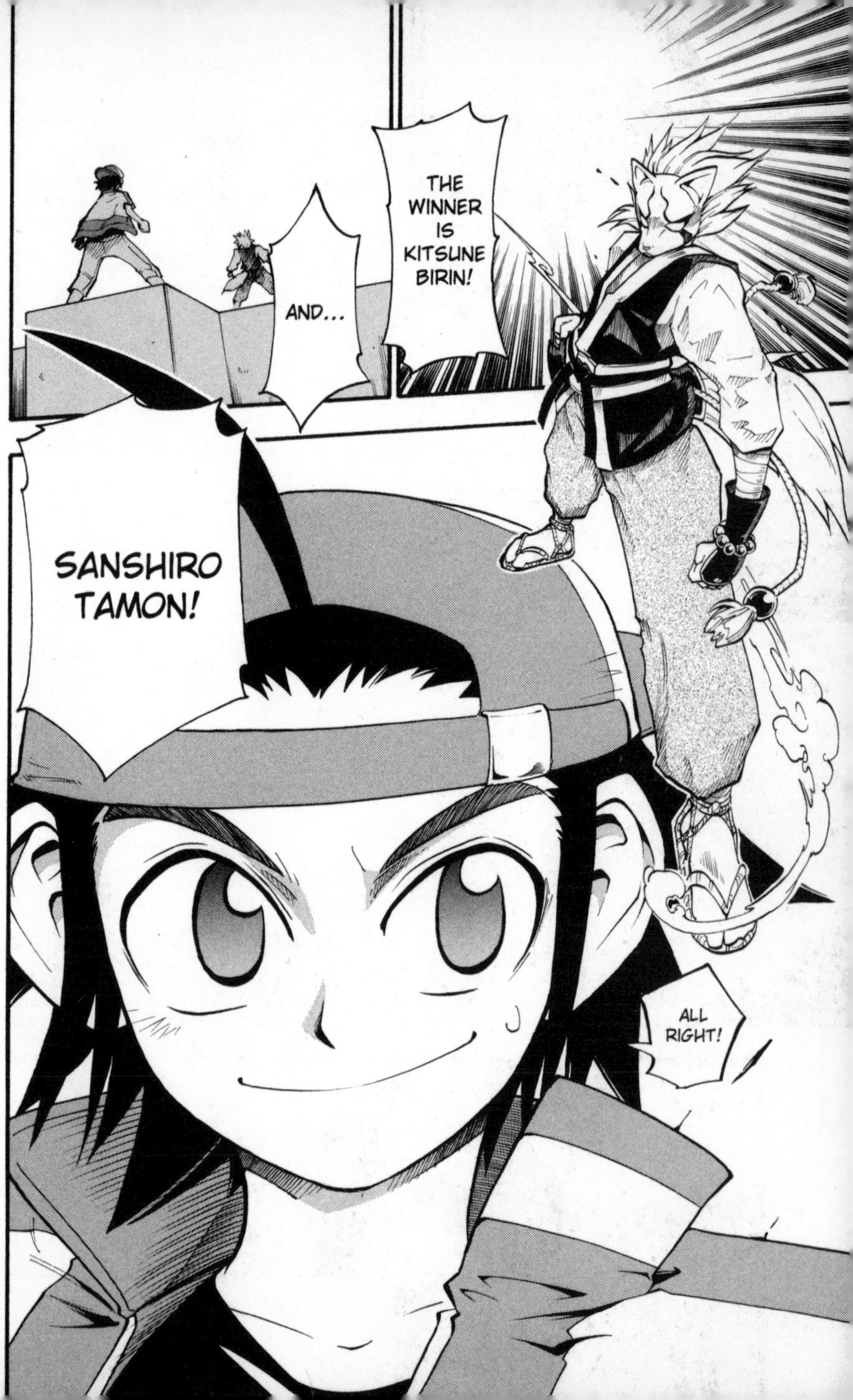
THE WINNER IS KITSUNE BIRIN!
AND...
SANSHIRO TAMON!
ALL RIGHT!

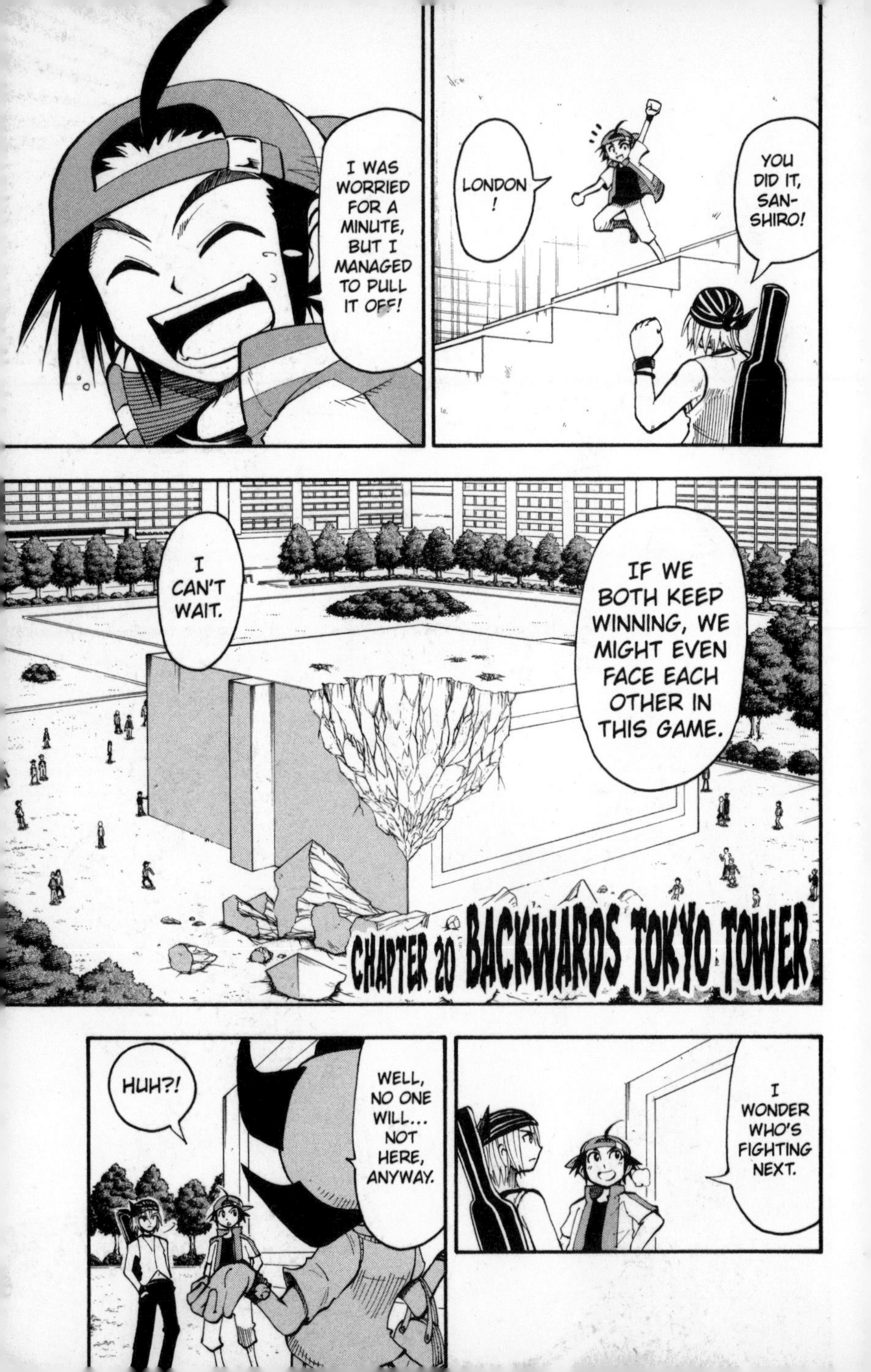
YOU DID IT, SAN-SHIRO!
LONDON!
I WAS WORRIED FOR A MINUTE, BUT I MANAGED TO PULL IT OFF!
IF WE BOTH KEEP WINNING, WE MIGHT EVEN FACE EACH OTHER IN THIS GAME.
I CAN'T WAIT.
CHAPTER 20 BACKWARDS TOKYO TOWER
I WONDER WHO'S FIGHTING NEXT.
WELL, NO ONE WILL... NOT HERE, ANYWAY.
HUH?!

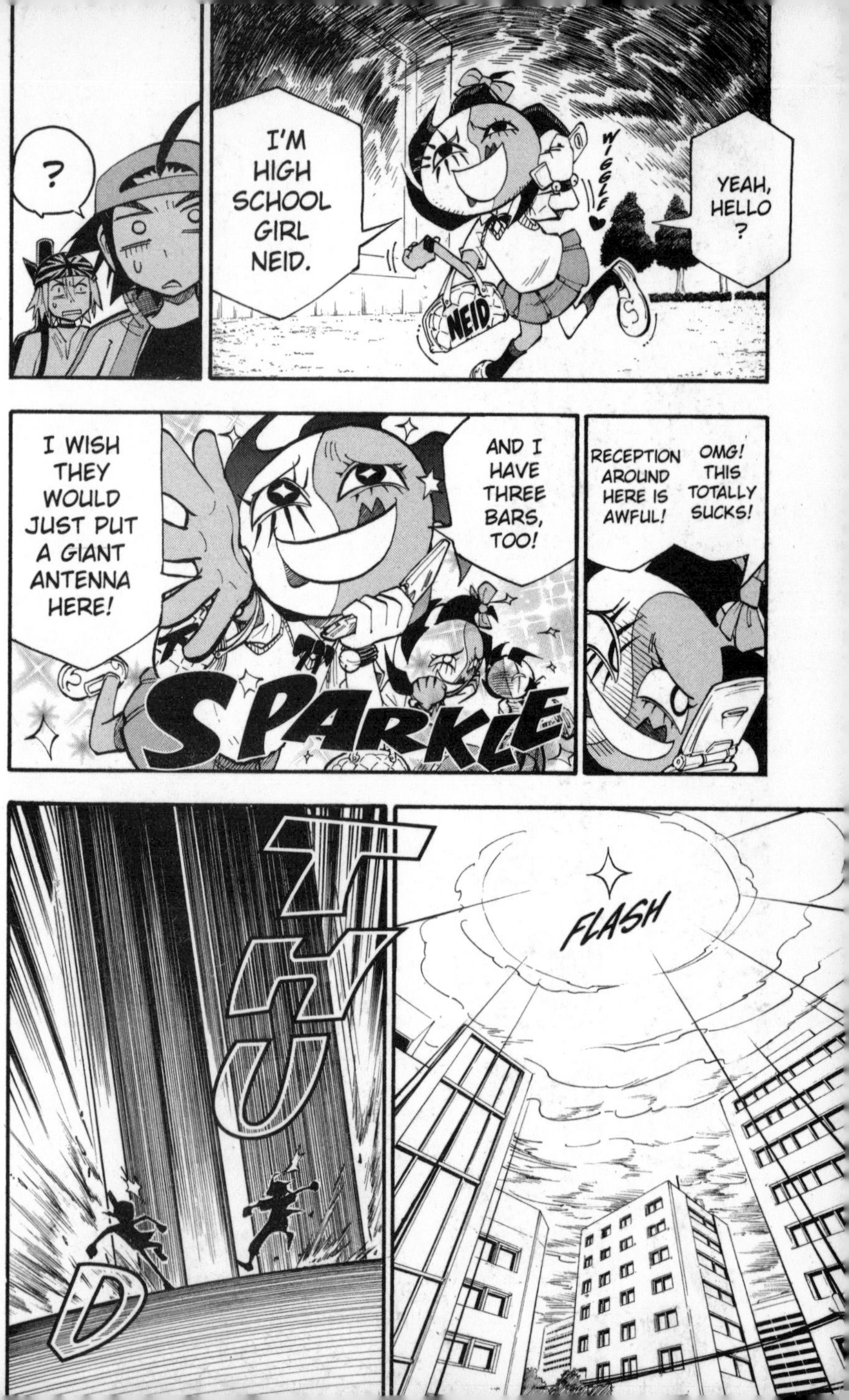
YEAH, HELLO ?
WIGGLE
I'M HIGH SCHOOL GIRL NEID.
NEID
?
OMG! THIS TOTALLY SUCKS!
RECEPTION AROUND HERE IS AWFUL!
AND I HAVE THREE BARS, TOO!
I WISH THEY WOULD JUST PUT A GIANT ANTENNA HERE!
SPARKLE
FLASH
THUD

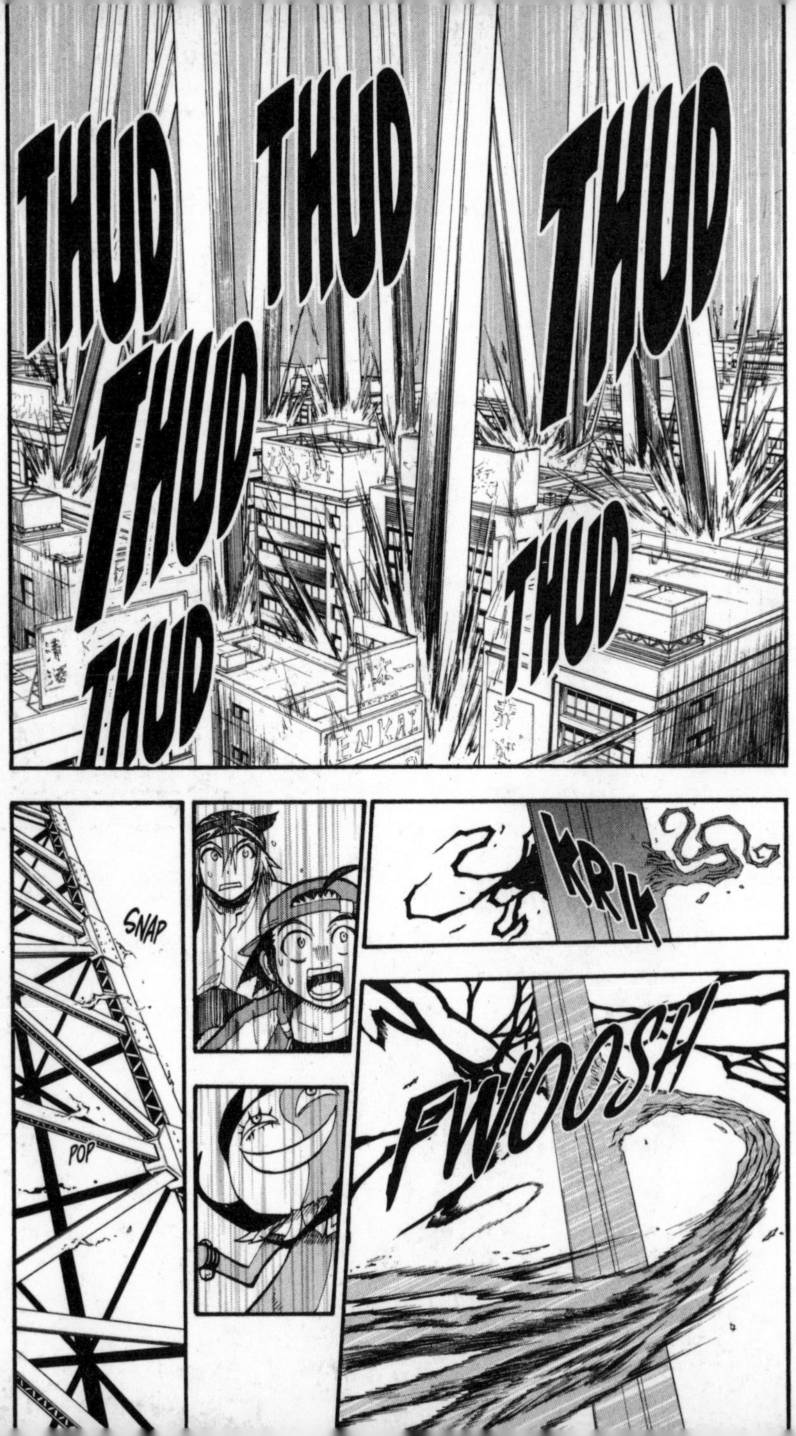
THUD
THUD
THUD
THUD
THUD
THUD
KRIK
FWOOSH
SNAP
POP

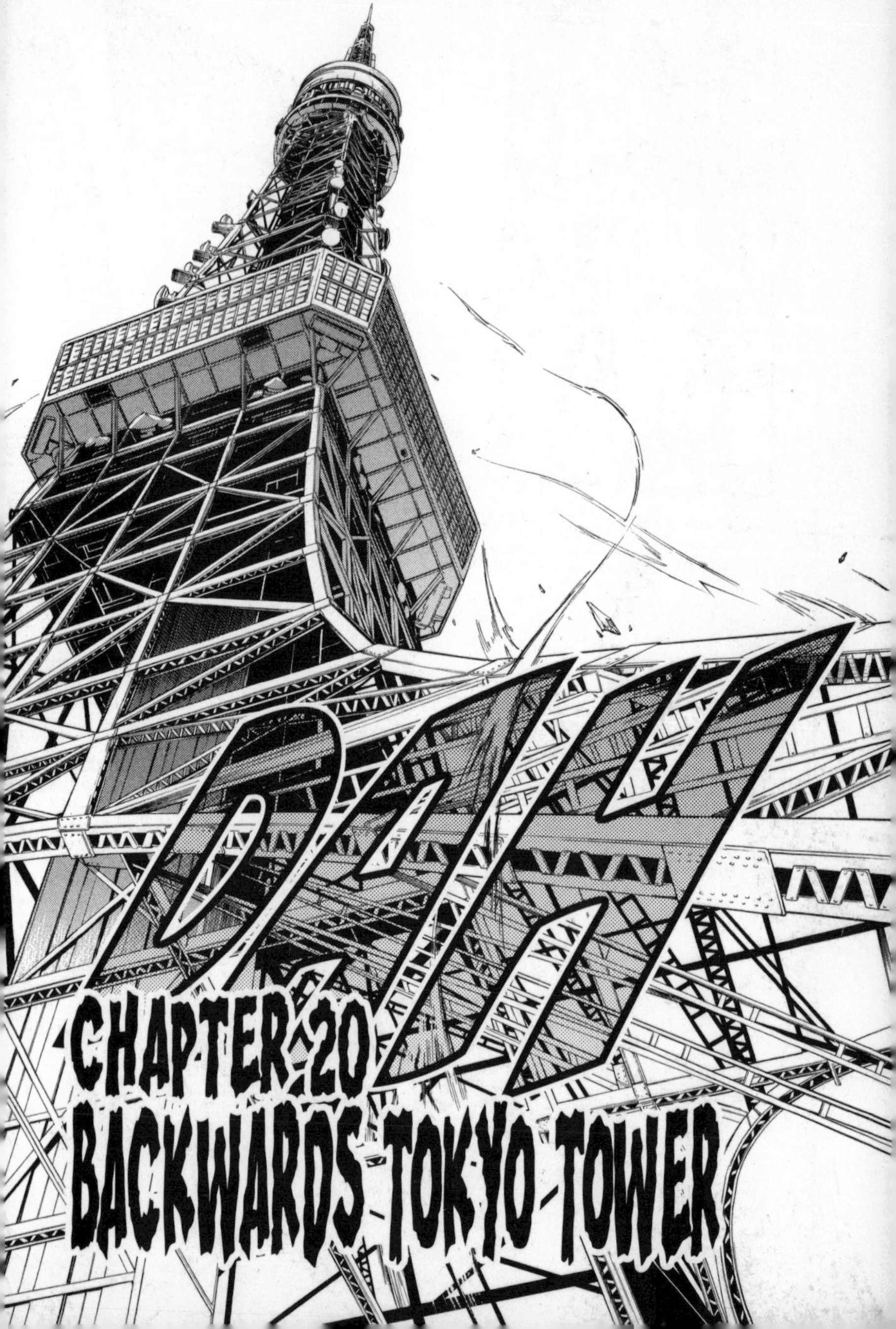
CHAPTER 20
BACKWARDS TOKYO TOWER

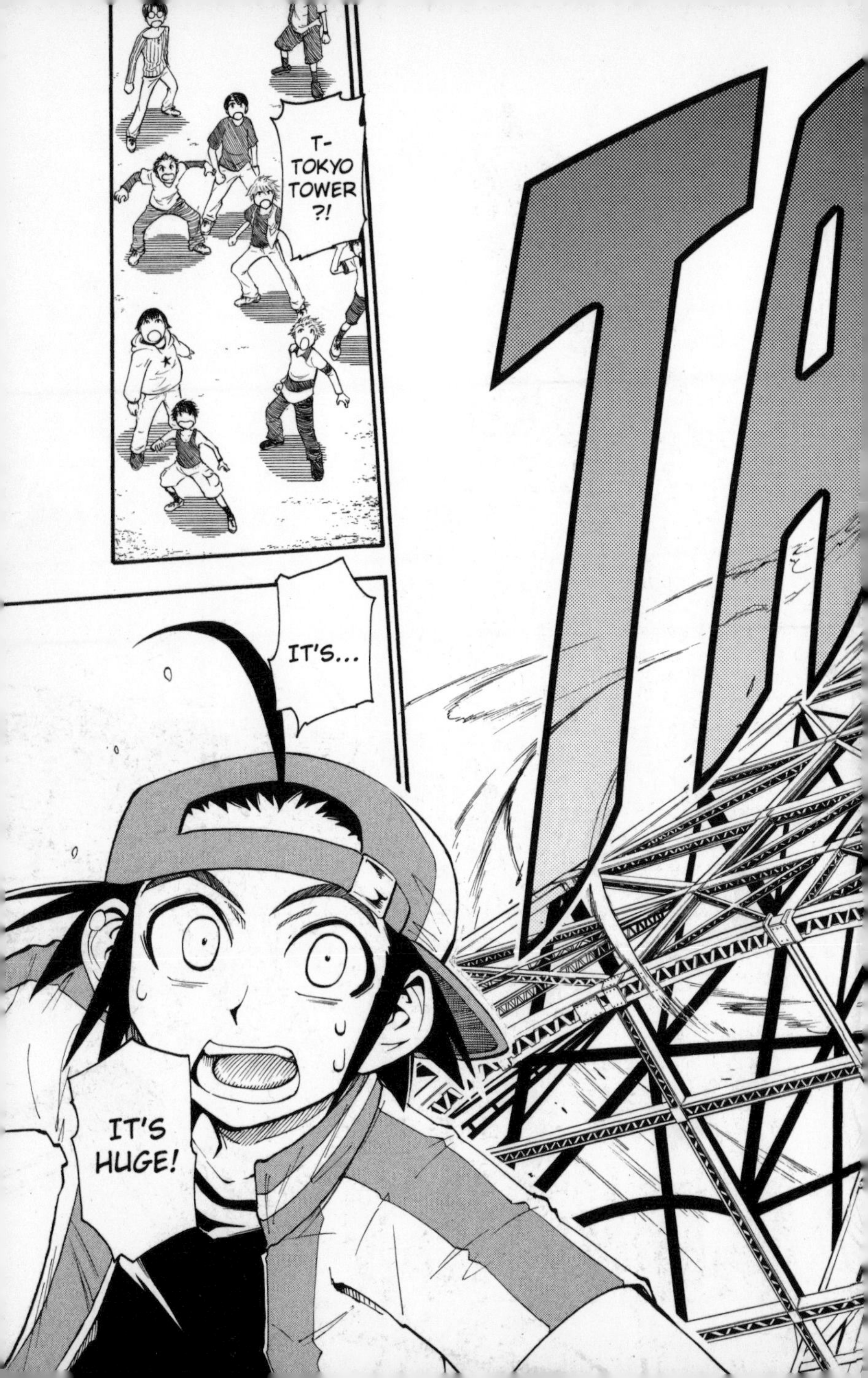
T-TOKYO TOWER?!
IT'S...
IT'S HUGE!

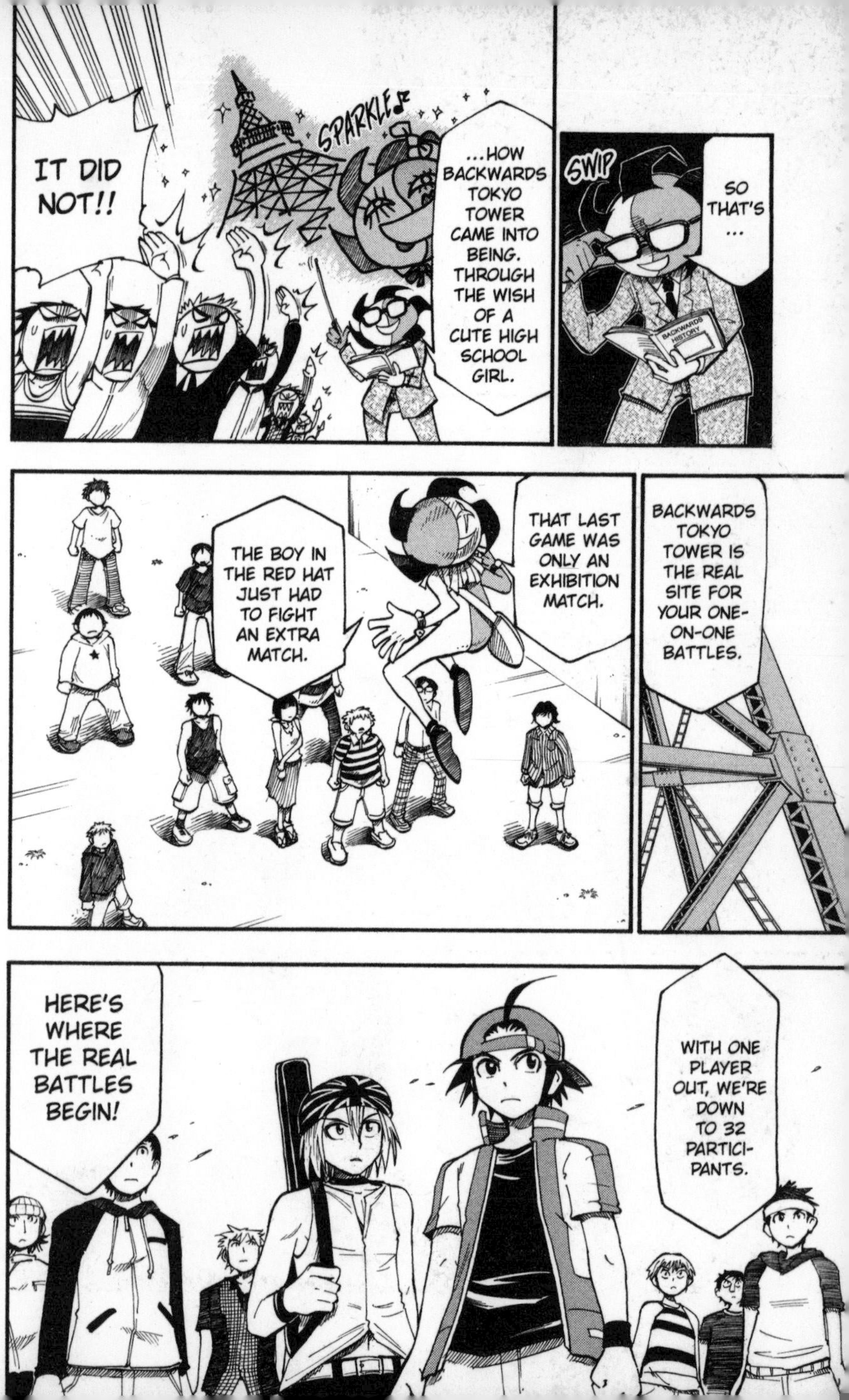
SWIP
SO THAT'S ...
BACKWARDS HISTORY
...HOW BACKWARDS TOKYO TOWER CAME INTO BEING. THROUGH THE WISH OF A CUTE HIGH SCHOOL GIRL.
SPARKLE
IT DID NOT!!
BACKWARDS TOKYO TOWER IS THE REAL SITE FOR YOUR ONE-ON-ONE BATTLES.
THAT LAST GAME WAS ONLY AN EXHIBITION MATCH.
THE BOY IN THE RED HAT JUST HAD TO FIGHT AN EXTRA MATCH.
WITH ONE PLAYER OUT, WE'RE DOWN TO 32 PARTICI-PANTS.
HERE'S WHERE THE REAL BATTLES BEGIN!

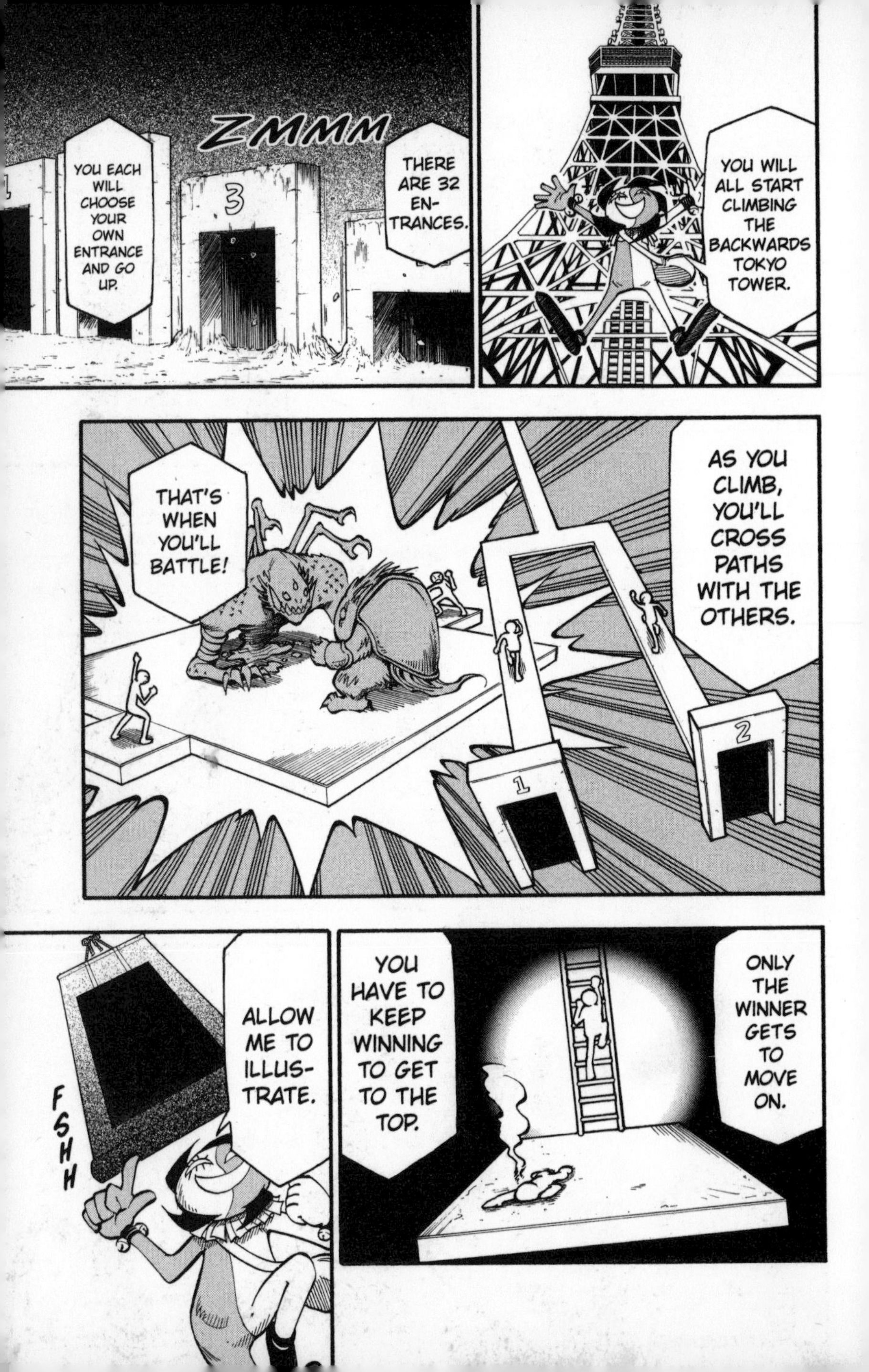
YOU WILL ALL START CLIMBING THE BACKWARDS TOKYO TOWER.
THERE ARE 32 EN-TRANCES.
ZMMMM
YOU EACH WILL CHOOSE YOUR OWN ENTRANCE AND GO UP.
AS YOU CLIMB, YOU'LL CROSS PATHS WITH THE OTHERS.
THAT'S WHEN YOU'LL BATTLE!
ONLY THE WINNER GETS TO MOVE ON.
YOU HAVE TO KEEP WINNING TO GET TO THE TOP.
ALLOW ME TO ILLUS-TRATE.
FSHH

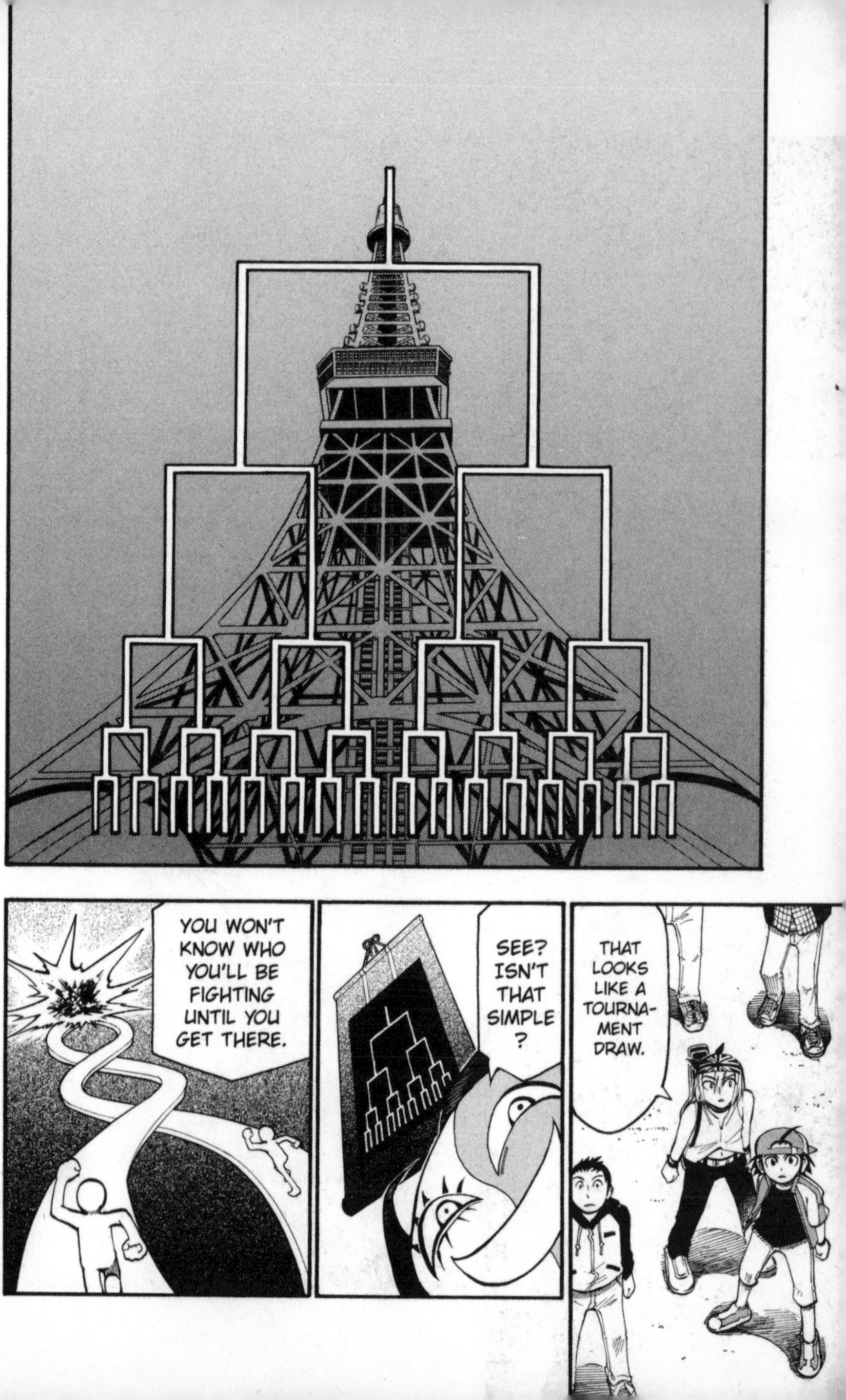
THAT LOOKS LIKE A TOURNAMENT DRAW.
SEE? ISN'T THAT SIMPLE?
YOU WON'T KNOW WHO YOU'LL BE FIGHTING UNTIL YOU GET THERE.

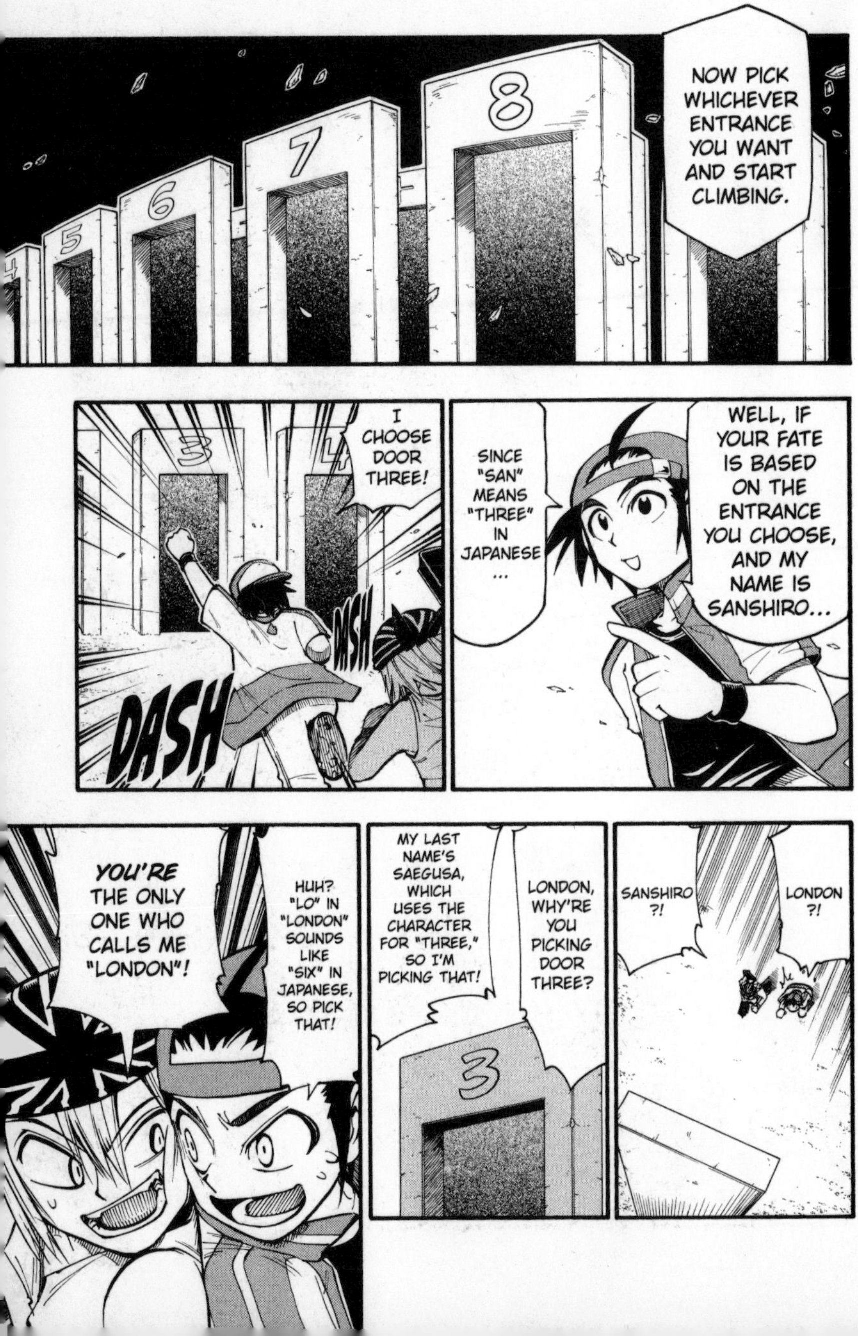
NOW PICK WHICHEVER ENTRANCE YOU WANT AND START CLIMBING.
WELL, IF YOUR FATE IS BASED ON THE ENTRANCE YOU CHOOSE, AND MY NAME IS SANSHIRO...
SINCE "SAN" MEANS "THREE" IN JAPANESE ...
I CHOOSE DOOR THREE!
DASH
DASH
LONDON ?!
SANSHIRO ?!
LONDON, WHY'RE YOU PICKING DOOR THREE?
MY LAST NAME'S SAEGUSA, WHICH USES THE CHARACTER FOR "THREE," SO I'M PICKING THAT!
HUH? "LO" IN "LONDON" SOUNDS LIKE "SIX" IN JAPANESE, SO PICK THAT!
YOU'RE THE ONLY ONE WHO CALLS ME "LONDON"!

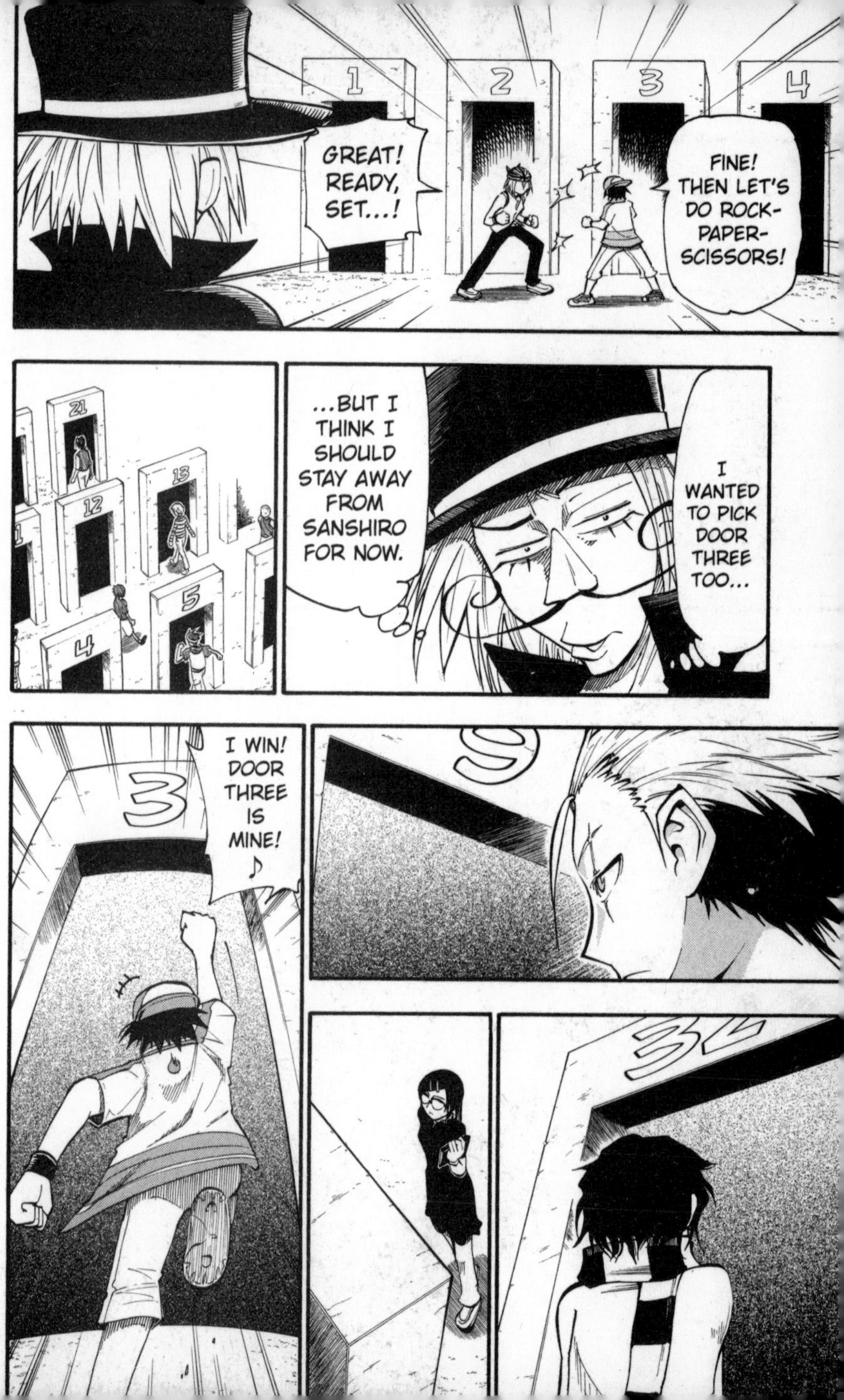
FINE! THEN LET'S DO ROCK-PAPER-SCISSORS!
GREAT! READY, SET...!
I WANTED TO PICK DOOR THREE TOO...
...BUT I THINK I SHOULD STAY AWAY FROM SANSHIRO FOR NOW.
I WIN! DOOR THREE IS MINE! ♪

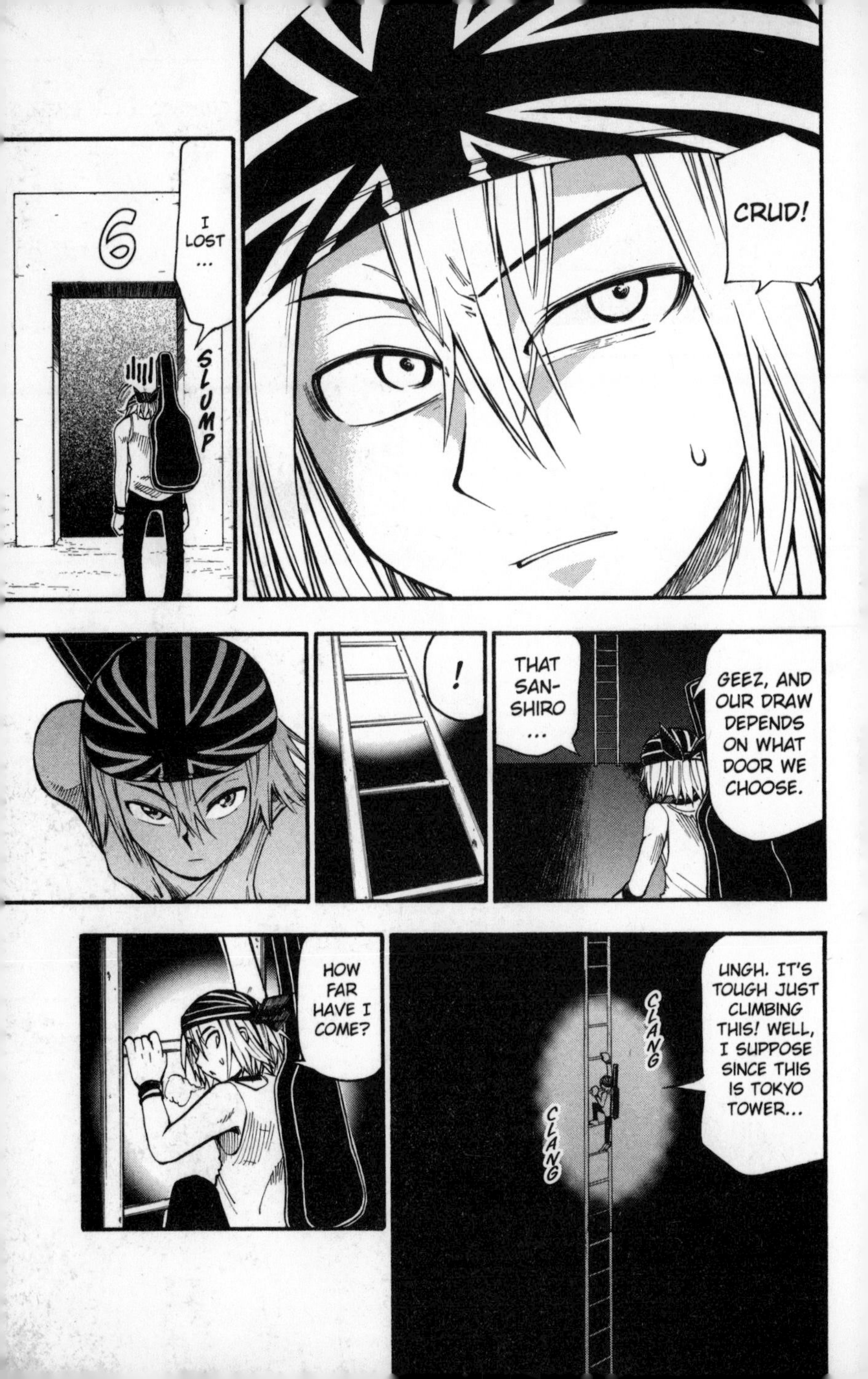
CRUD!
6
I LOST ...
SLUMP
GEEZ, AND OUR DRAW DEPENDS ON WHAT DOOR WE CHOOSE.
THAT SAN-SHIRO ...
!
UNGH. IT'S TOUGH JUST CLIMBING THIS! WELL, I SUPPOSE SINCE THIS IS TOKYO TOWER...
CLANG
CLANG
HOW FAR HAVE I COME?

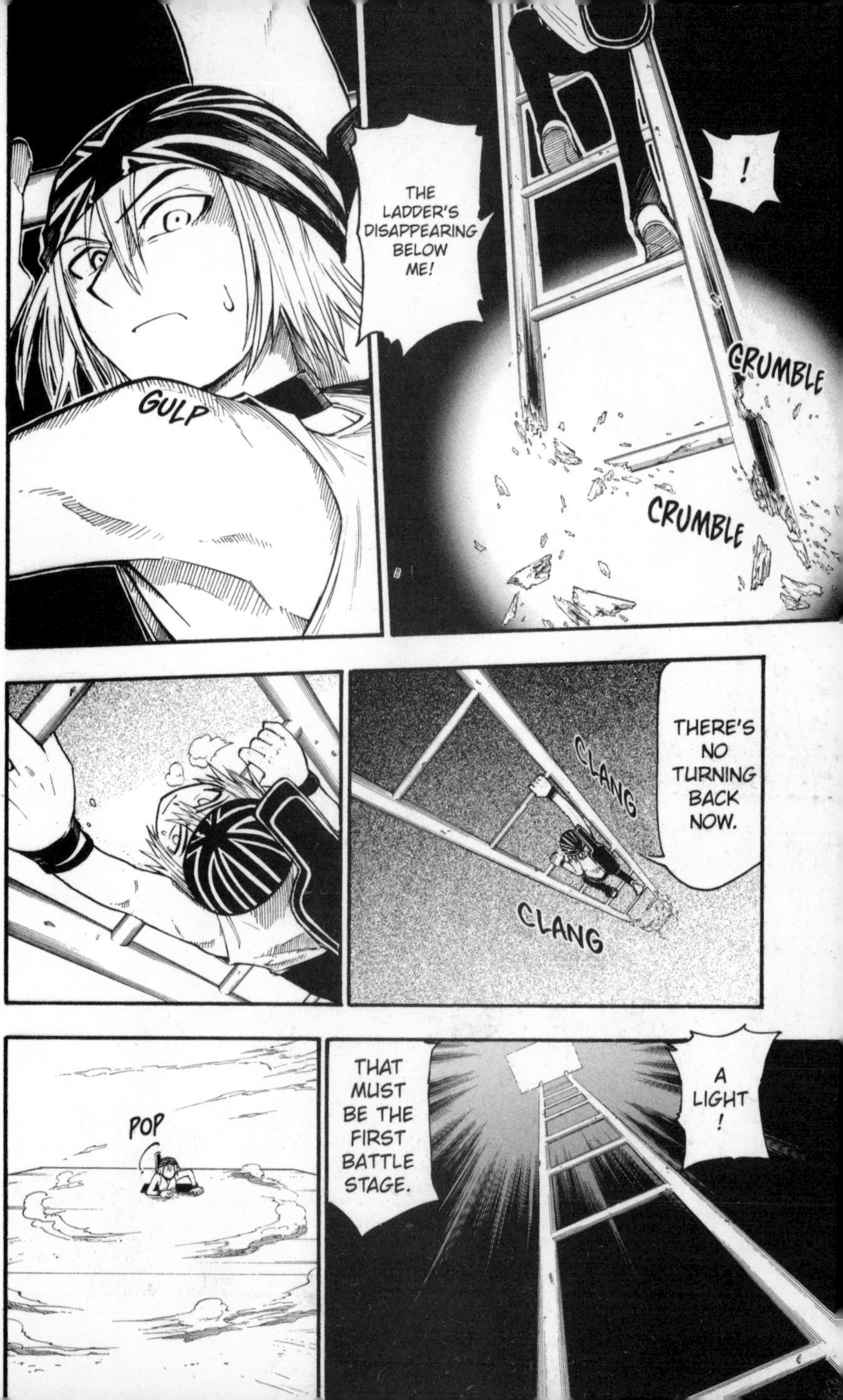
!
CRUMBLE
CRUMBLE
THE LADDER'S DISAPPEARING BELOW ME!
GULP
THERE'S NO TURNING BACK NOW.
CLANG
CLANG
A LIGHT!
THAT MUST BE THE FIRST BATTLE STAGE.
POP

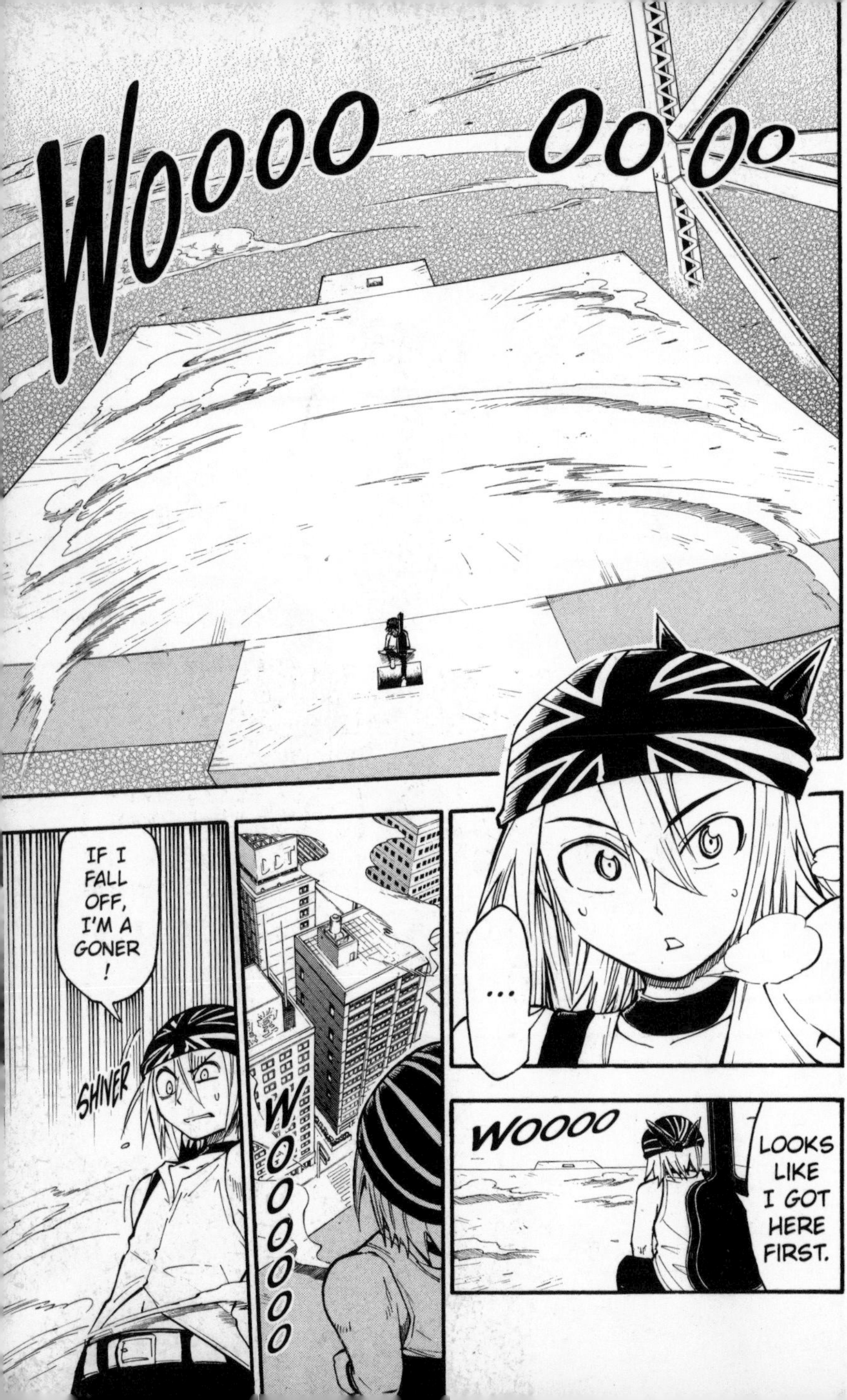
WOOOO OOOO
...
WOOOO
LOOKS LIKE I GOT HERE FIRST.
CCT
WOOOOOOOO
IF I FALL OFF, I'M A GONER!
SHIVER

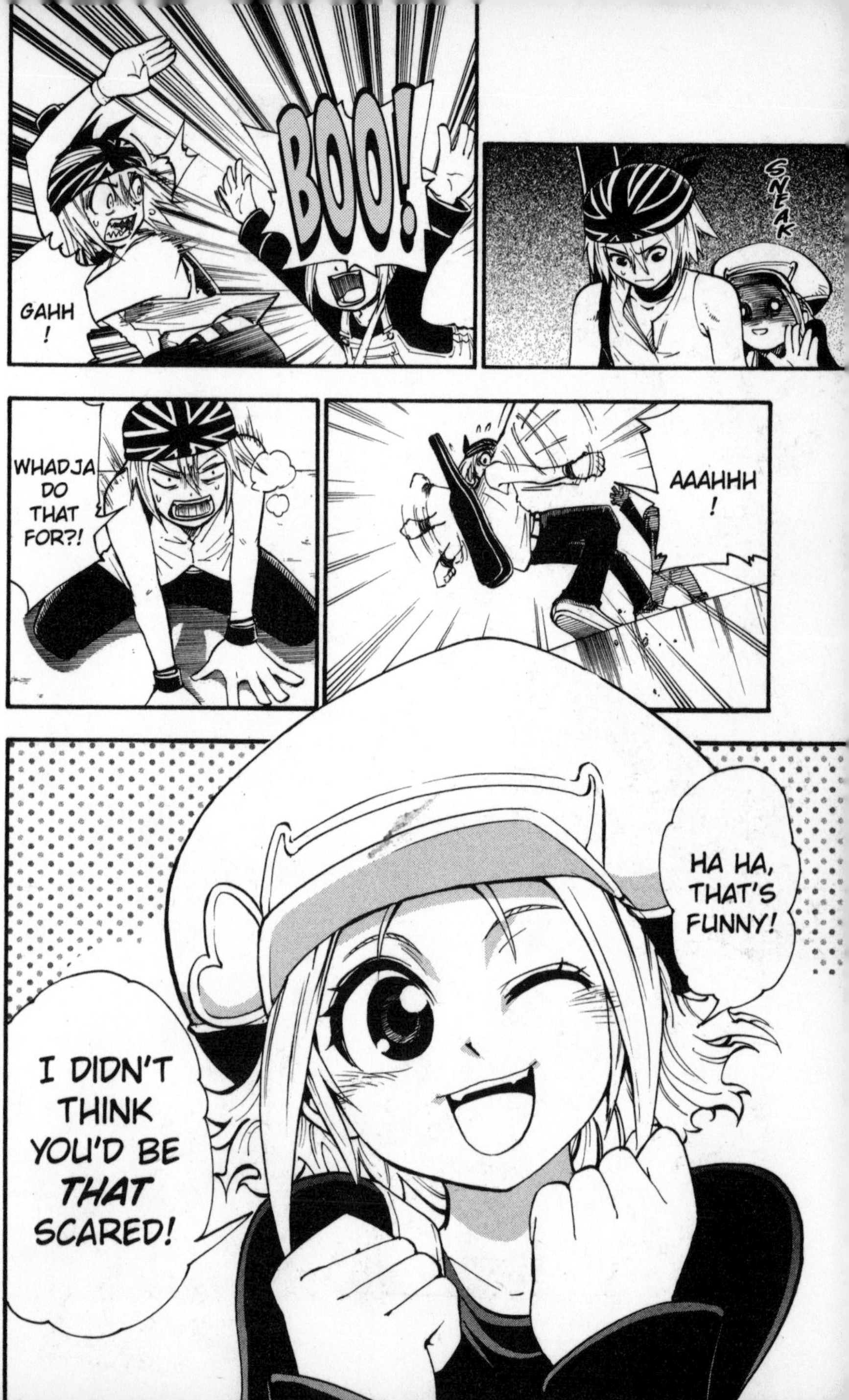
SNEAK
BOO!
GAHH!
AAAHHH!
WHADJA DO THAT FOR?!
HA HA, THAT'S FUNNY!
I DIDN'T THINK YOU'D BE *THAT* SCARED!

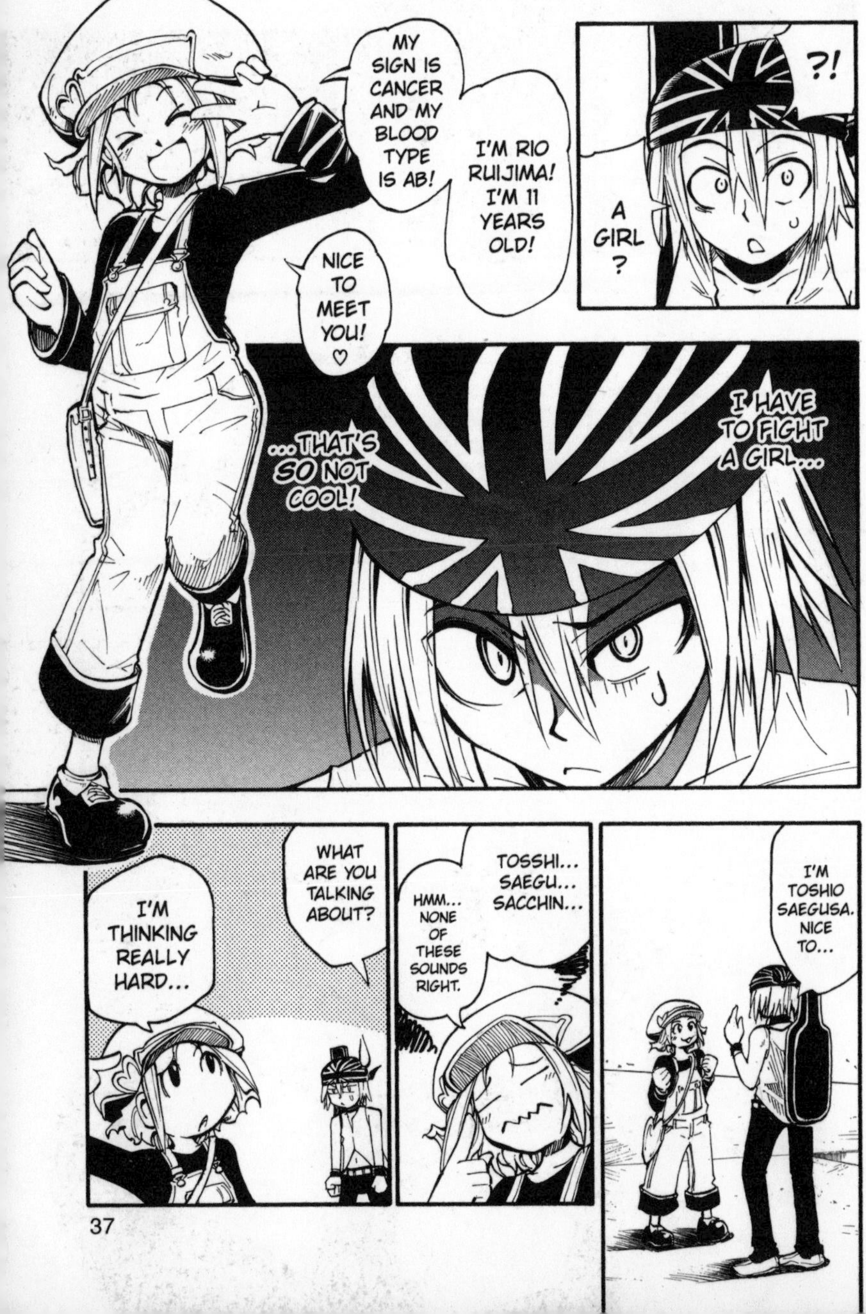
I'M RIO RUIJIMA! I'M 11 YEARS OLD!
MY SIGN IS CANCER AND MY BLOOD TYPE IS AB!
NICE TO MEET YOU! ♡
?!
A GIRL ?
I HAVE TO FIGHT A GIRL...
...THAT'S SO NOT COOL!
I'M TOSHIO SAEGUSA. NICE TO...
TOSSHI... SAEGU... SACCHIN...
HMM... NONE OF THESE SOUNDS RIGHT.
WHAT ARE YOU TALKING ABOUT?
I'M THINKING REALLY HARD...

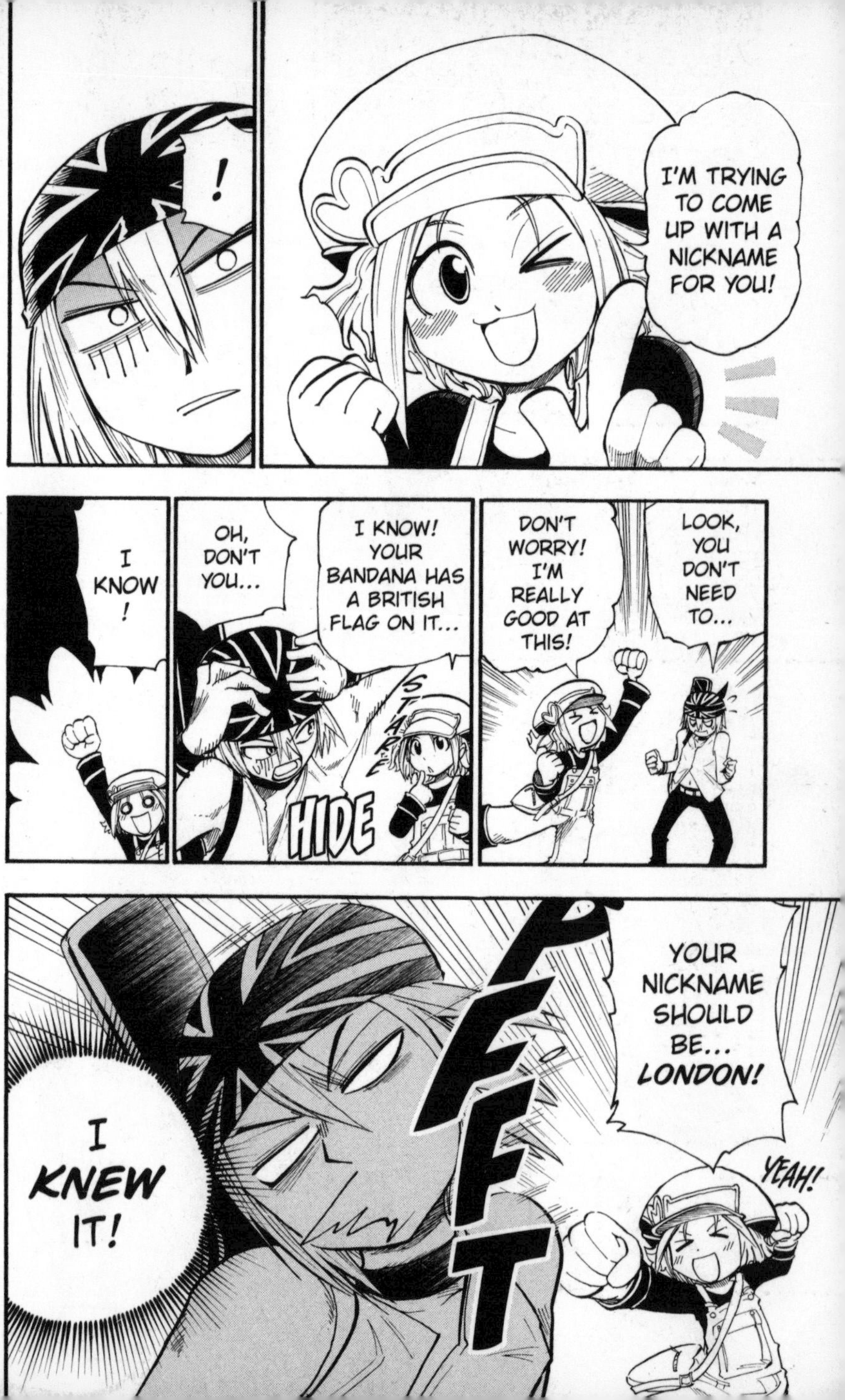
I'M TRYING TO COME UP WITH A NICKNAME FOR YOU!
!
LOOK, YOU DON'T NEED TO...
DON'T WORRY! I'M REALLY GOOD AT THIS!
I KNOW! YOUR BANDANA HAS A BRITISH FLAG ON IT...
OH, DON'T YOU...
STARE
HIDE
I KNOW!
YOUR NICKNAME SHOULD BE... LONDON!
YEAH!
PFFT
I KNEW IT!

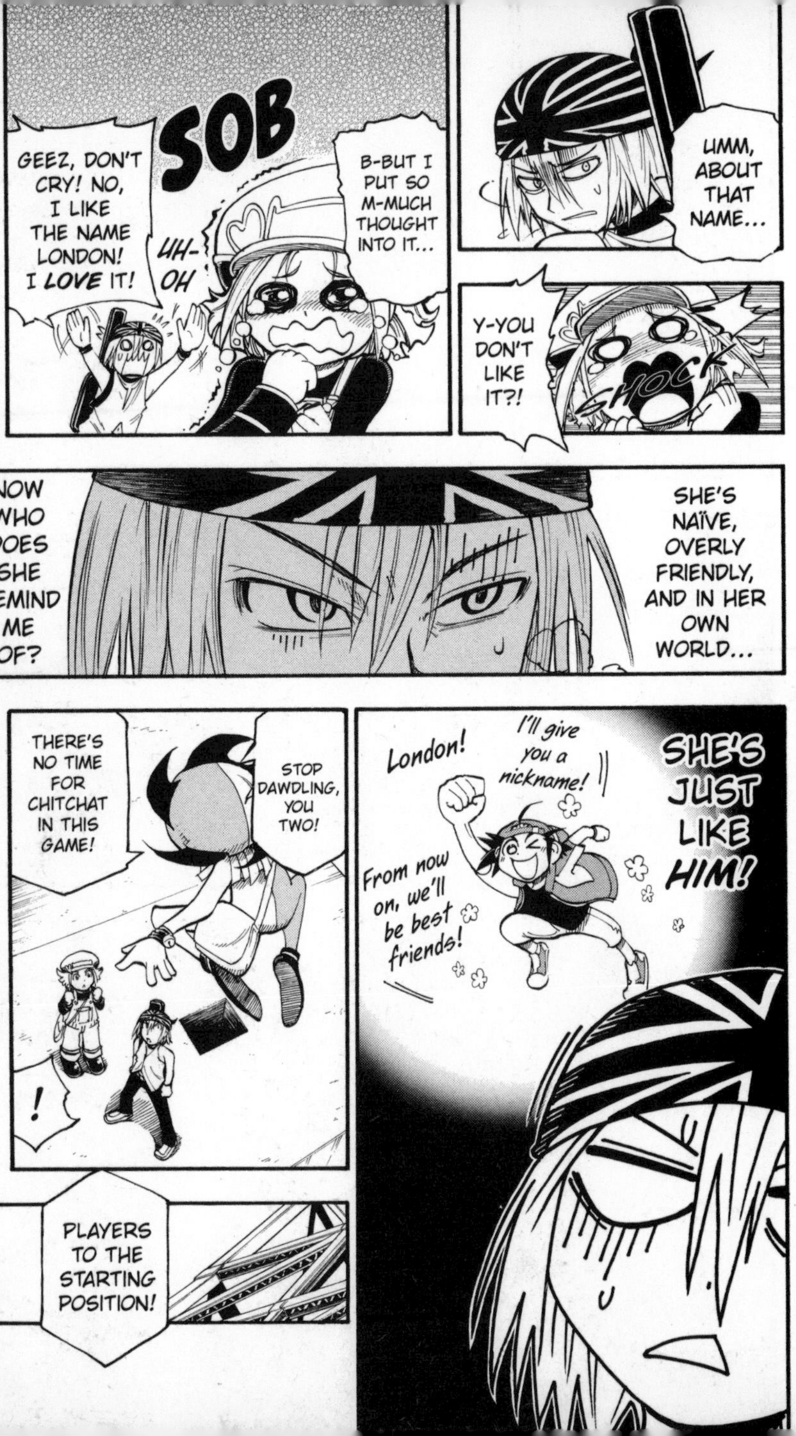
UMM, ABOUT THAT NAME...
Y-YOU DON'T LIKE IT?!
SHOCK
B-BUT I PUT SO M-MUCH THOUGHT INTO IT...
SOB
GEEZ, DON'T CRY! NO, I LIKE THE NAME LONDON! I *LOVE* IT!
UH-OH
SHE'S NAÏVE, OVERLY FRIENDLY, AND IN HER OWN WORLD...
NOW WHO DOES SHE REMIND ME OF?
SHE'S JUST LIKE *HIM!*
London!
I'll give you a nickname!
From now on, we'll be best friends!
STOP DAWDLING, YOU TWO!
THERE'S NO TIME FOR CHITCHAT IN THIS GAME!
!
PLAYERS TO THE STARTING POSITION!

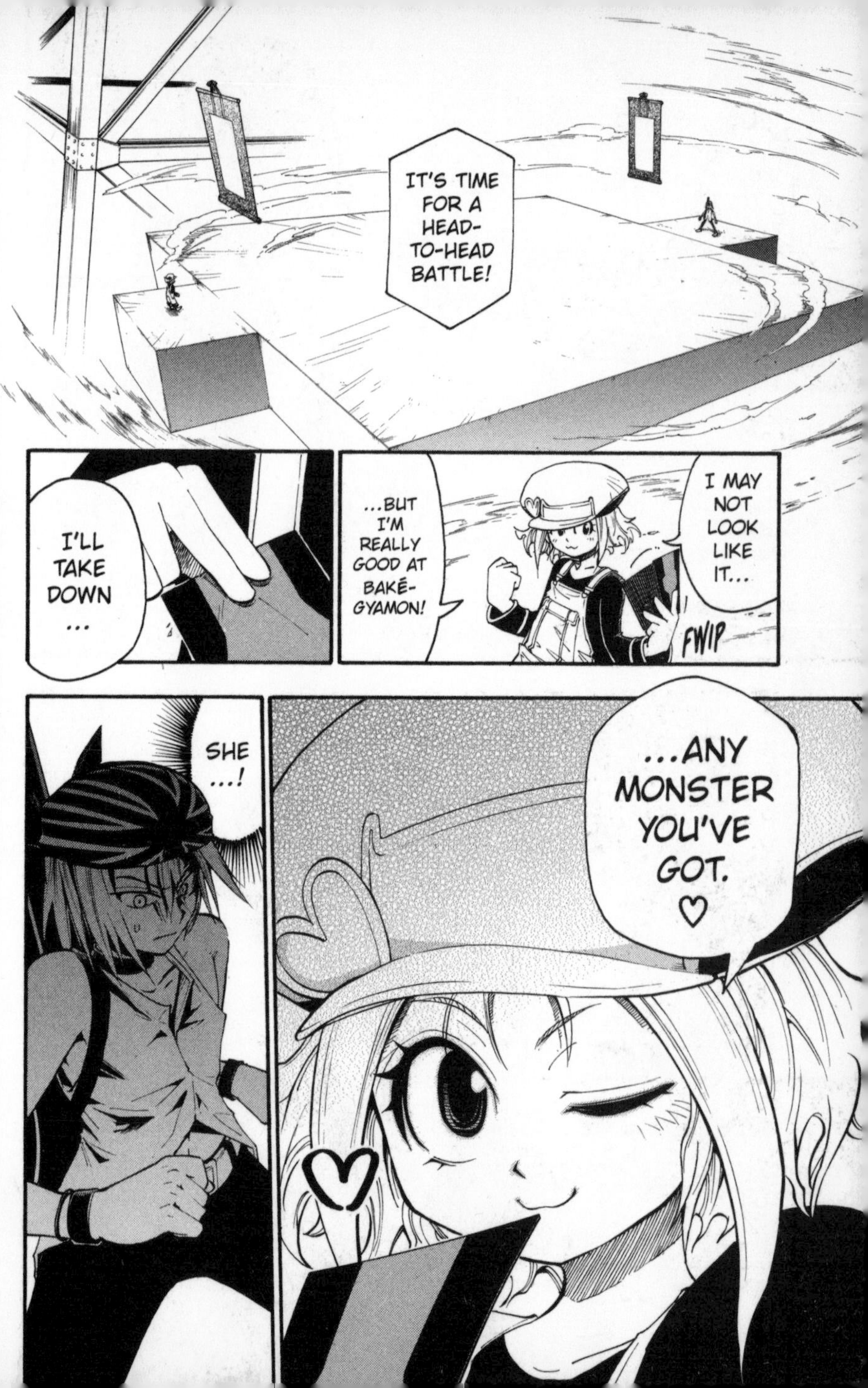
IT'S TIME FOR A HEAD-TO-HEAD BATTLE!
I MAY NOT LOOK LIKE IT...
FWIP
...BUT I'M REALLY GOOD AT BAKÉ-GYAMON!
I'LL TAKE DOWN ...
...ANY MONSTER YOU'VE GOT. ♡
SHE ...!

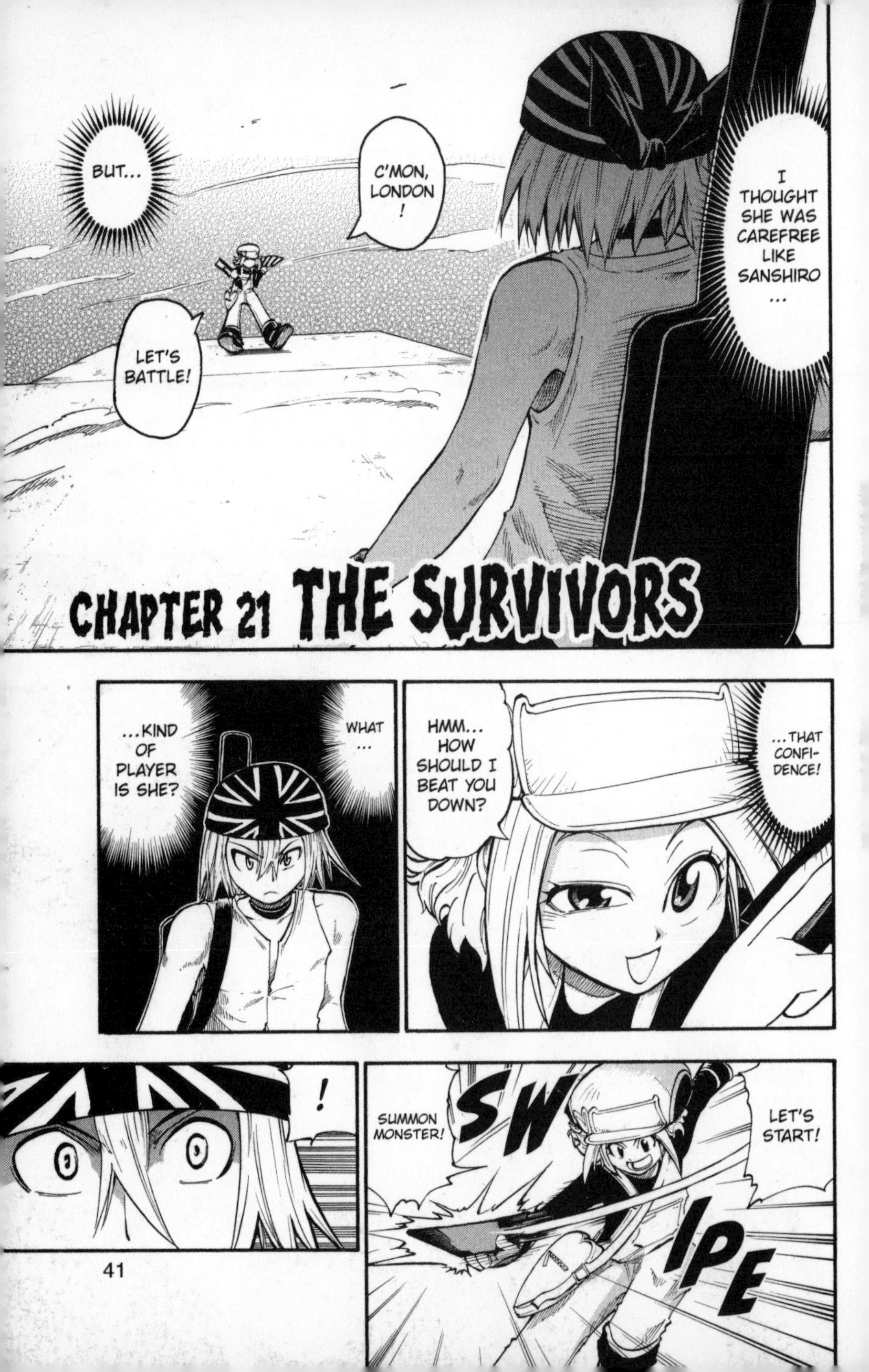
I THOUGHT SHE WAS CAREFREE LIKE SANSHIRO...
C'MON, LONDON!
BUT...
LET'S BATTLE!
CHAPTER 21 THE SURVIVORS
...THAT CONFIDENCE!
HMM... HOW SHOULD I BEAT YOU DOWN?
WHAT...
...KIND OF PLAYER IS SHE?
LET'S START!
SUMMON MONSTER!
SWIPE
!

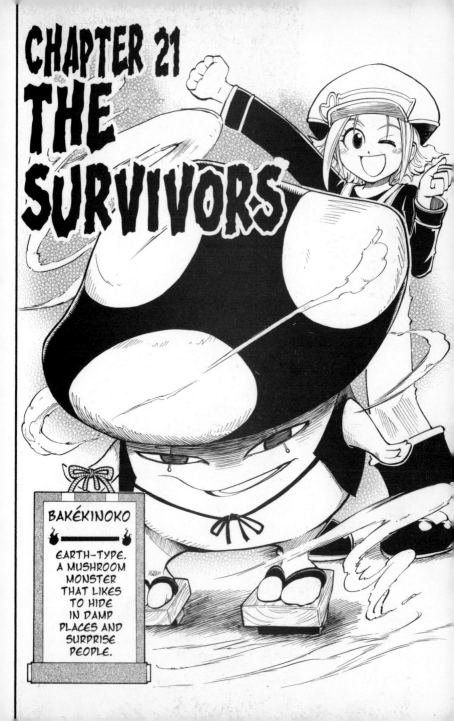

CHAPTER 21
THE SURVIVORS

BAKÉKINOKO

EARTH-TYPE.
A MUSHROOM
MONSTER
THAT LIKES
TO HIDE
IN DAMP
PLACES AND
SURPRISE
PEOPLE.

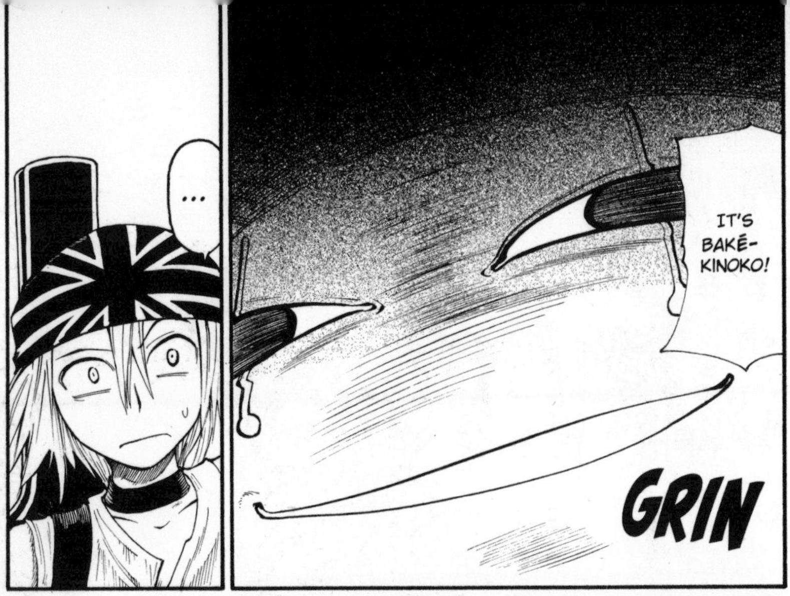
IT'S BAKÉ-KINOKO!
GRIN
...

"BAKÉ" MEANS "MONSTER" AND "KINOKO" MEANS "MUSHROOM."

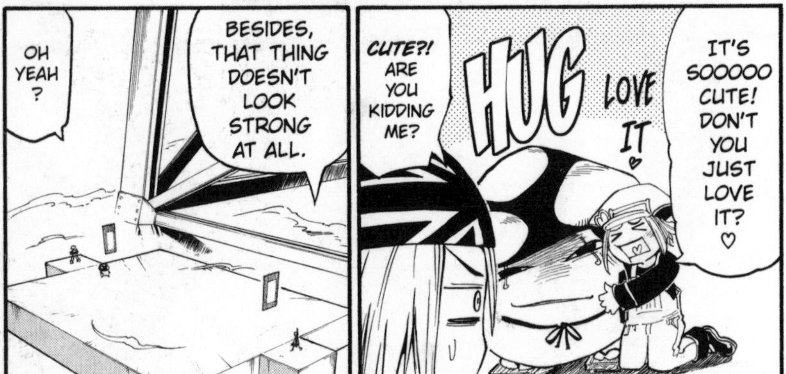
IT'S SOOOOO CUTE! DON'T YOU JUST LOVE IT? ♡
LOVE IT ♡
HUG
CUTE?! ARE YOU KIDDING ME?
BESIDES, THAT THING DOESN'T LOOK STRONG AT ALL.
OH YEAH?

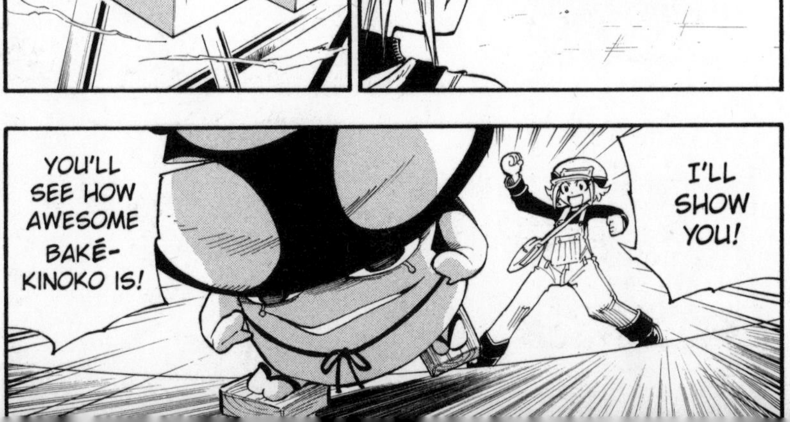
I'LL SHOW YOU!
YOU'LL SEE HOW AWESOME BAKÉ-KINOKO IS!

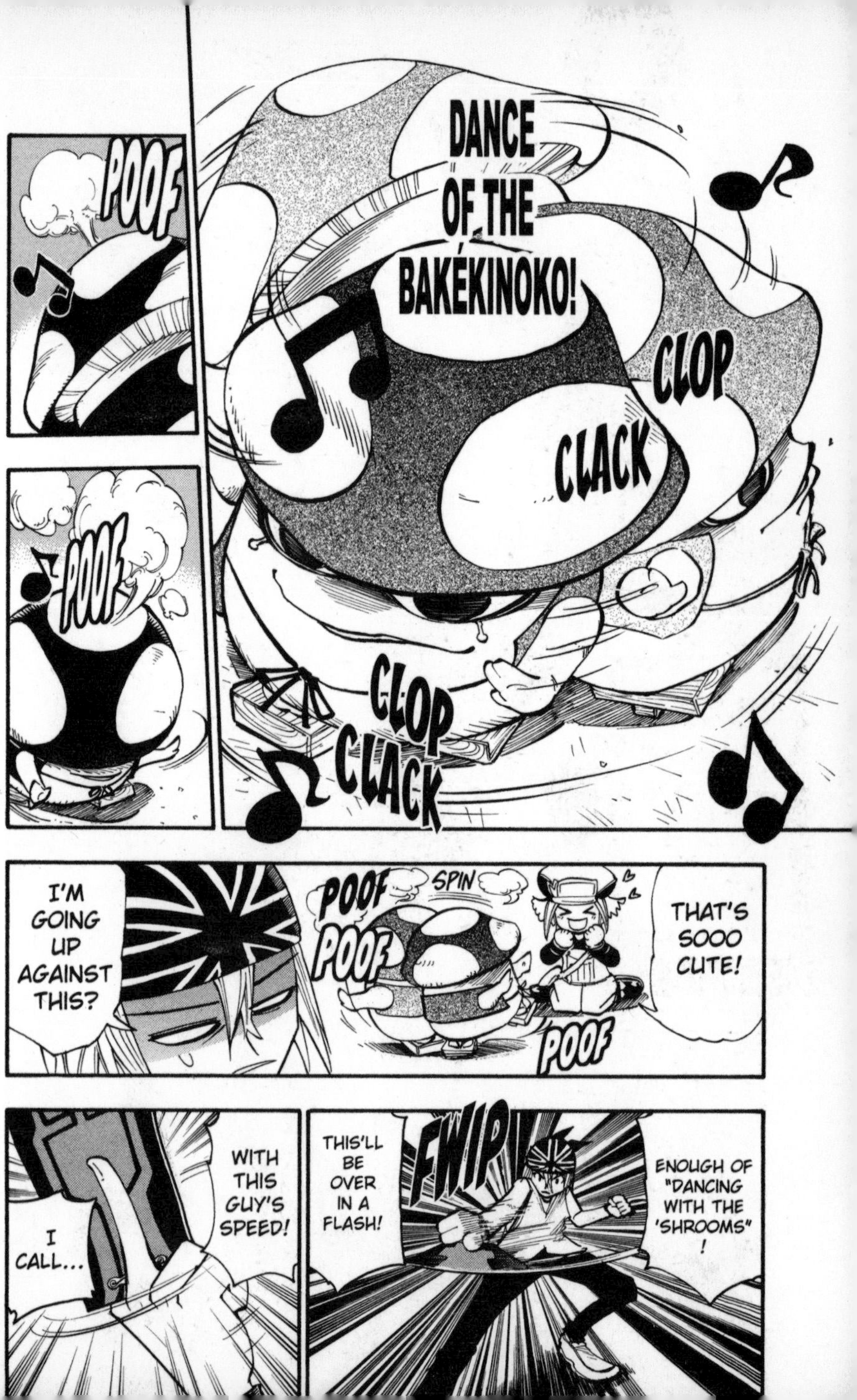
DANCE OF THE BAKÉKINOKO!
CLOP
CLACK
CLOP
CLACK
POOF
POOF
THAT'S SOOO CUTE!
SPIN
POOF
POOF
POOF
I'M GOING UP AGAINST THIS?
ENOUGH OF "DANCING WITH THE 'SHROOMS"!
FWIP
THIS'LL BE OVER IN A FLASH!
WITH THIS GUY'S SPEED!
I CALL...

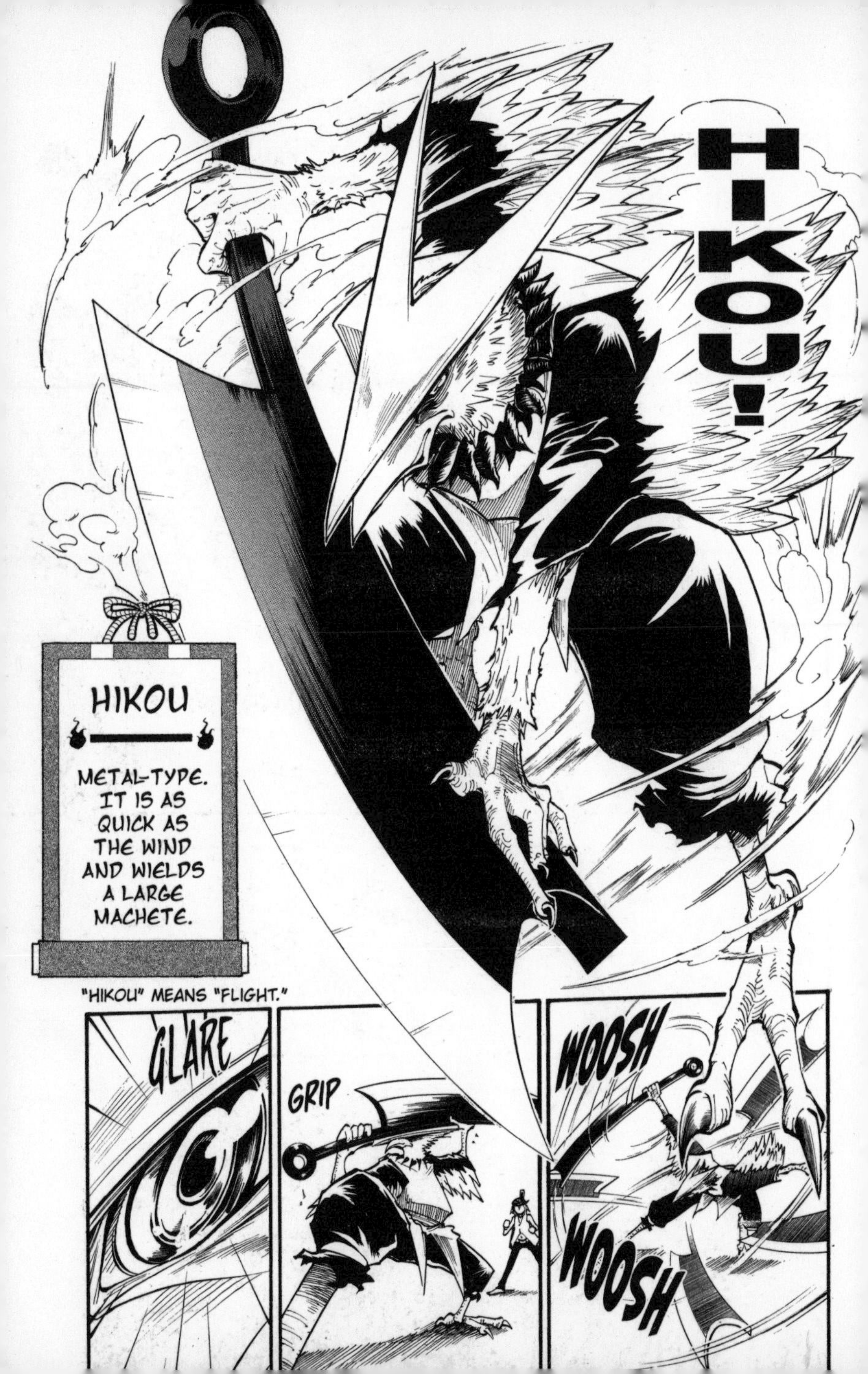
HIKOU!
HIKOU
METAL-TYPE. IT IS AS QUICK AS THE WIND AND WIELDS A LARGE MACHETE.
"HIKOU" MEANS "FLIGHT."
WOOSH
WOOSH
GRIP
GLARE

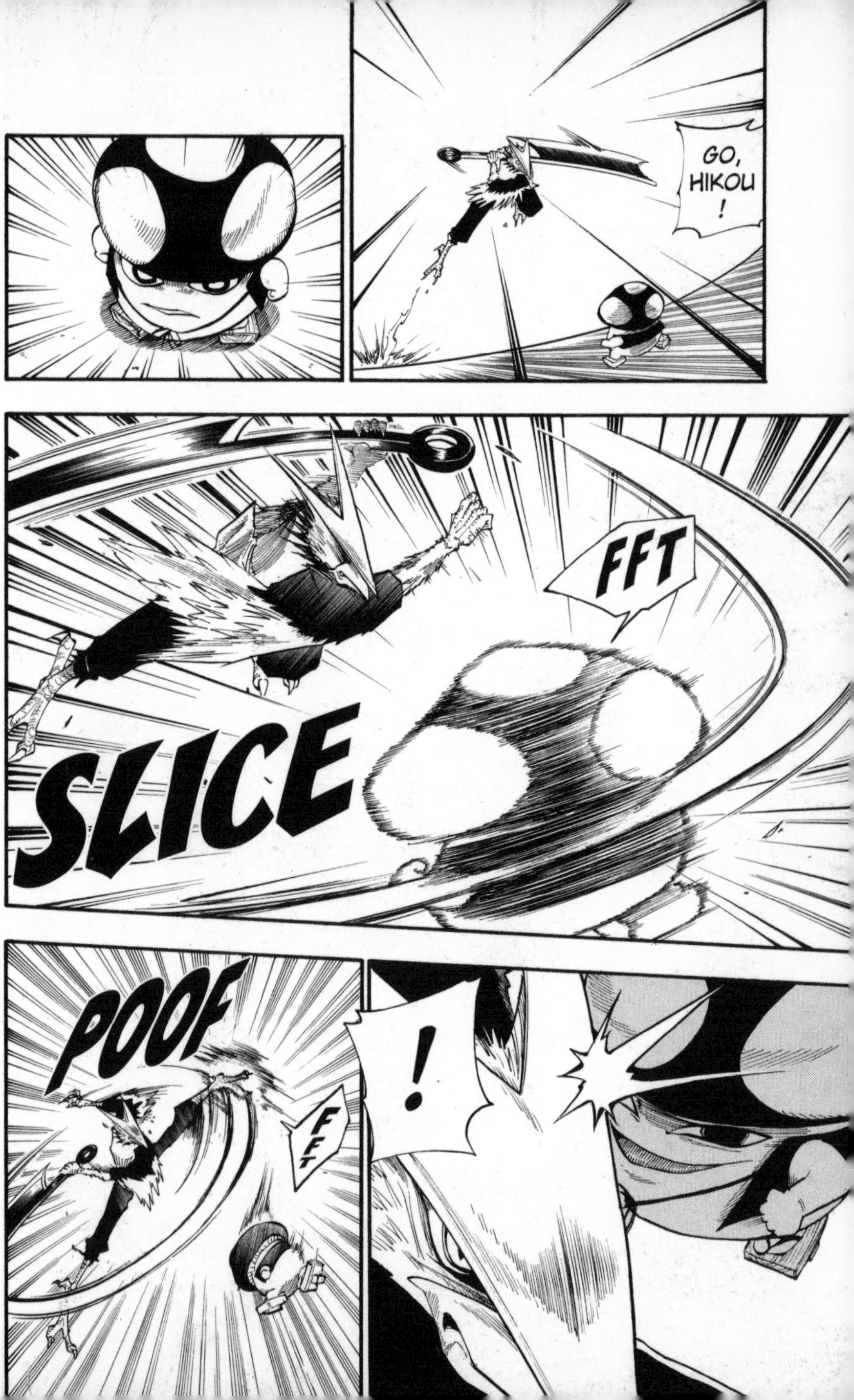
GO, HIKOU!
FFT
SLICE
!
POOF
FFT

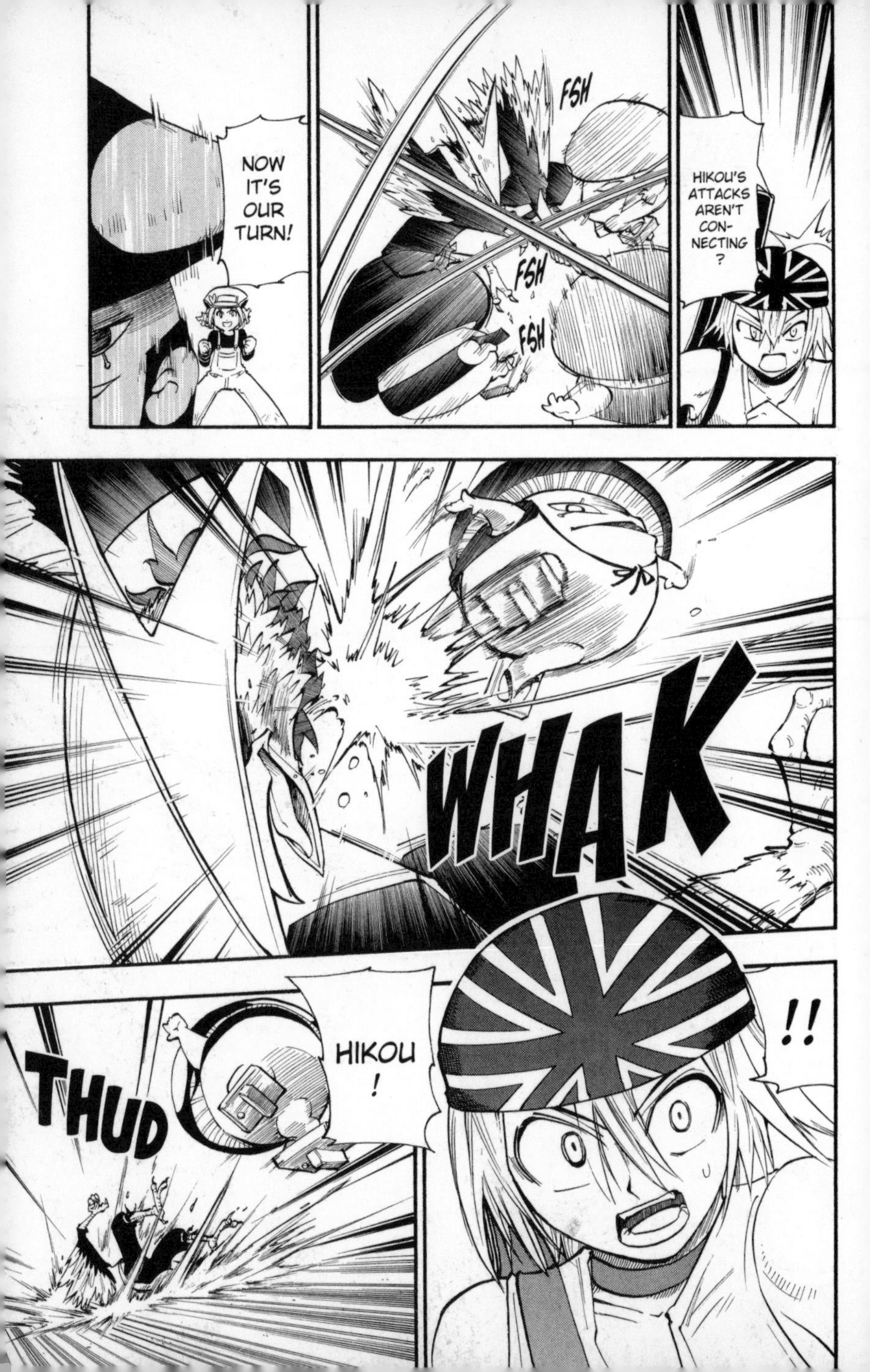
HIKOU'S ATTACKS AREN'T CON-NECTING?
FSH
FSH
FSH
NOW IT'S OUR TURN!
WHAK
!!
HIKOU!
THUD

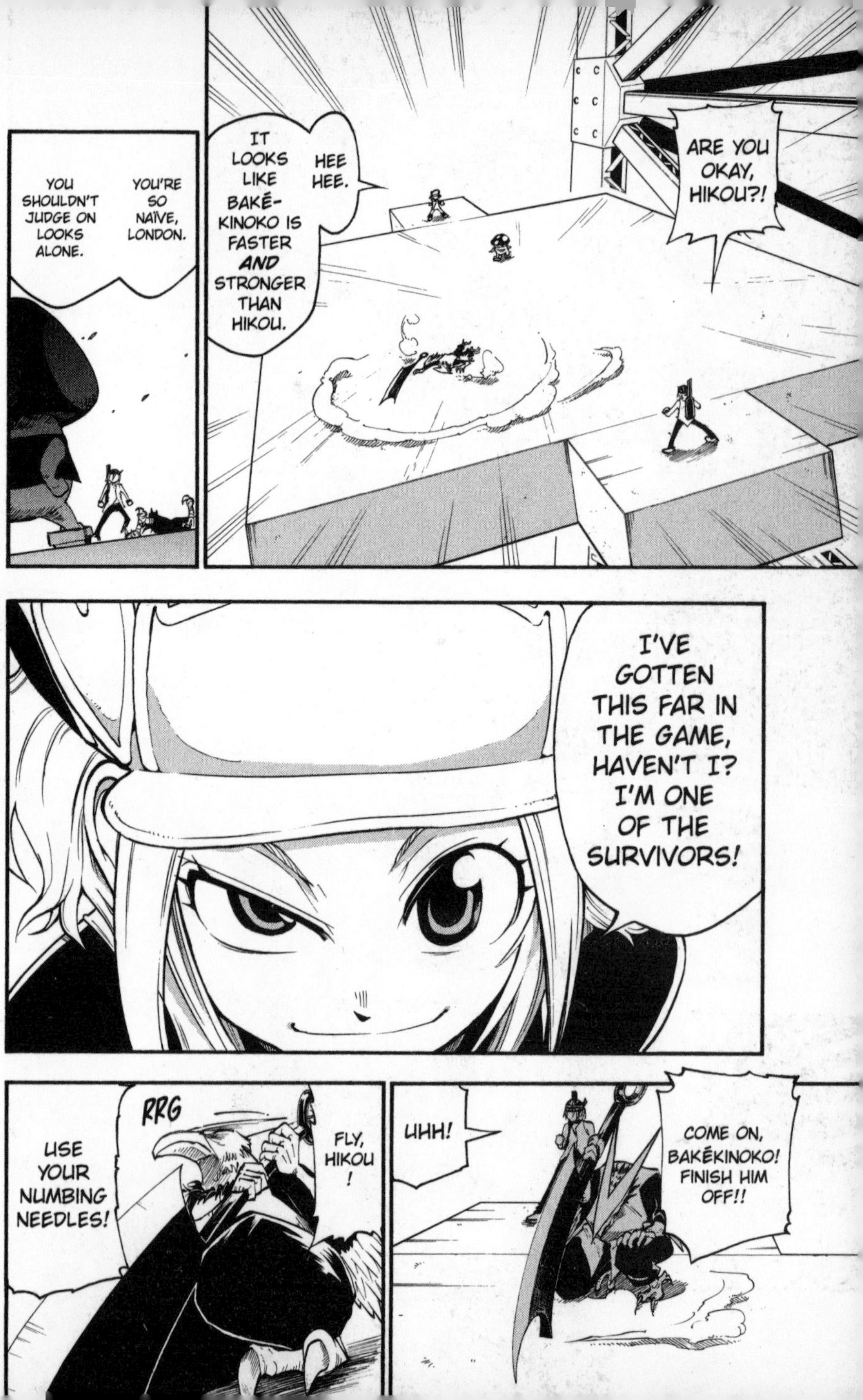
ARE YOU OKAY, HIKOU?!
HEE HEE.
IT LOOKS LIKE BAKÉ-KINOKO IS FASTER *AND* STRONGER THAN HIKOU.
YOU'RE SO NAÏVE, LONDON.
YOU SHOULDN'T JUDGE ON LOOKS ALONE.
I'VE GOTTEN THIS FAR IN THE GAME, HAVEN'T I? I'M ONE OF THE SURVIVORS!
COME ON, BAKÉKINOKO! FINISH HIM OFF!!
UHH!
FLY, HIKOU!
RRG
USE YOUR NUMBING NEEDLES!

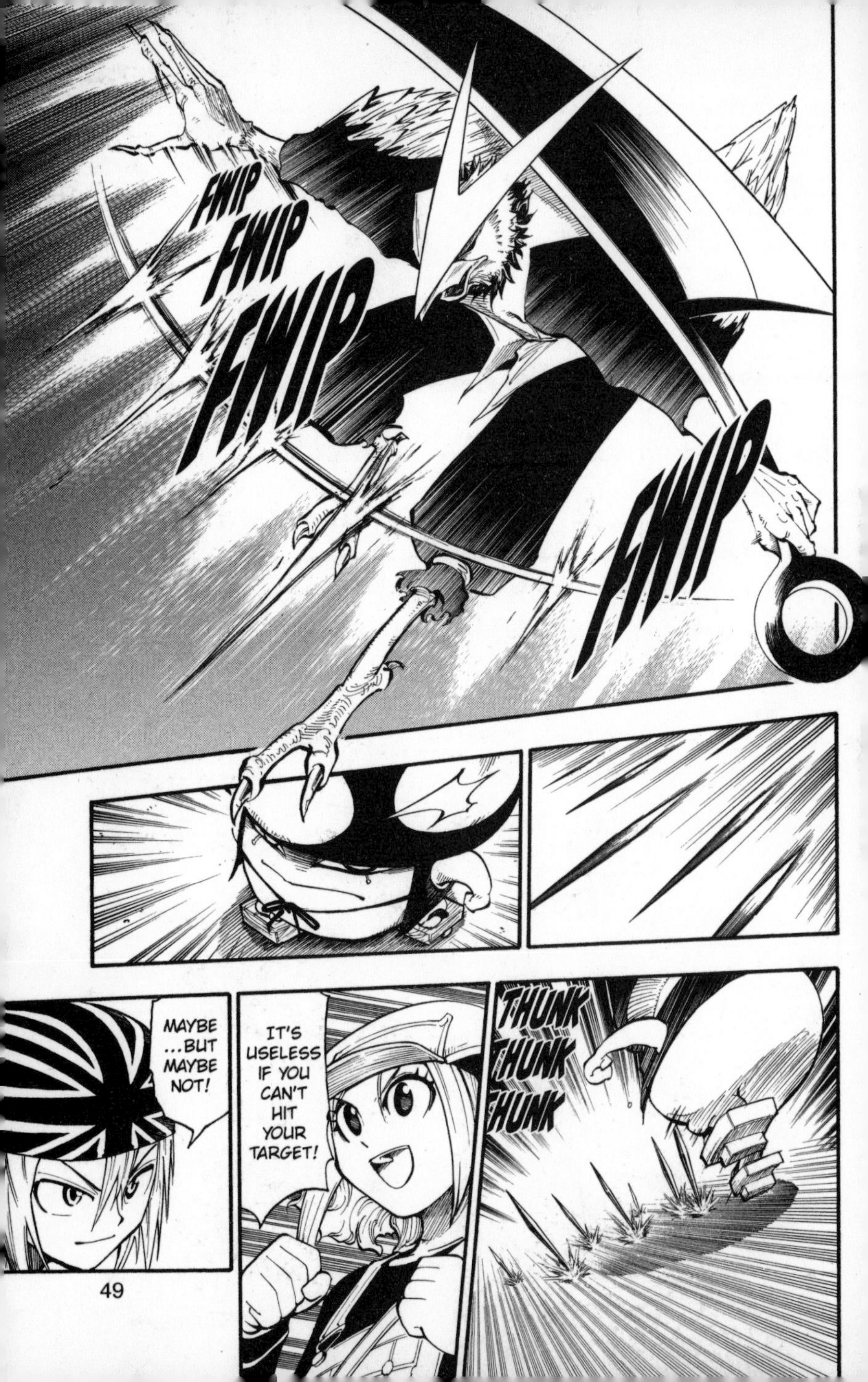
FWIP
FWIP
FWIP
FWIP
THUNK
THUNK
THUNK
IT'S USELESS IF YOU CAN'T HIT YOUR TARGET!
MAYBE ...BUT MAYBE NOT!

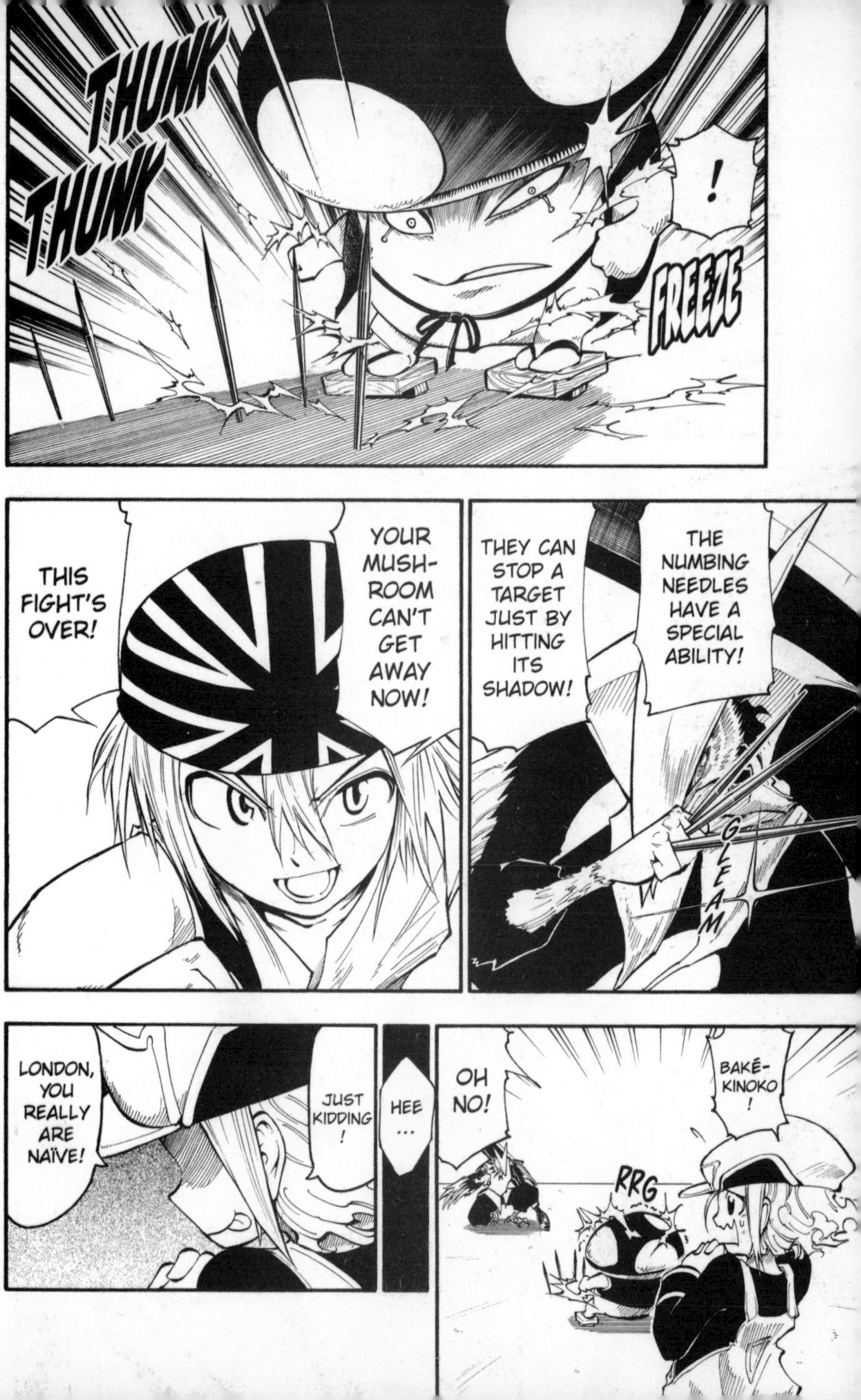
THUNK
THUNK
!
FREEZE
THE NUMBING NEEDLES HAVE A SPECIAL ABILITY!
THEY CAN STOP A TARGET JUST BY HITTING ITS SHADOW!
GLEAM
YOUR MUSH-ROOM CAN'T GET AWAY NOW!
THIS FIGHT'S OVER!
BAKÉ-KINOKO!
OH NO!
RRG
HEE...
JUST KIDDING!
LONDON, YOU REALLY ARE NAÏVE!

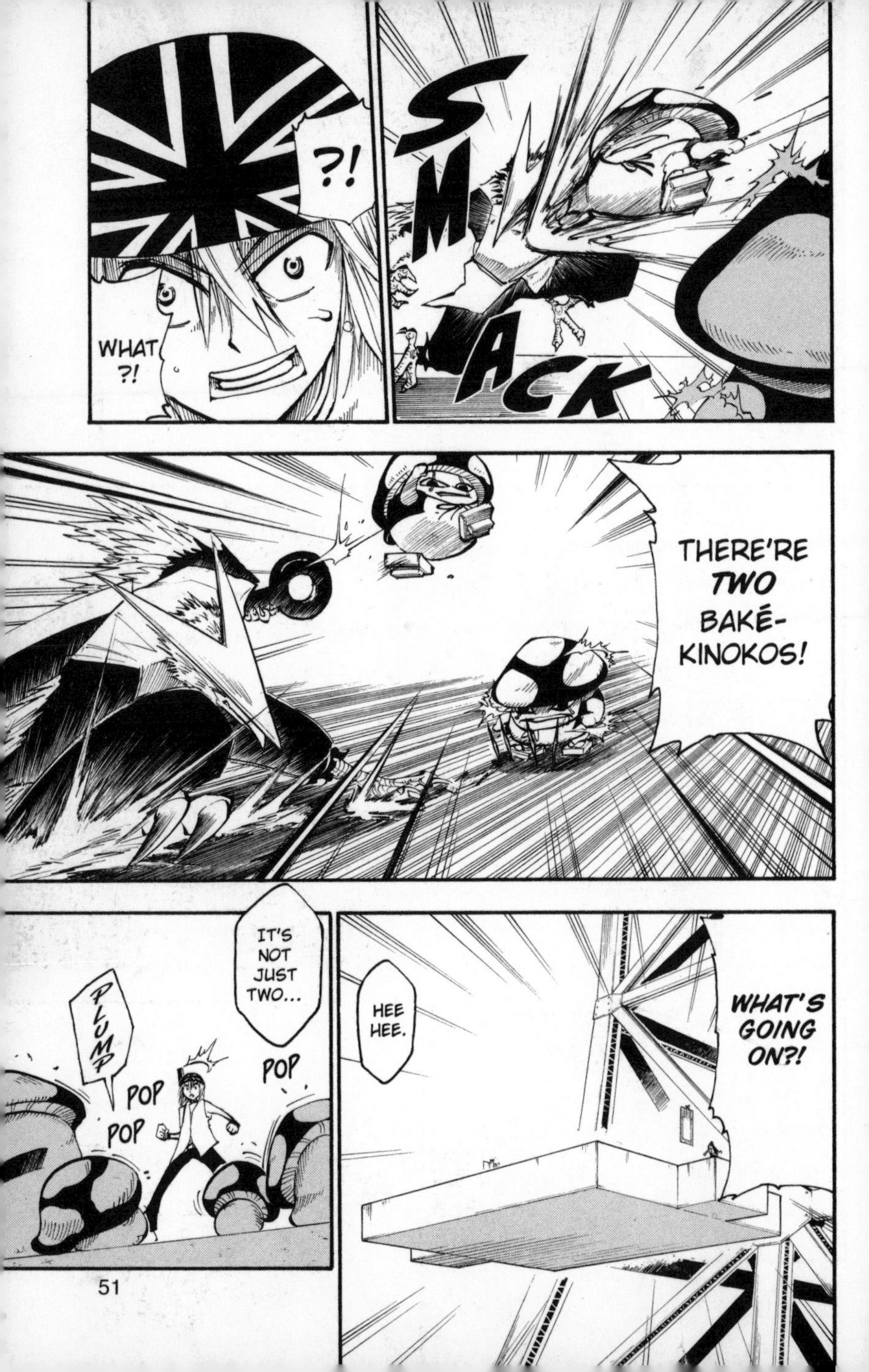
SMACK
?!
WHAT ?!
THERE'RE *TWO* BAKÉ-KINOKOS!
WHAT'S GOING ON?!
HEE HEE.
IT'S NOT JUST TWO...
PLUMP
POP
POP POP

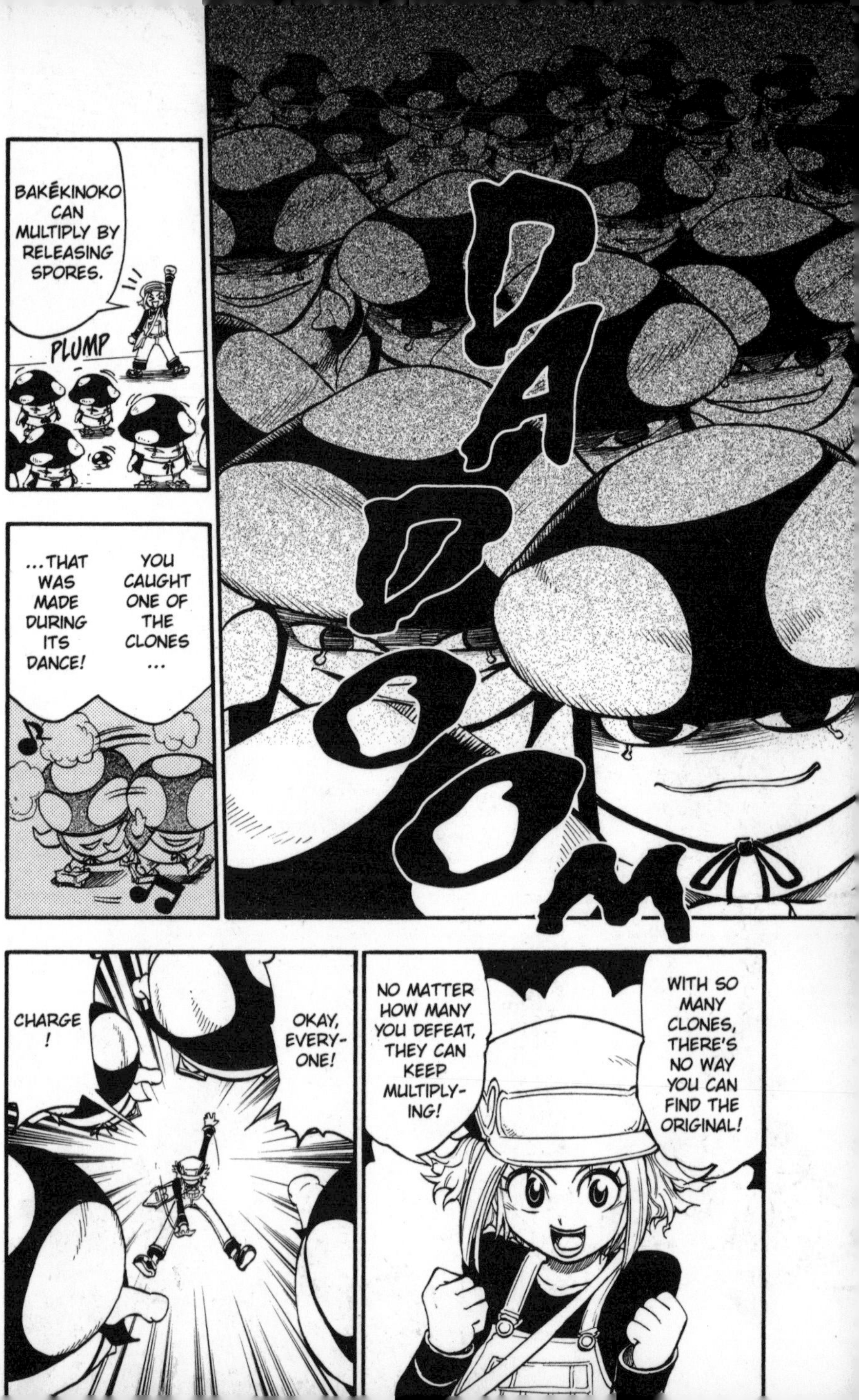
DADOOOM
BAKÉKINOKO CAN MULTIPLY BY RELEASING SPORES.
PLUMP
YOU CAUGHT ONE OF THE CLONES...
...THAT WAS MADE DURING ITS DANCE!
WITH SO MANY CLONES, THERE'S NO WAY YOU CAN FIND THE ORIGINAL!
NO MATTER HOW MANY YOU DEFEAT, THEY CAN KEEP MULTIPLY-ING!
OKAY, EVERY-ONE!
CHARGE!

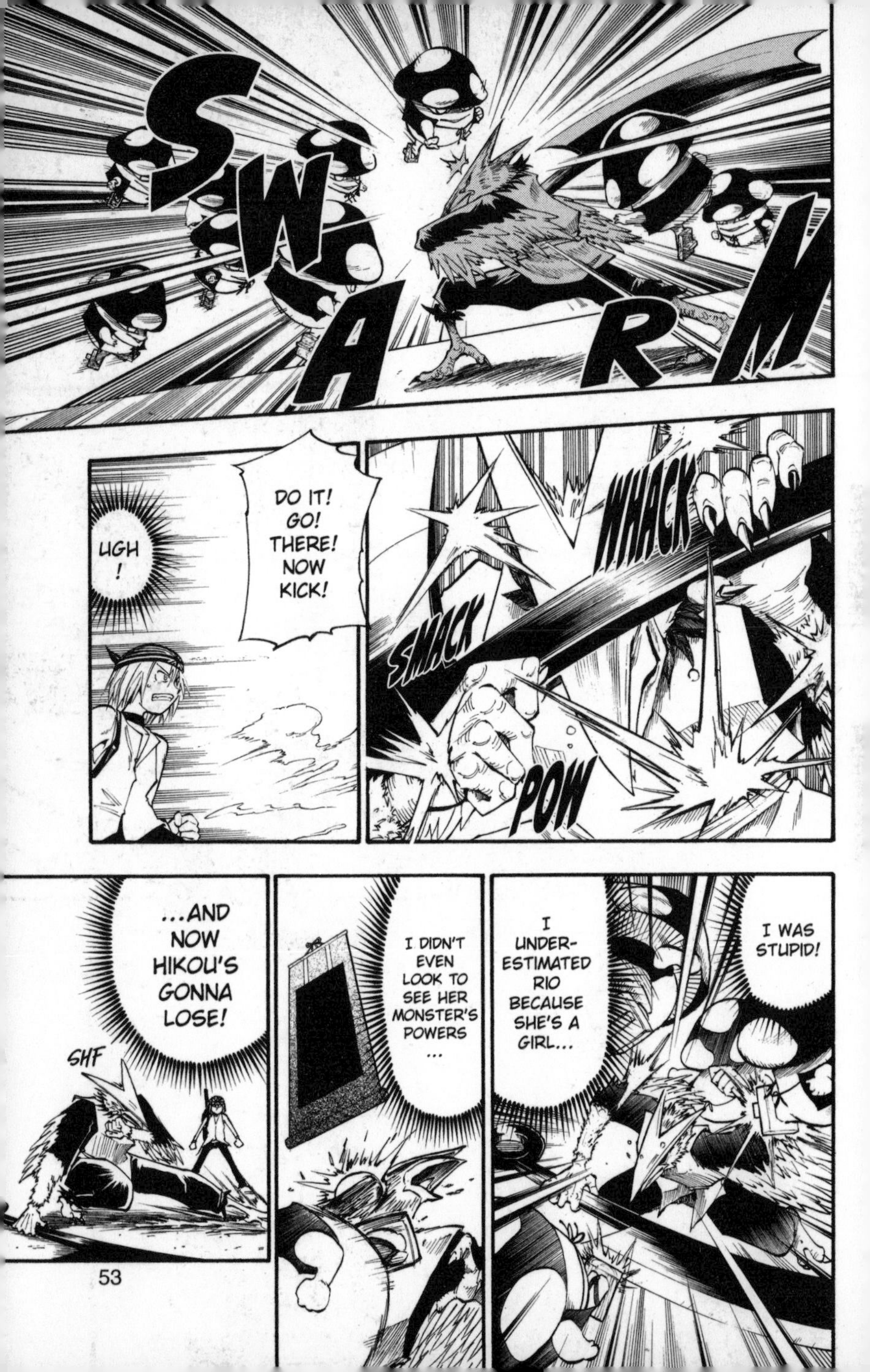
SWARM
WHACK
SMACK
POW
DO IT! GO! THERE! NOW KICK!
UGH!
I WAS STUPID!
I UNDER-ESTIMATED RIO BECAUSE SHE'S A GIRL...
I DIDN'T EVEN LOOK TO SEE HER MONSTER'S POWERS...
...AND NOW HIKOU'S GONNA LOSE!
SHF

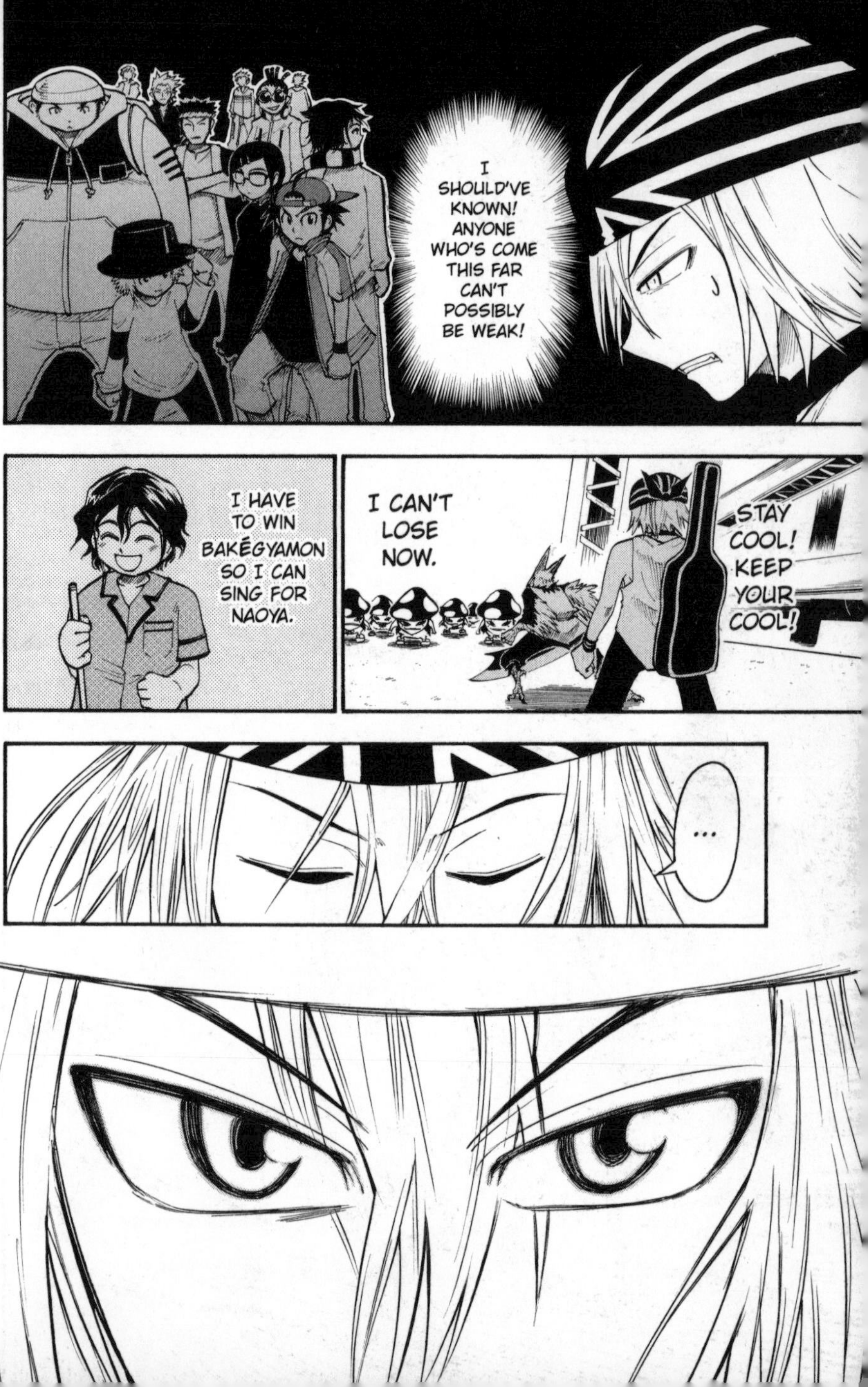
I SHOULD'VE KNOWN! ANYONE WHO'S COME THIS FAR CAN'T POSSIBLY BE WEAK!
STAY COOL! KEEP YOUR COOL!
I CAN'T LOSE NOW.
I HAVE TO WIN BAKÉGYAMON SO I CAN SING FOR NAOYA.
...

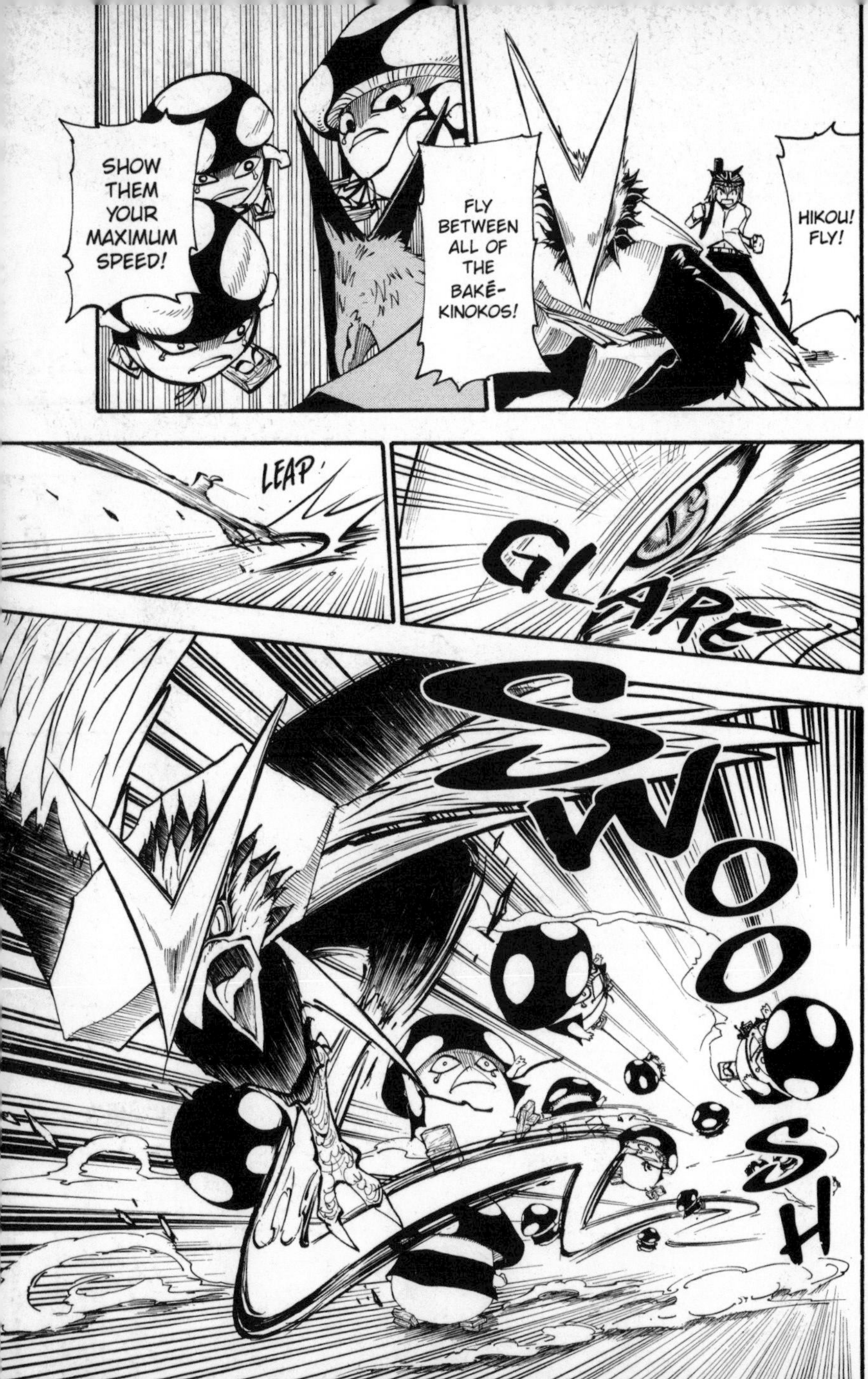
HIKOU! FLY!
FLY BETWEEN ALL OF THE BAKÉ-KINOKOS!
SHOW THEM YOUR MAXIMUM SPEED!
GLARE
LEAP
SWOOOSH

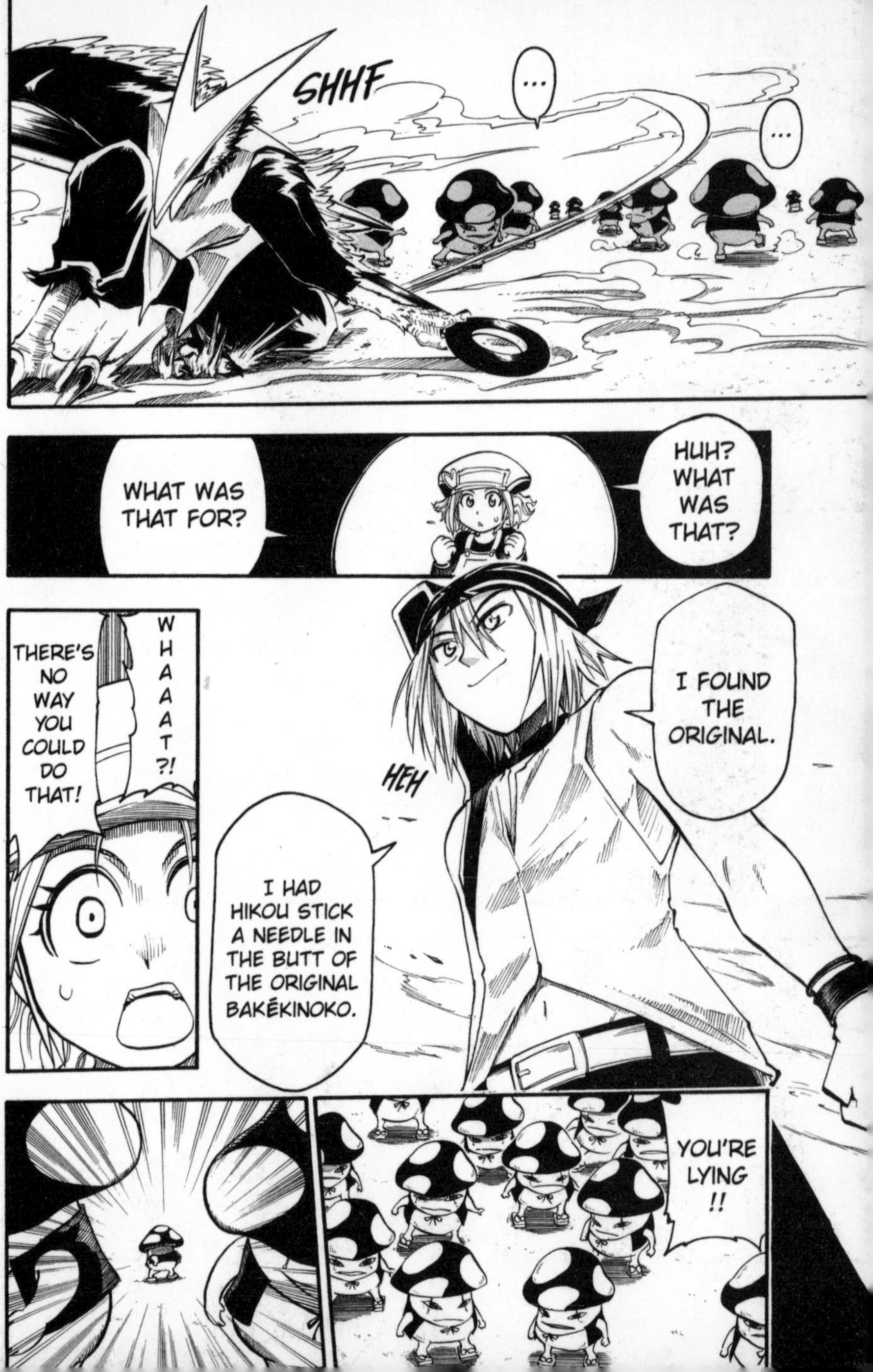
...
...
SHHF
HUH? WHAT WAS THAT?
WHAT WAS THAT FOR?
I FOUND THE ORIGINAL.
HEH
I HAD HIKOU STICK A NEEDLE IN THE BUTT OF THE ORIGINAL BAKÉKINOKO.
WHAAAAT?!
THERE'S NO WAY YOU COULD DO THAT!
YOU'RE LYING!!

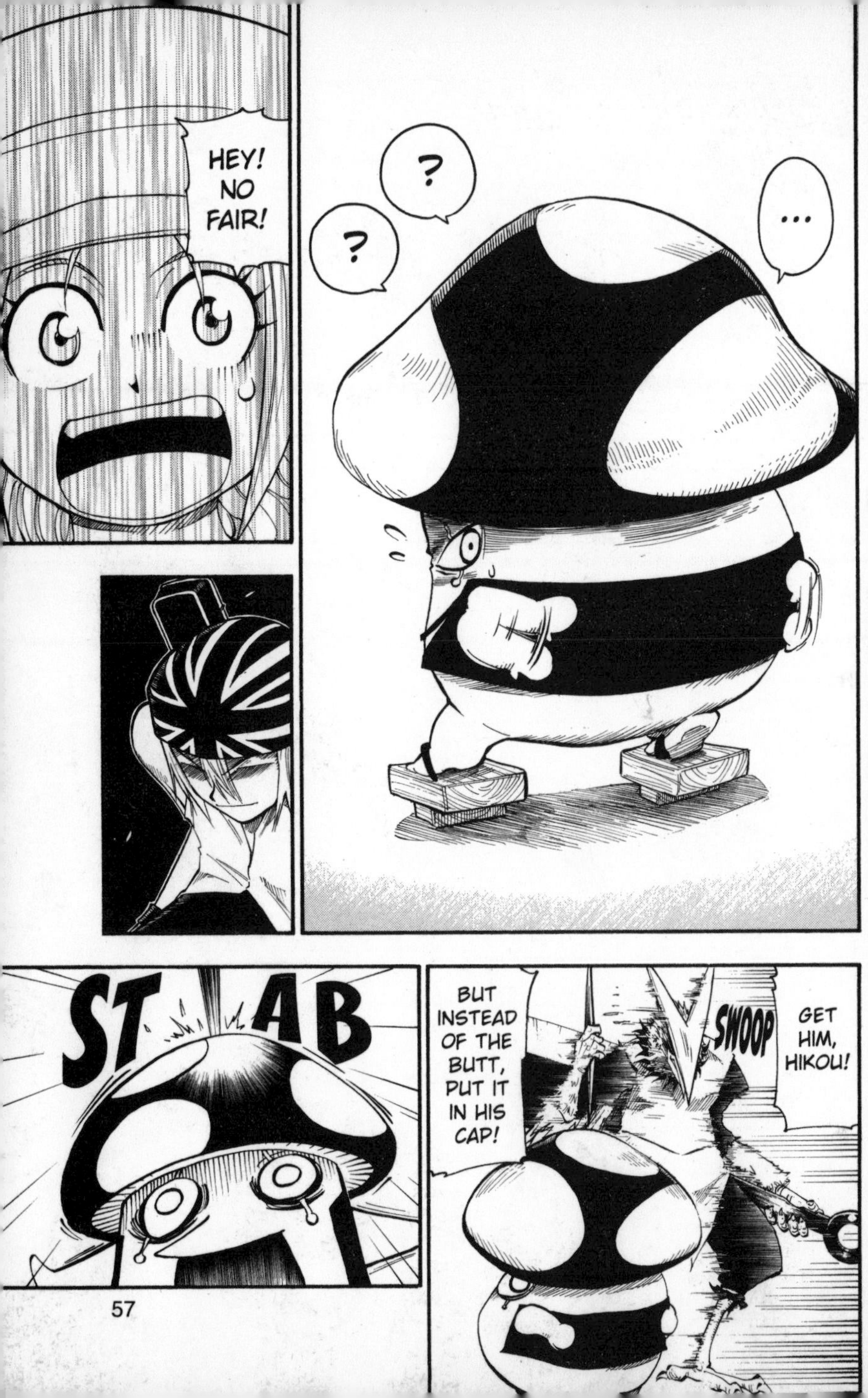
...
?
?
HEY! NO FAIR!
GET HIM, HIKOU!
SWOOP
BUT INSTEAD OF THE BUTT, PUT IT IN HIS CAP!
STAB

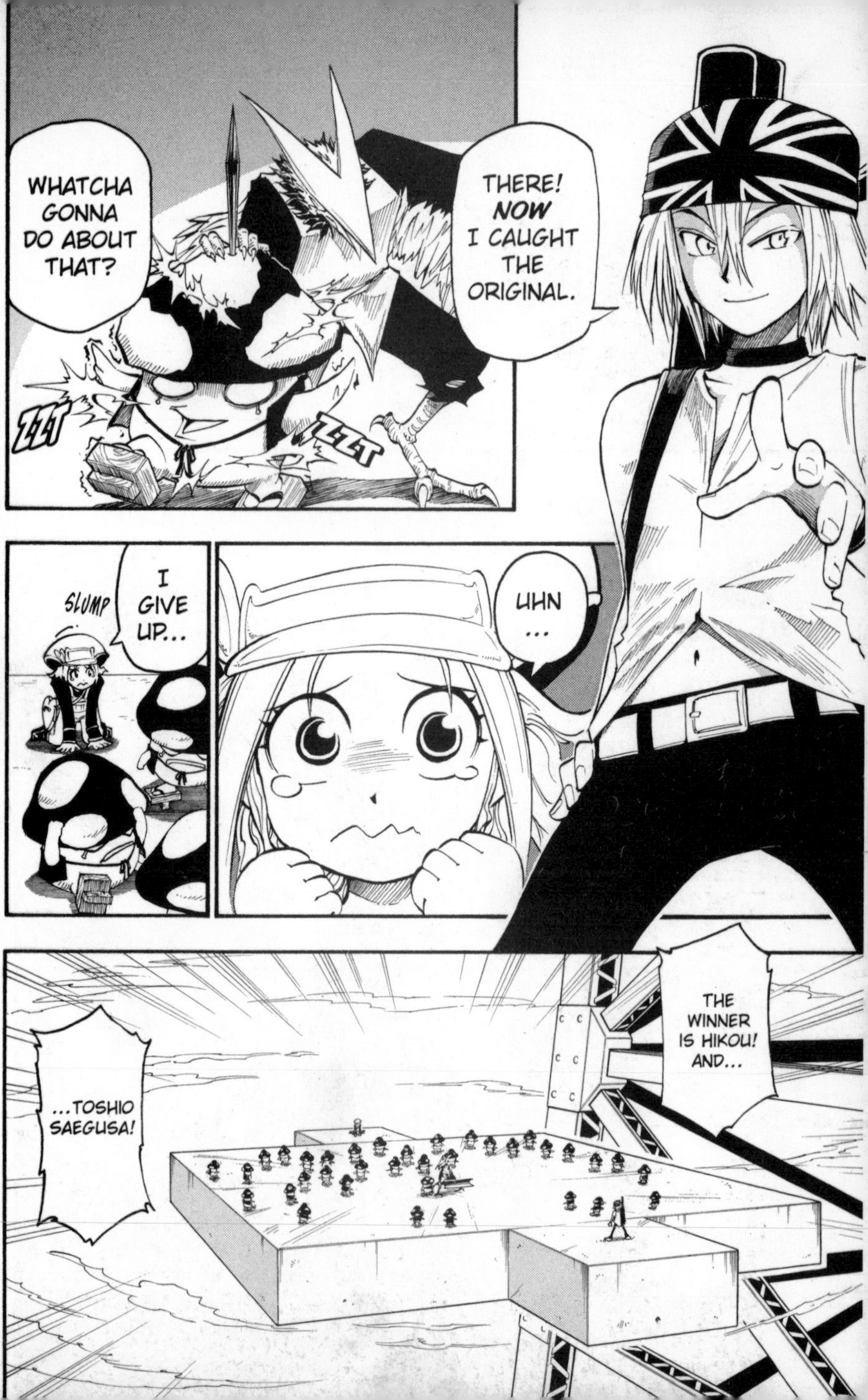
THERE! NOW I CAUGHT THE ORIGINAL.
WHATCHA GONNA DO ABOUT THAT?
ZZZT
ZZZT
UHN ...
I GIVE UP...
SLUMP
THE WINNER IS HIKOU! AND...
...TOSHIO SAEGUSA!

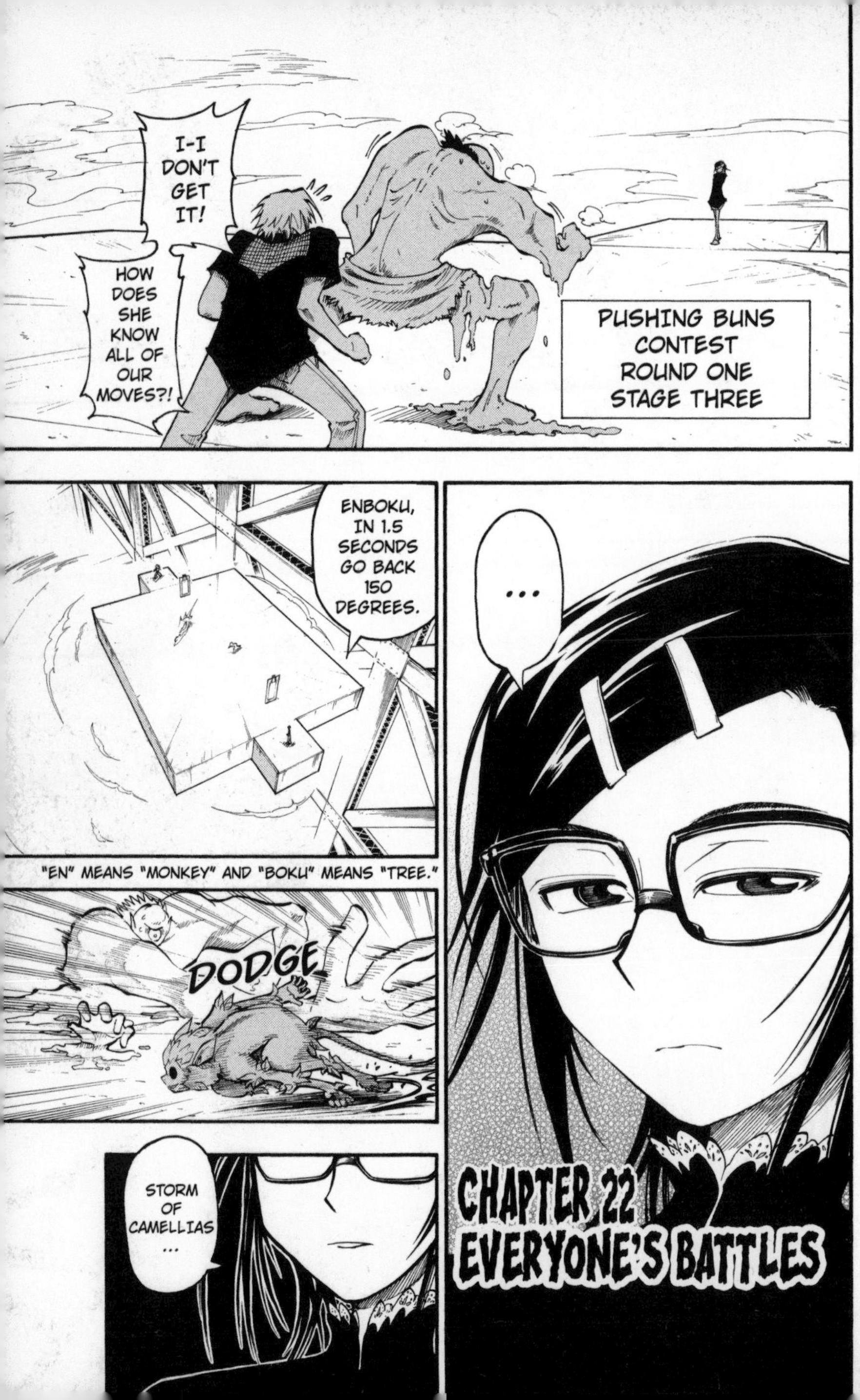
PUSHING BUNS CONTEST ROUND ONE STAGE THREE
I-I DON'T GET IT!
HOW DOES SHE KNOW ALL OF OUR MOVES?!
...
CHAPTER 22 EVERYONE'S BATTLES
ENBOKU, IN 1.5 SECONDS GO BACK 150 DEGREES.
"EN" MEANS "MONKEY" AND "BOKU" MEANS "TREE."
DODGE
STORM OF CAMELLIAS ...

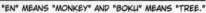

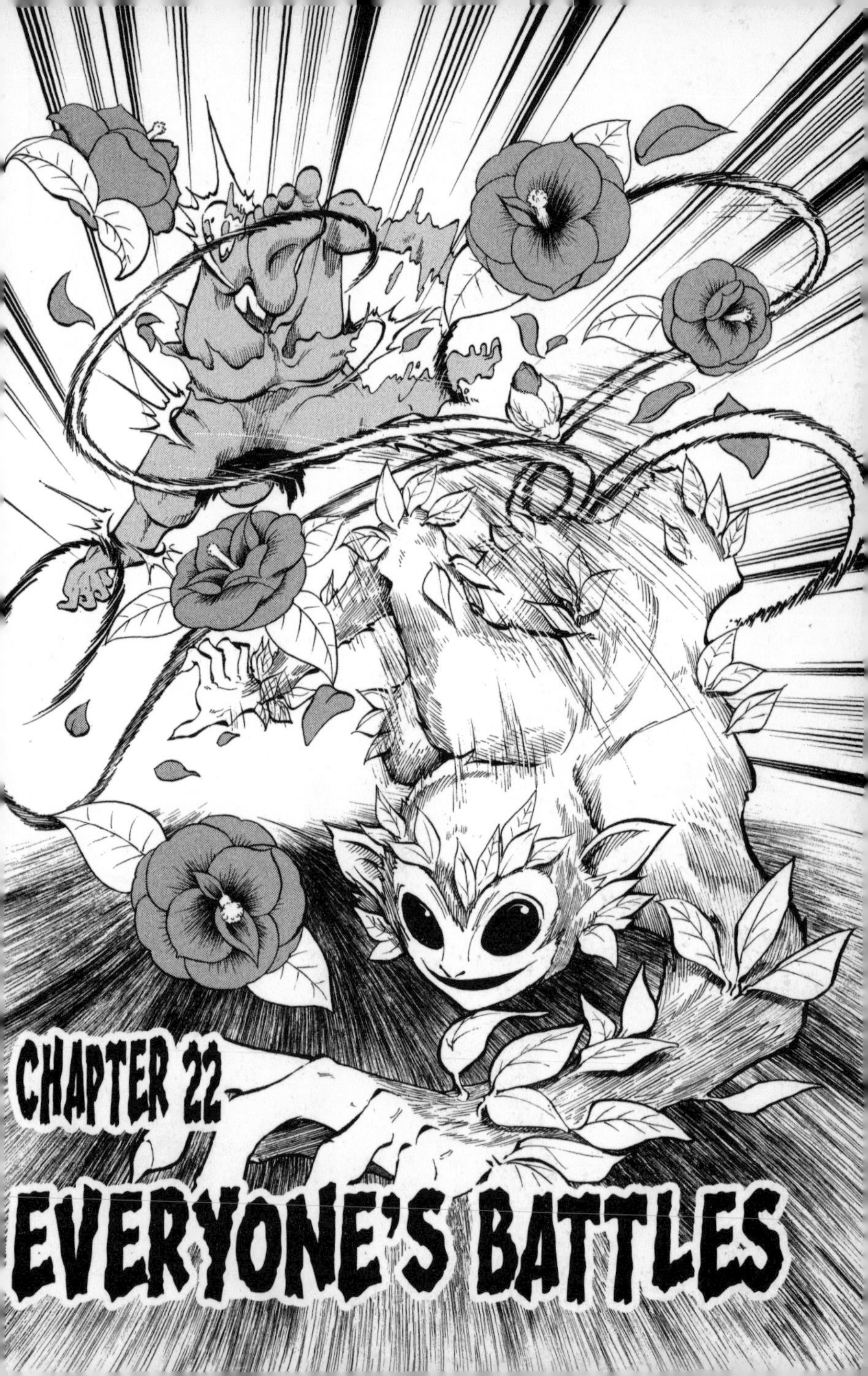
CHAPTER 22
EVERYONE'S BATTLES

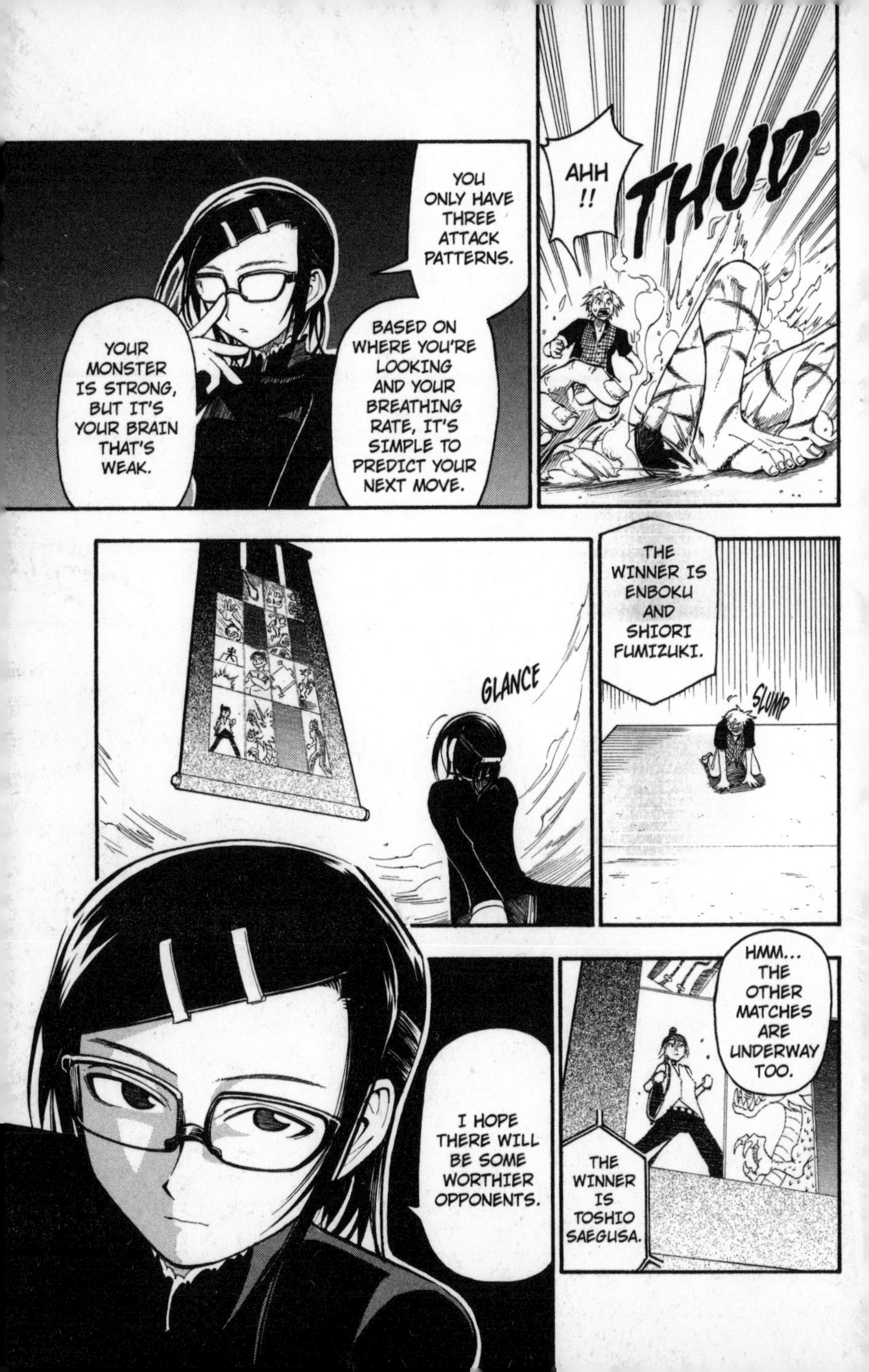
AHH!!
THUD
YOU ONLY HAVE THREE ATTACK PATTERNS.
BASED ON WHERE YOU'RE LOOKING AND YOUR BREATHING RATE, IT'S SIMPLE TO PREDICT YOUR NEXT MOVE.
YOUR MONSTER IS STRONG, BUT IT'S YOUR BRAIN THAT'S WEAK.
THE WINNER IS ENBOKU AND SHIORI FUMIZUKI.
SLUMP
GLANCE
HMM... THE OTHER MATCHES ARE UNDERWAY TOO.
THE WINNER IS TOSHIO SAEGUSA.
I HOPE THERE WILL BE SOME WORTHIER OPPONENTS.

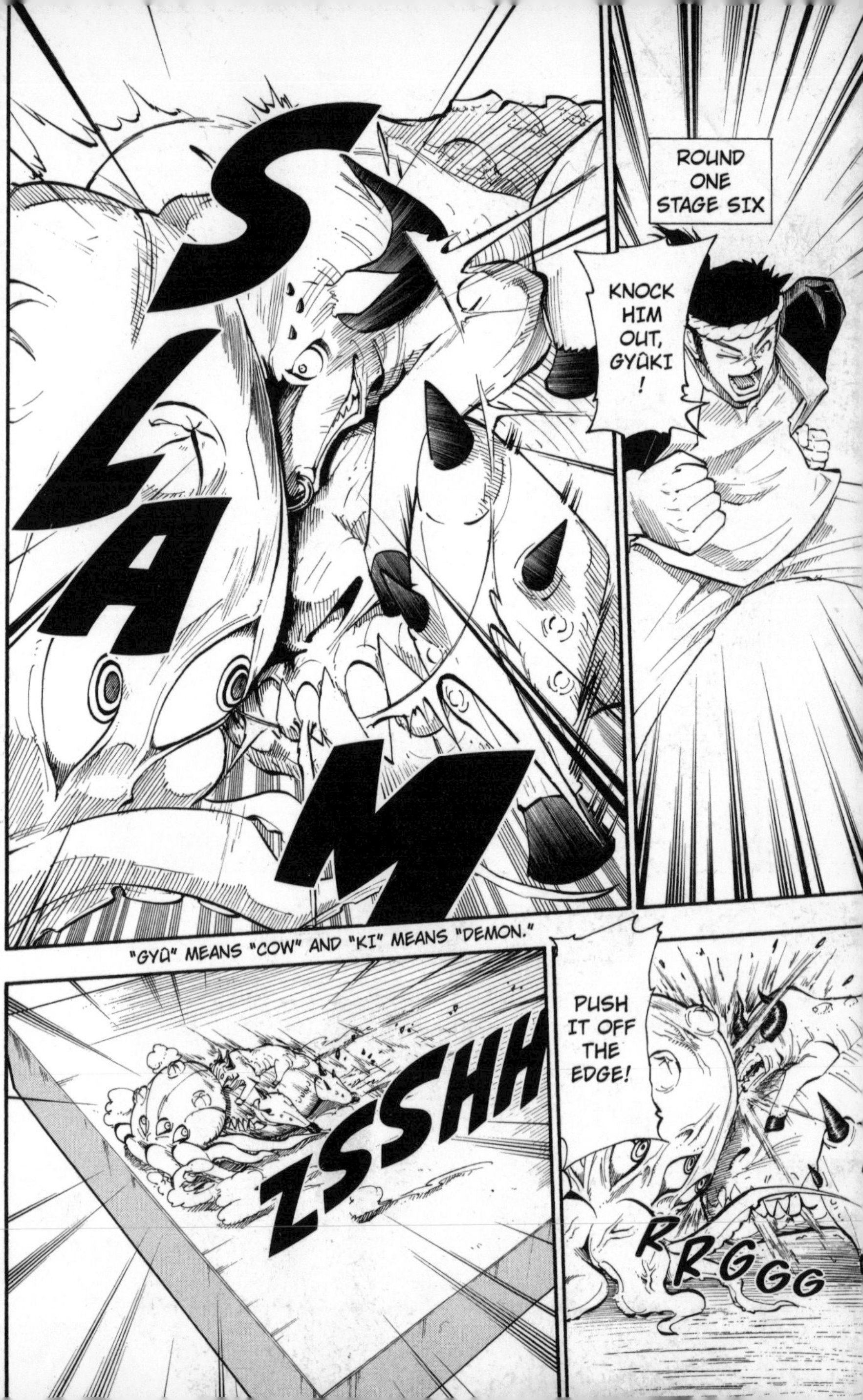
ROUND ONE STAGE SIX
KNOCK HIM OUT, GYÛKI!
SLAM
"GYÛ" MEANS "COW" AND "KI" MEANS "DEMON."
PUSH IT OFF THE EDGE!
RRGGGG
ZSSHH

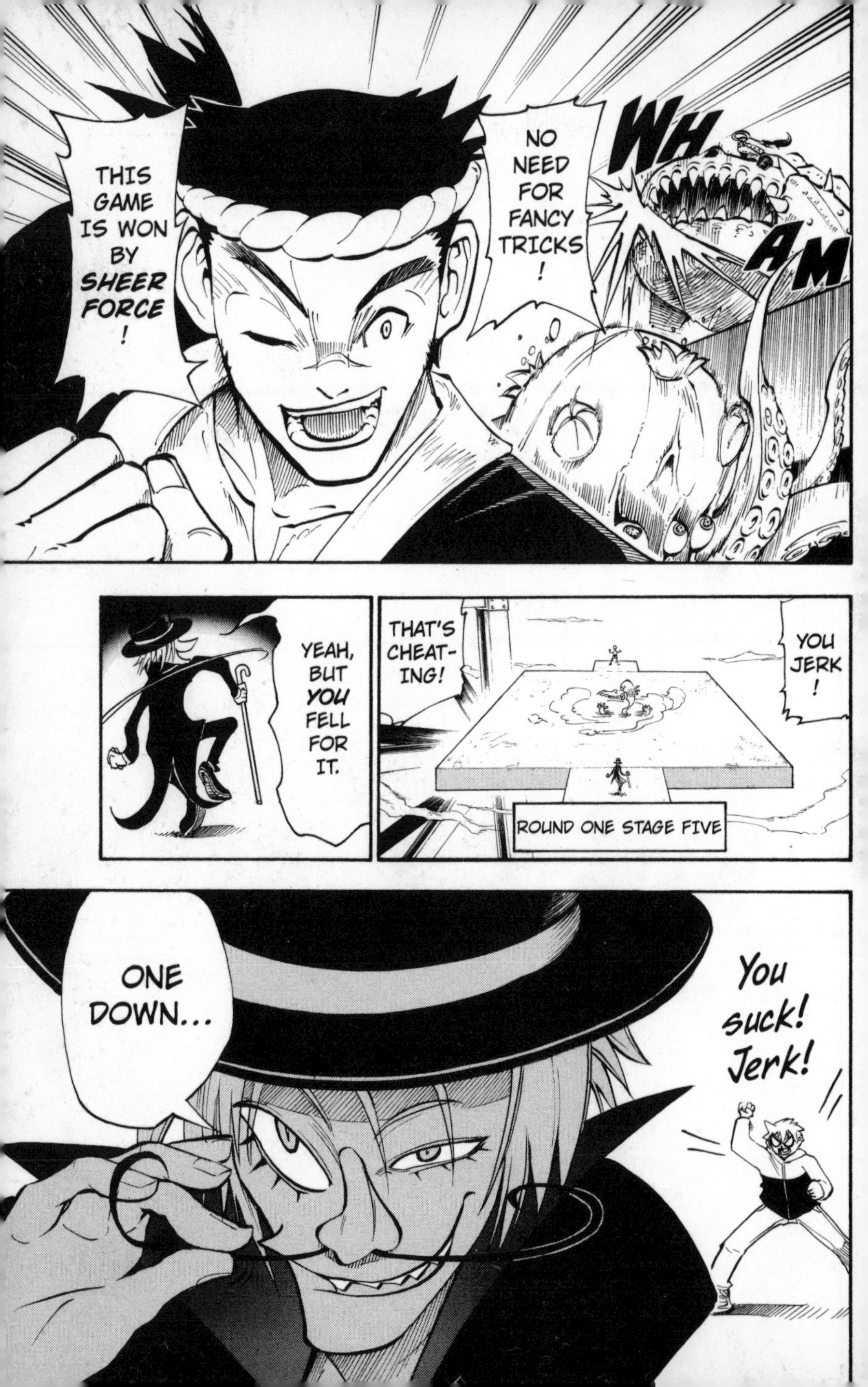
WHAM
NO NEED FOR FANCY TRICKS!
THIS GAME IS WON BY SHEER FORCE!
YOU JERK!
THAT'S CHEAT-ING!
ROUND ONE STAGE FIVE
YEAH, BUT YOU FELL FOR IT.
You suck! Jerk!
ONE DOWN...

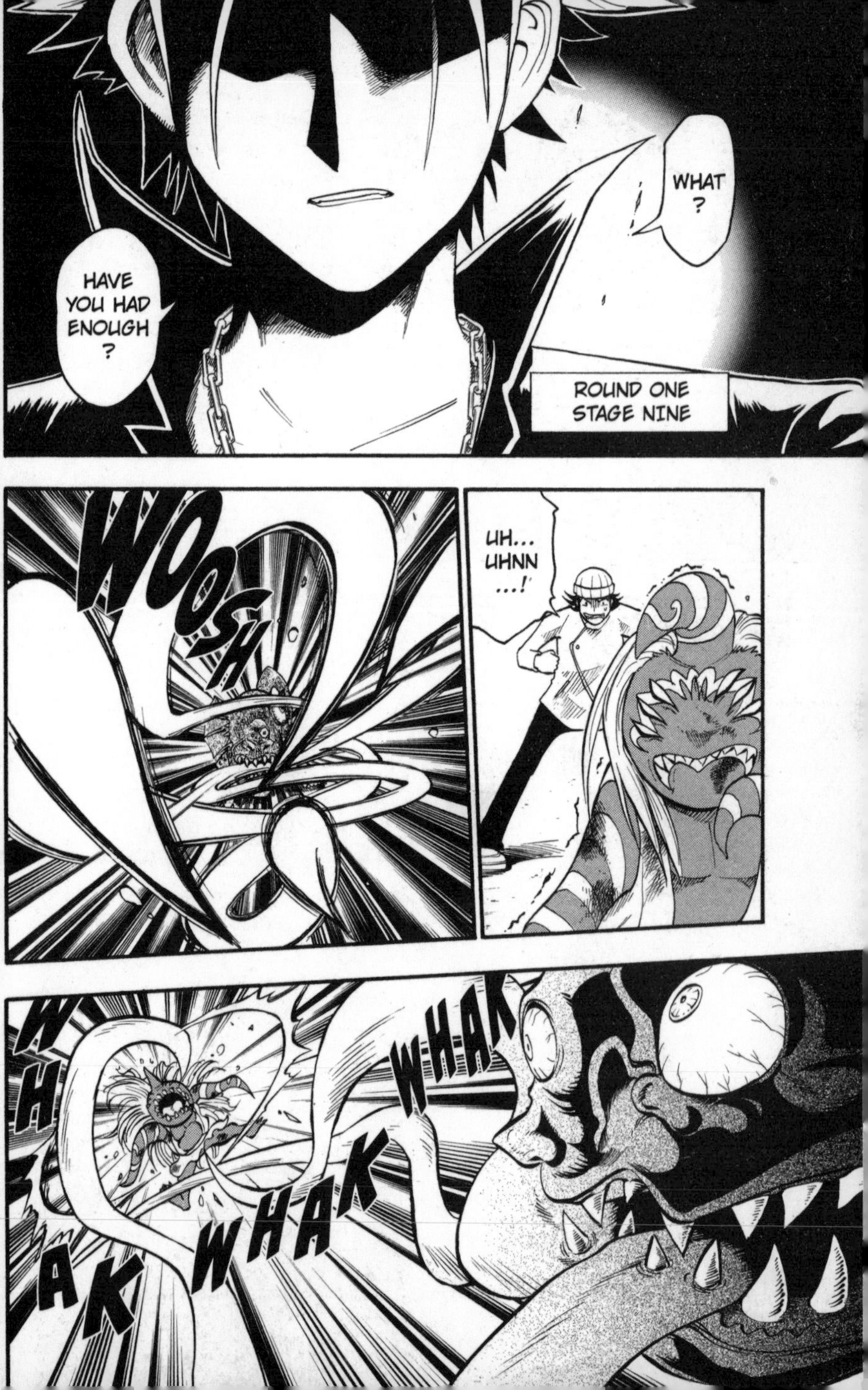
WHAT ?
HAVE YOU HAD ENOUGH ?
ROUND ONE STAGE NINE
UH... UHNN ...!
WOOSH
WHAK
WHAK
WHAK
WHAK

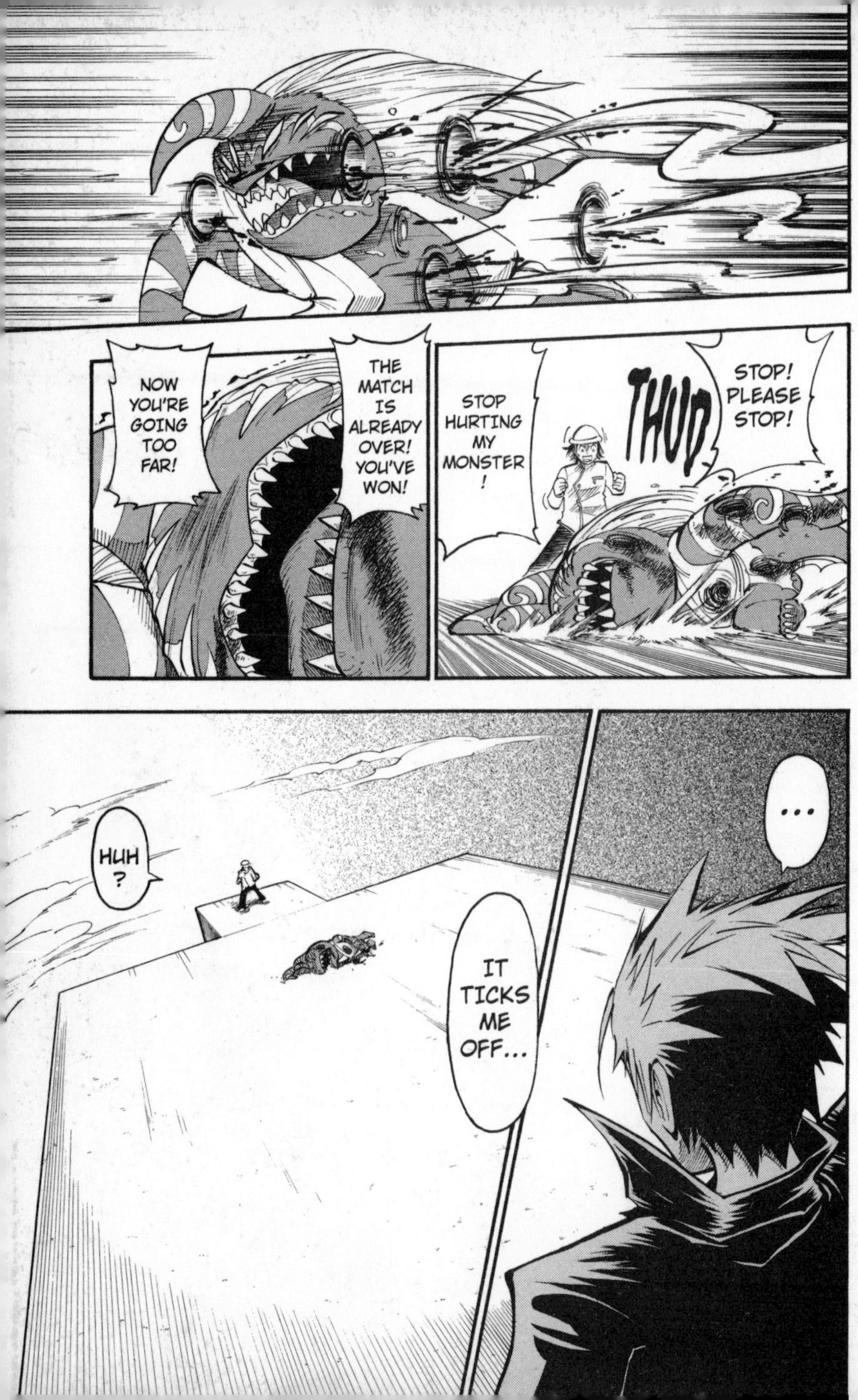
STOP! PLEASE STOP!
THUD
STOP HURTING MY MONSTER!
THE MATCH IS ALREADY OVER! YOU'VE WON!
NOW YOU'RE GOING TOO FAR!
...
IT TICKS ME OFF...
HUH?

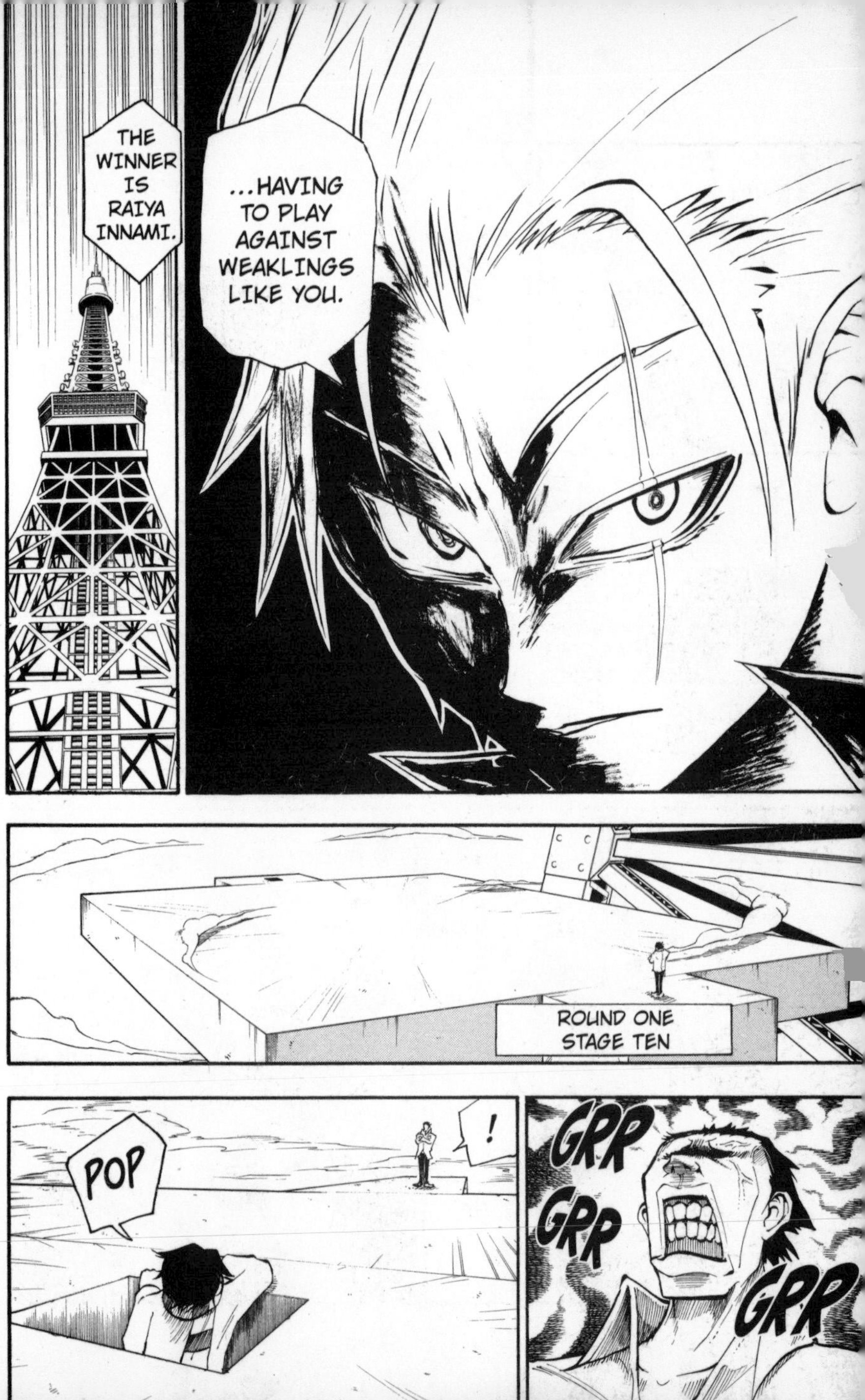
...HAVING TO PLAY AGAINST WEAKLINGS LIKE YOU.
THE WINNER IS RAIYA INNAMI.
ROUND ONE STAGE TEN
GRR
GRR
GRR
!
POP

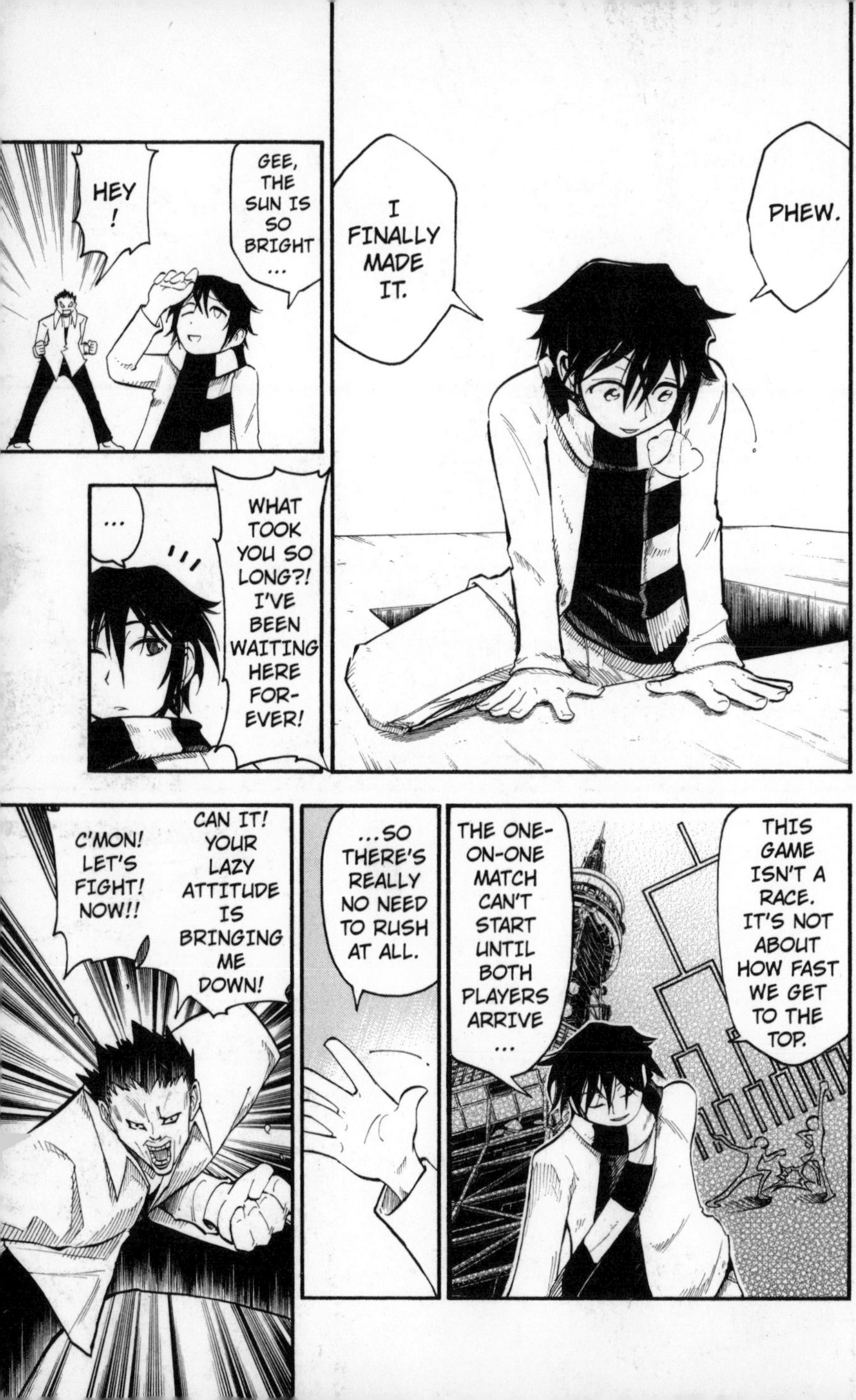

PHEW.
I FINALLY MADE IT.
GEE, THE SUN IS SO BRIGHT...
HEY!
WHAT TOOK YOU SO LONG?! I'VE BEEN WAITING HERE FOR-EVER!
...
THIS GAME ISN'T A RACE. IT'S NOT ABOUT HOW FAST WE GET TO THE TOP.
THE ONE-ON-ONE MATCH CAN'T START UNTIL BOTH PLAYERS ARRIVE...
...SO THERE'S REALLY NO NEED TO RUSH AT ALL.
CAN IT! YOUR LAZY ATTITUDE IS BRINGING ME DOWN!
C'MON! LET'S FIGHT! NOW!!

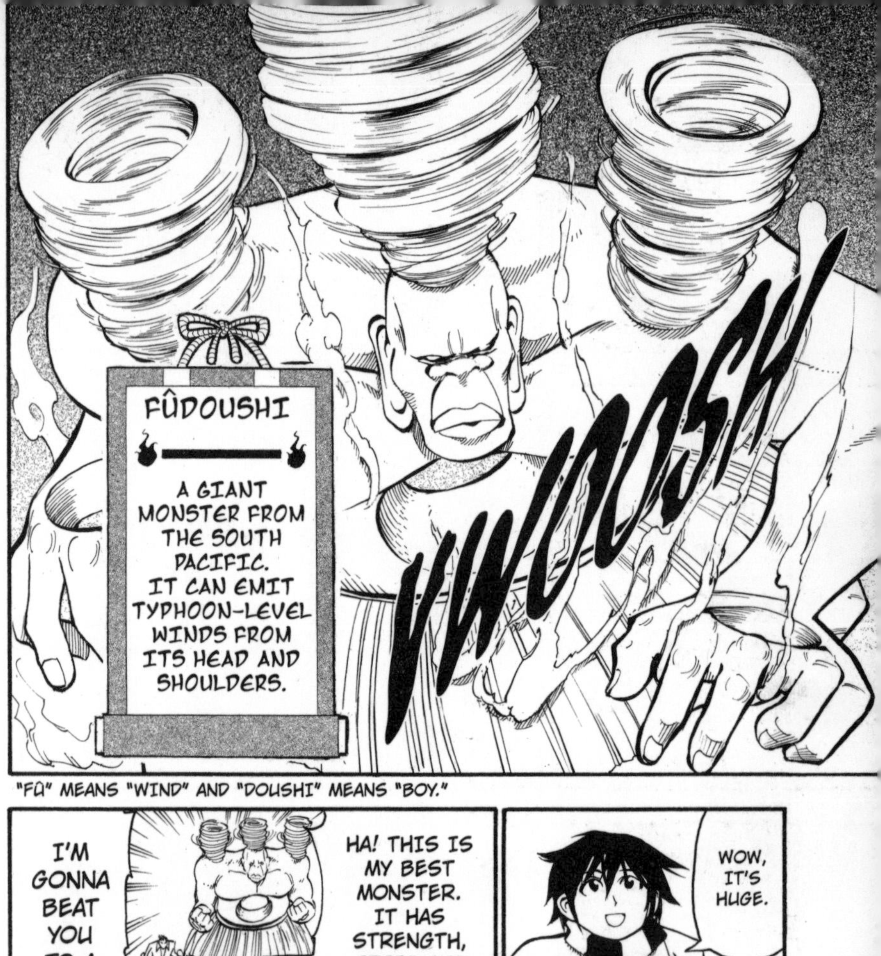
FÛDOUSHI
A GIANT MONSTER FROM THE SOUTH PACIFIC. IT CAN EMIT TYPHOON-LEVEL WINDS FROM ITS HEAD AND SHOULDERS.
VWOOSH

"FÛ" MEANS "WIND" AND "DOUSHI" MEANS "BOY."

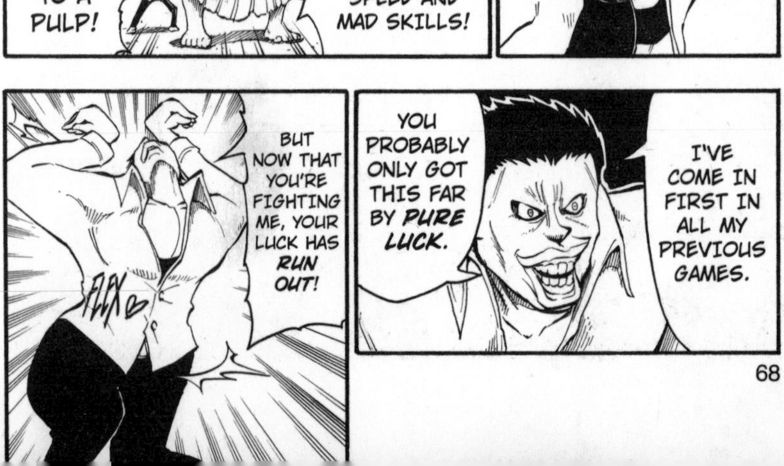
WOW, IT'S HUGE.
HA! THIS IS MY BEST MONSTER. IT HAS STRENGTH, SPEED AND MAD SKILLS!
I'M GONNA BEAT YOU TO A PULP!
I'VE COME IN FIRST IN ALL MY PREVIOUS GAMES.
YOU PROBABLY ONLY GOT THIS FAR BY *PURE LUCK*.
BUT NOW THAT YOU'RE FIGHTING ME, YOUR LUCK HAS *RUN OUT*!
FLEX

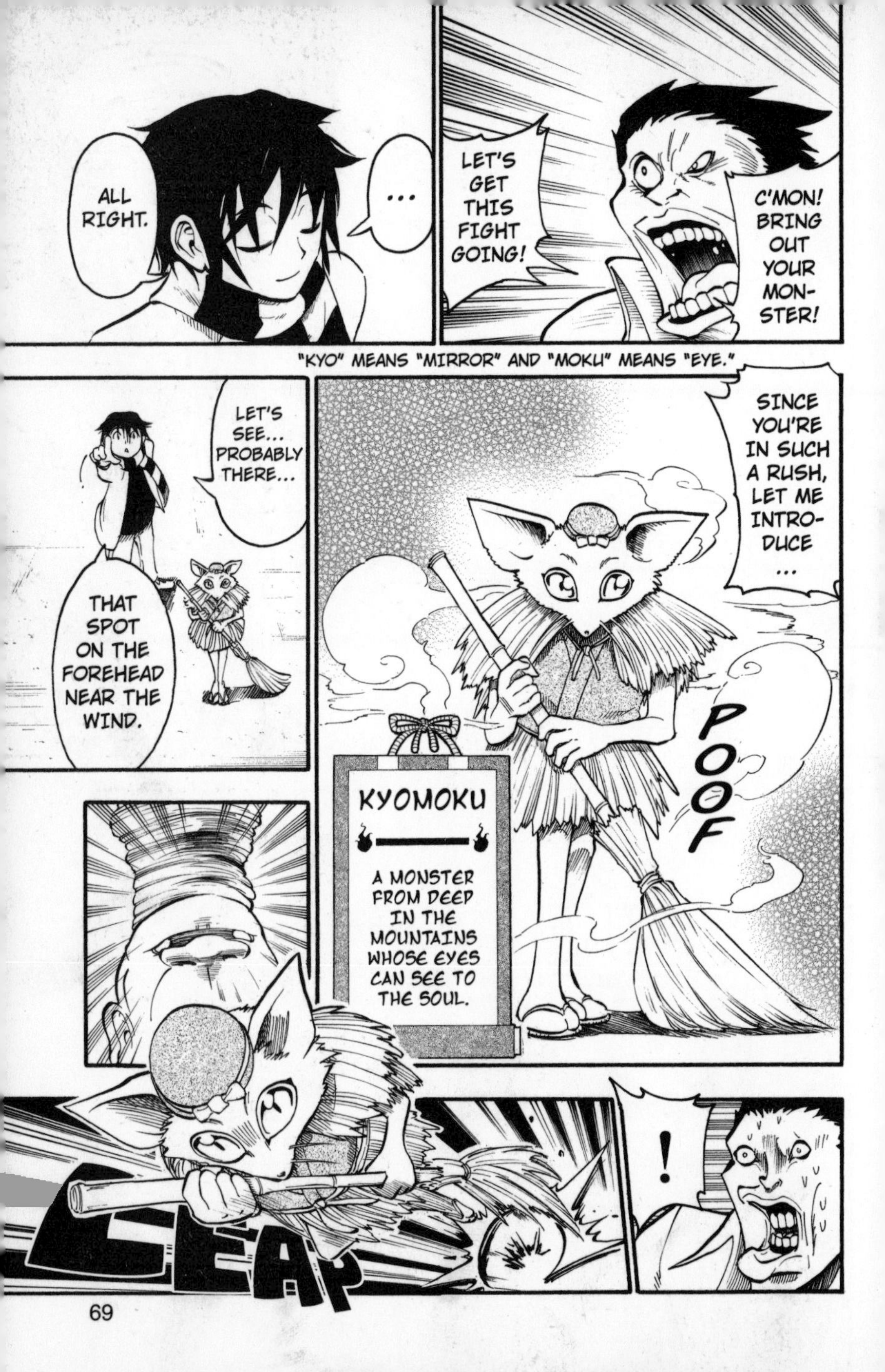
C'MON! BRING OUT YOUR MON-STER!
LET'S GET THIS FIGHT GOING!
...
ALL RIGHT.
"KYO" MEANS "MIRROR" AND "MOKU" MEANS "EYE."
SINCE YOU'RE IN SUCH A RUSH, LET ME INTRO-DUCE ...
POOF
KYOMOKU
A MONSTER FROM DEEP IN THE MOUNTAINS WHOSE EYES CAN SEE TO THE SOUL.
LET'S SEE... PROBABLY THERE...
THAT SPOT ON THE FOREHEAD NEAR THE WIND.
!
LEAP

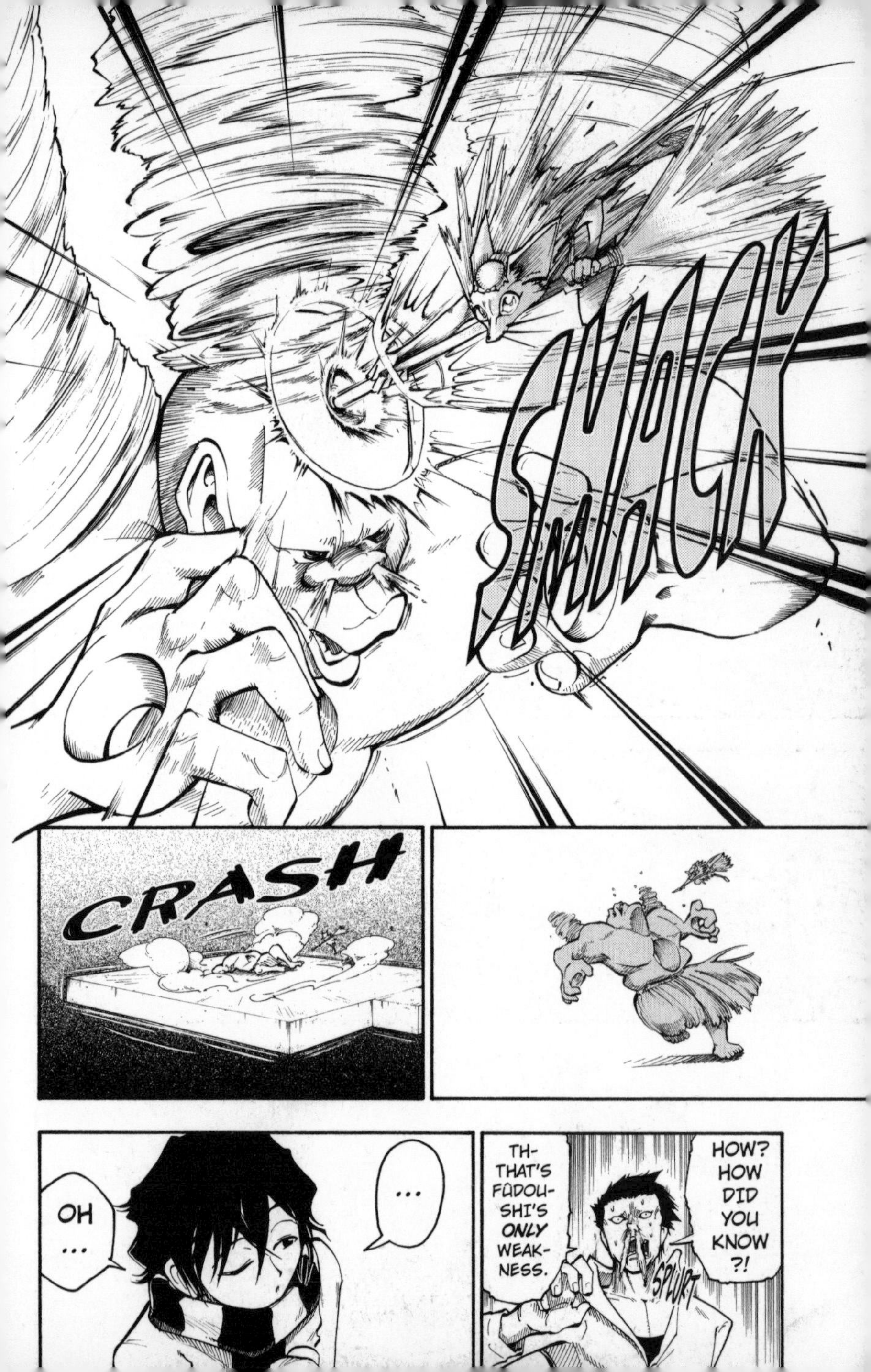
SMACK
CRASH
HOW? HOW DID YOU KNOW ?!
SPLURT
TH- THAT'S FŪDOU-SHI'S ONLY WEAK-NESS.
...
OH ...

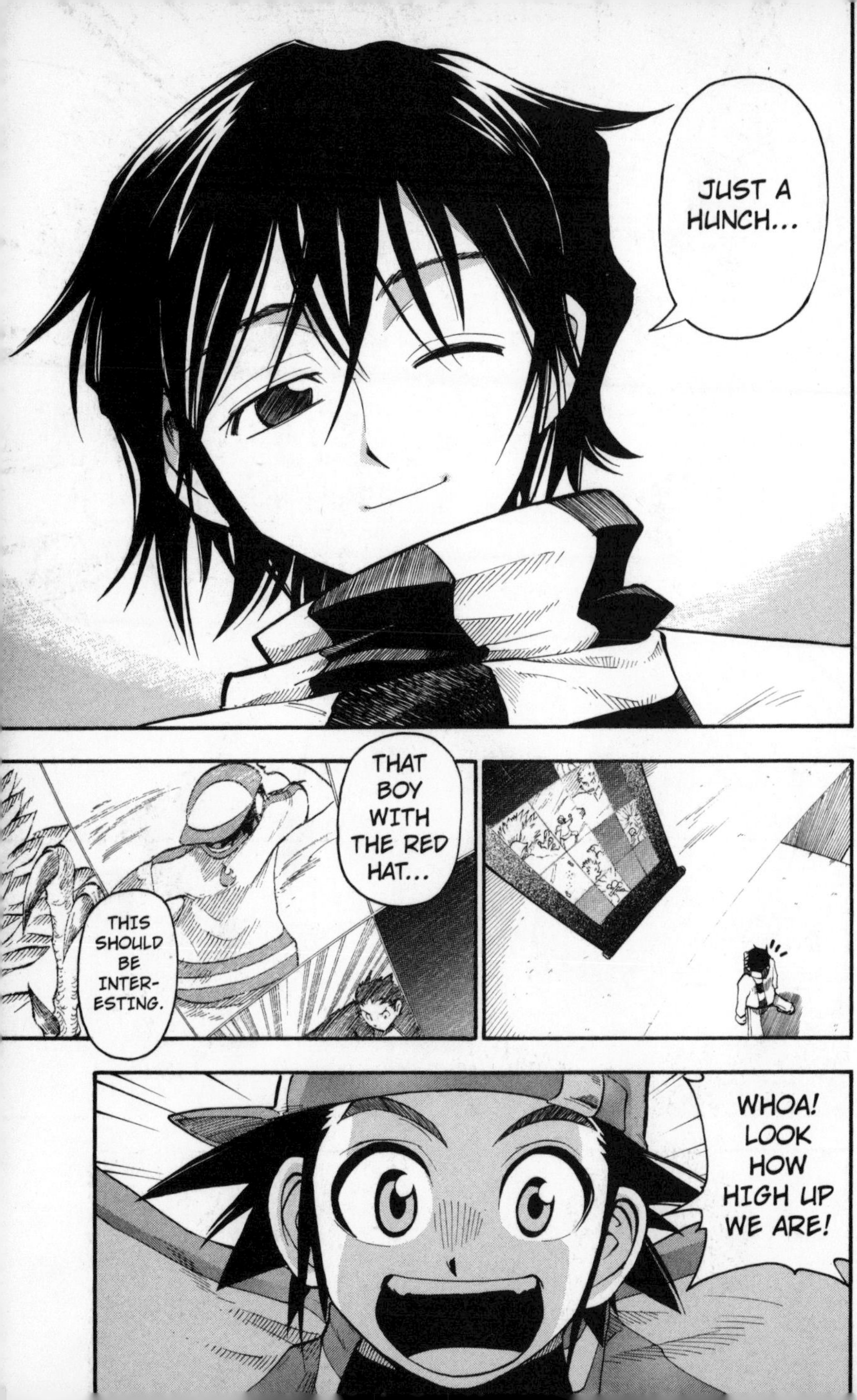
JUST A HUNCH...
THAT BOY WITH THE RED HAT...
THIS SHOULD BE INTER-ESTING.
WHOA! LOOK HOW HIGH UP WE ARE!

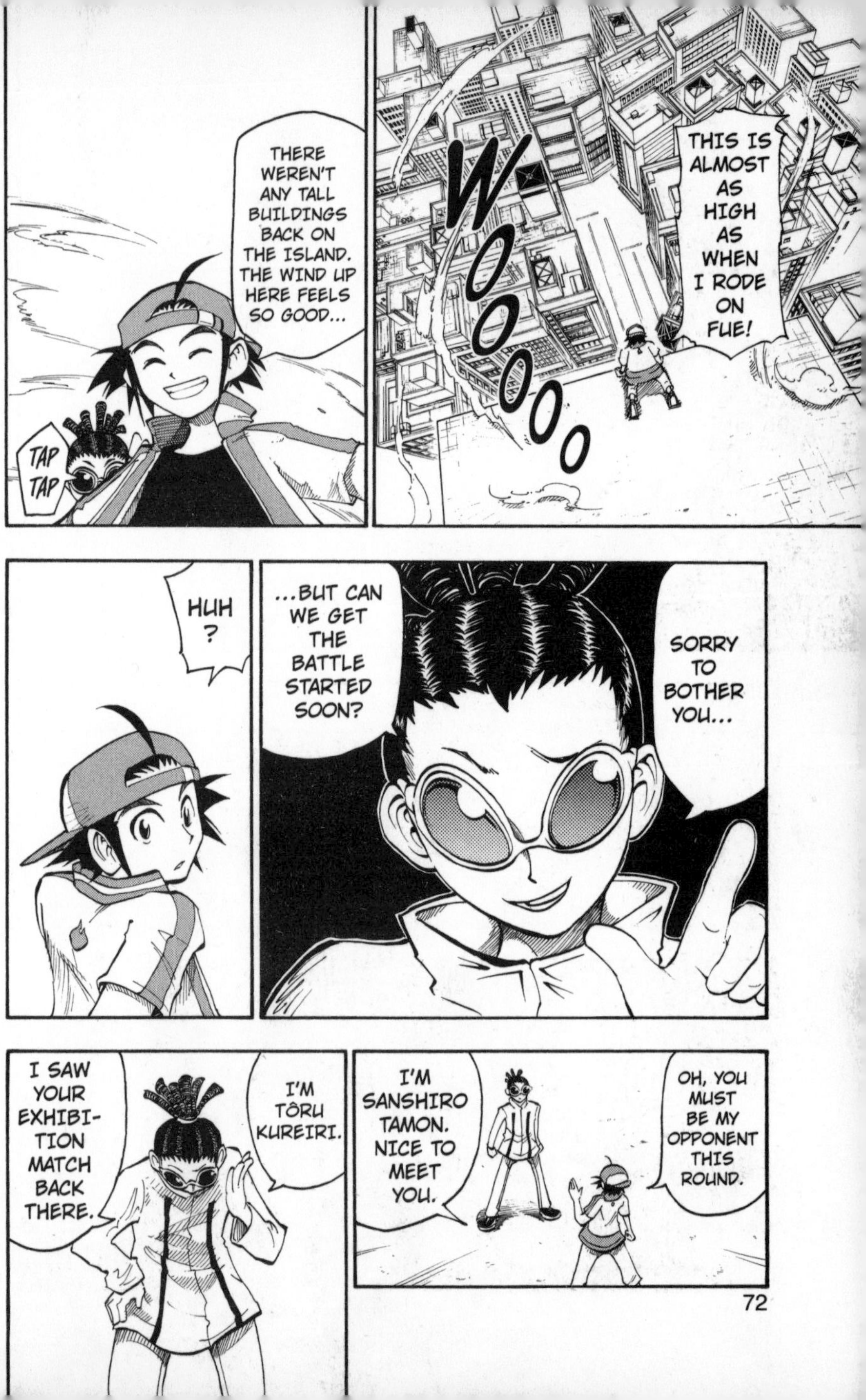
THIS IS ALMOST AS HIGH AS WHEN I RODE ON FUE!
WOOOOOO
THERE WEREN'T ANY TALL BUILDINGS BACK ON THE ISLAND. THE WIND UP HERE FEELS SO GOOD...
TAP TAP
SORRY TO BOTHER YOU...
...BUT CAN WE GET THE BATTLE STARTED SOON?
HUH?
OH, YOU MUST BE MY OPPONENT THIS ROUND.
I'M SANSHIRO TAMON. NICE TO MEET YOU.
I'M TÔRU KUREIRI.
I SAW YOUR EXHIBI-TION MATCH BACK THERE.

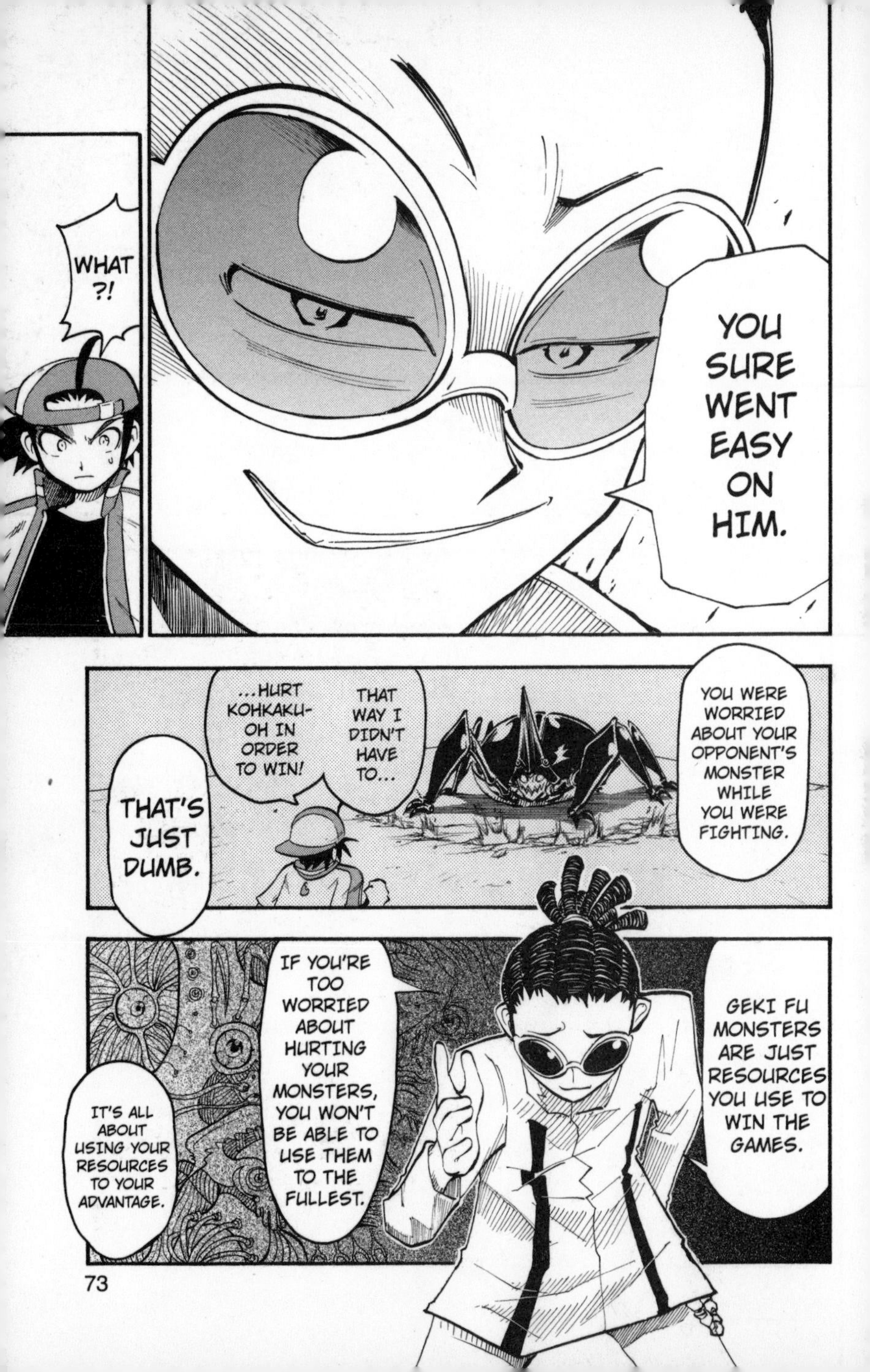
YOU SURE WENT EASY ON HIM.
WHAT ?!
YOU WERE WORRIED ABOUT YOUR OPPONENT'S MONSTER WHILE YOU WERE FIGHTING.
THAT WAY I DIDN'T HAVE TO...
...HURT KOHKAKU-OH IN ORDER TO WIN!
THAT'S JUST DUMB.
GEKI FU MONSTERS ARE JUST RESOURCES YOU USE TO WIN THE GAMES.
IF YOU'RE TOO WORRIED ABOUT HURTING YOUR MONSTERS, YOU WON'T BE ABLE TO USE THEM TO THE FULLEST.
IT'S ALL ABOUT USING YOUR RESOURCES TO YOUR ADVANTAGE.

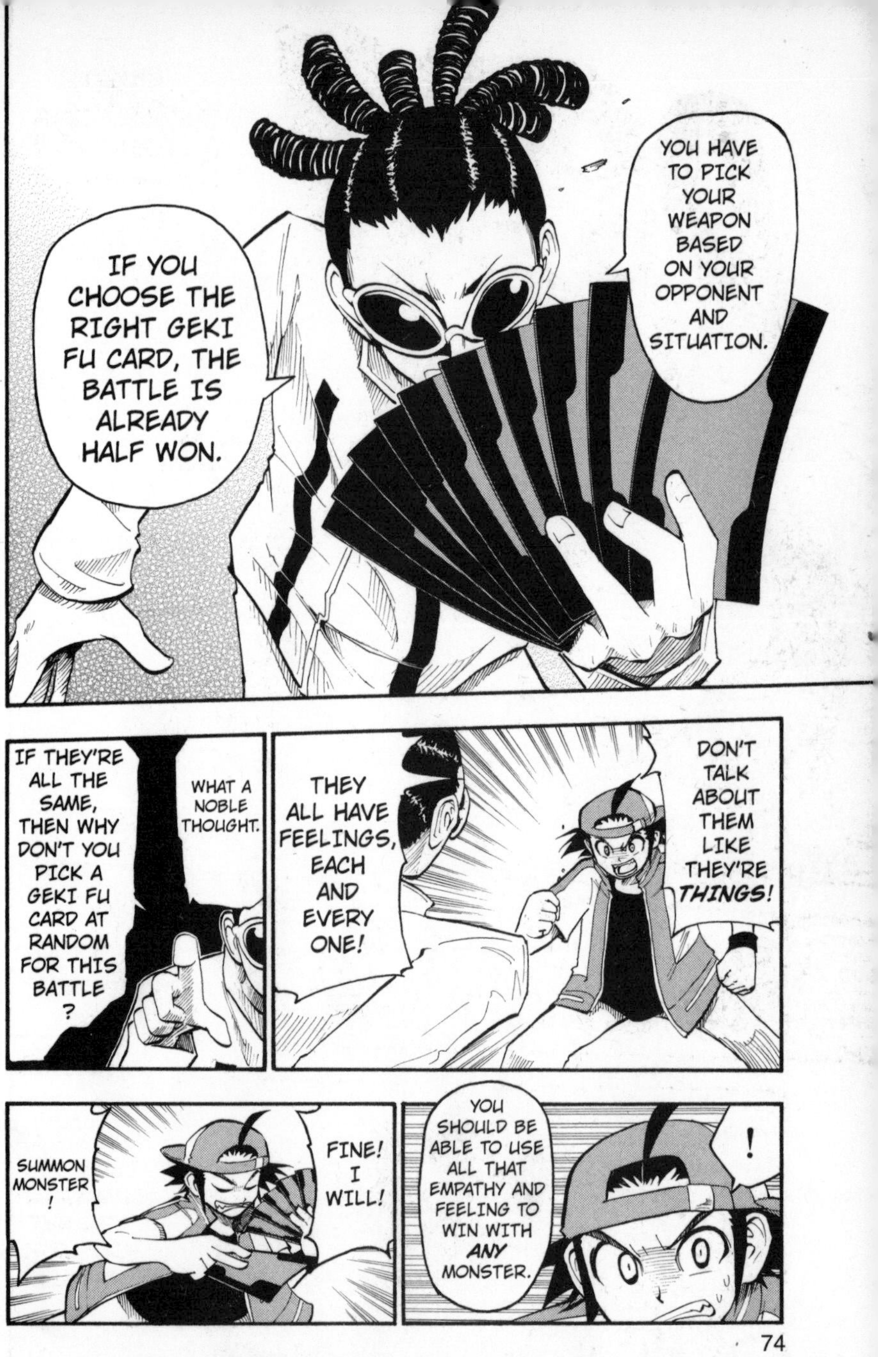
YOU HAVE TO PICK YOUR WEAPON BASED ON YOUR OPPONENT AND SITUATION.
IF YOU CHOOSE THE RIGHT GEKI FU CARD, THE BATTLE IS ALREADY HALF WON.
DON'T TALK ABOUT THEM LIKE THEY'RE *THINGS*!
THEY ALL HAVE FEELINGS, EACH AND EVERY ONE!
WHAT A NOBLE THOUGHT.
IF THEY'RE ALL THE SAME, THEN WHY DON'T YOU PICK A GEKI FU CARD AT RANDOM FOR THIS BATTLE?
!
YOU SHOULD BE ABLE TO USE ALL THAT EMPATHY AND FEELING TO WIN WITH *ANY* MONSTER.
FINE! I WILL!
SUMMON MONSTER!

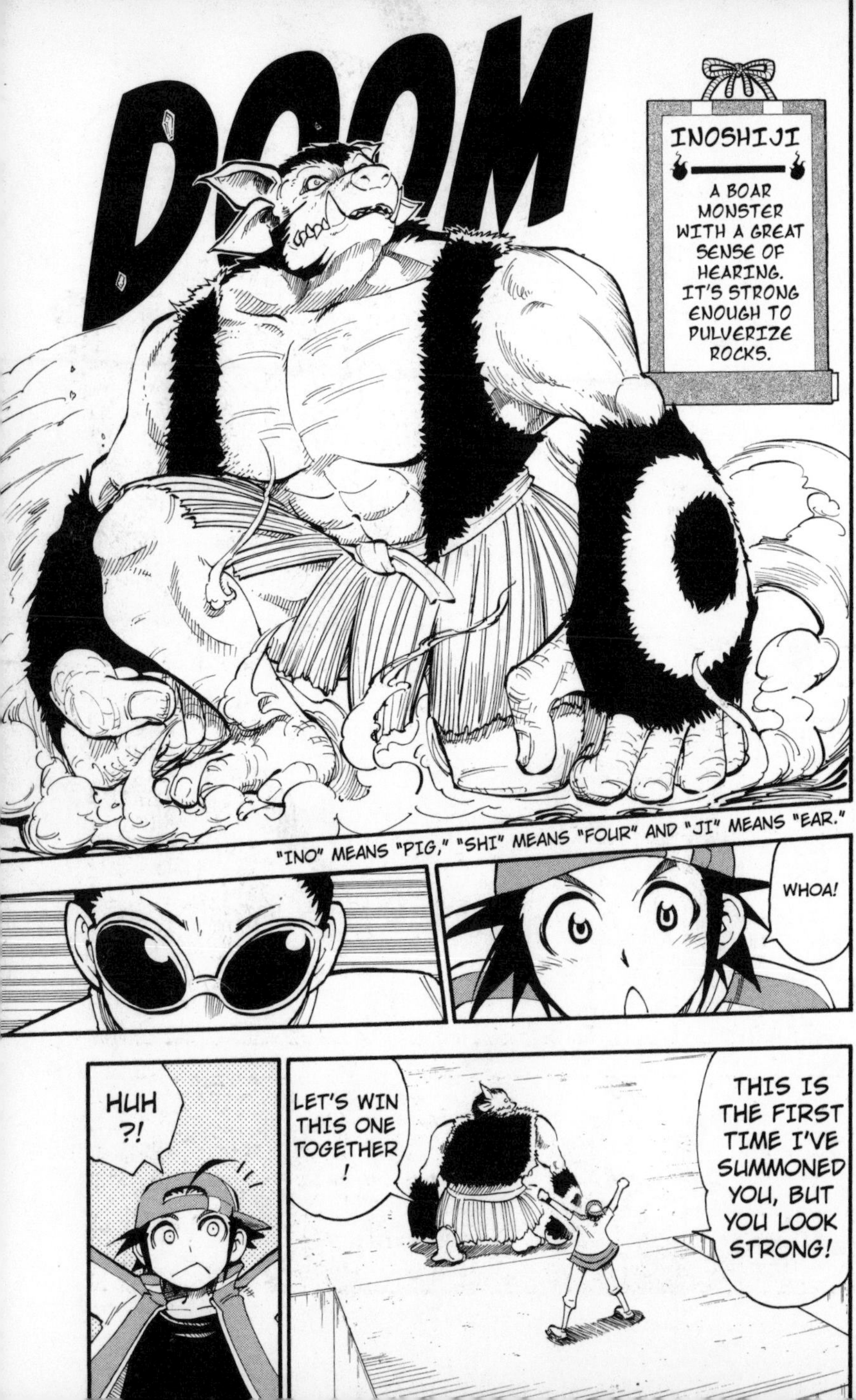
DOOM
INOSHIJI
A BOAR MONSTER WITH A GREAT SENSE OF HEARING. IT'S STRONG ENOUGH TO PULVERIZE ROCKS.
"INO" MEANS "PIG," "SHI" MEANS "FOUR" AND "JI" MEANS "EAR."
WHOA!
THIS IS THE FIRST TIME I'VE SUMMONED YOU, BUT YOU LOOK STRONG!
LET'S WIN THIS ONE TOGETHER!
HUH ?!

DON'T TELL ME...

POINT POINT

GROAN

WHAT? WHAT'S WRONG?

W-OOOOO

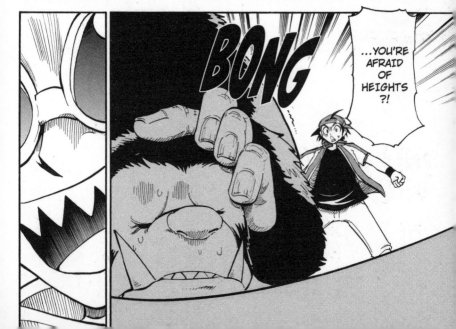

BONG

...YOU'RE AFRAID OF HEIGHTS?!

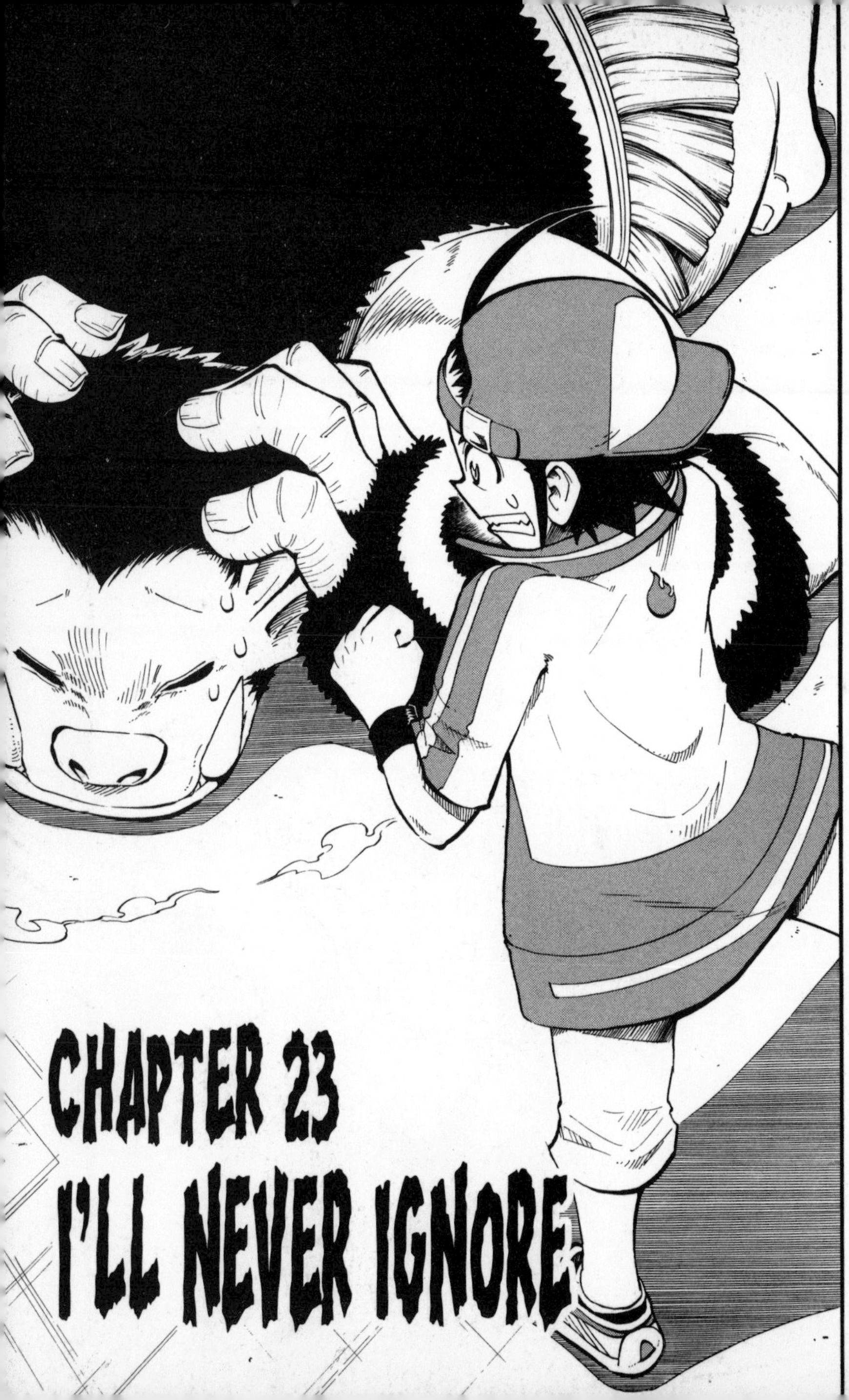
CHAPTER 23
I'LL NEVER IGNORE

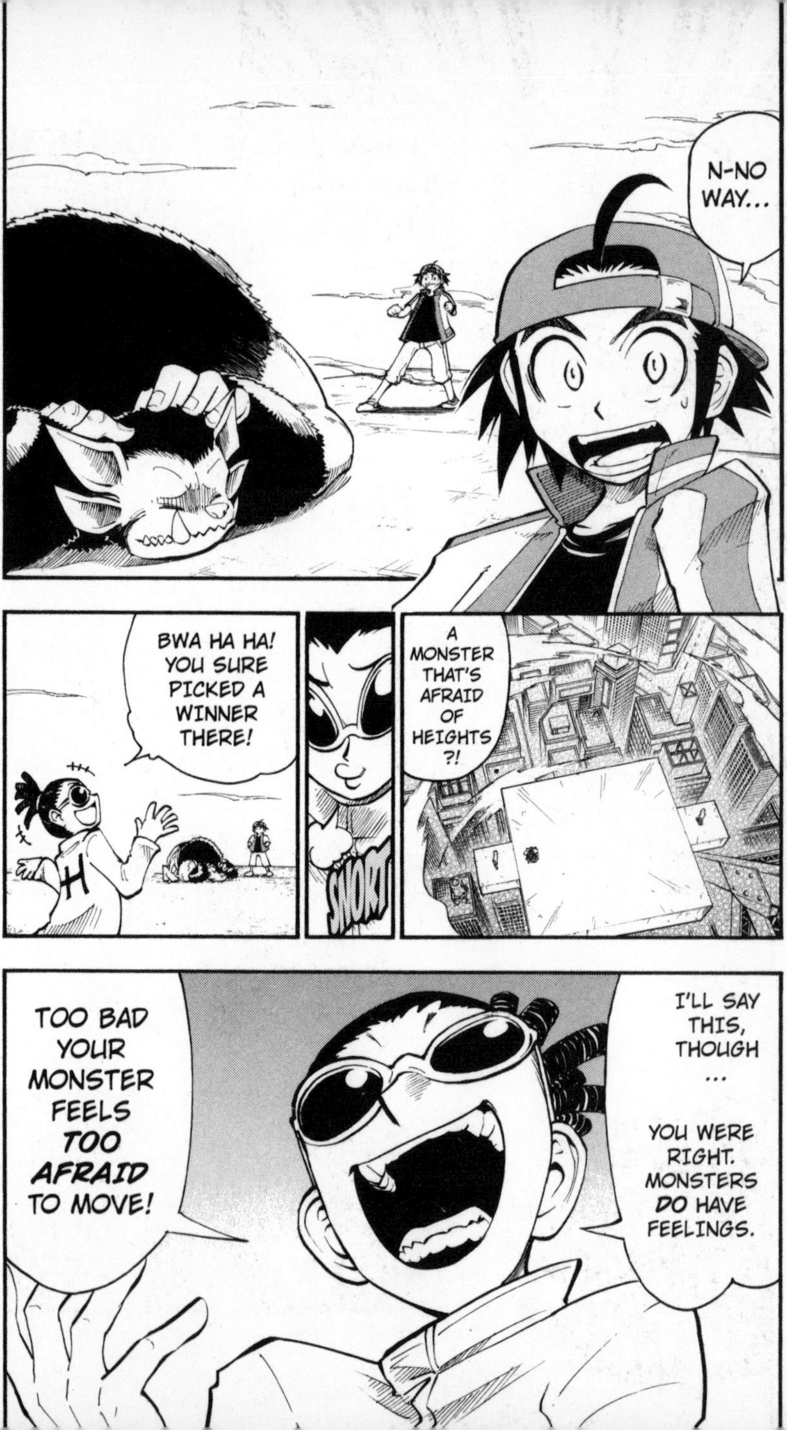
N-NO WAY...
A MONSTER THAT'S AFRAID OF HEIGHTS ?!
SNORT
BWA HA HA! YOU SURE PICKED A WINNER THERE!
I'LL SAY THIS, THOUGH ...
YOU WERE RIGHT. MONSTERS DO HAVE FEELINGS.
TOO BAD YOUR MONSTER FEELS TOO AFRAID TO MOVE!

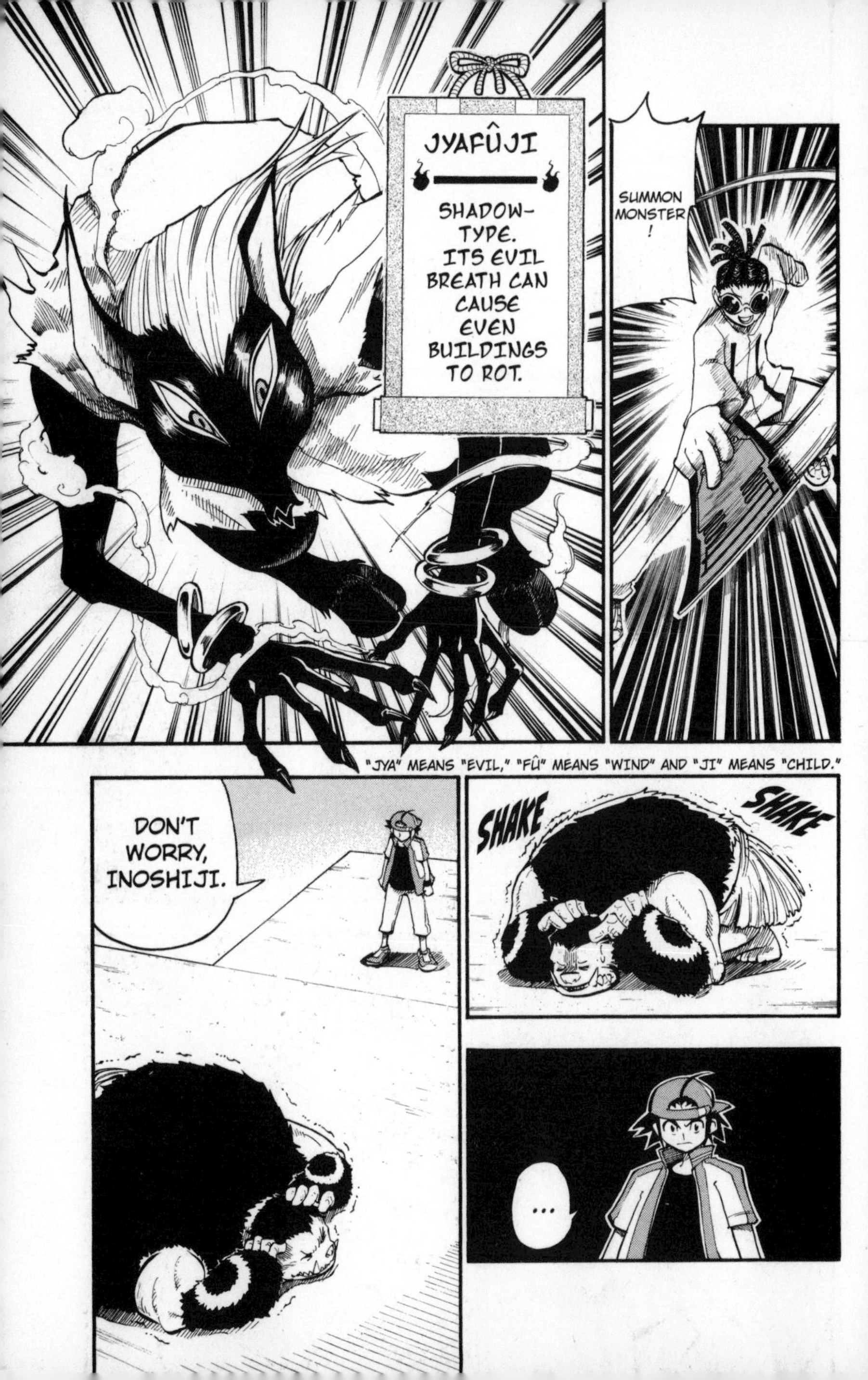
SUMMON MONSTER!
JYAFÛJI
SHADOW-TYPE. ITS EVIL BREATH CAN CAUSE EVEN BUILDINGS TO ROT.
"JYA" MEANS "EVIL," "FÛ" MEANS "WIND" AND "JI" MEANS "CHILD."
SHAKE
SHAKE
...
DON'T WORRY, INOSHIJI.

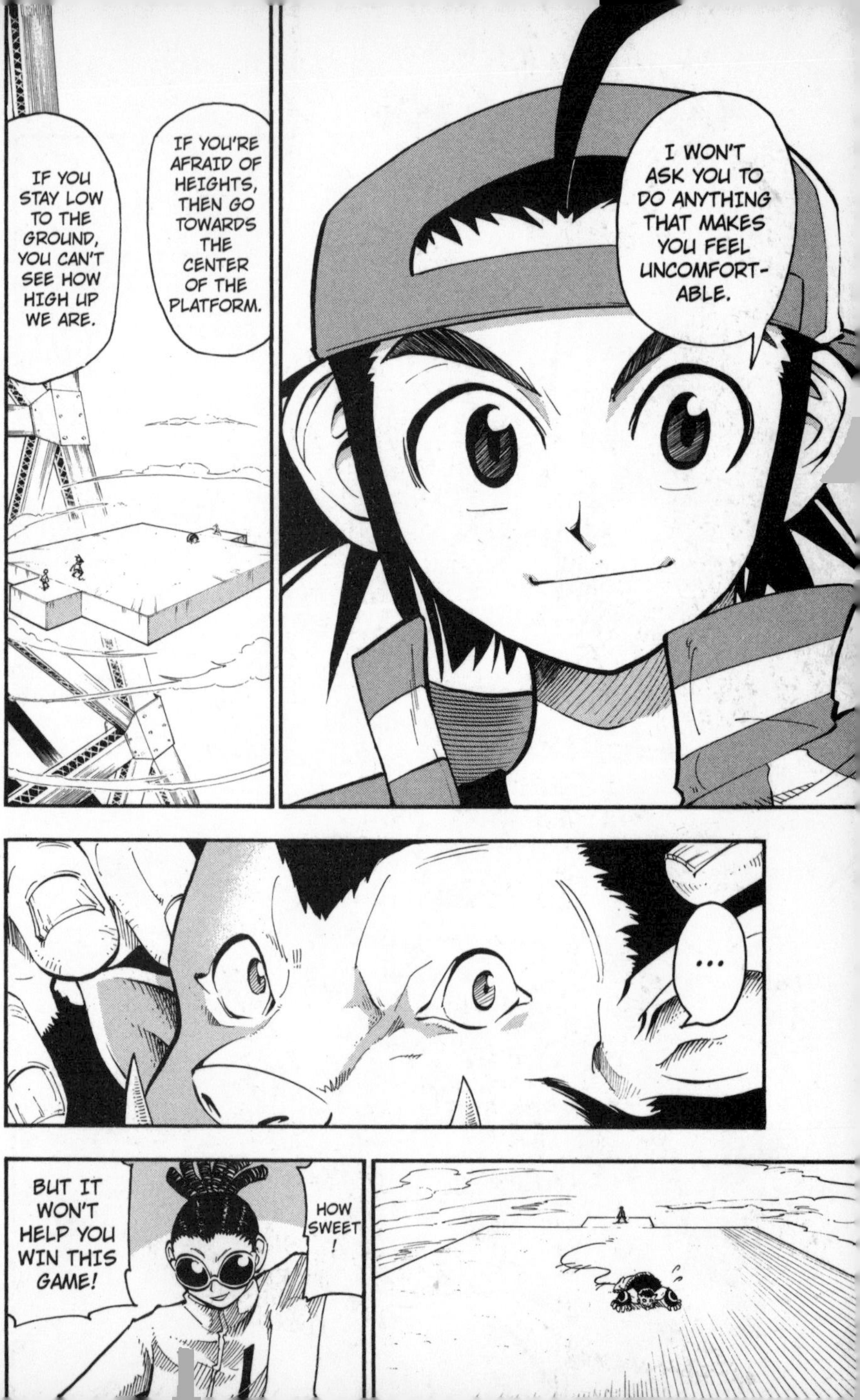
I WON'T ASK YOU TO DO ANYTHING THAT MAKES YOU FEEL UNCOMFORT-ABLE.
IF YOU'RE AFRAID OF HEIGHTS, THEN GO TOWARDS THE CENTER OF THE PLATFORM.
IF YOU STAY LOW TO THE GROUND, YOU CAN'T SEE HOW HIGH UP WE ARE.
...
HOW SWEET!
BUT IT WON'T HELP YOU WIN THIS GAME!

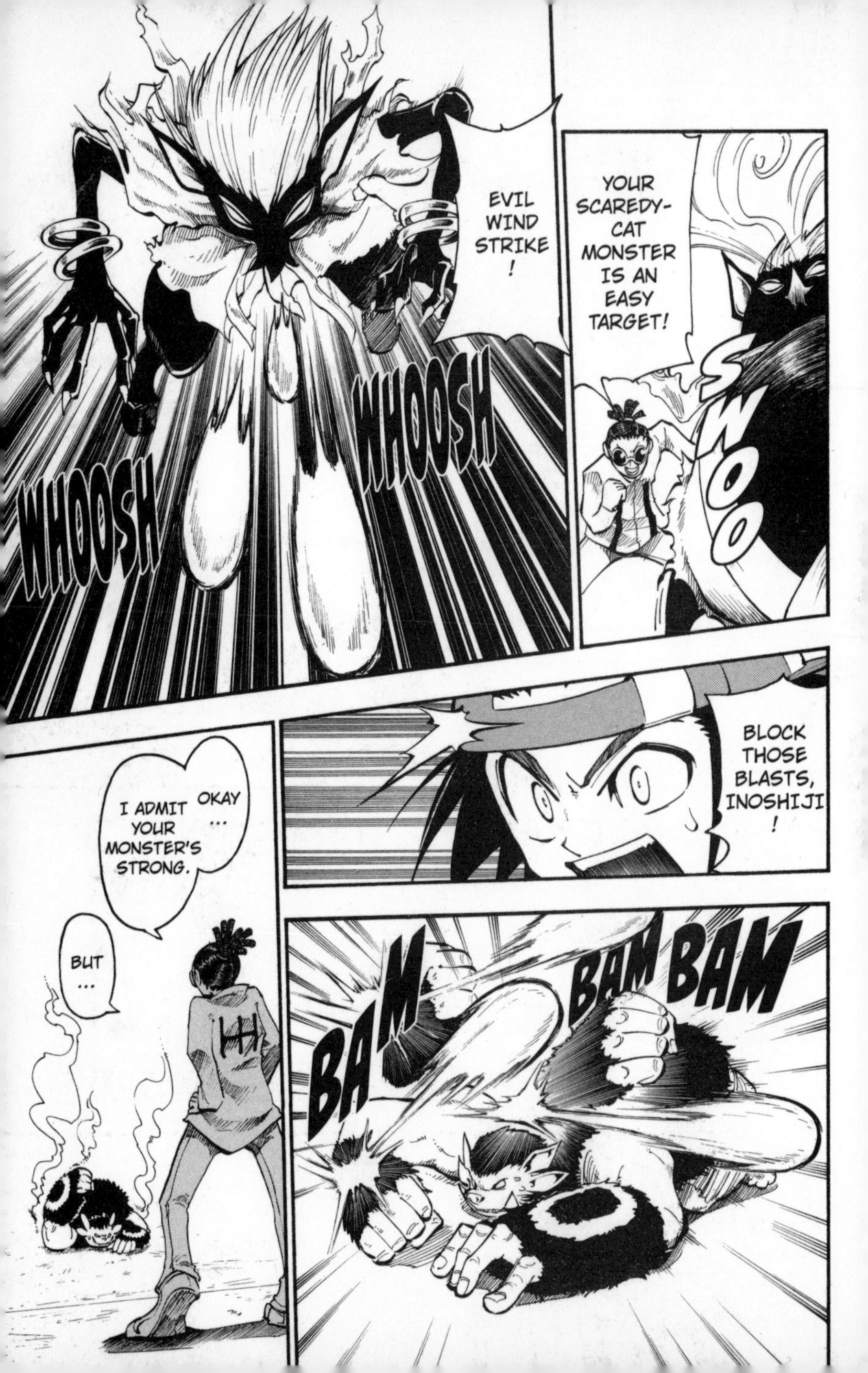
YOUR SCAREDY-CAT MONSTER IS AN EASY TARGET!
SWOO
EVIL WIND STRIKE!
WHOOSH
WHOOSH
BLOCK THOSE BLASTS, INOSHIJI!
BAM BAM
BAM
OKAY...
I ADMIT YOUR MONSTER'S STRONG.
BUT...

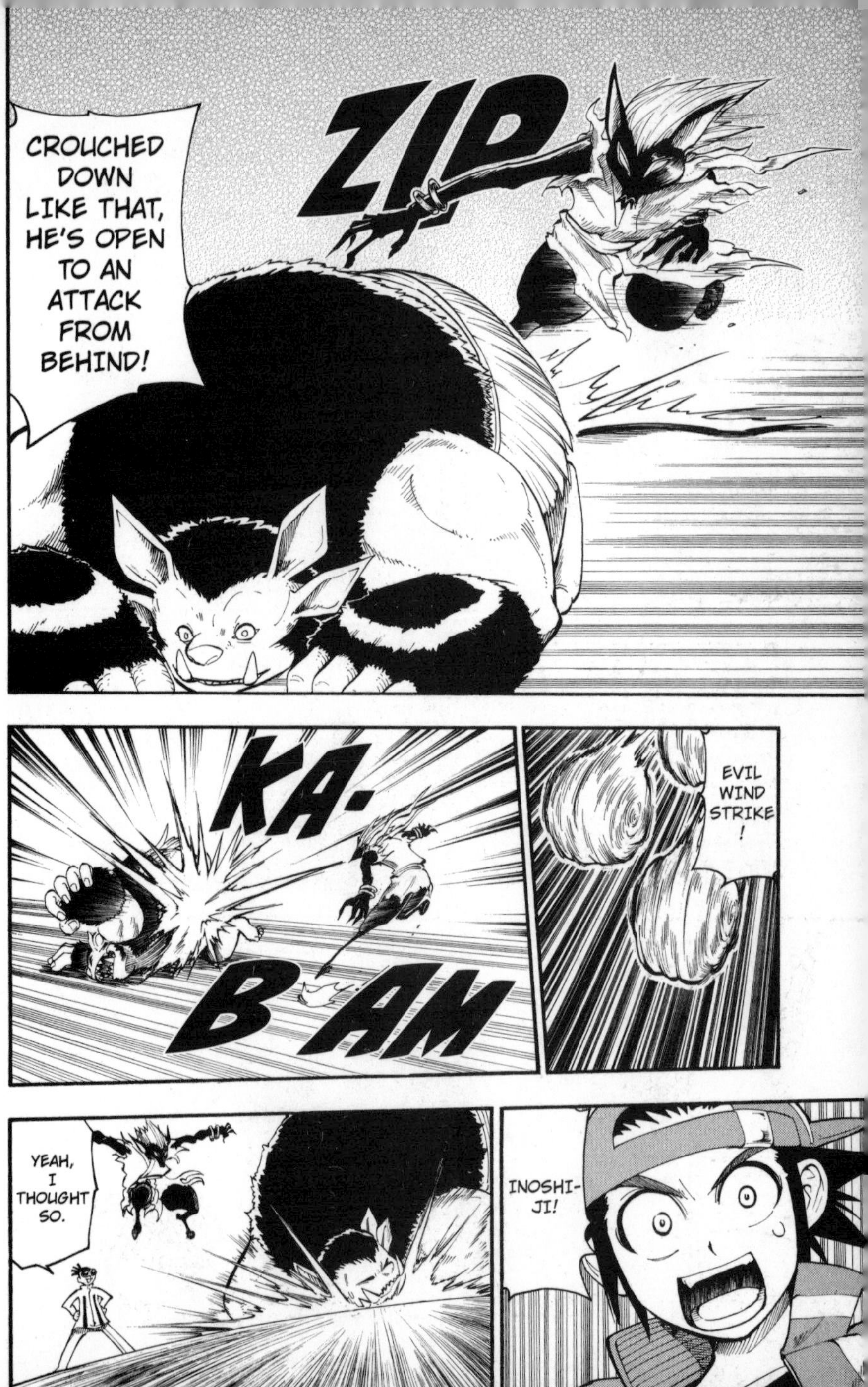
ZIP
CROUCHED DOWN LIKE THAT, HE'S OPEN TO AN ATTACK FROM BEHIND!
EVIL WIND STRIKE!
KA-BAM
INOSHIJI!
YEAH, I THOUGHT SO.

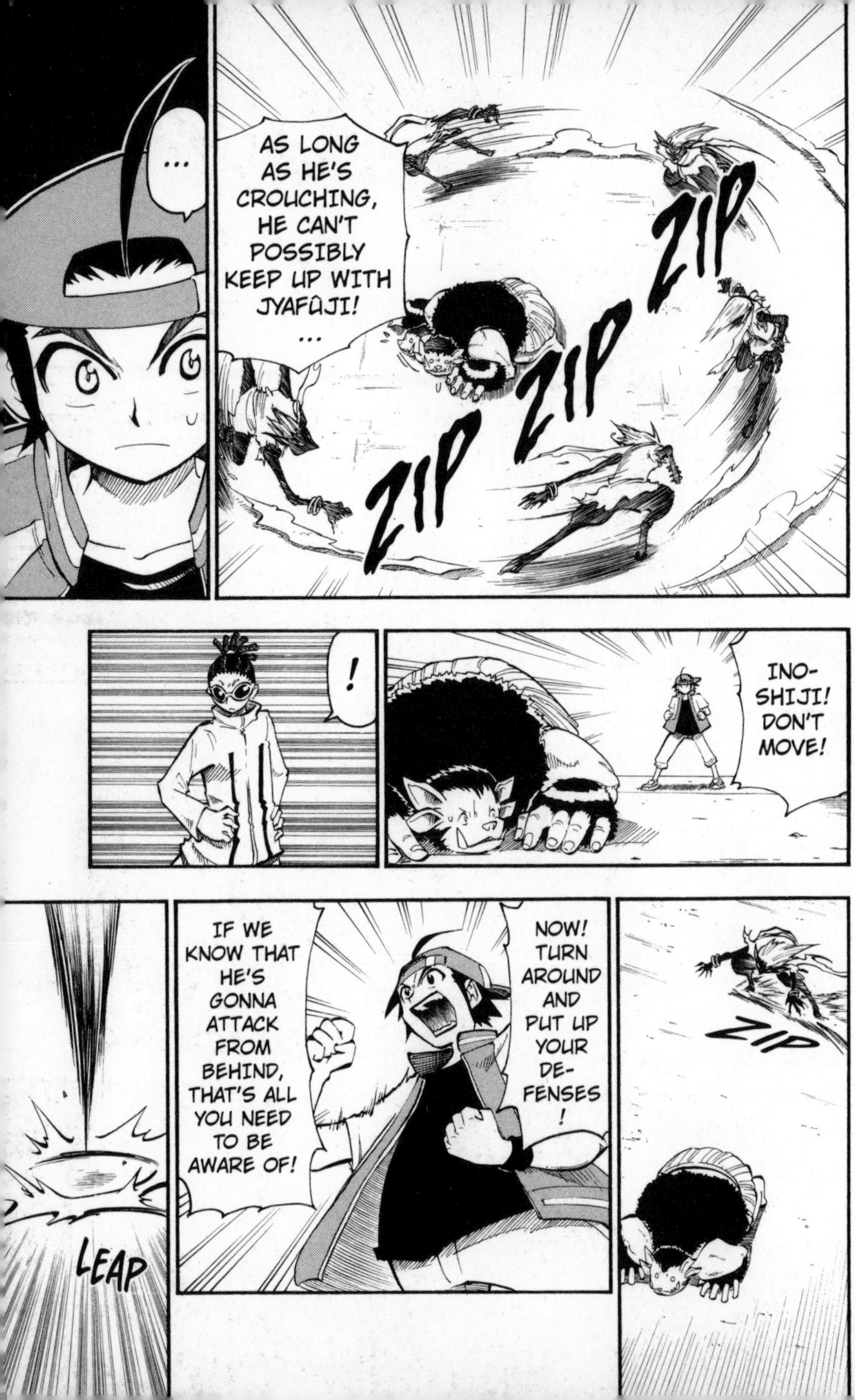
AS LONG AS HE'S CROUCHING, HE CAN'T POSSIBLY KEEP UP WITH JYAFÛJI! ...
ZIP ZIP ZIP ZIP
...
INO-SHIJI! DON'T MOVE!
!
ZIP
NOW! TURN AROUND AND PUT UP YOUR DE-FENSES!
IF WE KNOW THAT HE'S GONNA ATTACK FROM BEHIND, THAT'S ALL YOU NEED TO BE AWARE OF!
LEAP

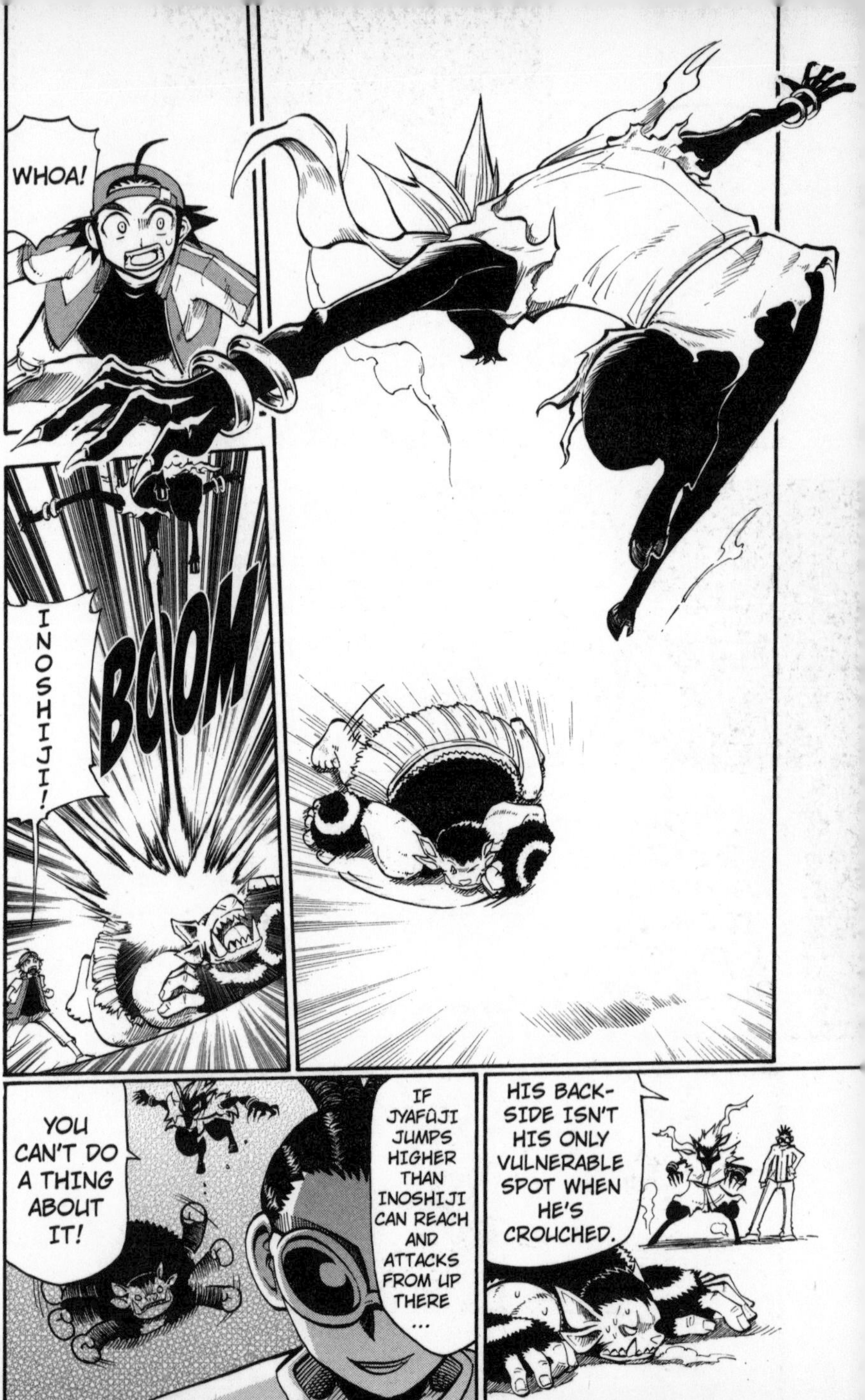
WHOA!
BOOM
INOSHIJI!
HIS BACKSIDE ISN'T HIS ONLY VULNERABLE SPOT WHEN HE'S CROUCHED.
IF JYAFŪJI JUMPS HIGHER THAN INOSHIJI CAN REACH AND ATTACKS FROM UP THERE ...
YOU CAN'T DO A THING ABOUT IT!

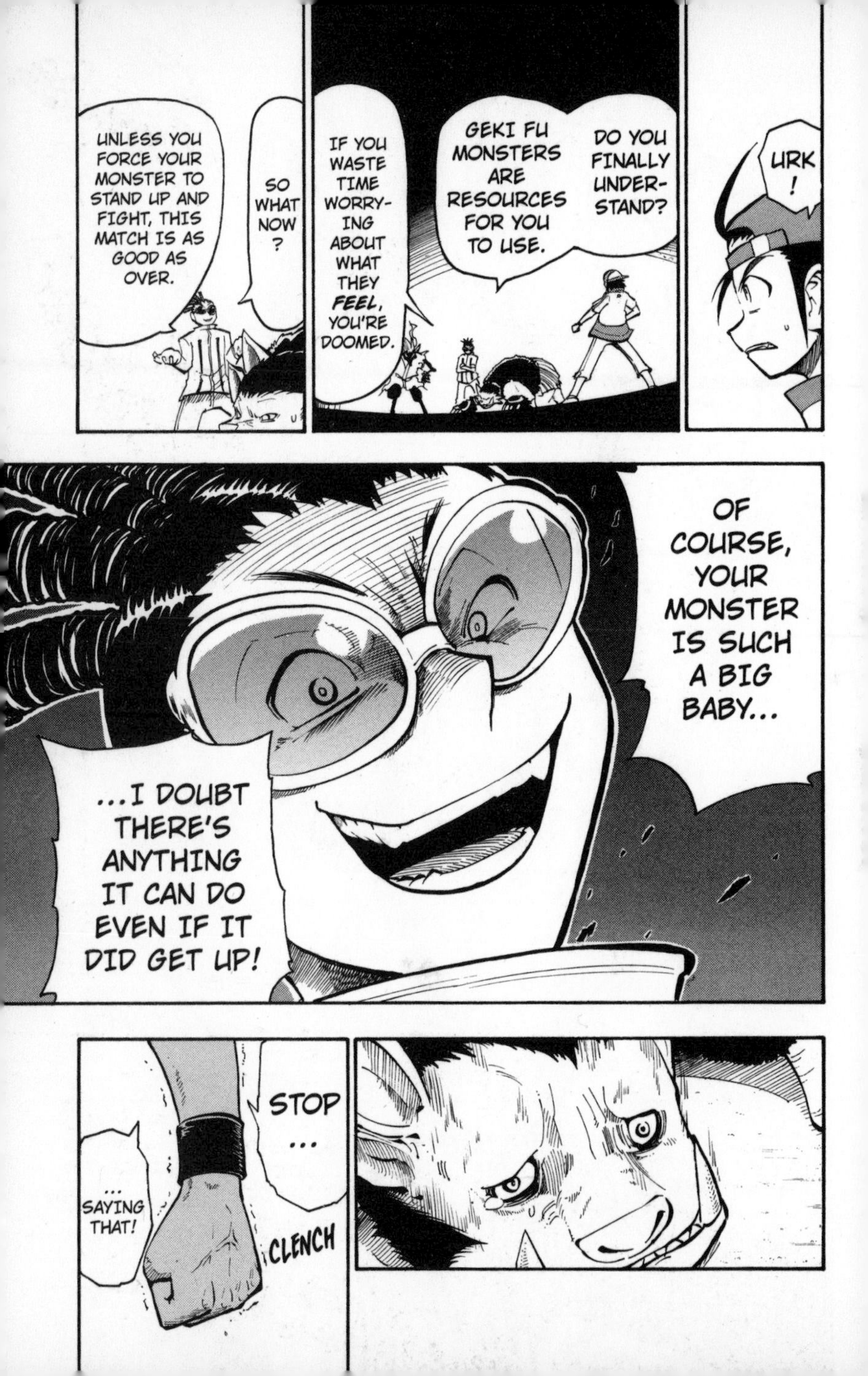
URK!
DO YOU FINALLY UNDER-STAND?
GEKI FU MONSTERS ARE RESOURCES FOR YOU TO USE.
IF YOU WASTE TIME WORRY-ING ABOUT WHAT THEY *FEEL*, YOU'RE DOOMED.
SO WHAT NOW?
UNLESS YOU FORCE YOUR MONSTER TO STAND UP AND FIGHT, THIS MATCH IS AS GOOD AS OVER.
OF COURSE, YOUR MONSTER IS SUCH A BIG BABY...
...I DOUBT THERE'S ANYTHING IT CAN DO EVEN IF IT DID GET UP!
STOP...
CLENCH
...SAYING THAT!

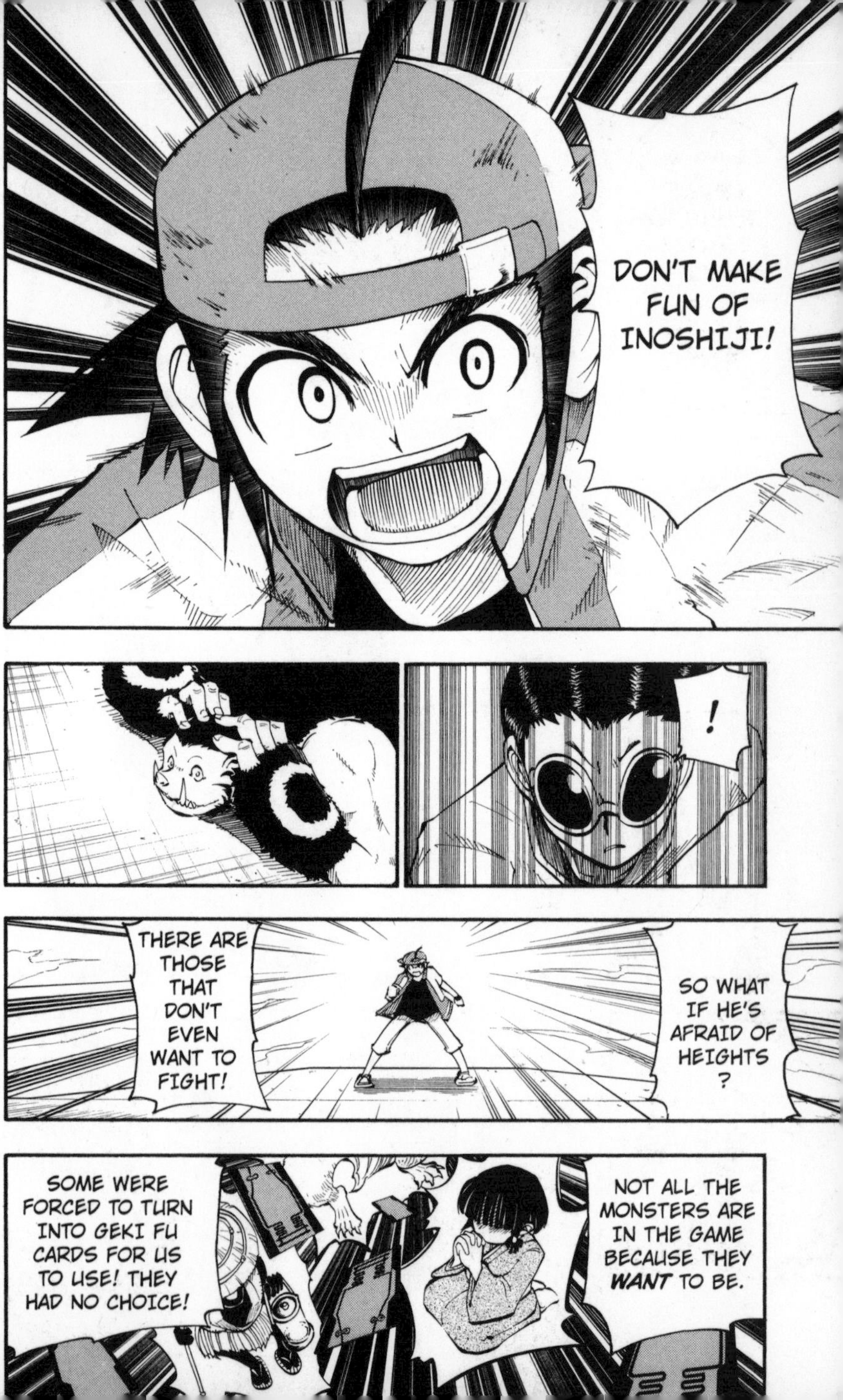
DON'T MAKE FUN OF INOSHIJI!
!
SO WHAT IF HE'S AFRAID OF HEIGHTS?
THERE ARE THOSE THAT DON'T EVEN WANT TO FIGHT!
NOT ALL THE MONSTERS ARE IN THE GAME BECAUSE THEY *WANT* TO BE.
SOME WERE FORCED TO TURN INTO GEKI FU CARDS FOR US TO USE! THEY HAD NO CHOICE!

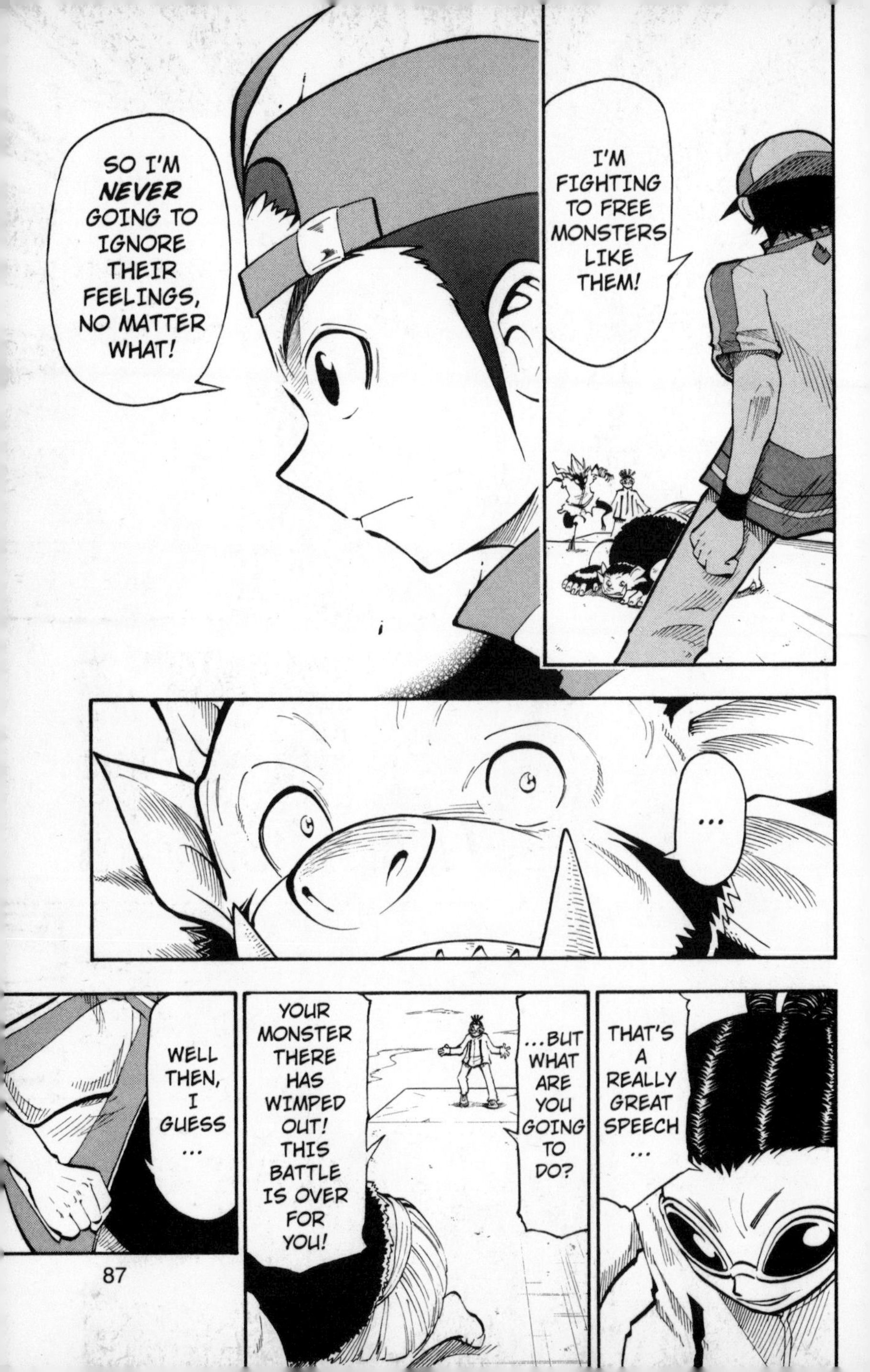
I'M FIGHTING TO FREE MONSTERS LIKE THEM!
SO I'M ***NEVER*** GOING TO IGNORE THEIR FEELINGS, NO MATTER WHAT!
...
THAT'S A REALLY GREAT SPEECH...
...BUT WHAT ARE YOU GOING TO DO?
YOUR MONSTER THERE HAS WIMPED OUT! THIS BATTLE IS OVER FOR YOU!
WELL THEN, I GUESS...

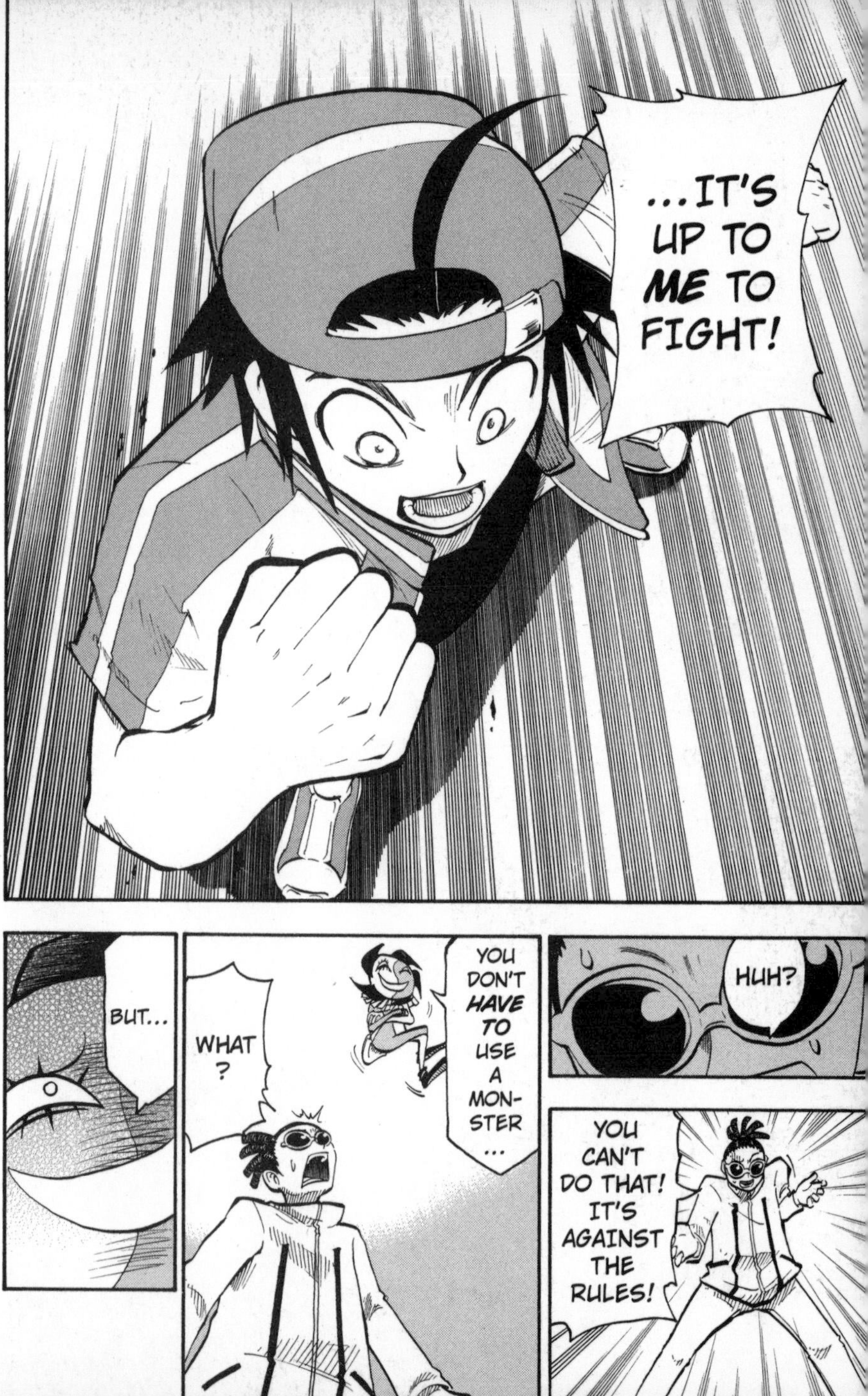
...IT'S UP TO ME TO FIGHT!
HUH?
YOU CAN'T DO THAT! IT'S AGAINST THE RULES!
YOU DON'T HAVE TO USE A MONSTER...
WHAT?
BUT...

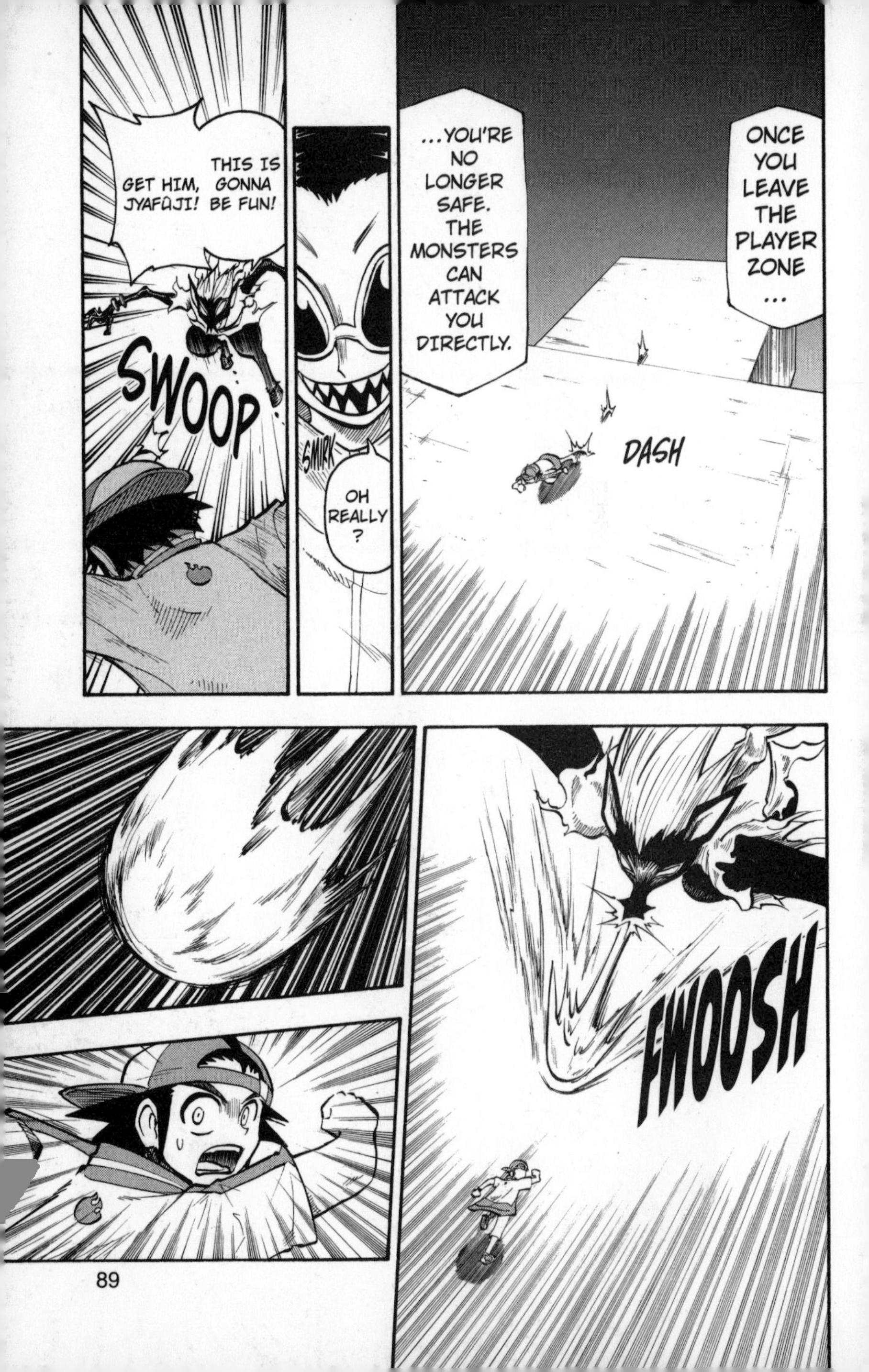

ONCE YOU LEAVE THE PLAYER ZONE...
...YOU'RE NO LONGER SAFE. THE MONSTERS CAN ATTACK YOU DIRECTLY.
DASH
SMIRK
OH REALLY?
THIS IS GONNA BE FUN!
GET HIM, JYAFŪJI!
SWOOP
FWOOSH

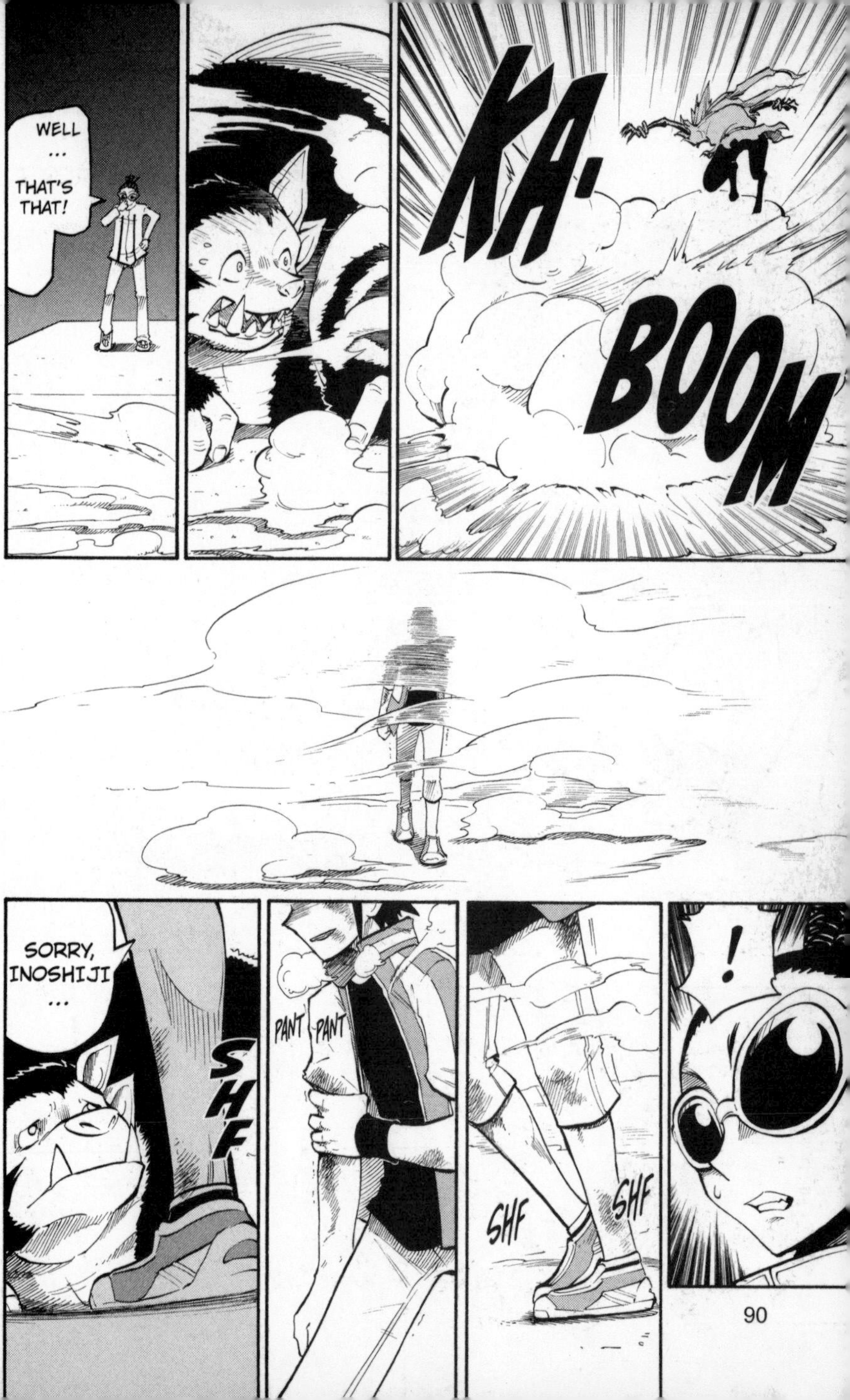
KA-BOOM
WELL ... THAT'S THAT!
!
SHF
SHF
PANT PANT
SORRY, INOSHIJI ...
SHF

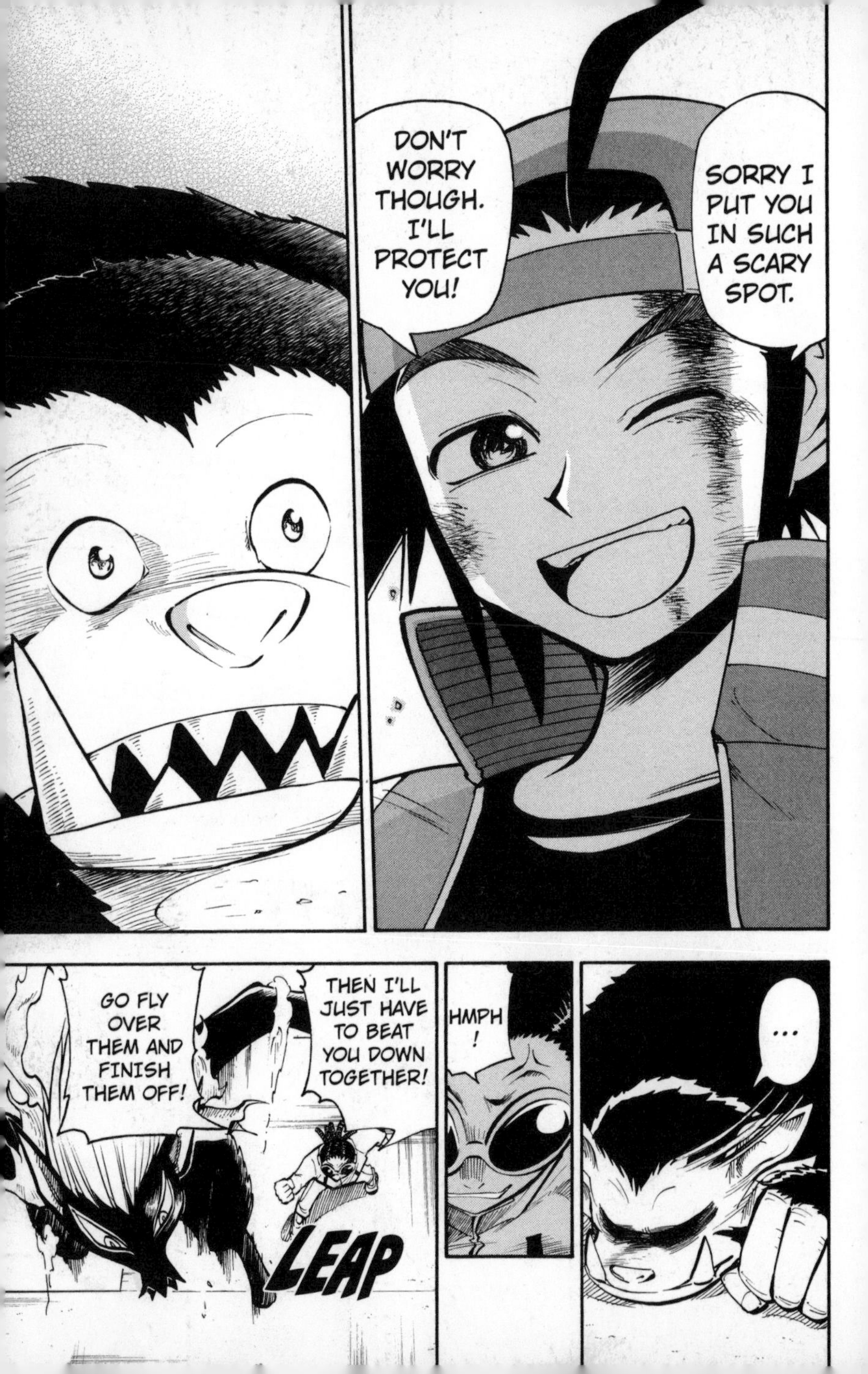
SORRY I PUT YOU IN SUCH A SCARY SPOT.
DON'T WORRY THOUGH. I'LL PROTECT YOU!
...
HMPH!
THEN I'LL JUST HAVE TO BEAT YOU DOWN TOGETHER!
GO FLY OVER THEM AND FINISH THEM OFF!
LEAP

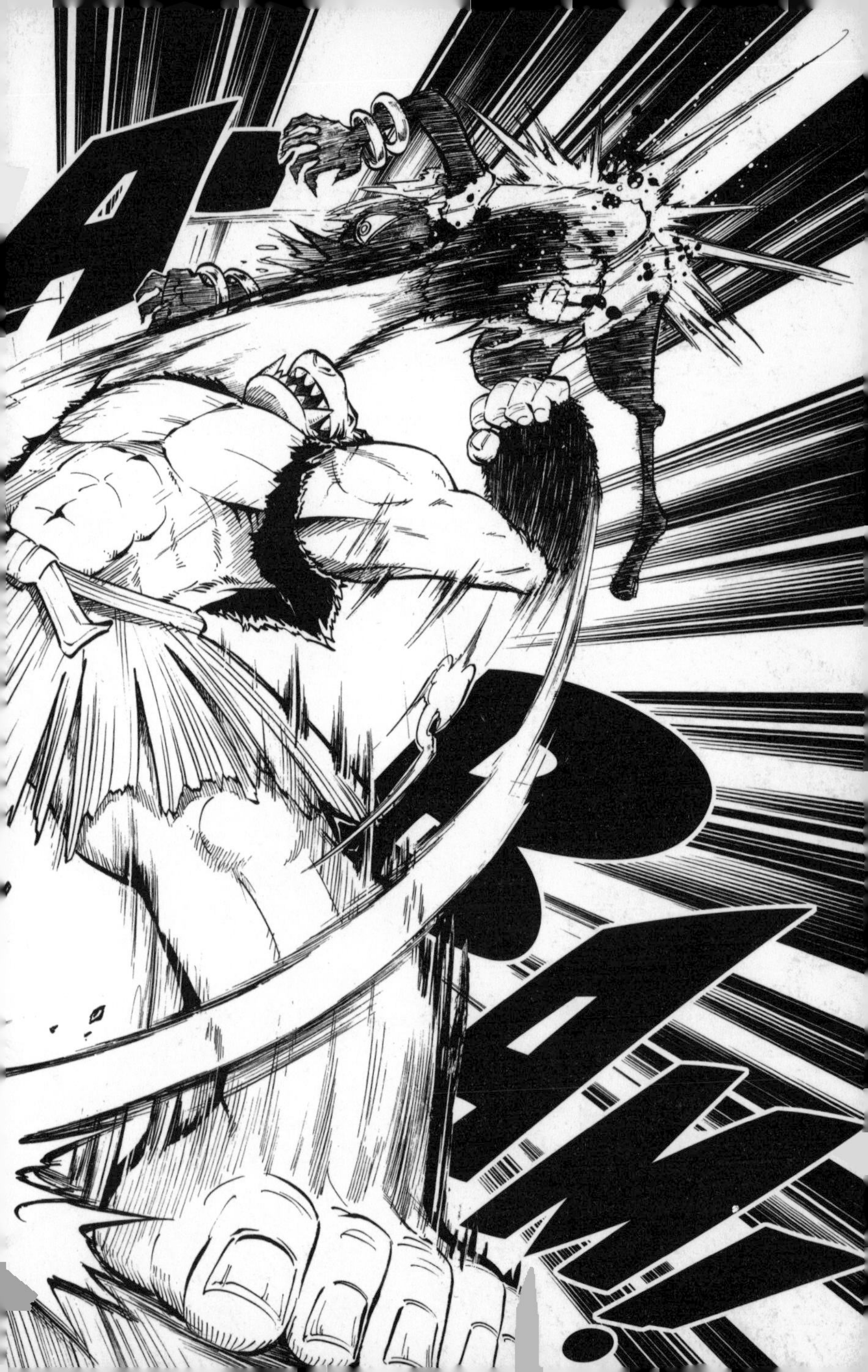

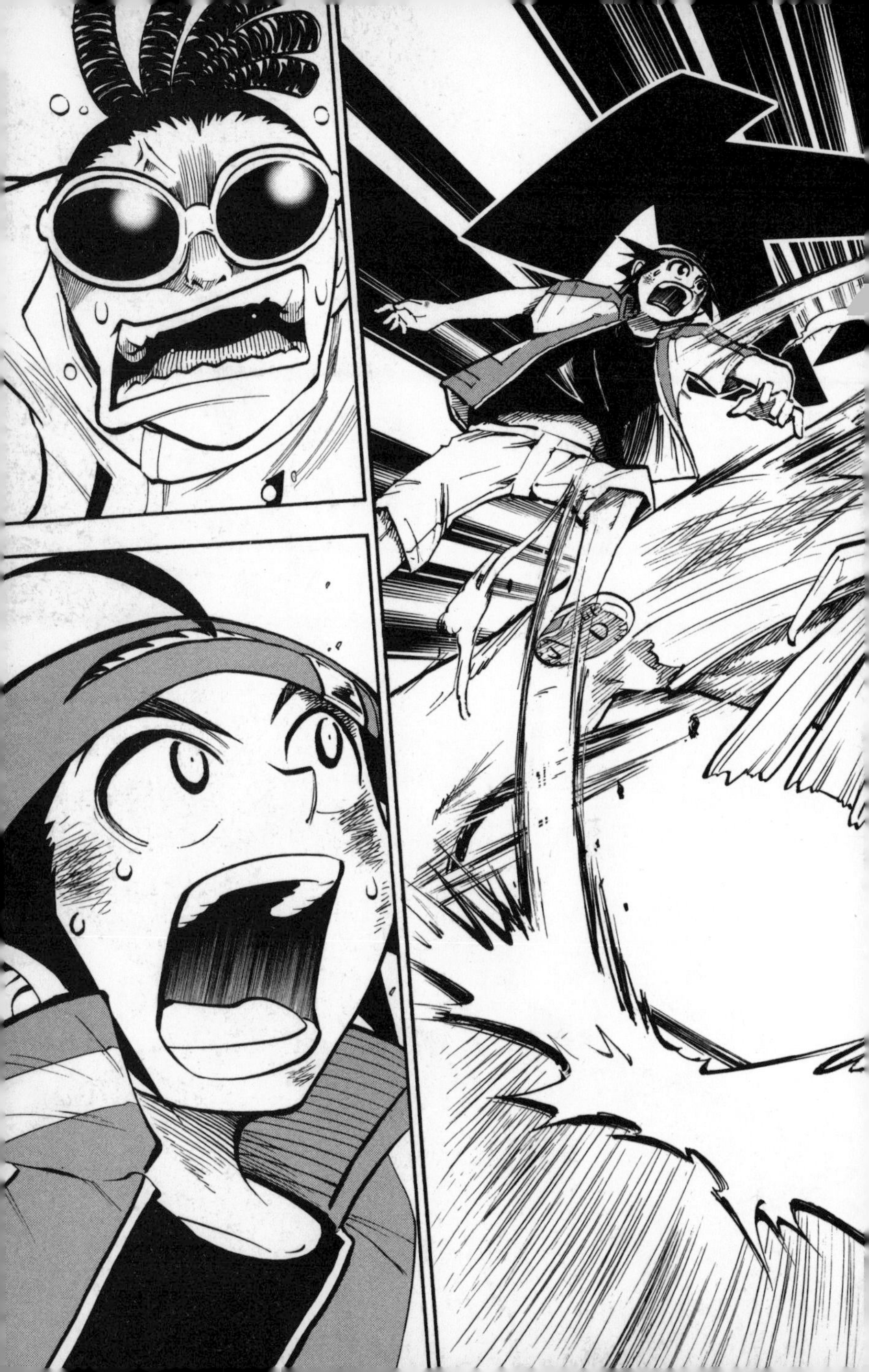

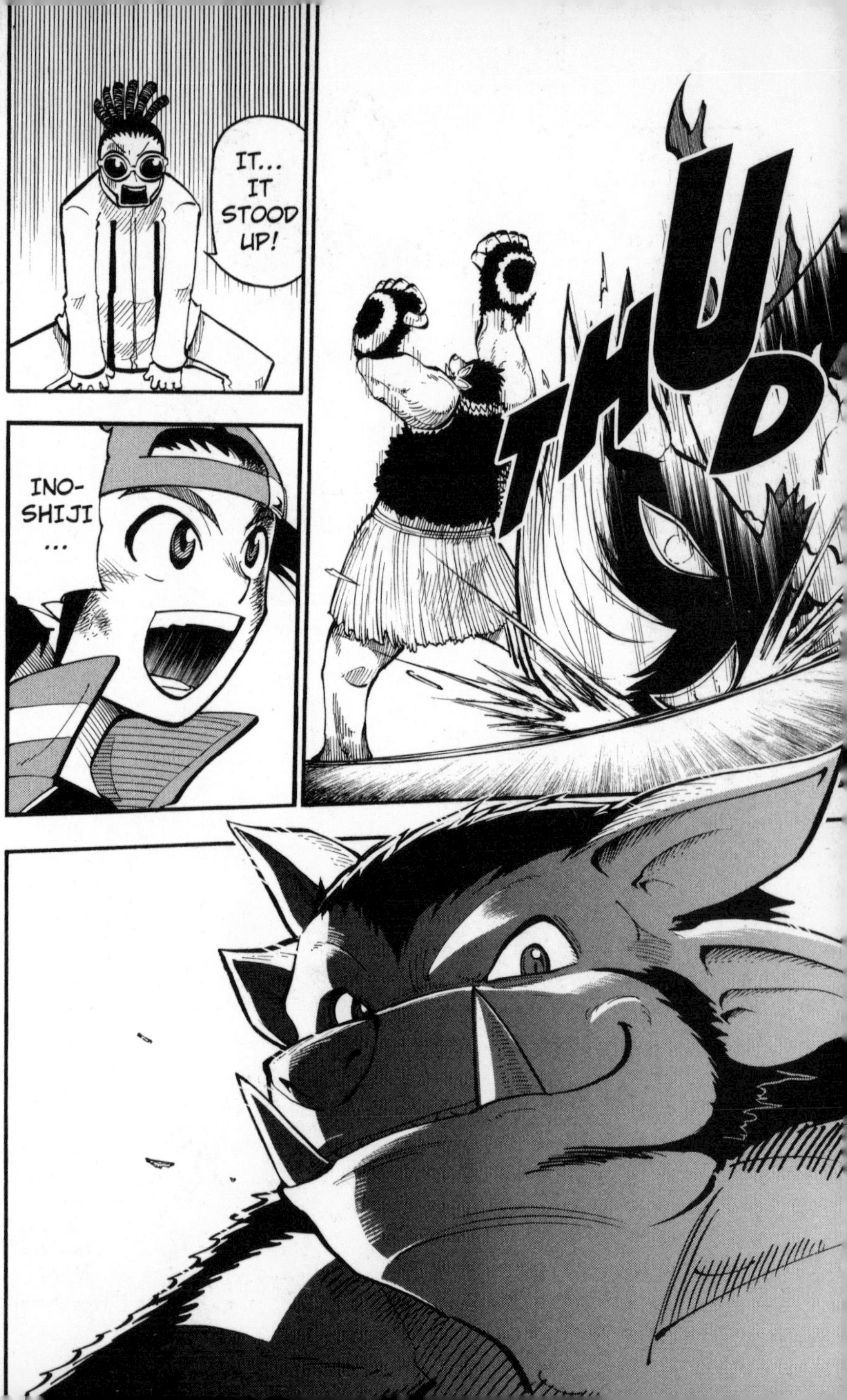
THUD
IT... IT STOOD UP!
INO-SHIJI...

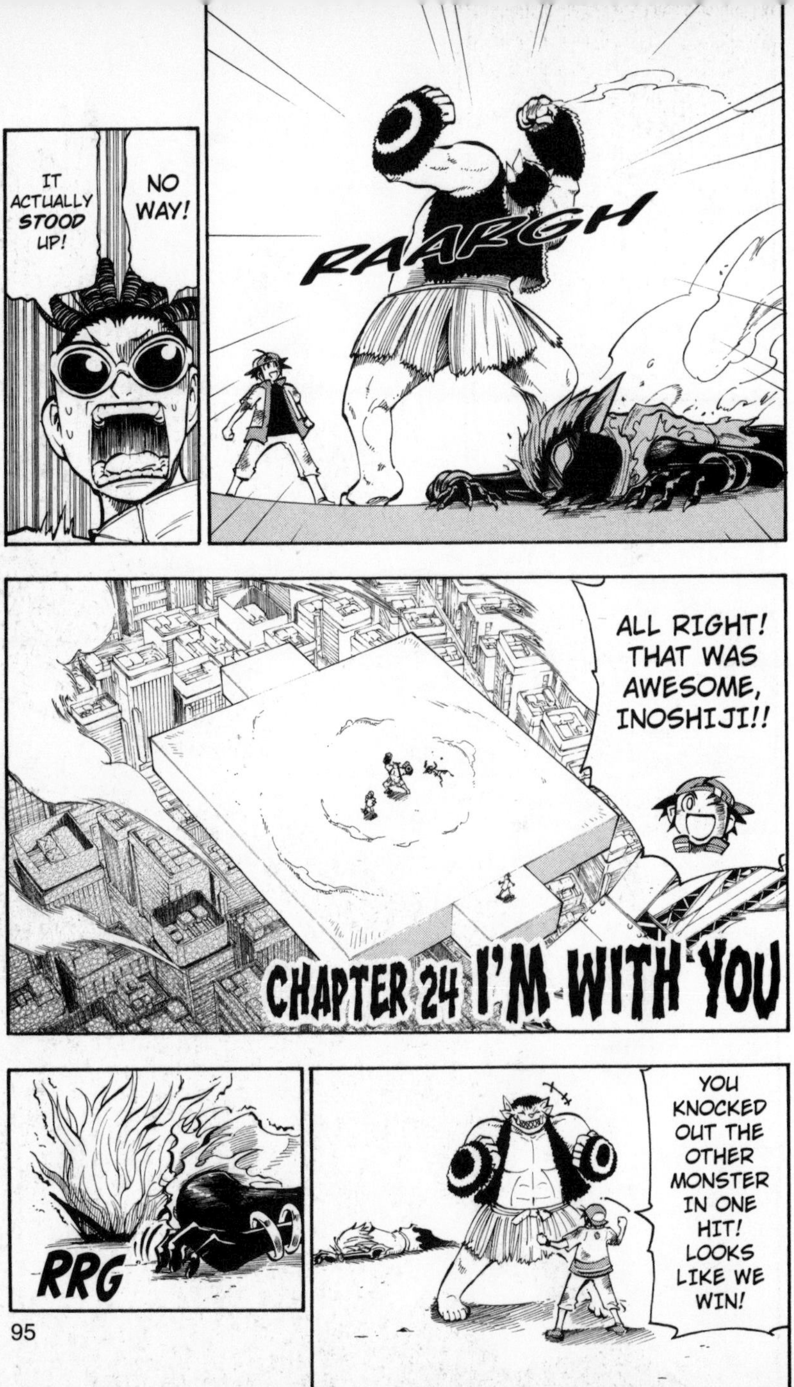
RAARGH
NO WAY!
IT ACTUALLY STOOD UP!
ALL RIGHT! THAT WAS AWESOME, INOSHIJI!!
CHAPTER 24 I'M WITH YOU
YOU KNOCKED OUT THE OTHER MONSTER IN ONE HIT! LOOKS LIKE WE WIN!
RRG

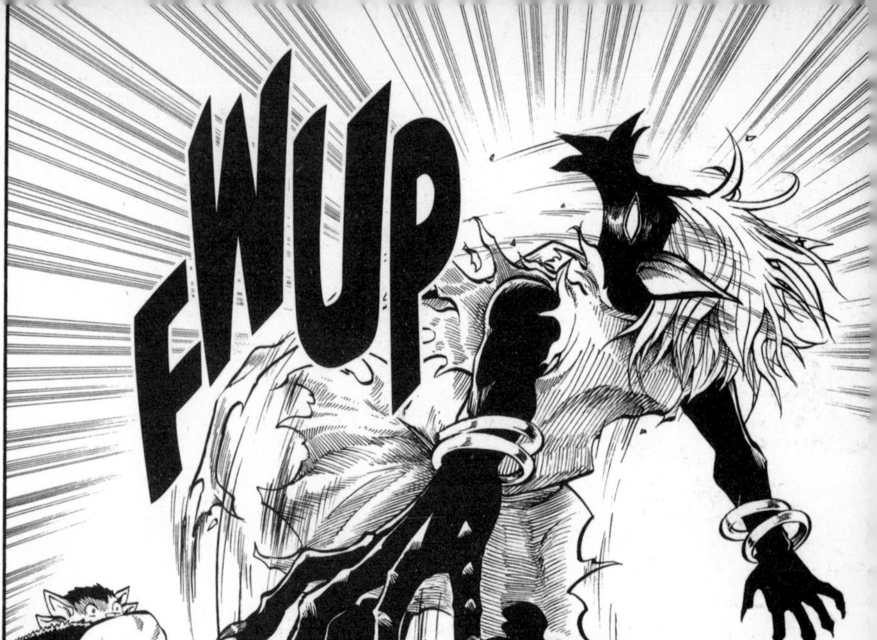
FWUP

CHAPTER 24 I'M WITH YOU

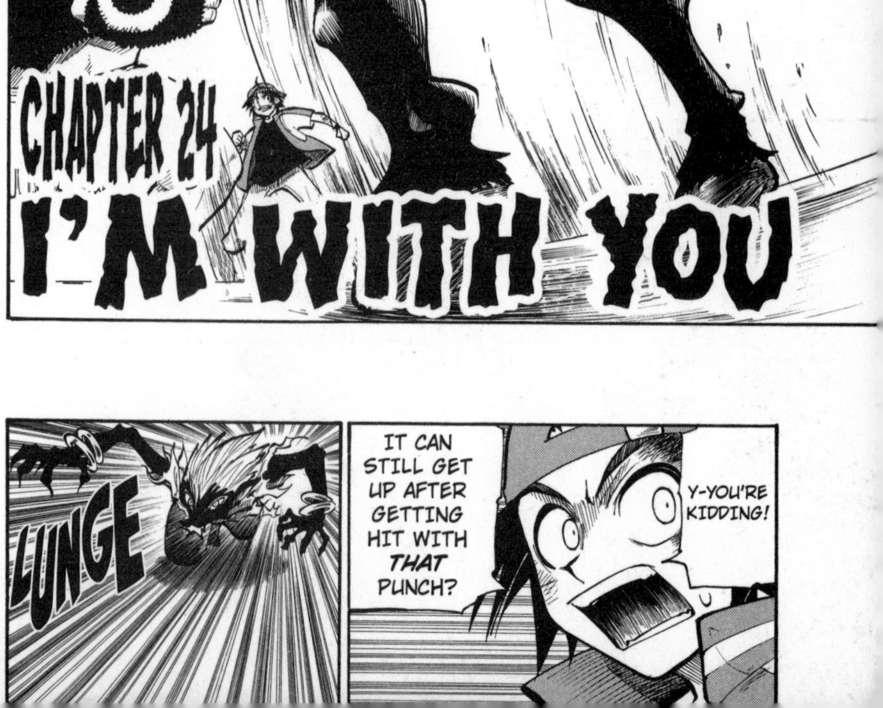
IT CAN STILL GET UP AFTER GETTING HIT WITH *THAT* PUNCH?
Y-YOU'RE KIDDING!
LUNGE

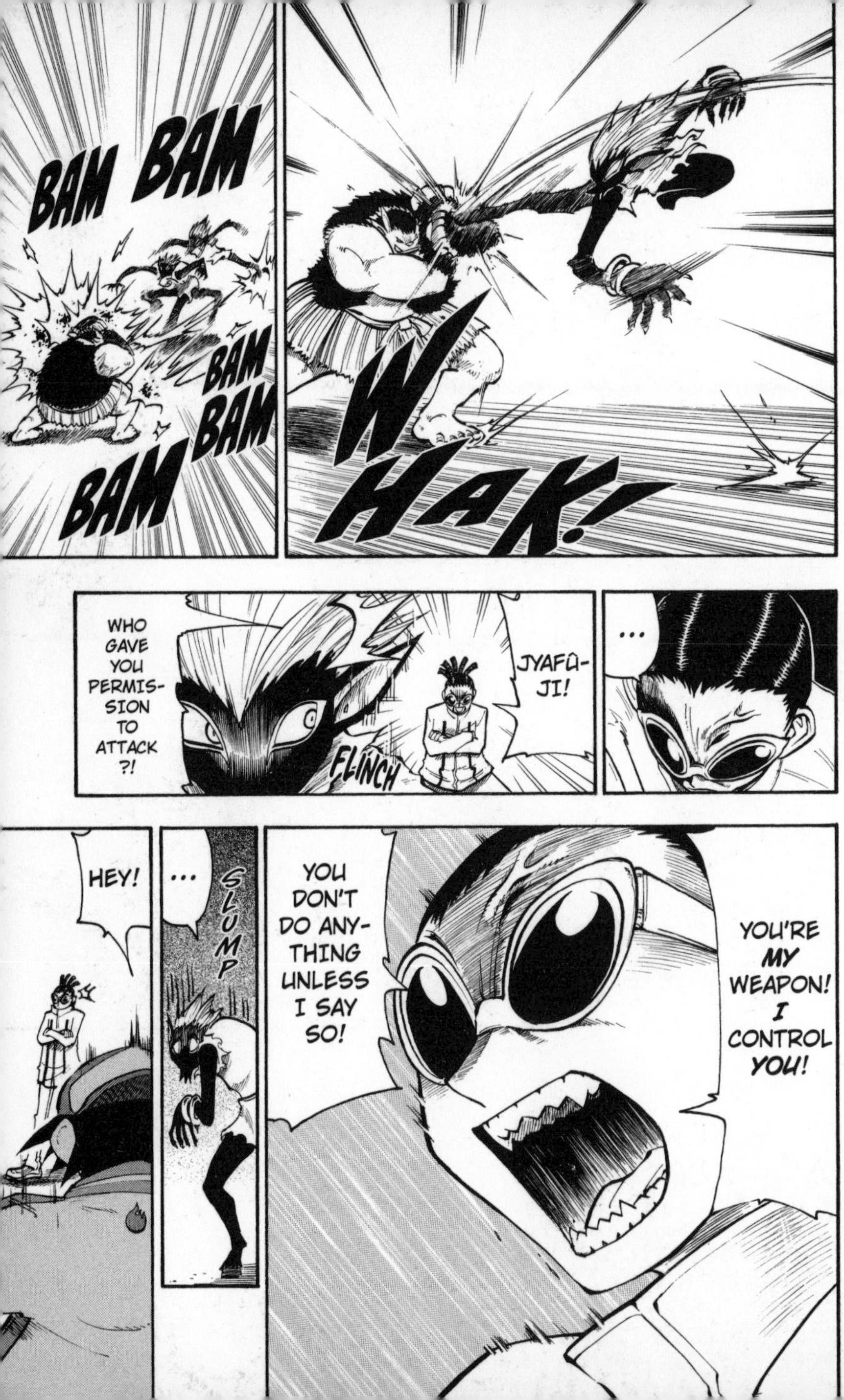
WHAK!
BAM BAM
BAM BAM
BAM
...
JYAFÛ-JI!
WHO GAVE YOU PERMISSION TO ATTACK?!
FLINCH
YOU'RE MY WEAPON! I CONTROL YOU!
YOU DON'T DO ANYTHING UNLESS I SAY SO!
...
SLUMP
HEY!

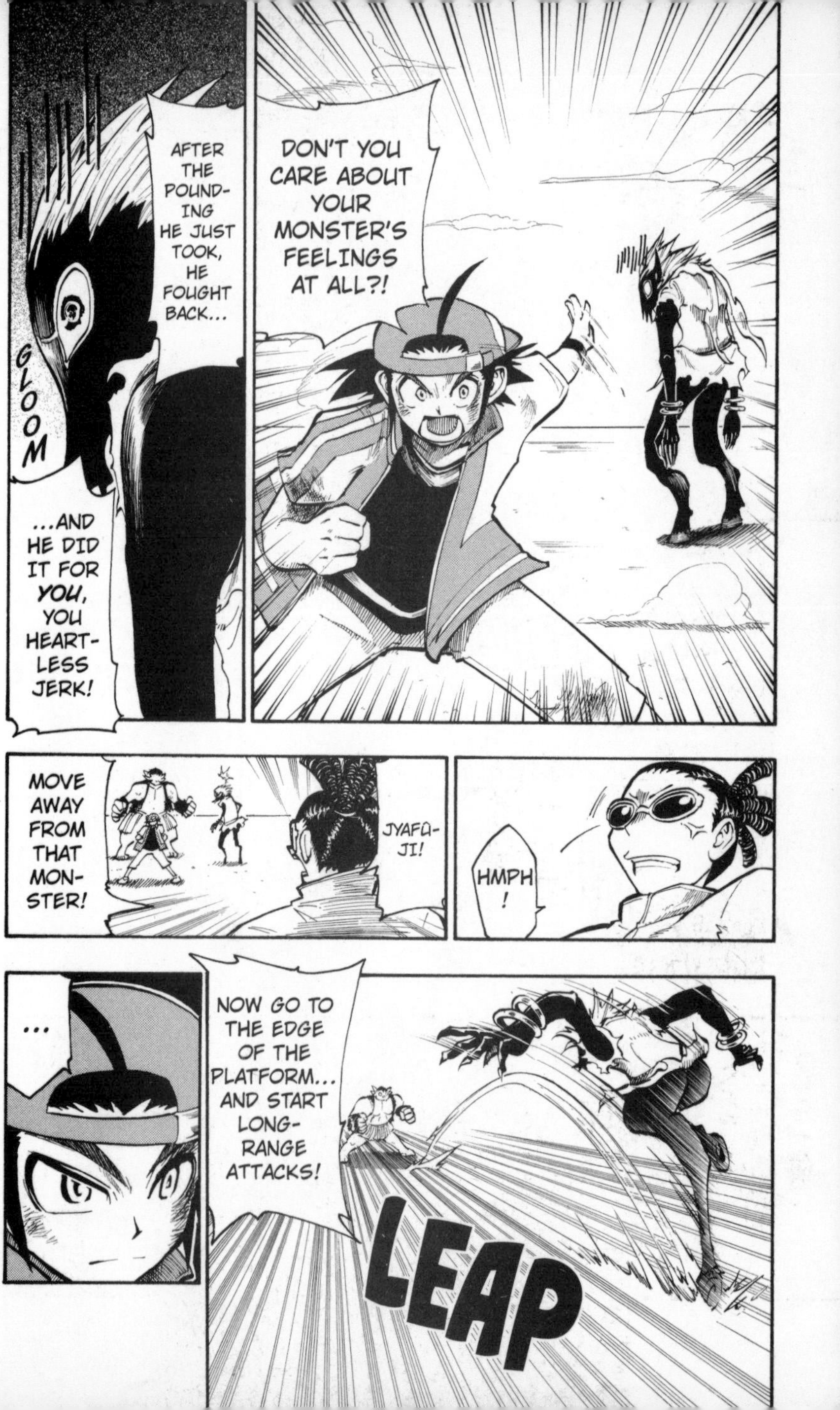
DON'T YOU CARE ABOUT YOUR MONSTER'S FEELINGS AT ALL?!
AFTER THE POUNDING HE JUST TOOK, HE FOUGHT BACK...
GLOOM
...AND HE DID IT FOR *YOU*, YOU HEARTLESS JERK!
HMPH!
JYAFŪJI!
MOVE AWAY FROM THAT MONSTER!
NOW GO TO THE EDGE OF THE PLATFORM... AND START LONG-RANGE ATTACKS!
LEAP
...

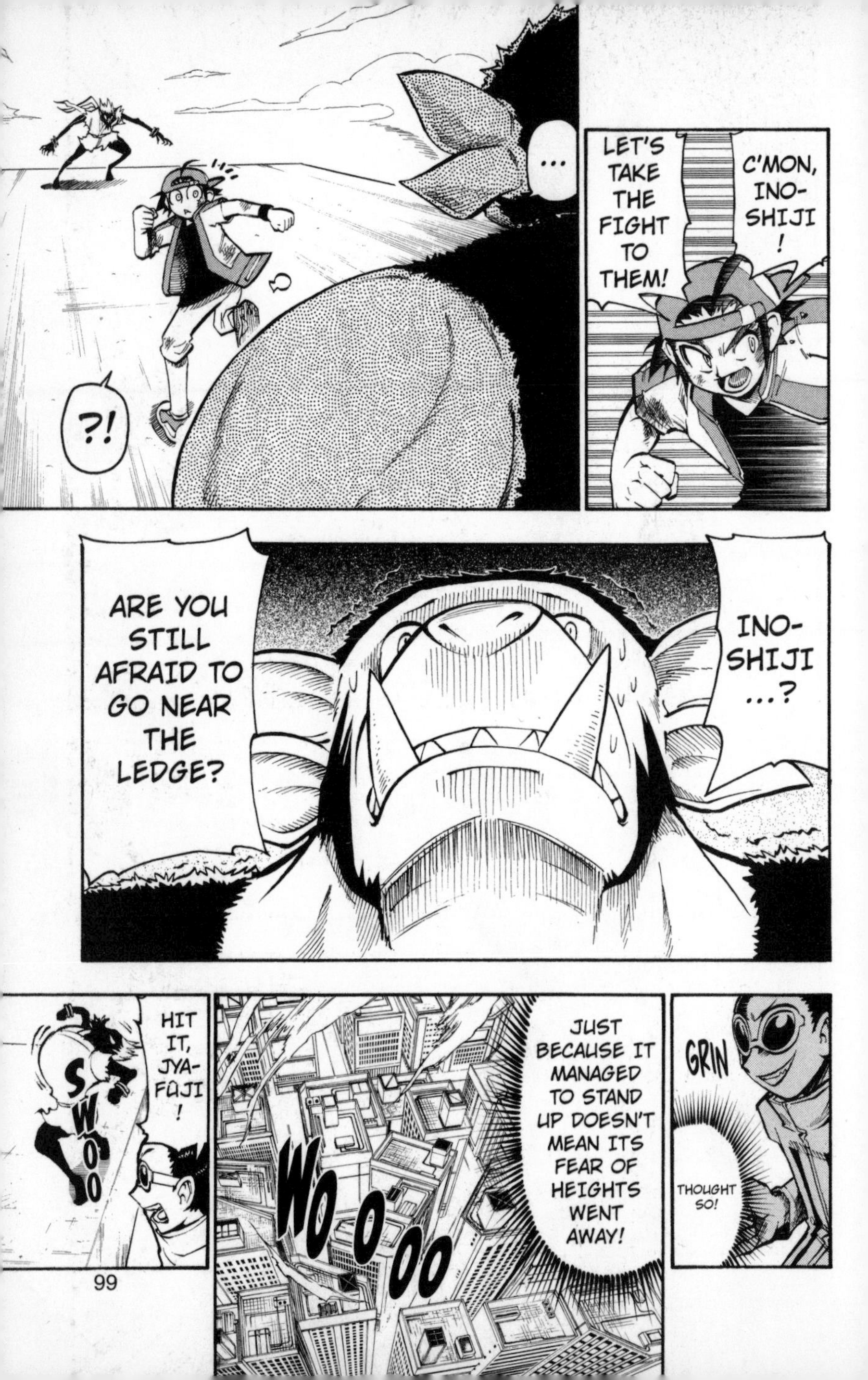
C'MON, INO-SHIJI!
LET'S TAKE THE FIGHT TO THEM!
...
?!
INO-SHIJI...?
ARE YOU STILL AFRAID TO GO NEAR THE LEDGE?
GRIN
THOUGHT SO!
JUST BECAUSE IT MANAGED TO STAND UP DOESN'T MEAN ITS FEAR OF HEIGHTS WENT AWAY!
WOOOO
HIT IT, JYA-FUJI!
SWOOO

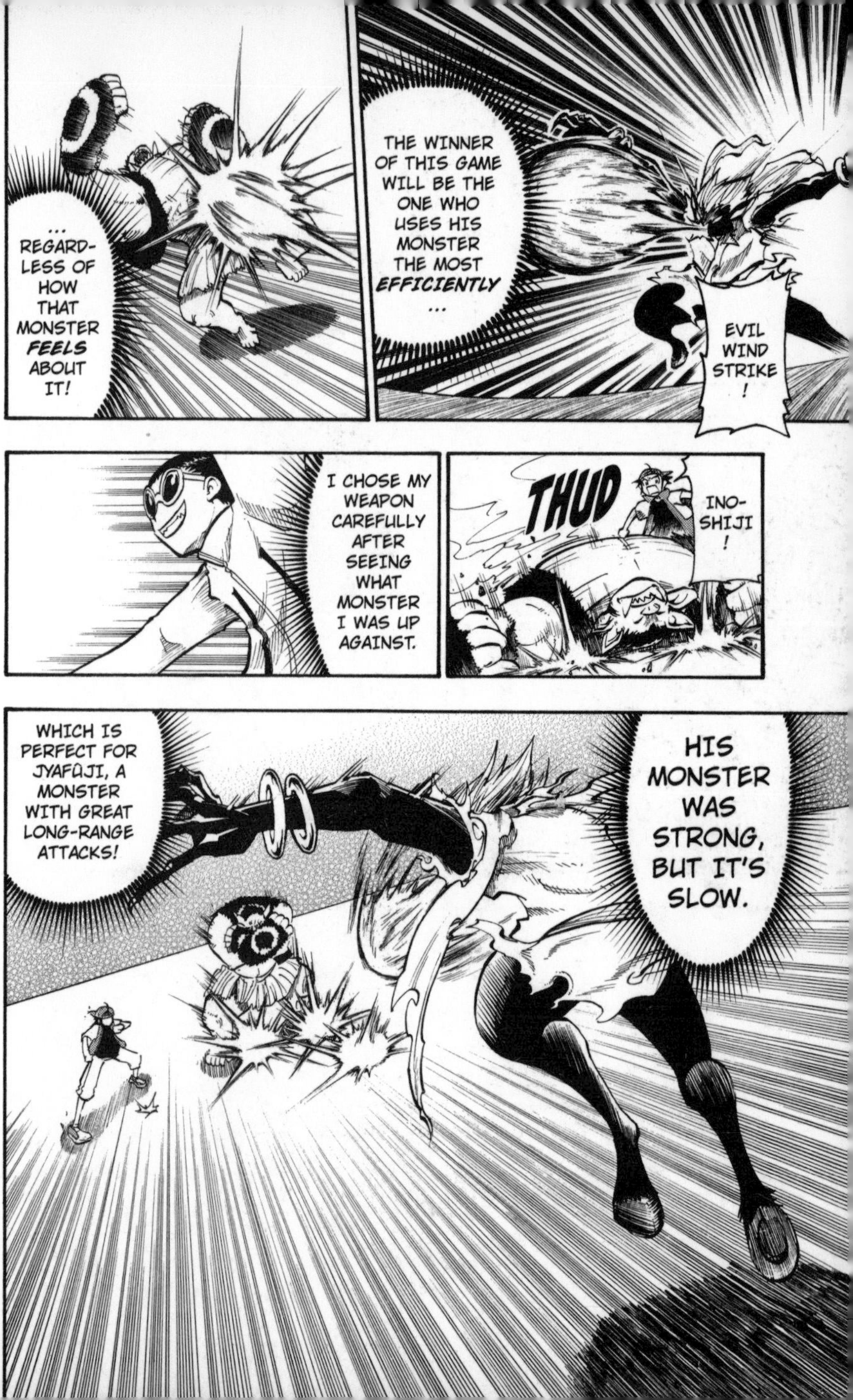
THE WINNER OF THIS GAME WILL BE THE ONE WHO USES HIS MONSTER THE MOST *EFFICIENTLY* ...
EVIL WIND STRIKE!
... REGARDLESS OF HOW THAT MONSTER *FEELS* ABOUT IT!
THUD
INO-SHIJI!
I CHOSE MY WEAPON CAREFULLY AFTER SEEING WHAT MONSTER I WAS UP AGAINST.
HIS MONSTER WAS STRONG, BUT IT'S SLOW.
WHICH IS PERFECT FOR JYAFÛJI, A MONSTER WITH GREAT LONG-RANGE ATTACKS!

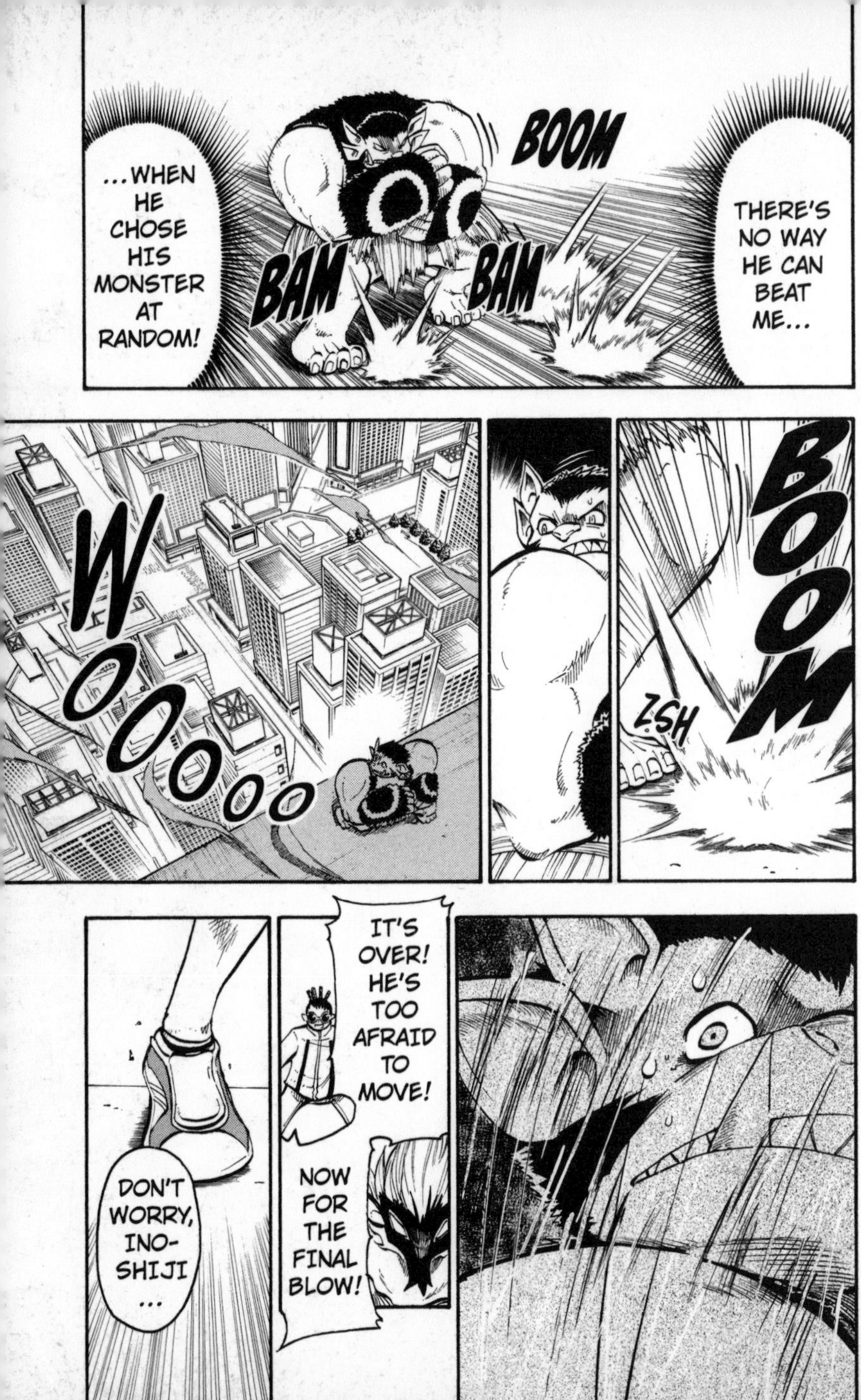
THERE'S NO WAY HE CAN BEAT ME...
BOOM
BAM
BAM
...WHEN HE CHOSE HIS MONSTER AT RANDOM!
BOOM
ZSH
WOOOOOO
IT'S OVER! HE'S TOO AFRAID TO MOVE!
NOW FOR THE FINAL BLOW!
DON'T WORRY, INO-SHIJI ...

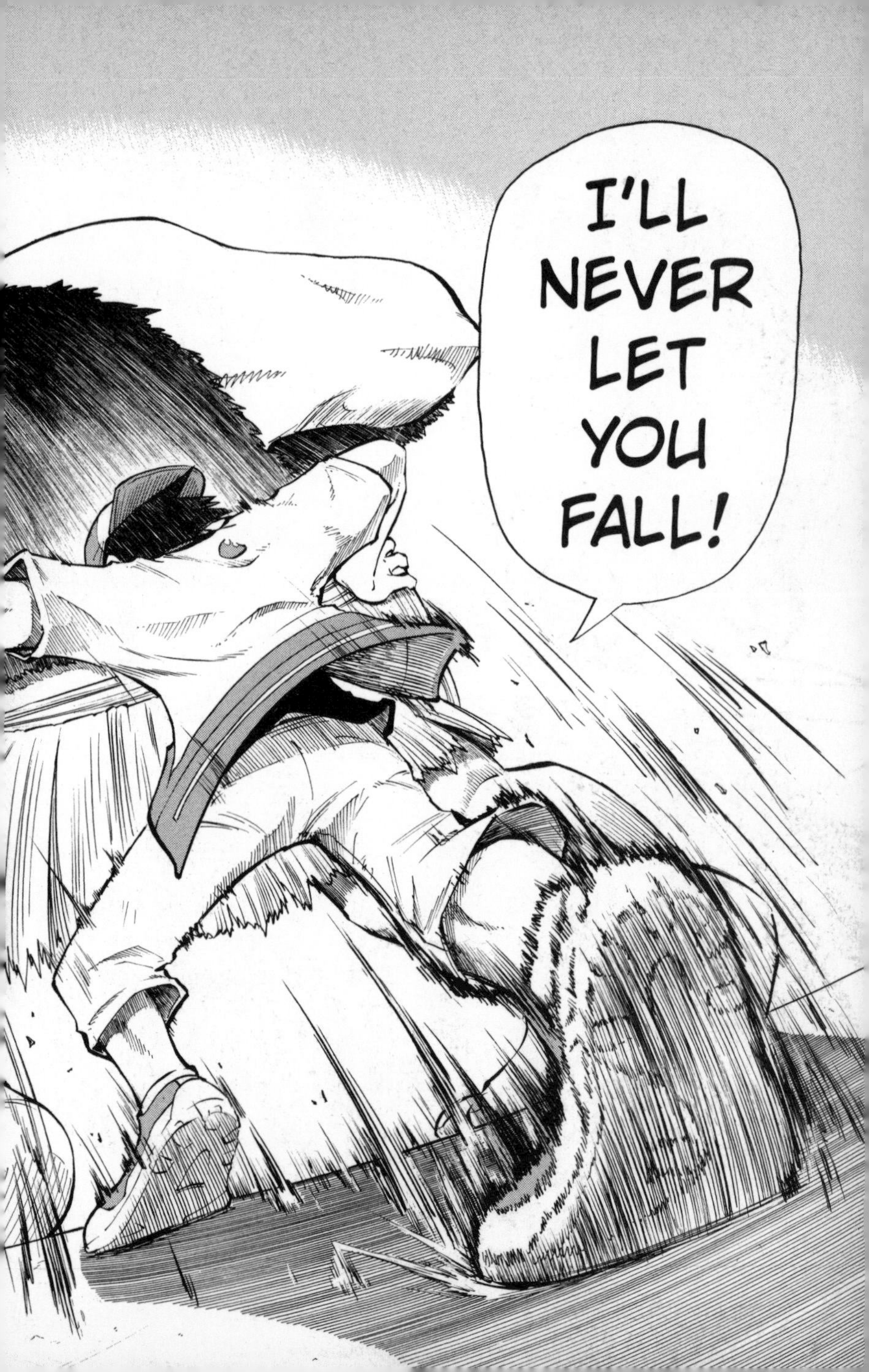
I'LL NEVER LET YOU FALL!

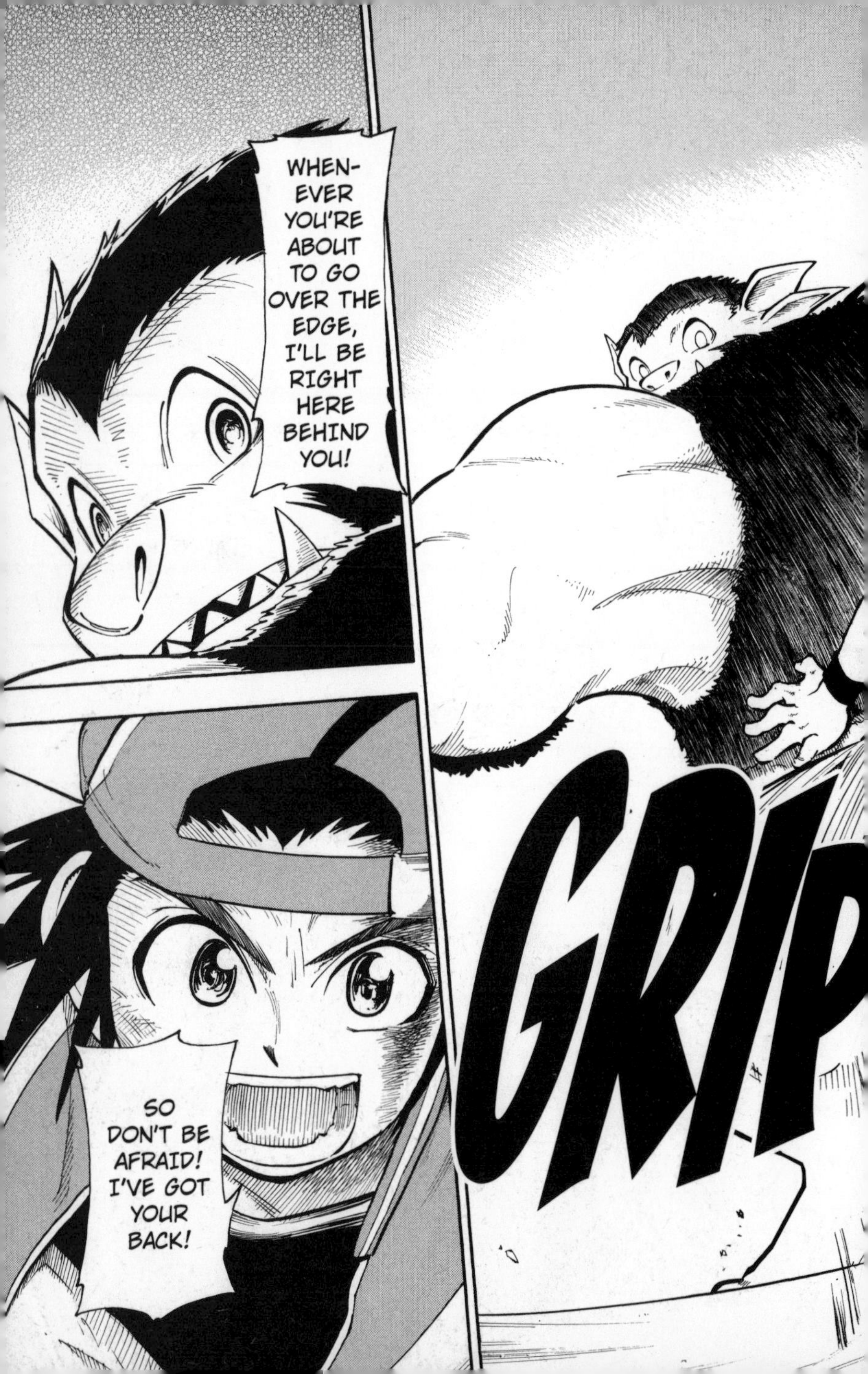
GRIP
WHEN-EVER YOU'RE ABOUT TO GO OVER THE EDGE, I'LL BE RIGHT HERE BEHIND YOU!
SO DON'T BE AFRAID! I'VE GOT YOUR BACK!

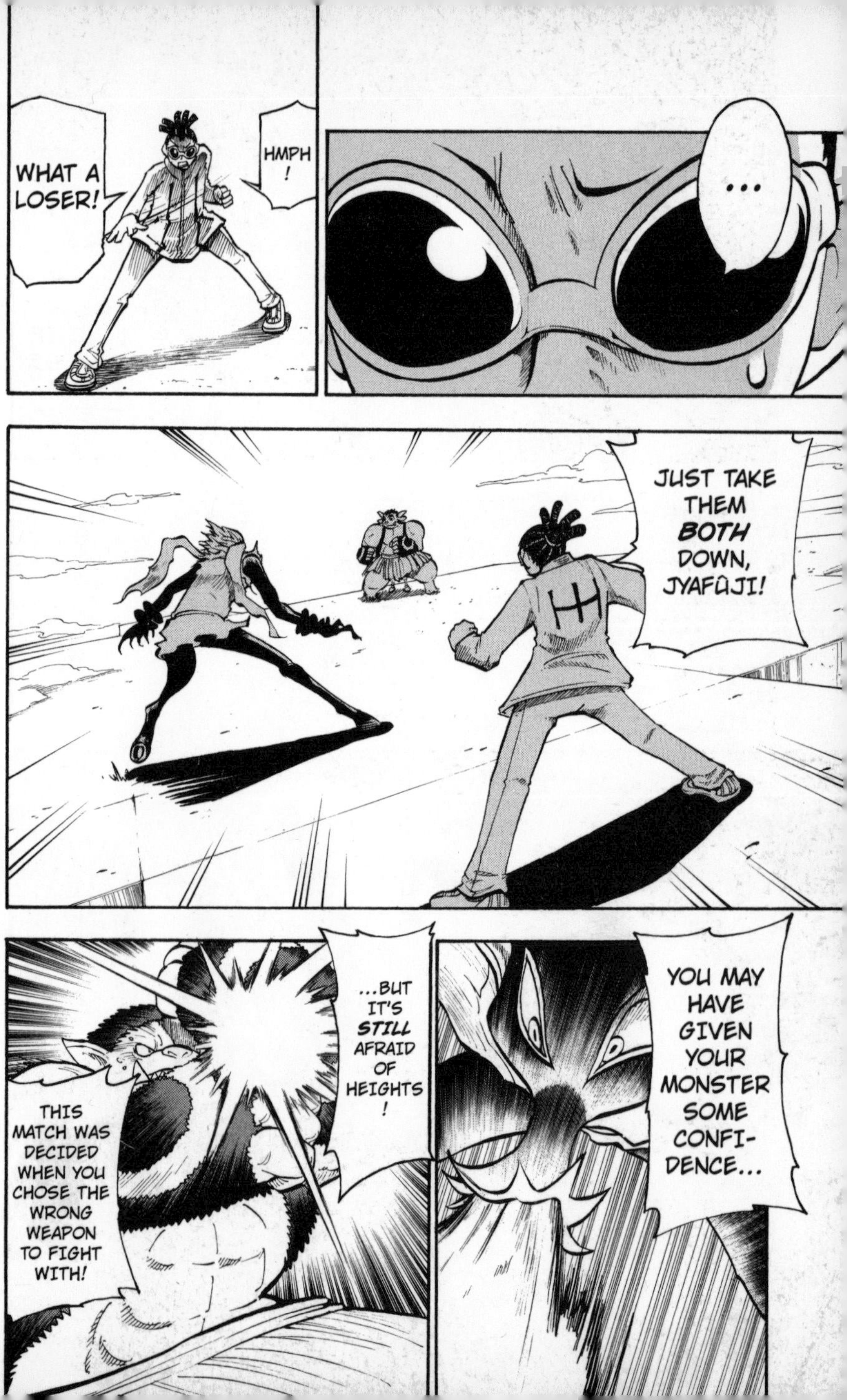
...
HMPH!
WHAT A LOSER!
JUST TAKE THEM *BOTH* DOWN, JYAFÛJI!
YOU MAY HAVE GIVEN YOUR MONSTER SOME CONFIDENCE...
...BUT IT'S *STILL* AFRAID OF HEIGHTS!
THIS MATCH WAS DECIDED WHEN YOU CHOSE THE WRONG WEAPON TO FIGHT WITH!

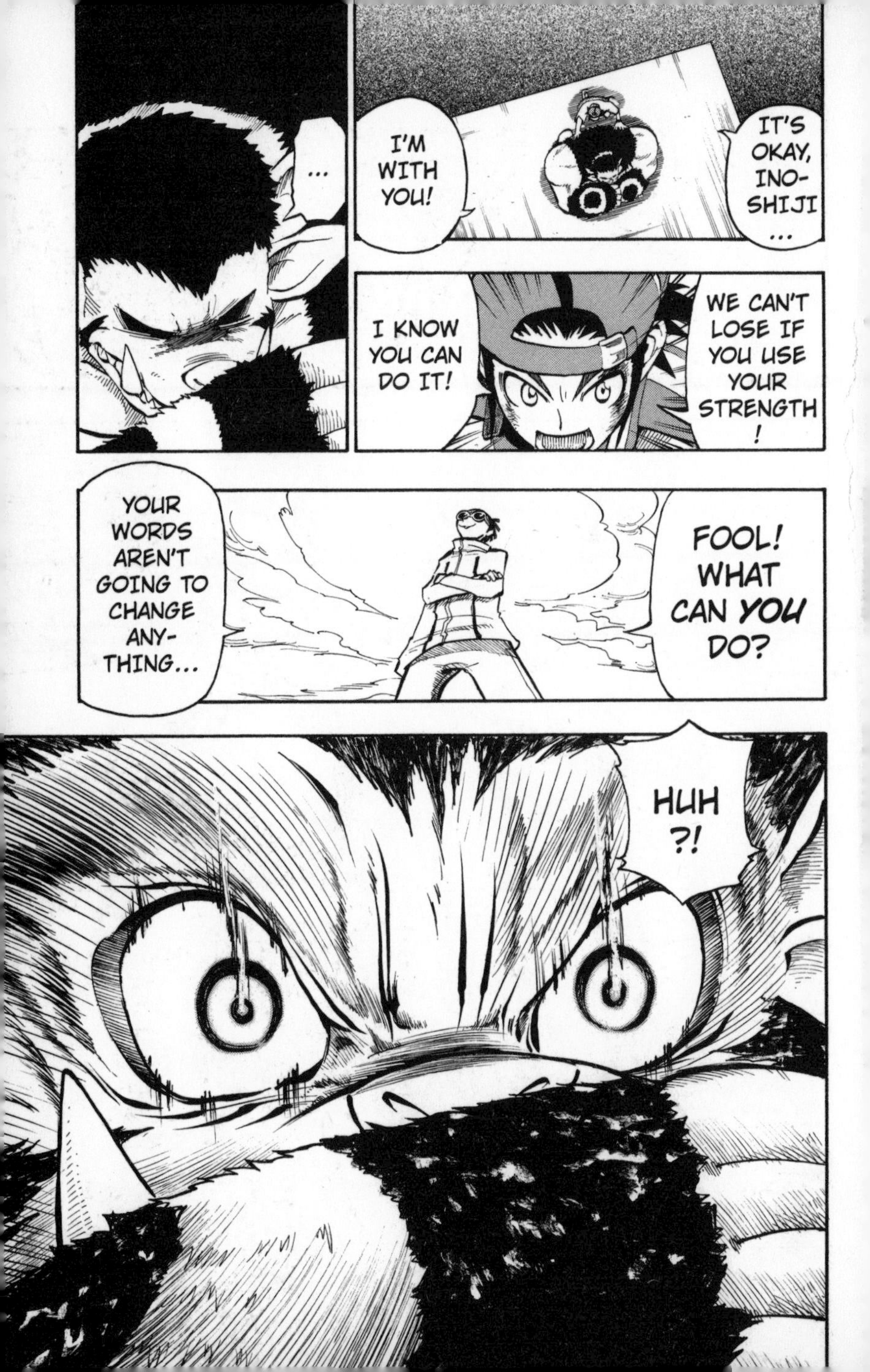
IT'S OKAY, INO-SHIJI...
I'M WITH YOU!
WE CAN'T LOSE IF YOU USE YOUR STRENGTH!
I KNOW YOU CAN DO IT!
...
FOOL! WHAT CAN YOU DO?
YOUR WORDS AREN'T GOING TO CHANGE ANYTHING...
HUH?!

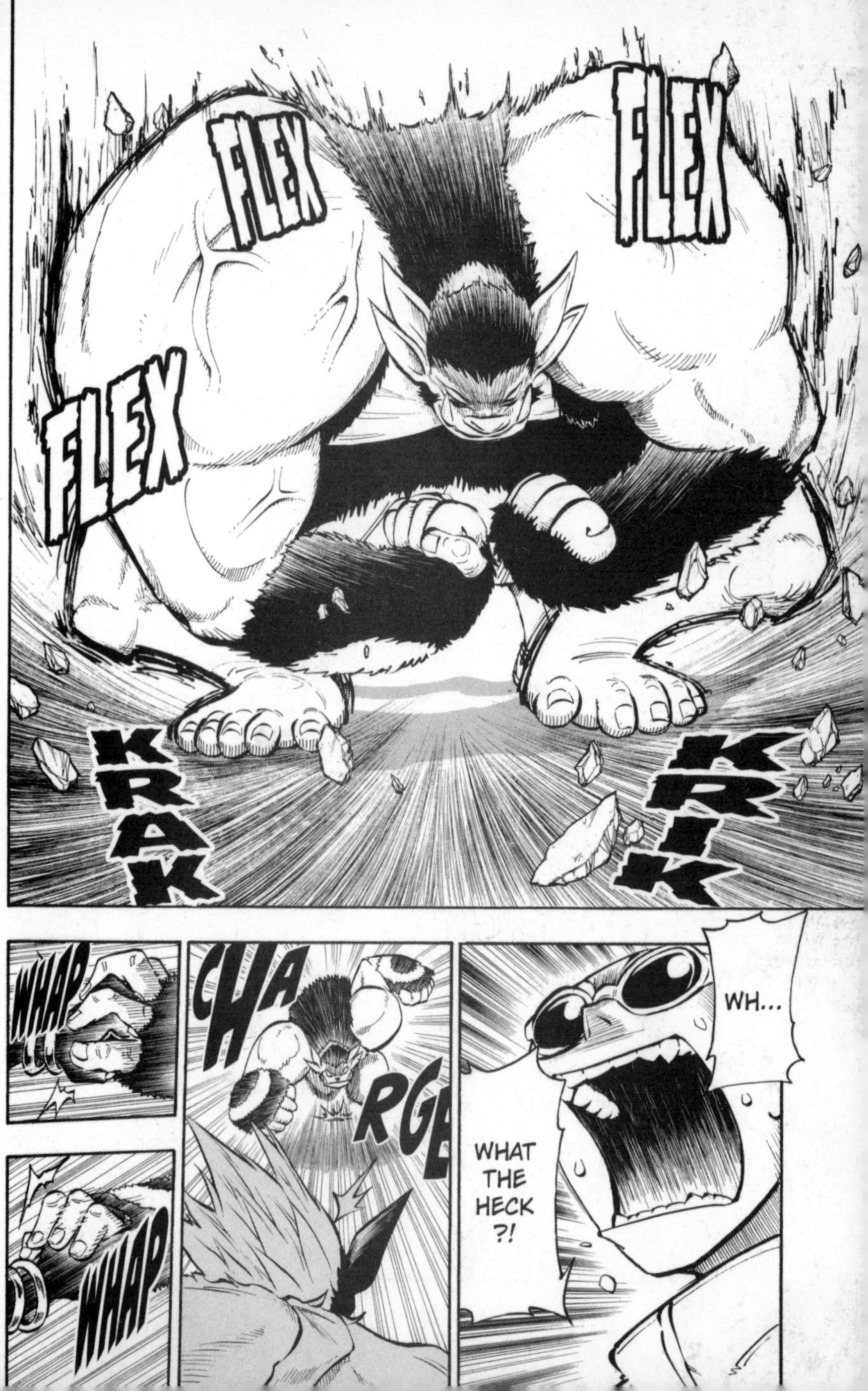
FLEX
FLEX
FLEX
KRIK
KRAK
WH...
WHAT THE HECK ?!
CHARGE
WHAP
WHAP

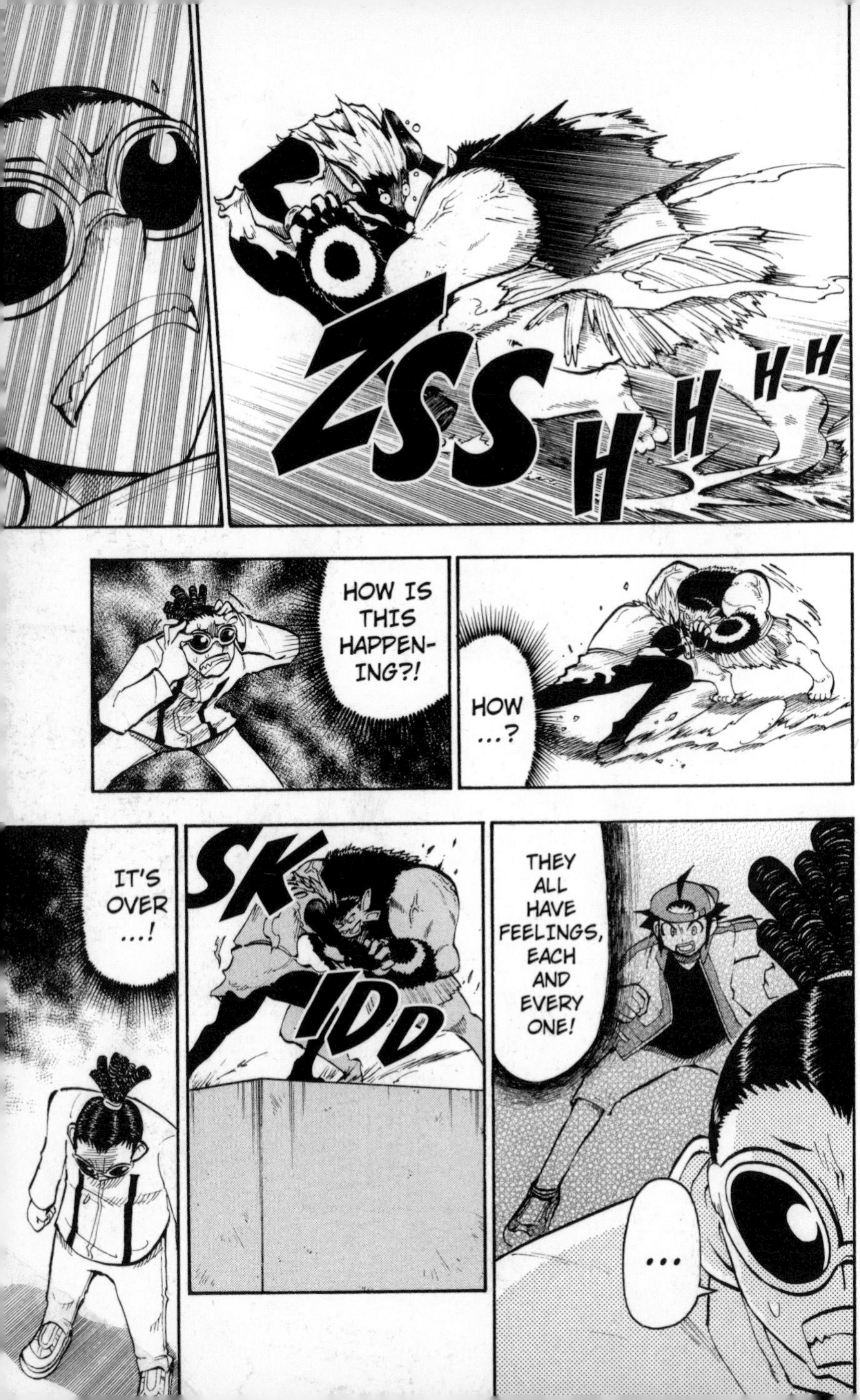
ZSSHHHH
HOW ...?
HOW IS THIS HAPPENING?!
THEY ALL HAVE FEELINGS, EACH AND EVERY ONE!
...
SKIDD
IT'S OVER ...!

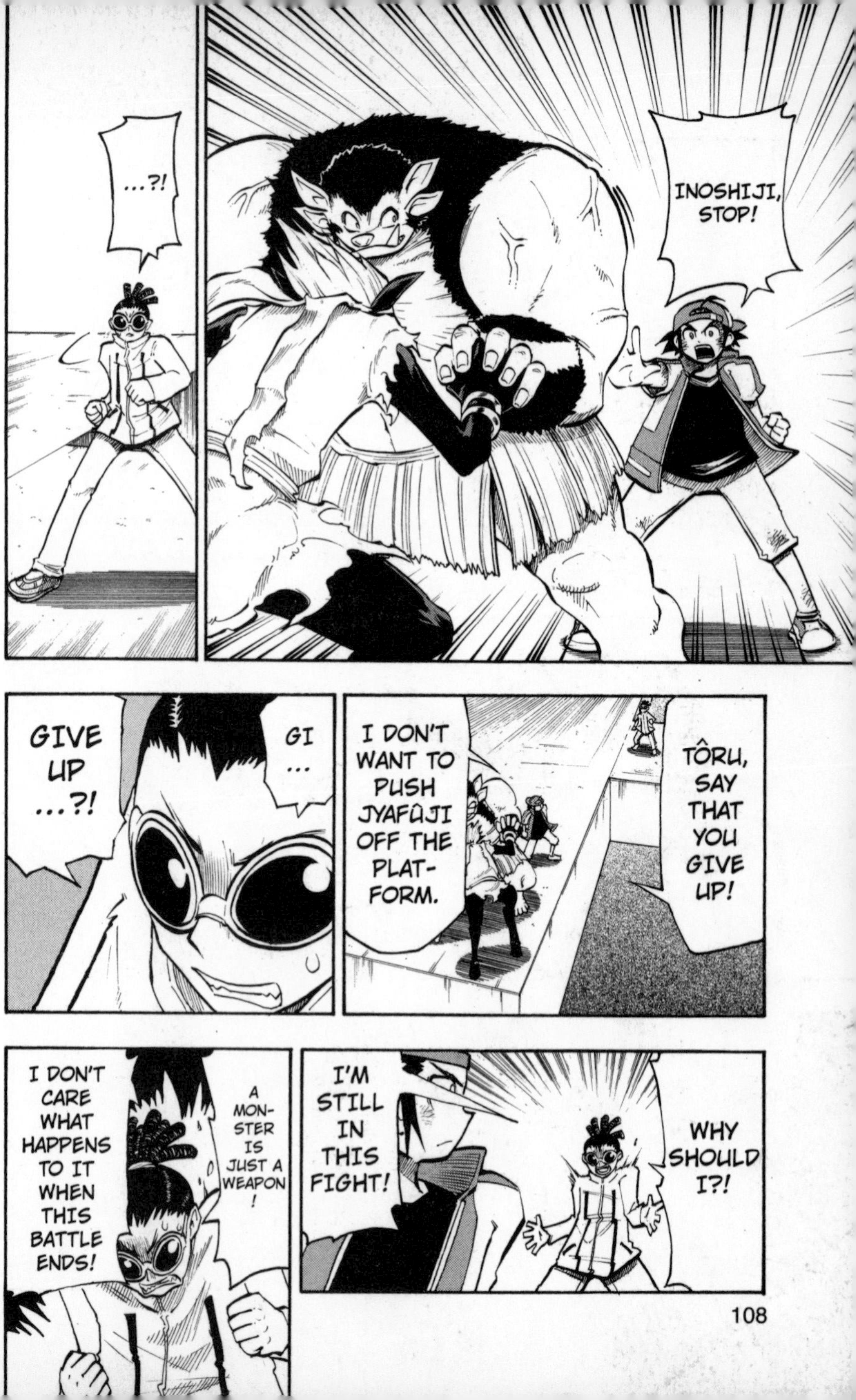

INOSHIJI, STOP!
...?!
TÔRU, SAY THAT YOU GIVE UP!
I DON'T WANT TO PUSH JYAFÛJI OFF THE PLATFORM.
GI ...
GIVE UP ...?!
WHY SHOULD I?!
I'M STILL IN THIS FIGHT!
A MONSTER IS JUST A WEAPON!
I DON'T CARE WHAT HAPPENS TO IT WHEN THIS BATTLE ENDS!

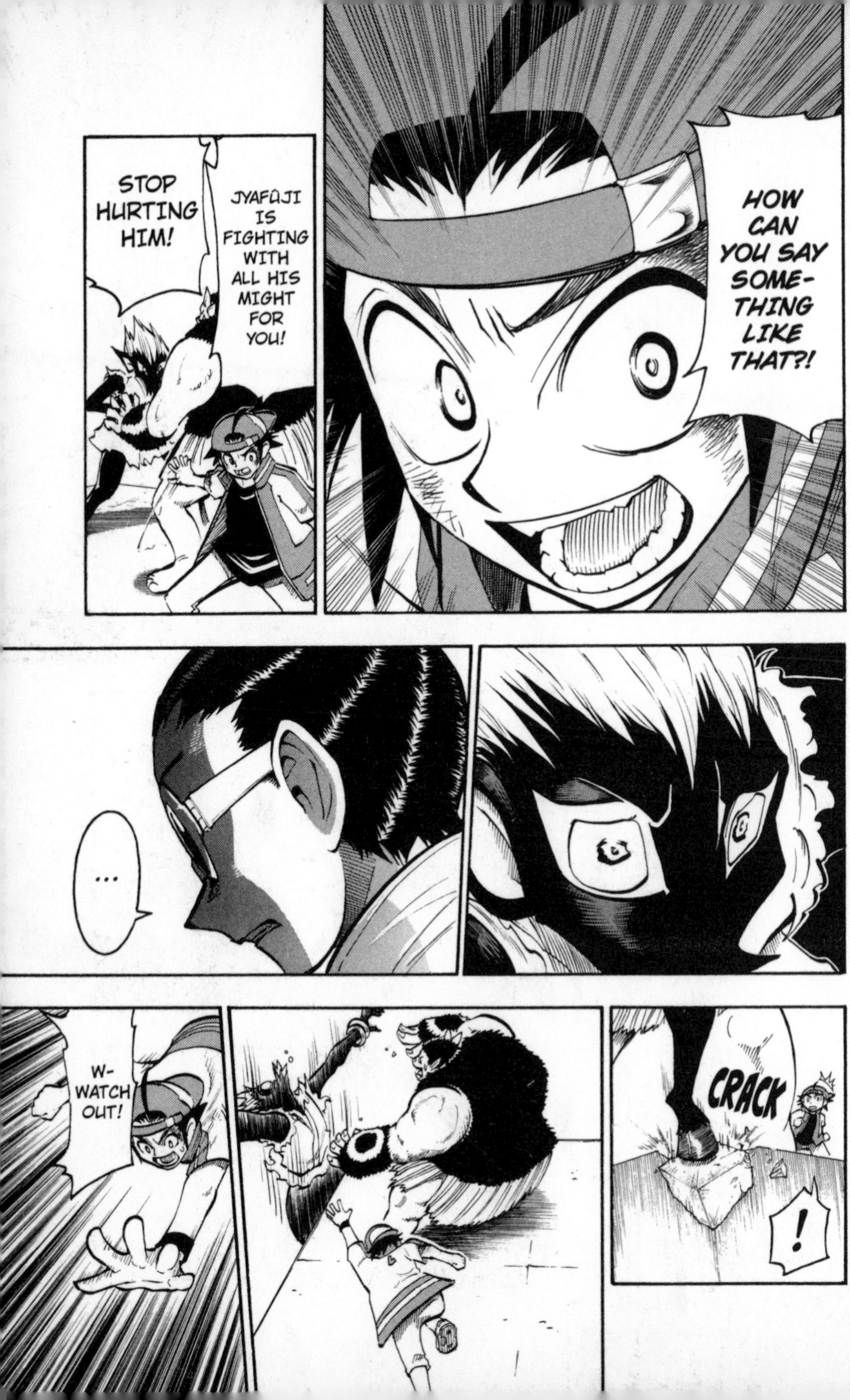
HOW CAN YOU SAY SOME-THING LIKE THAT?!
JYAFÛJI IS FIGHTING WITH ALL HIS MIGHT FOR YOU!
STOP HURTING HIM!
...
CRACK
!
W-WATCH OUT!

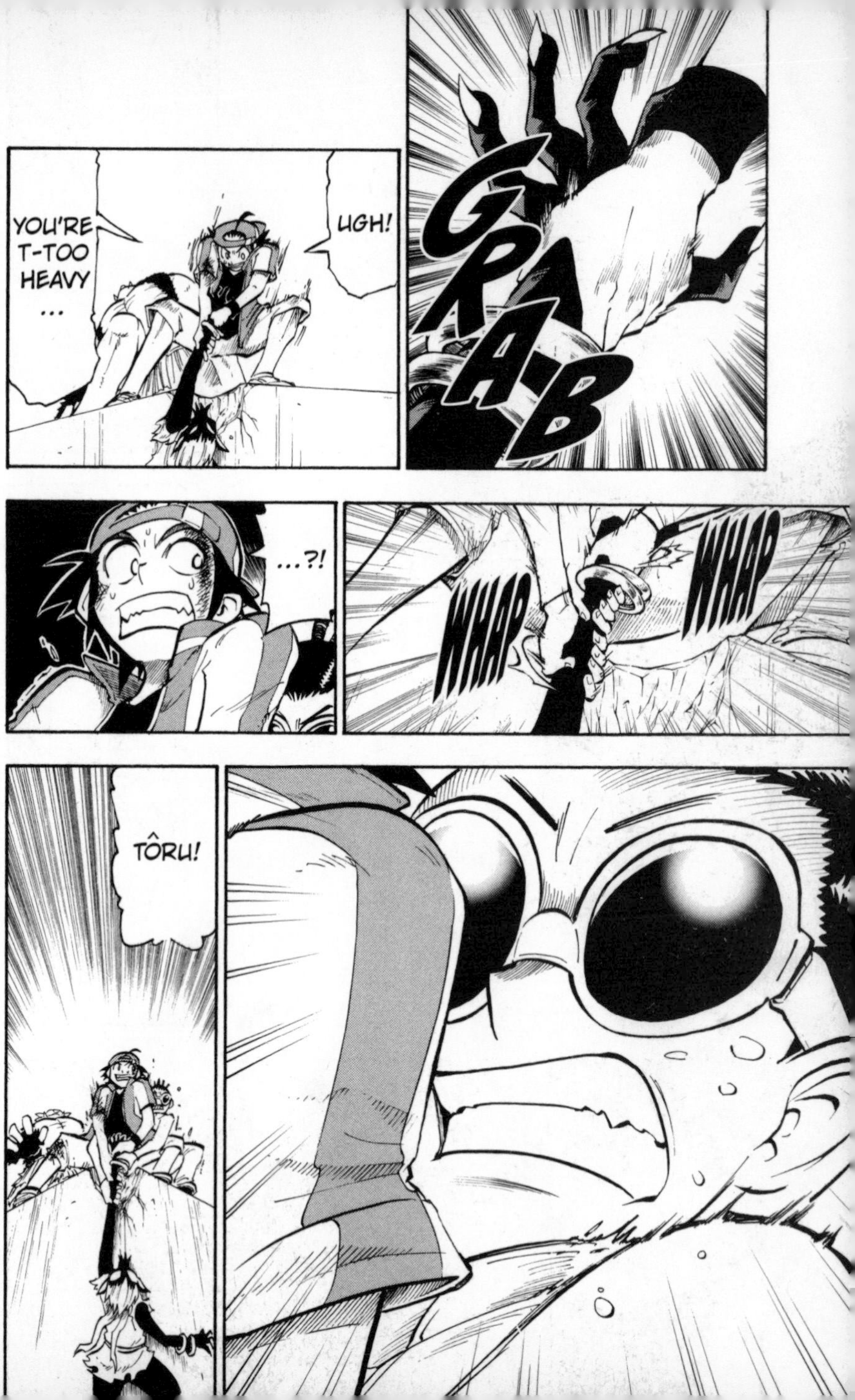
GRA-AB
UGH!
YOU'RE T-TOO HEAVY ...
WHAP WHAP
...?!
TÔRU!

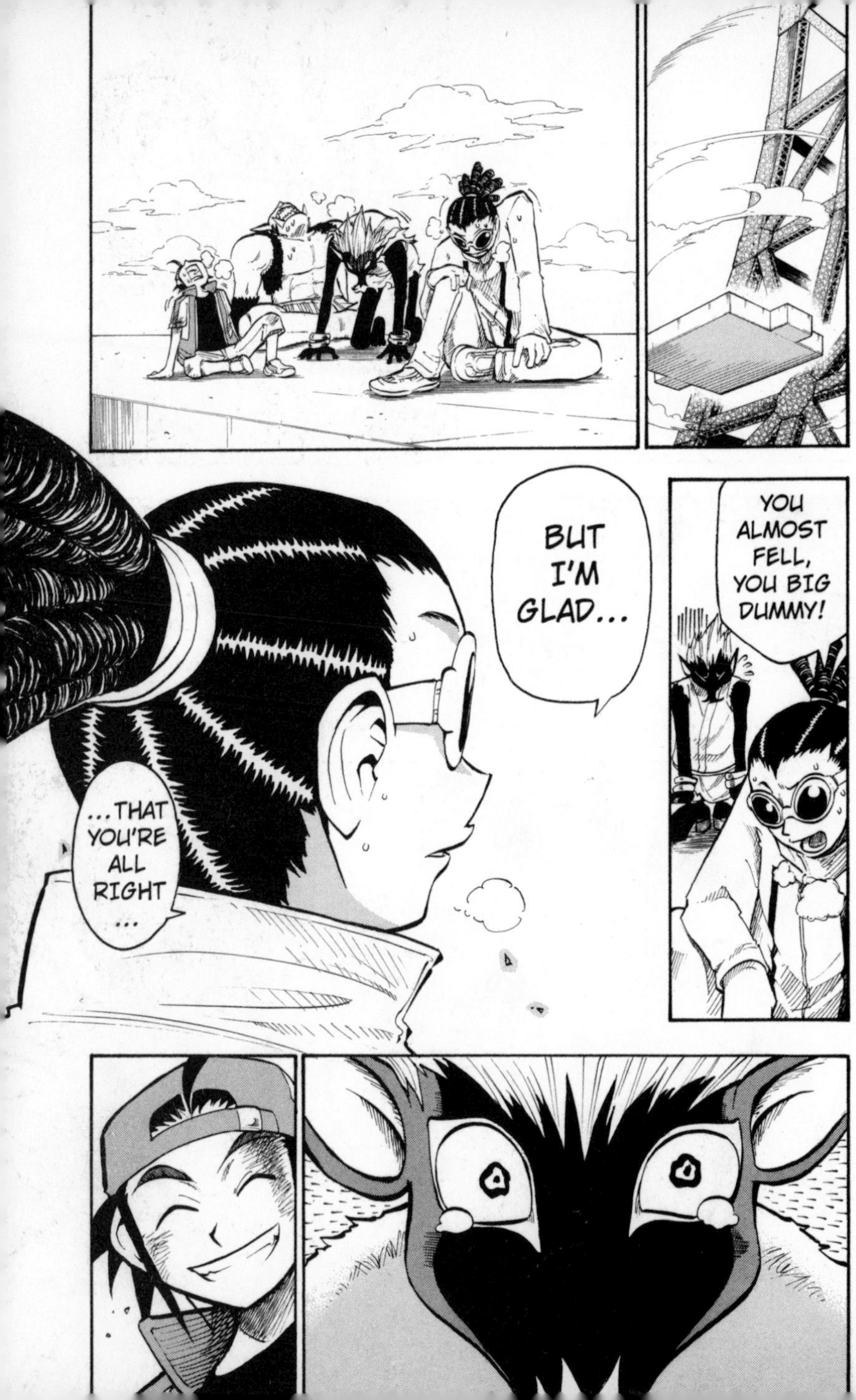
YOU ALMOST FELL, YOU BIG DUMMY!
BUT I'M GLAD...
...THAT YOU'RE ALL RIGHT ...

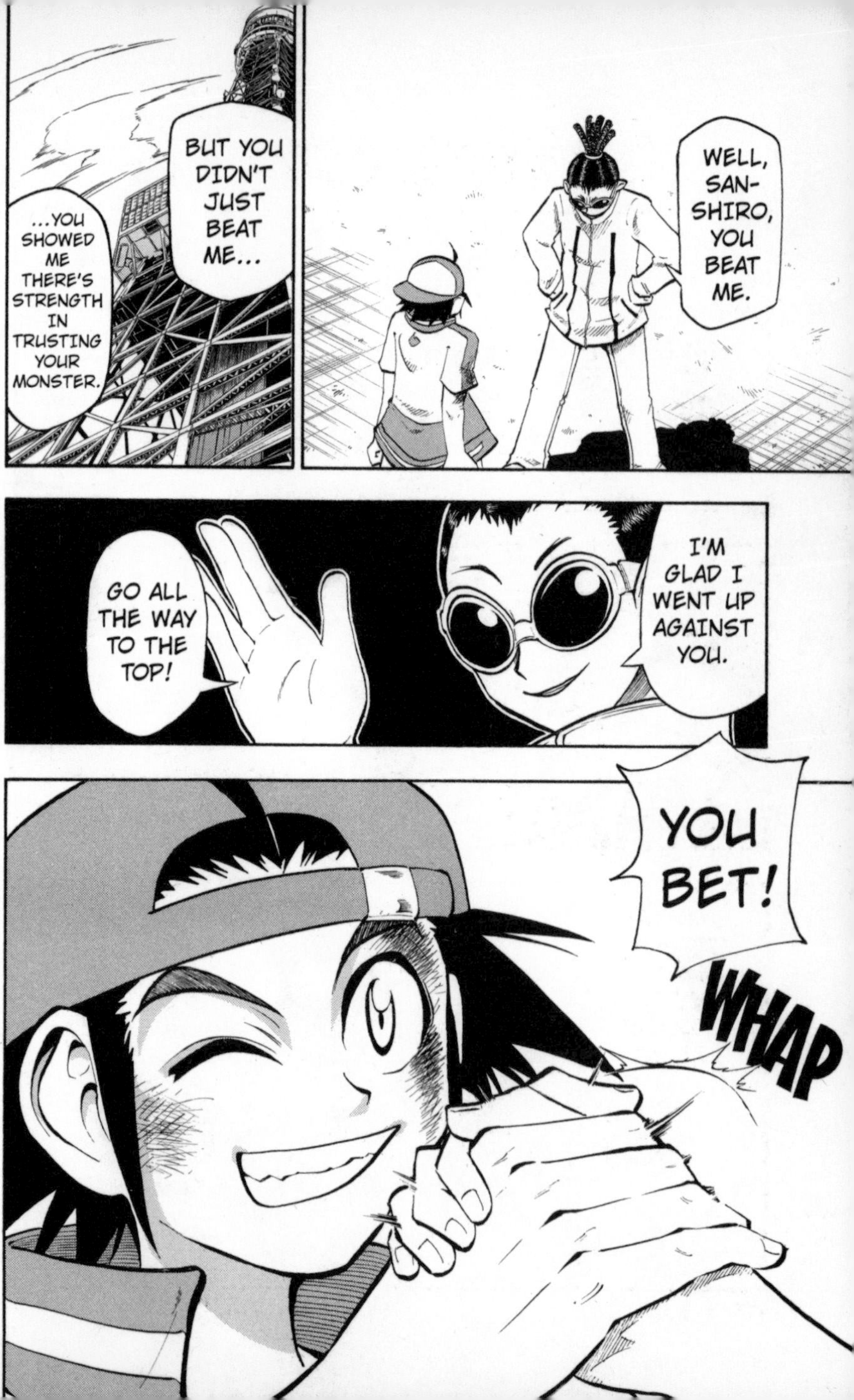
WELL, SAN-SHIRO, YOU BEAT ME.
BUT YOU DIDN'T JUST BEAT ME...
...YOU SHOWED ME THERE'S STRENGTH IN TRUSTING YOUR MONSTER.
I'M GLAD I WENT UP AGAINST YOU.
GO ALL THE WAY TO THE TOP!
YOU BET!
WHAP

BAKÉGYAMON DIARY 1 DRAWING

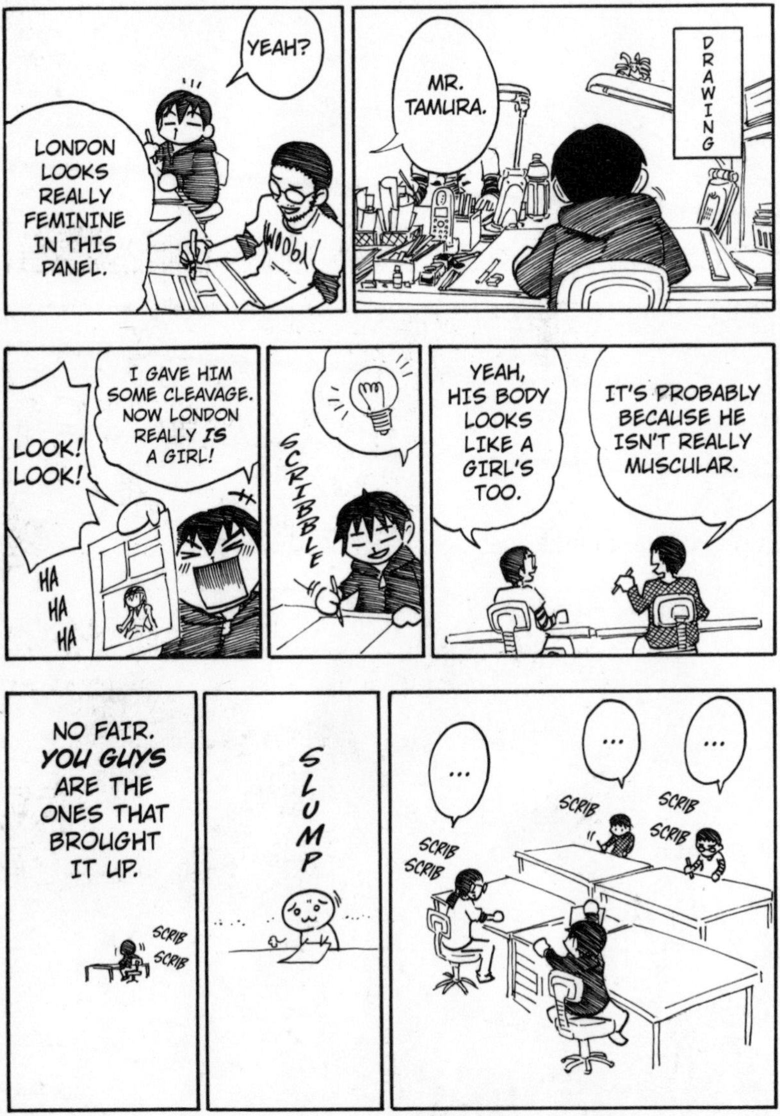
DRAWING
MR. TAMURA.
YEAH?
LONDON LOOKS REALLY FEMININE IN THIS PANEL.
IT'S PROBABLY BECAUSE HE ISN'T REALLY MUSCULAR.
YEAH, HIS BODY LOOKS LIKE A GIRL'S TOO.
SCRIBBLE
I GAVE HIM SOME CLEAVAGE. NOW LONDON REALLY IS A GIRL!
LOOK! LOOK!
HA HA HA
...
...
...
SCRIB
SCRIB SCRIB
SCRIB SCRIB
SLUMP
NO FAIR. YOU GUYS ARE THE ONES THAT BROUGHT IT UP.
SCRIB SCRIB

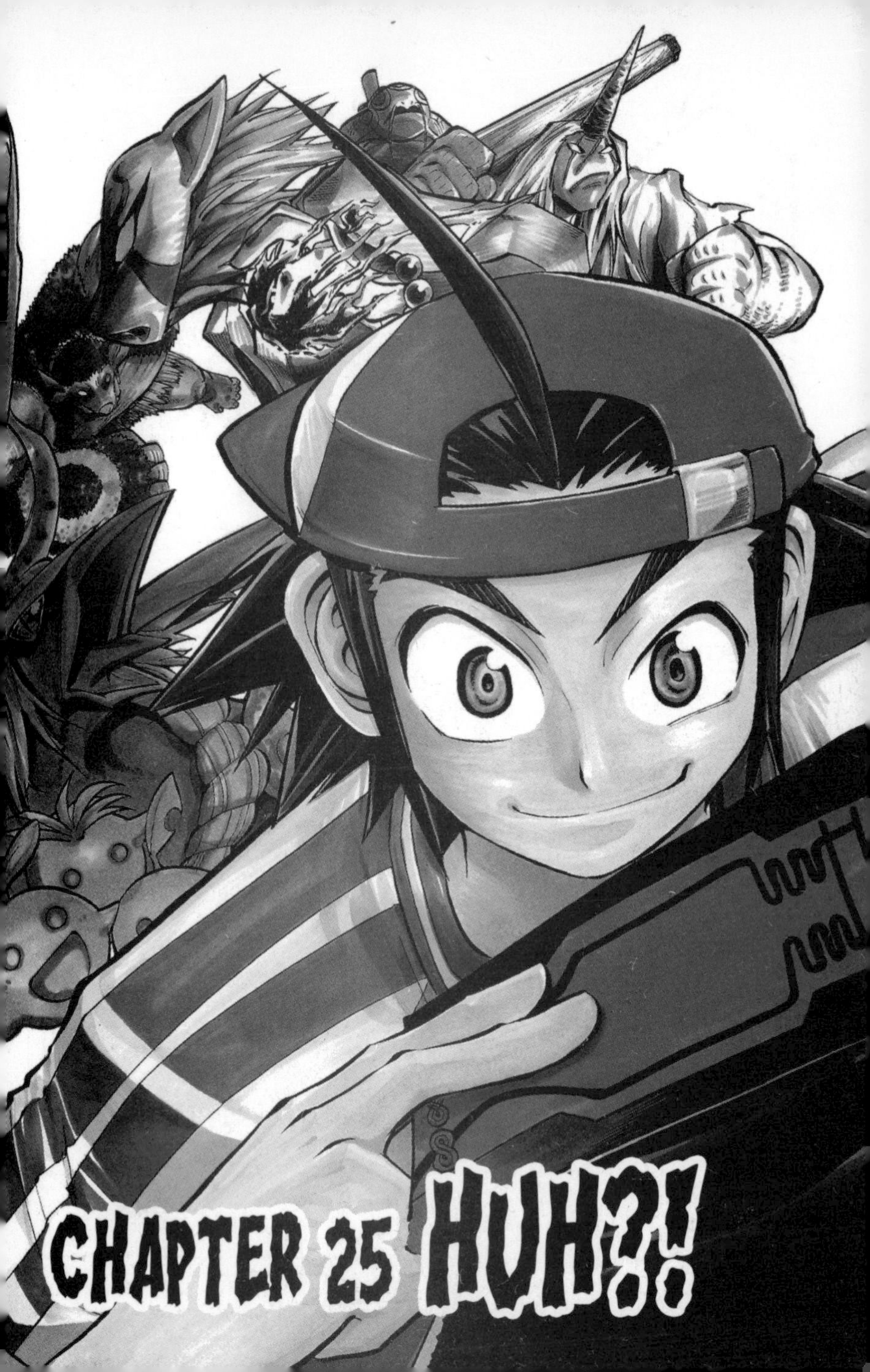
CHAPTER 25 HUH?!

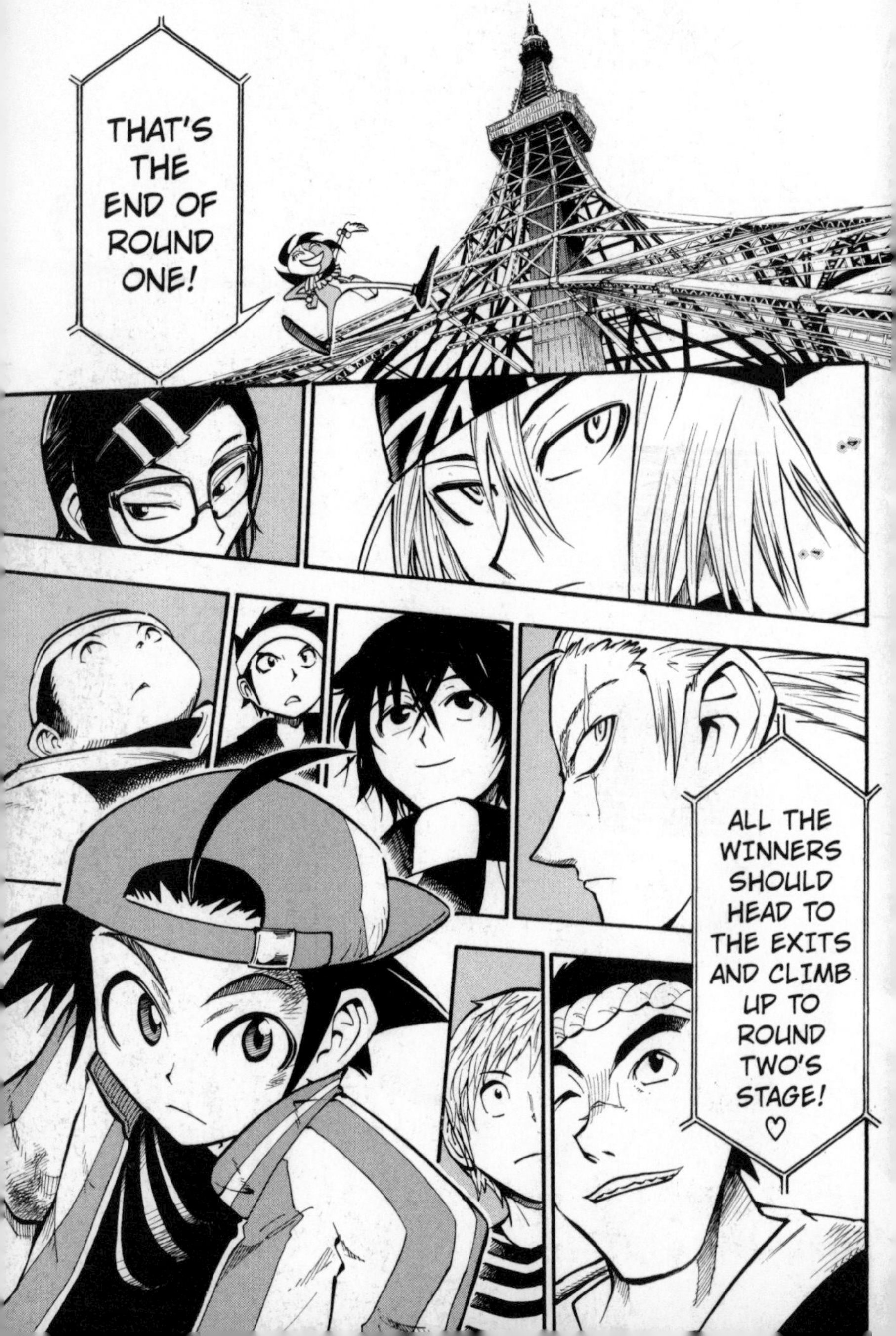
THAT'S THE END OF ROUND ONE!
ALL THE WINNERS SHOULD HEAD TO THE EXITS AND CLIMB UP TO ROUND TWO'S STAGE! ♡

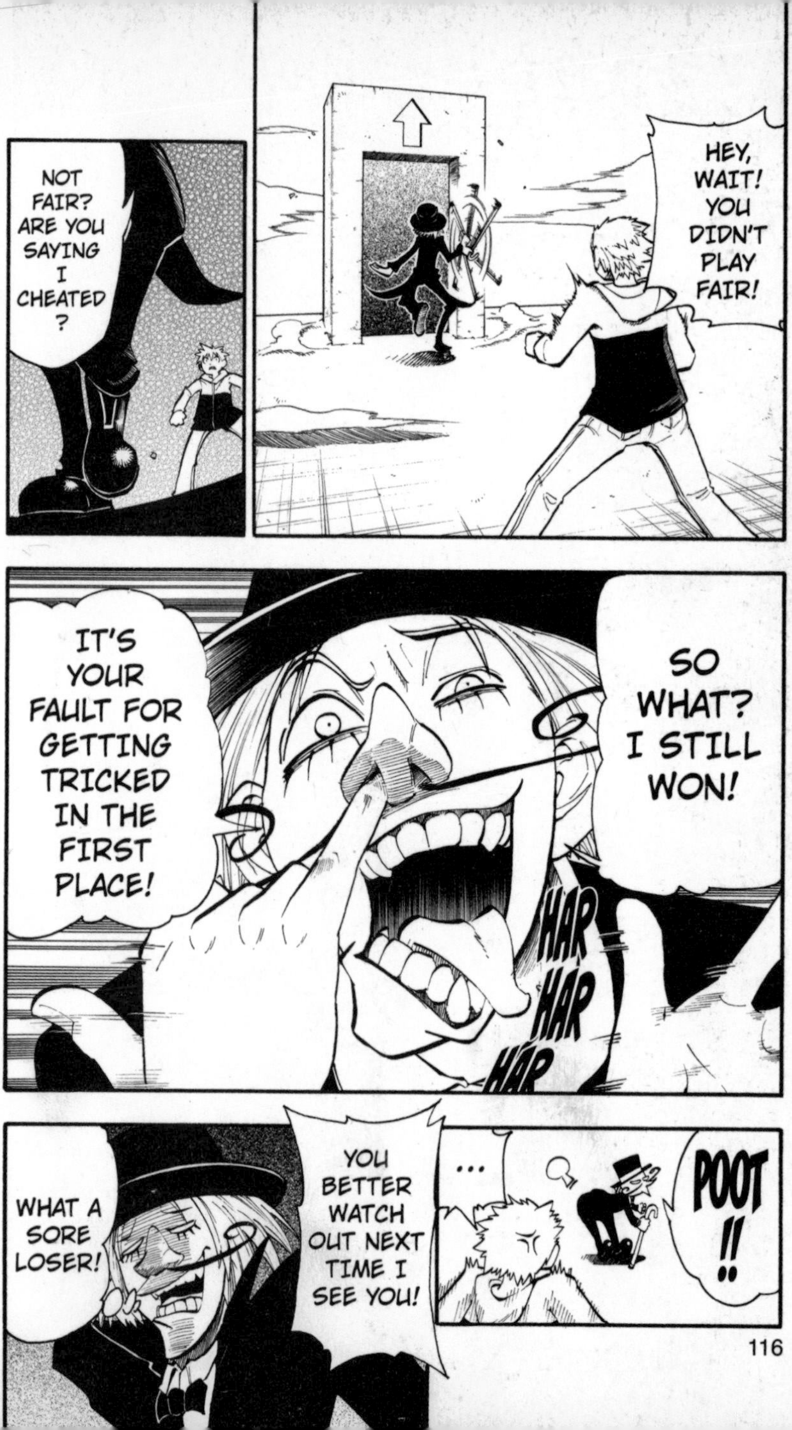
HEY, WAIT! YOU DIDN'T PLAY FAIR!
NOT FAIR? ARE YOU SAYING I CHEATED?
SO WHAT? I STILL WON!
IT'S YOUR FAULT FOR GETTING TRICKED IN THE FIRST PLACE!
HAR HAR HAR
POOT!!
...
YOU BETTER WATCH OUT NEXT TIME I SEE YOU!
WHAT A SORE LOSER!

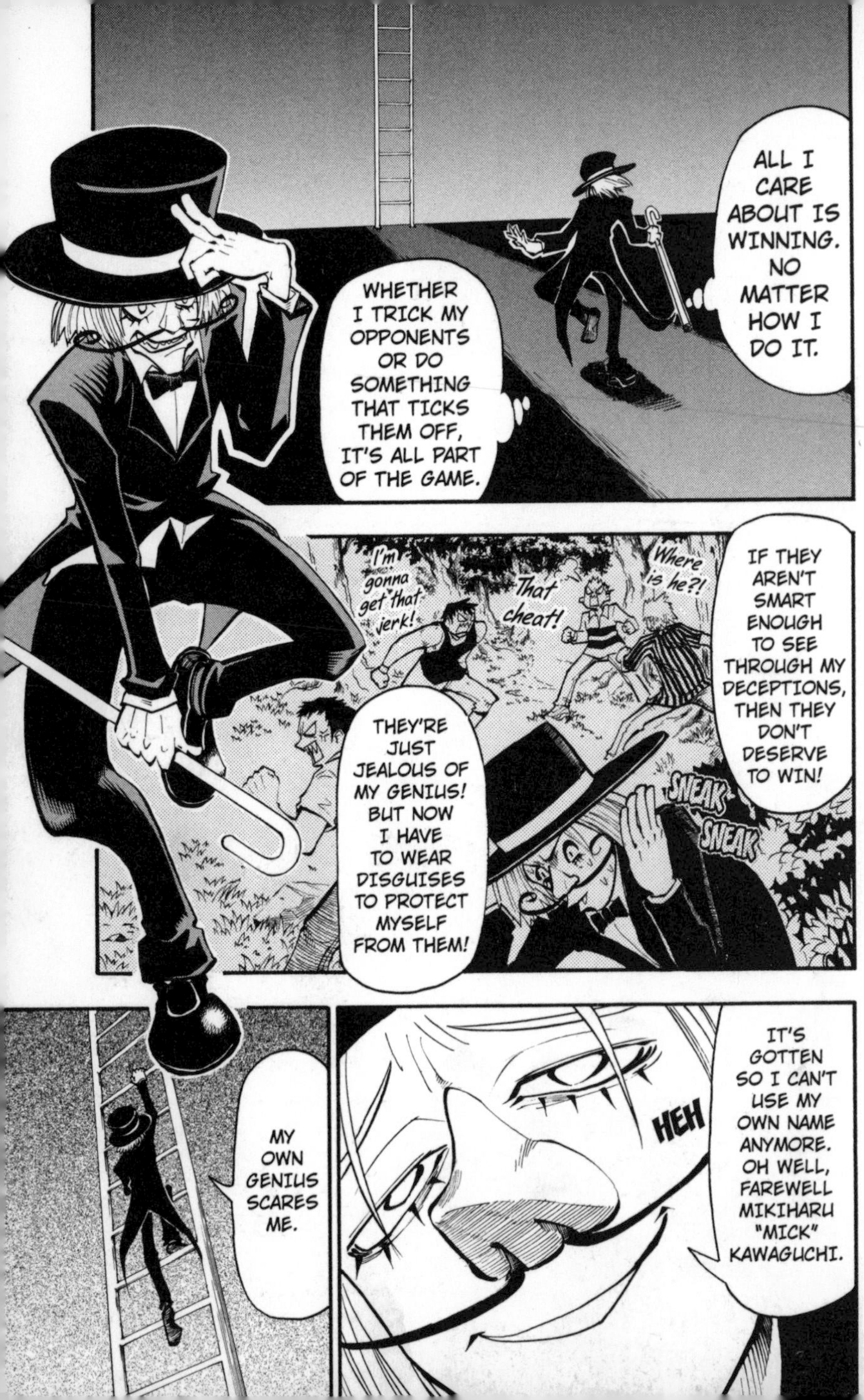

ALL I CARE ABOUT IS WINNING. NO MATTER HOW I DO IT.
WHETHER I TRICK MY OPPONENTS OR DO SOMETHING THAT TICKS THEM OFF, IT'S ALL PART OF THE GAME.
IF THEY AREN'T SMART ENOUGH TO SEE THROUGH MY DECEPTIONS, THEN THEY DON'T DESERVE TO WIN!
Where is he?!
That cheat!
I'm gonna get that jerk!
THEY'RE JUST JEALOUS OF MY GENIUS! BUT NOW I HAVE TO WEAR DISGUISES TO PROTECT MYSELF FROM THEM!
SNEAK
SNEAK
IT'S GOTTEN SO I CAN'T USE MY OWN NAME ANYMORE. OH WELL, FAREWELL MIKIHARU "MICK" KAWAGUCHI.
HEH
MY OWN GENIUS SCARES ME.

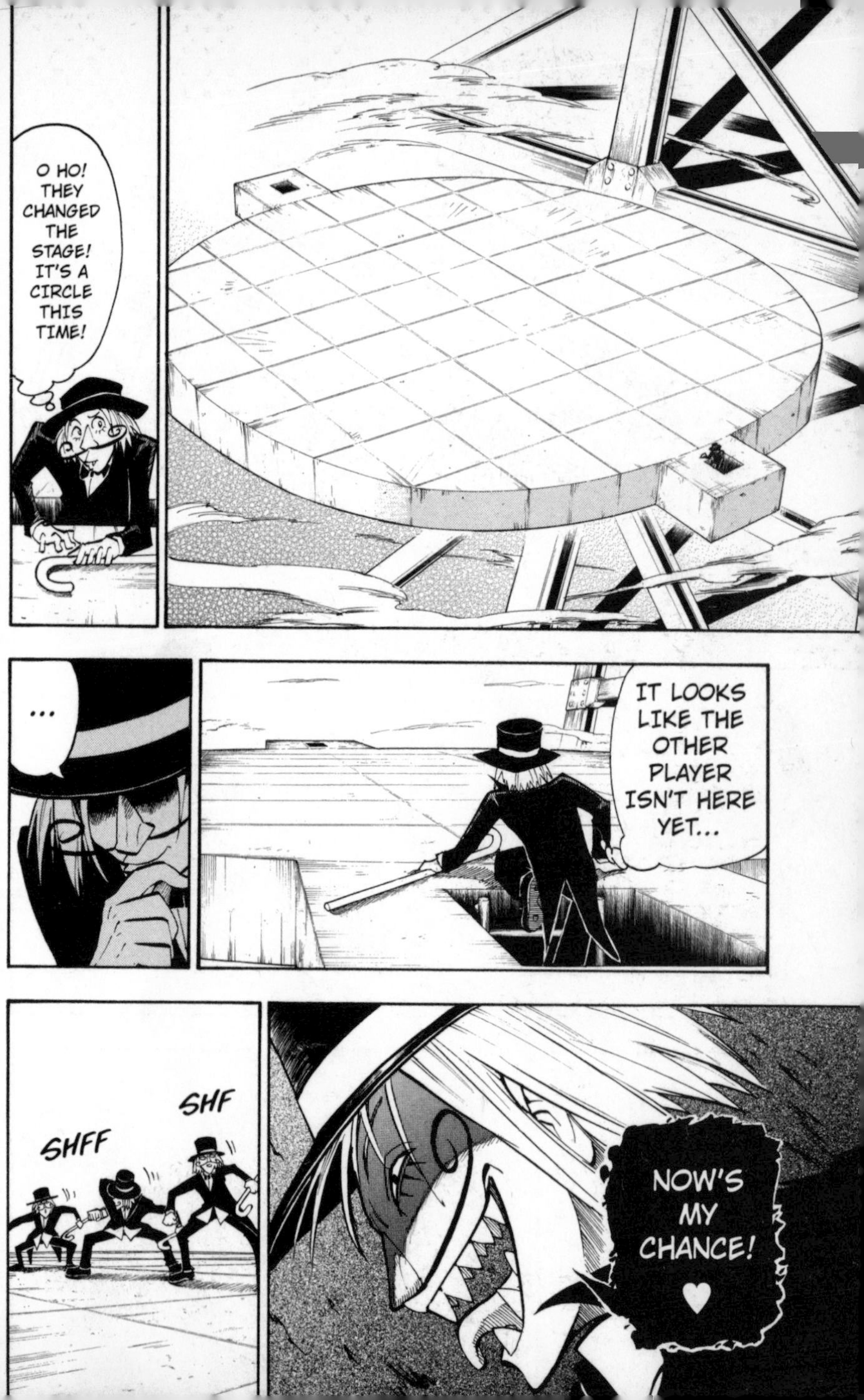
O HO! THEY CHANGED THE STAGE! IT'S A CIRCLE THIS TIME!
IT LOOKS LIKE THE OTHER PLAYER ISN'T HERE YET...
...
NOW'S MY CHANCE! ♥
SHF
SHFF

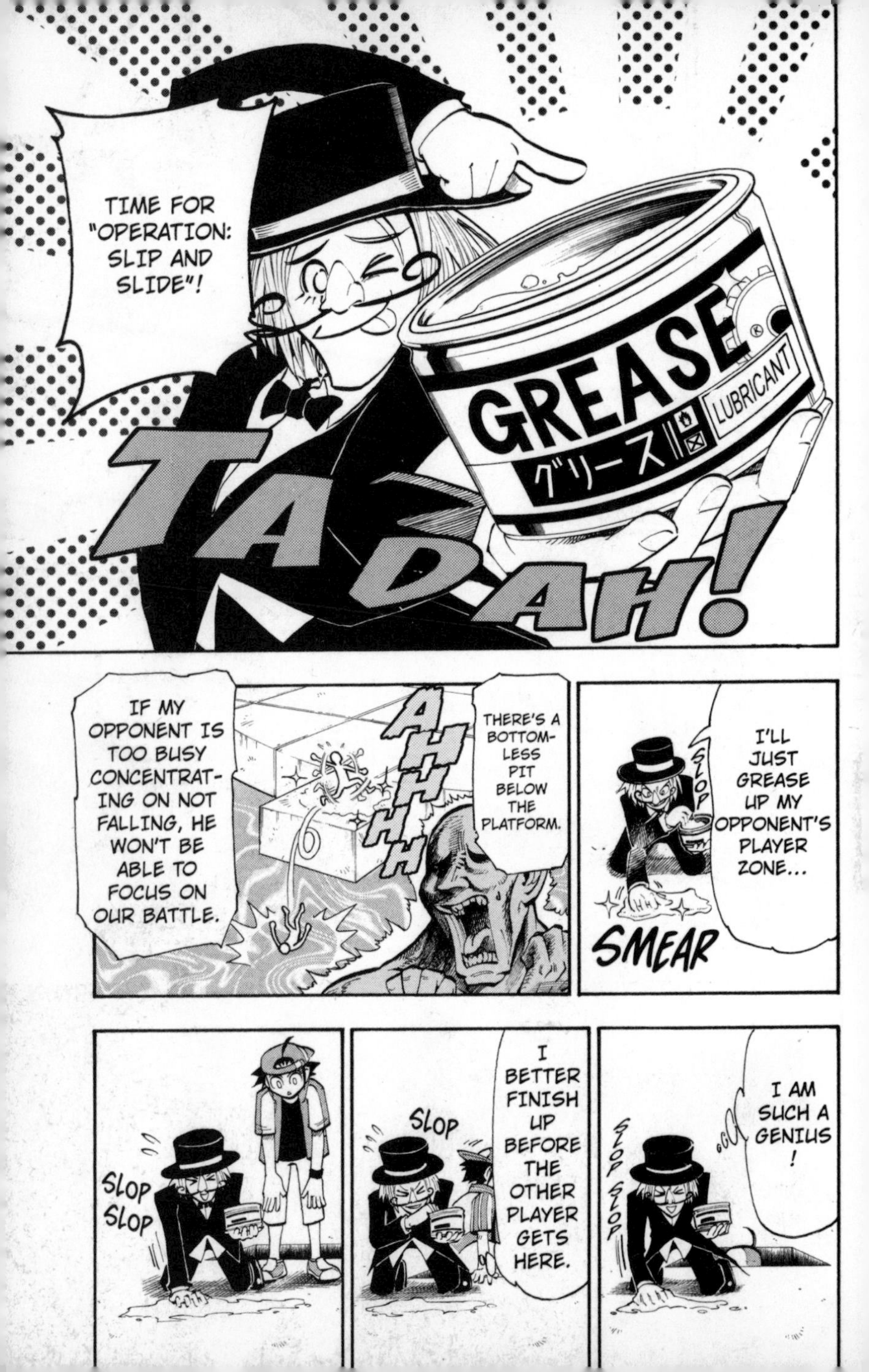
TIME FOR "OPERATION: SLIP AND SLIDE"!
GREASE
グリース
LUBRICANT
TA DAH!
I'LL JUST GREASE UP MY OPPONENT'S PLAYER ZONE...
SLOP
SMEAR
THERE'S A BOTTOM-LESS PIT BELOW THE PLATFORM.
AHHHHH
IF MY OPPONENT IS TOO BUSY CONCENTRAT-ING ON NOT FALLING, HE WON'T BE ABLE TO FOCUS ON OUR BATTLE.
I AM SUCH A GENIUS!
SLOP SLOP
I BETTER FINISH UP BEFORE THE OTHER PLAYER GETS HERE.
SLOP
SLOP SLOP

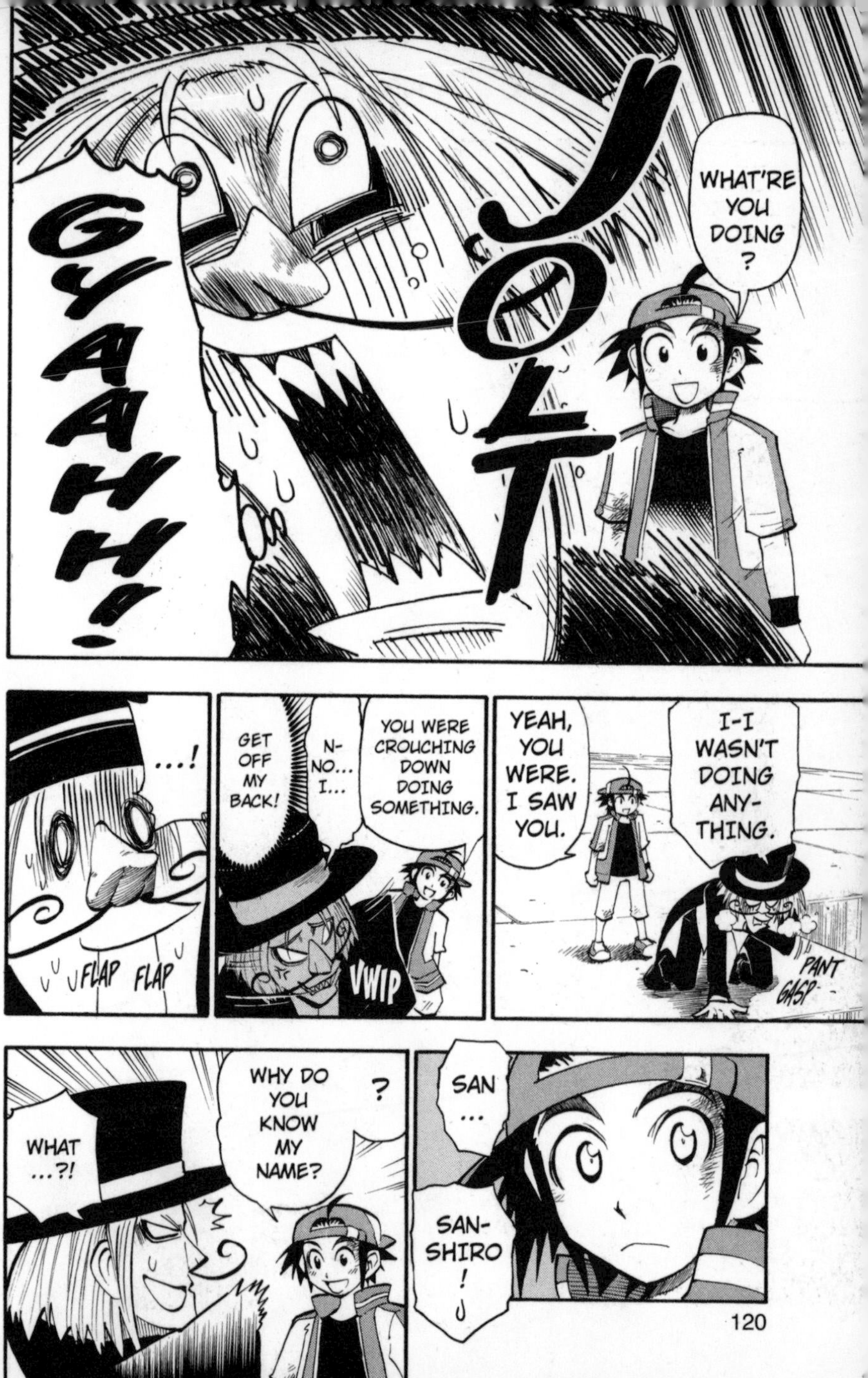
WHAT'RE YOU DOING?
JOLT
GYAAHH!
I-I WASN'T DOING ANY-THING.
PANT GASP
YEAH, YOU WERE. I SAW YOU.
YOU WERE CROUCHING DOWN DOING SOMETHING.
N-NO... I...
GET OFF MY BACK!
VWIP
...!
FLAP FLAP
SAN...
SAN-SHIRO!
?
WHY DO YOU KNOW MY NAME?
WHAT...?!

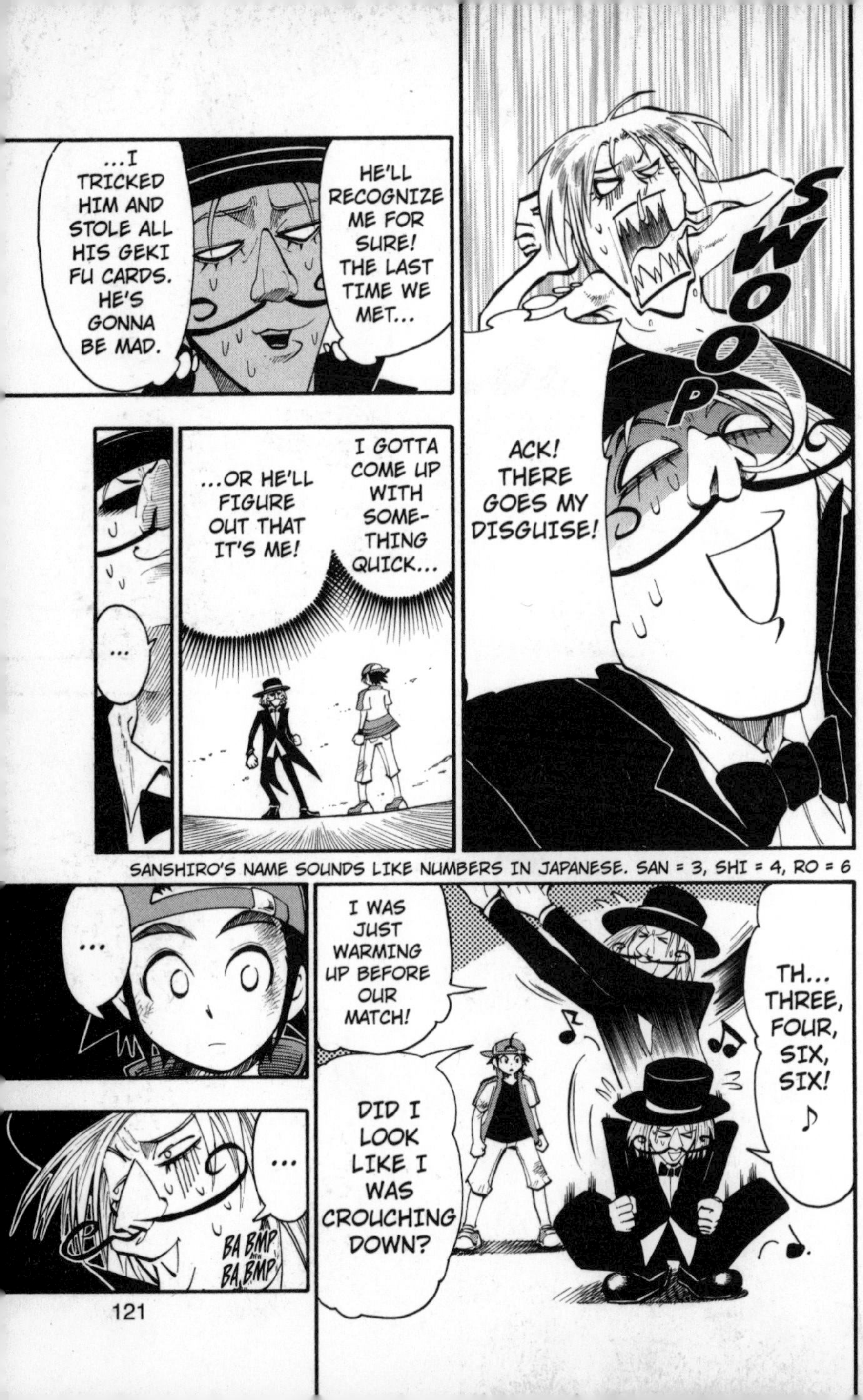
SWOOP
ACK! THERE GOES MY DISGUISE!
HE'LL RECOGNIZE ME FOR SURE! THE LAST TIME WE MET...
...I TRICKED HIM AND STOLE ALL HIS GEKI FU CARDS. HE'S GONNA BE MAD.
I GOTTA COME UP WITH SOME-THING QUICK...
...OR HE'LL FIGURE OUT THAT IT'S ME!
...
SANSHIRO'S NAME SOUNDS LIKE NUMBERS IN JAPANESE. SAN = 3, SHI = 4, RO = 6
TH... THREE, FOUR, SIX, SIX!
I WAS JUST WARMING UP BEFORE OUR MATCH!
DID I LOOK LIKE I WAS CROUCHING DOWN?
...
...
BA BMP BA BMP

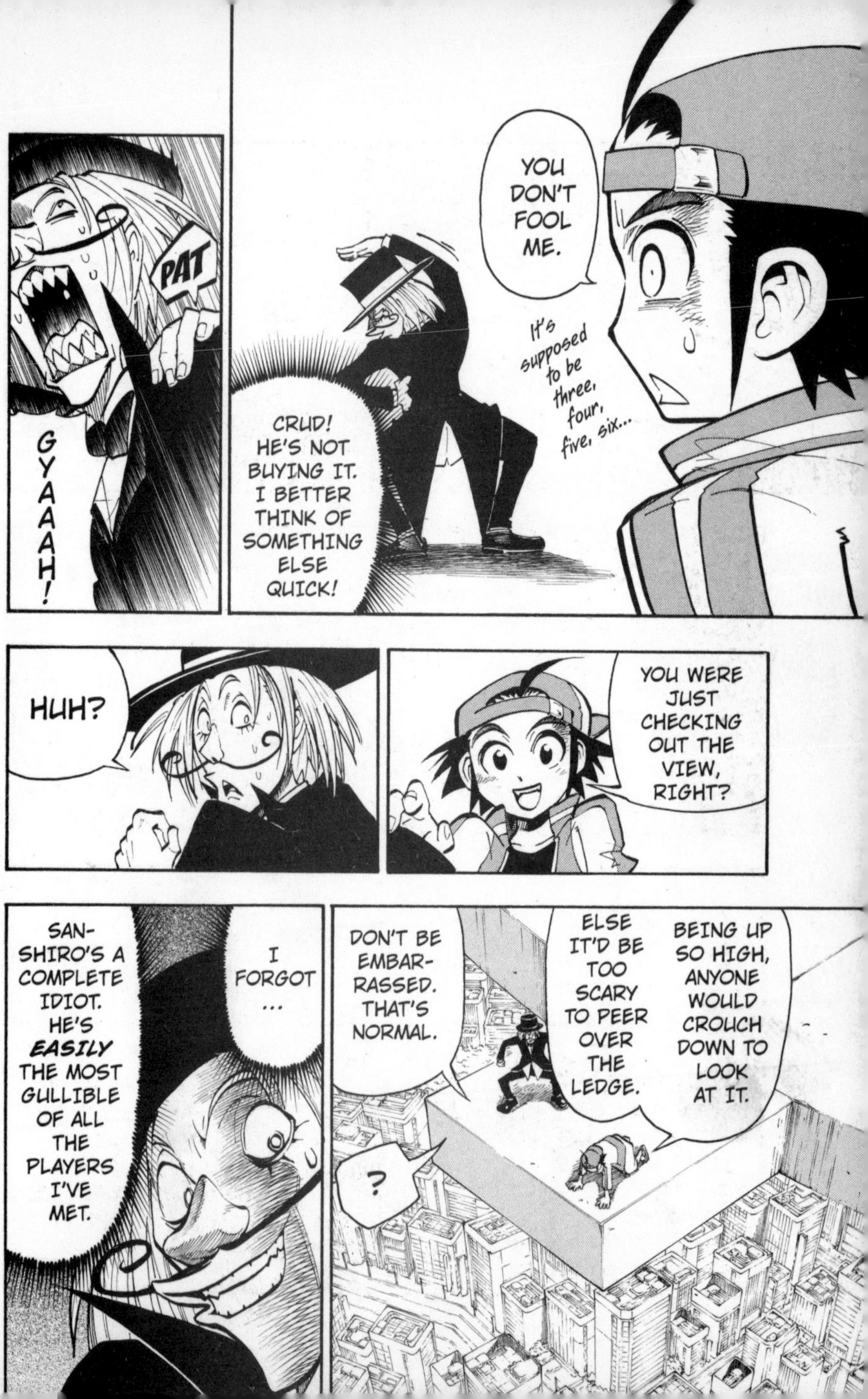
YOU DON'T FOOL ME.
It's supposed to be three, four, five, six...
CRUD! HE'S NOT BUYING IT. I BETTER THINK OF SOMETHING ELSE QUICK!
PAT
GYAAAAH!
YOU WERE JUST CHECKING OUT THE VIEW, RIGHT?
HUH?
BEING UP SO HIGH, ANYONE WOULD CROUCH DOWN TO LOOK AT IT.
ELSE IT'D BE TOO SCARY TO PEER OVER THE LEDGE.
DON'T BE EMBARRASSED. THAT'S NORMAL.
?
I FORGOT...
SAN-SHIRO'S A COMPLETE IDIOT. HE'S *EASILY* THE MOST GULLIBLE OF ALL THE PLAYERS I'VE MET.

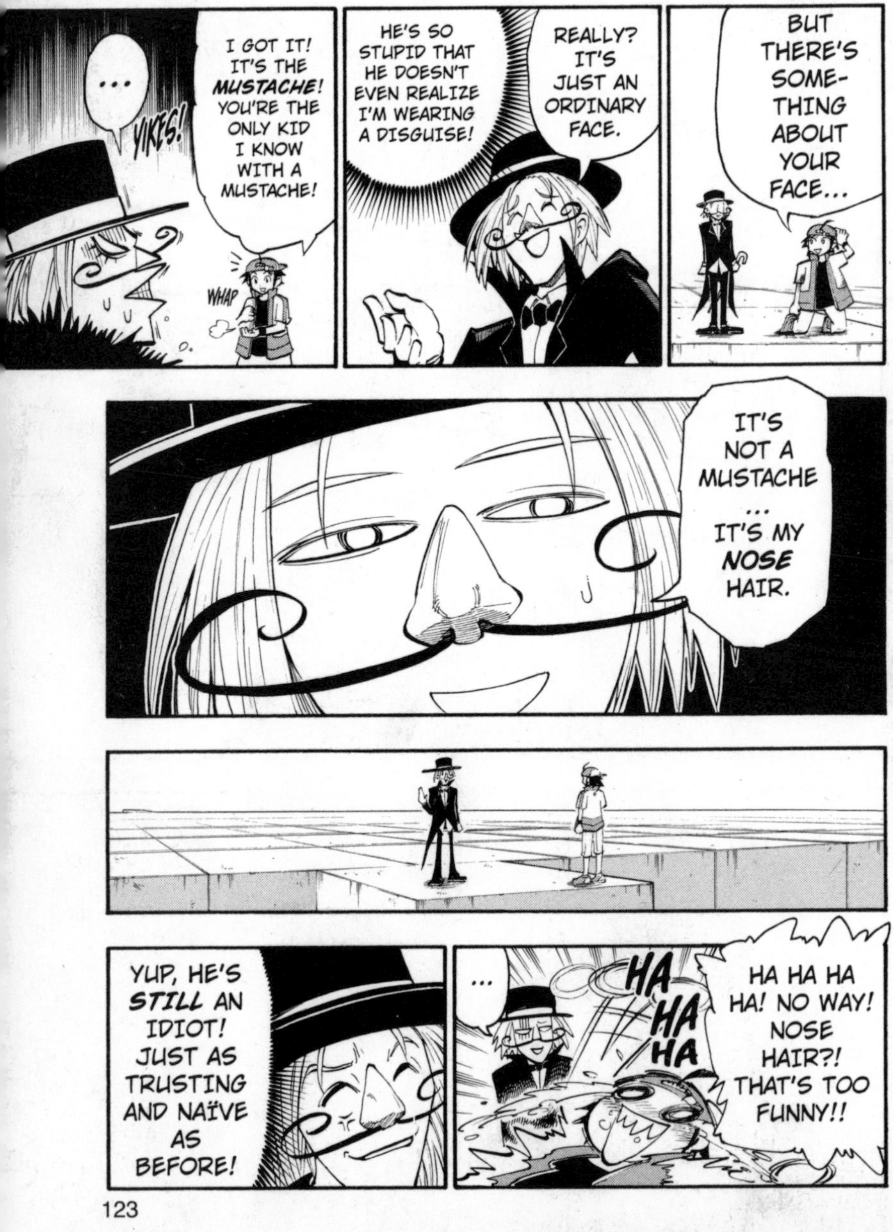
BUT THERE'S SOME-THING ABOUT YOUR FACE...
REALLY? IT'S JUST AN ORDINARY FACE.
HE'S SO STUPID THAT HE DOESN'T EVEN REALIZE I'M WEARING A DISGUISE!
I GOT IT! IT'S THE MUSTACHE! YOU'RE THE ONLY KID I KNOW WITH A MUSTACHE!
...
YIKES!
WHAP
IT'S NOT A MUSTACHE ... IT'S MY NOSE HAIR.
HA HA HA HA! NO WAY! NOSE HAIR?! THAT'S TOO FUNNY!!
HA HA HA
...
YUP, HE'S STILL AN IDIOT! JUST AS TRUSTING AND NAÏVE AS BEFORE!

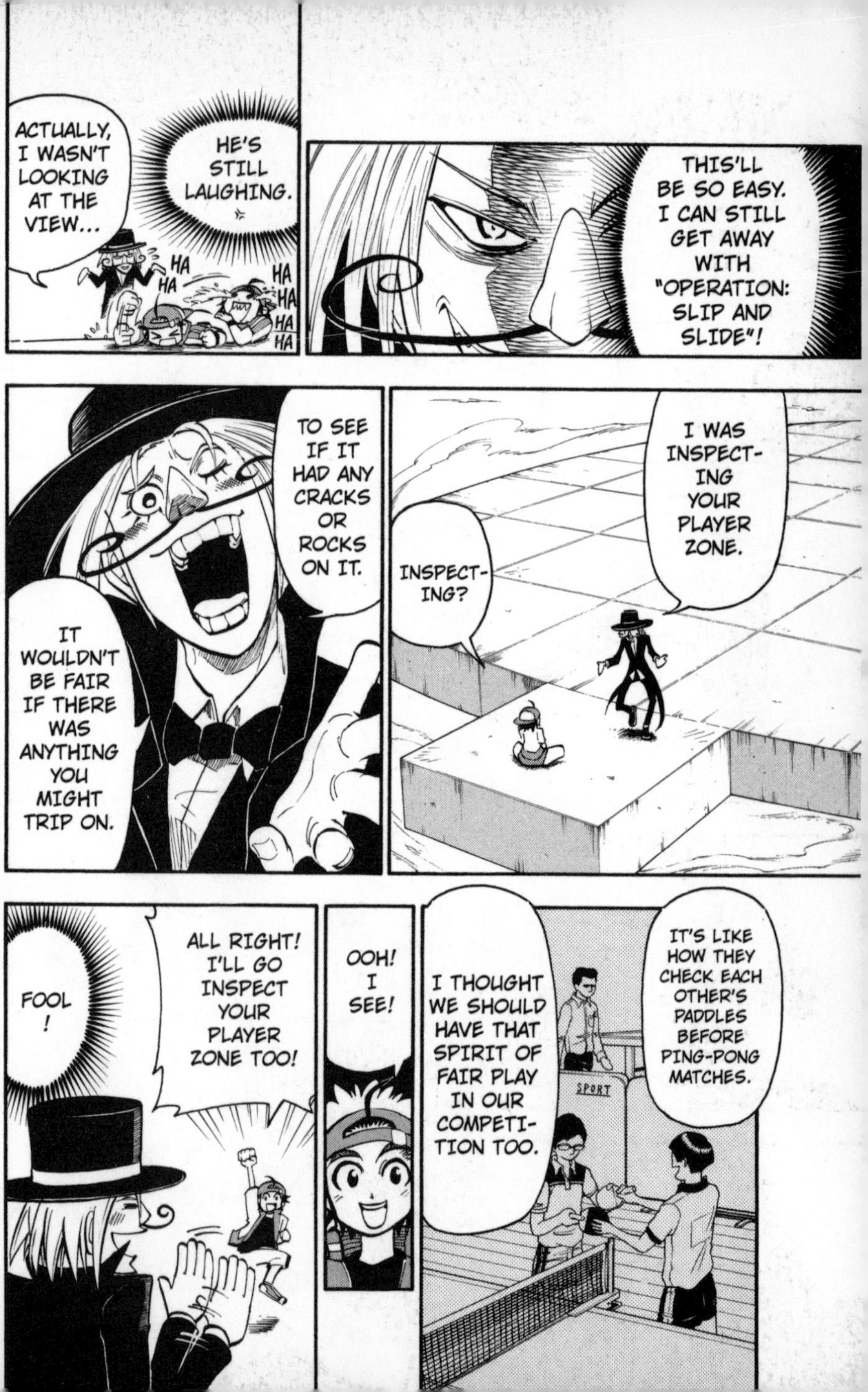
THIS'LL BE SO EASY. I CAN STILL GET AWAY WITH "OPERATION: SLIP AND SLIDE"!
HE'S STILL LAUGHING.
ACTUALLY, I WASN'T LOOKING AT THE VIEW...
HA HA HA HA HA HA HA
I WAS INSPECTING YOUR PLAYER ZONE.
INSPECTING?
TO SEE IF IT HAD ANY CRACKS OR ROCKS ON IT.
IT WOULDN'T BE FAIR IF THERE WAS ANYTHING YOU MIGHT TRIP ON.
IT'S LIKE HOW THEY CHECK EACH OTHER'S PADDLES BEFORE PING-PONG MATCHES.
SPORT
I THOUGHT WE SHOULD HAVE THAT SPIRIT OF FAIR PLAY IN OUR COMPETITION TOO.
OOH! I SEE!
ALL RIGHT! I'LL GO INSPECT YOUR PLAYER ZONE TOO!
FOOL!

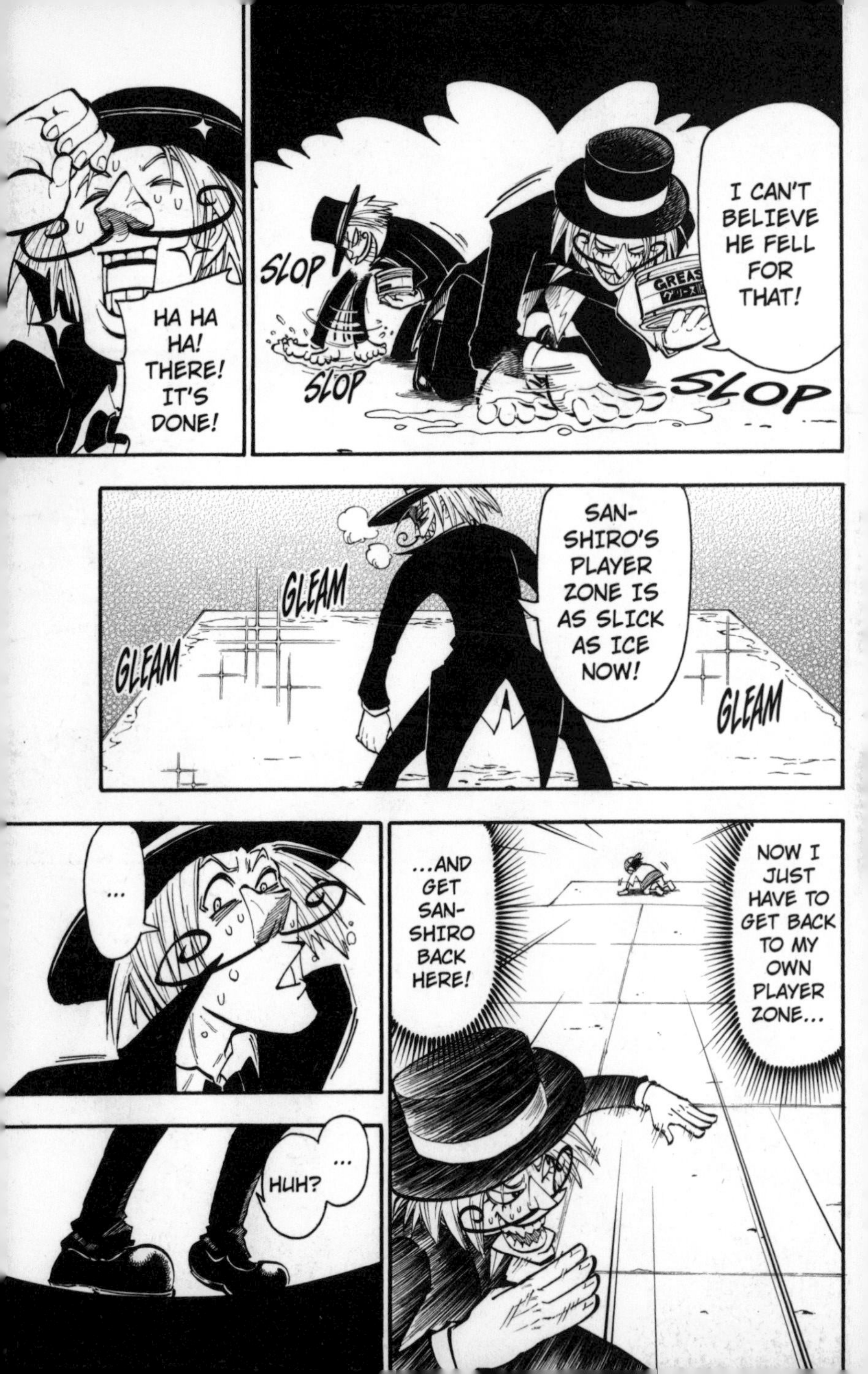
I CAN'T BELIEVE HE FELL FOR THAT!
SLOP
SLOP
SLOP
HA HA HA! THERE! IT'S DONE!
SAN-SHIRO'S PLAYER ZONE IS AS SLICK AS ICE NOW!
GLEAM
GLEAM
GLEAM
NOW I JUST HAVE TO GET BACK TO MY OWN PLAYER ZONE...
...AND GET SAN-SHIRO BACK HERE!
...
... HUH?

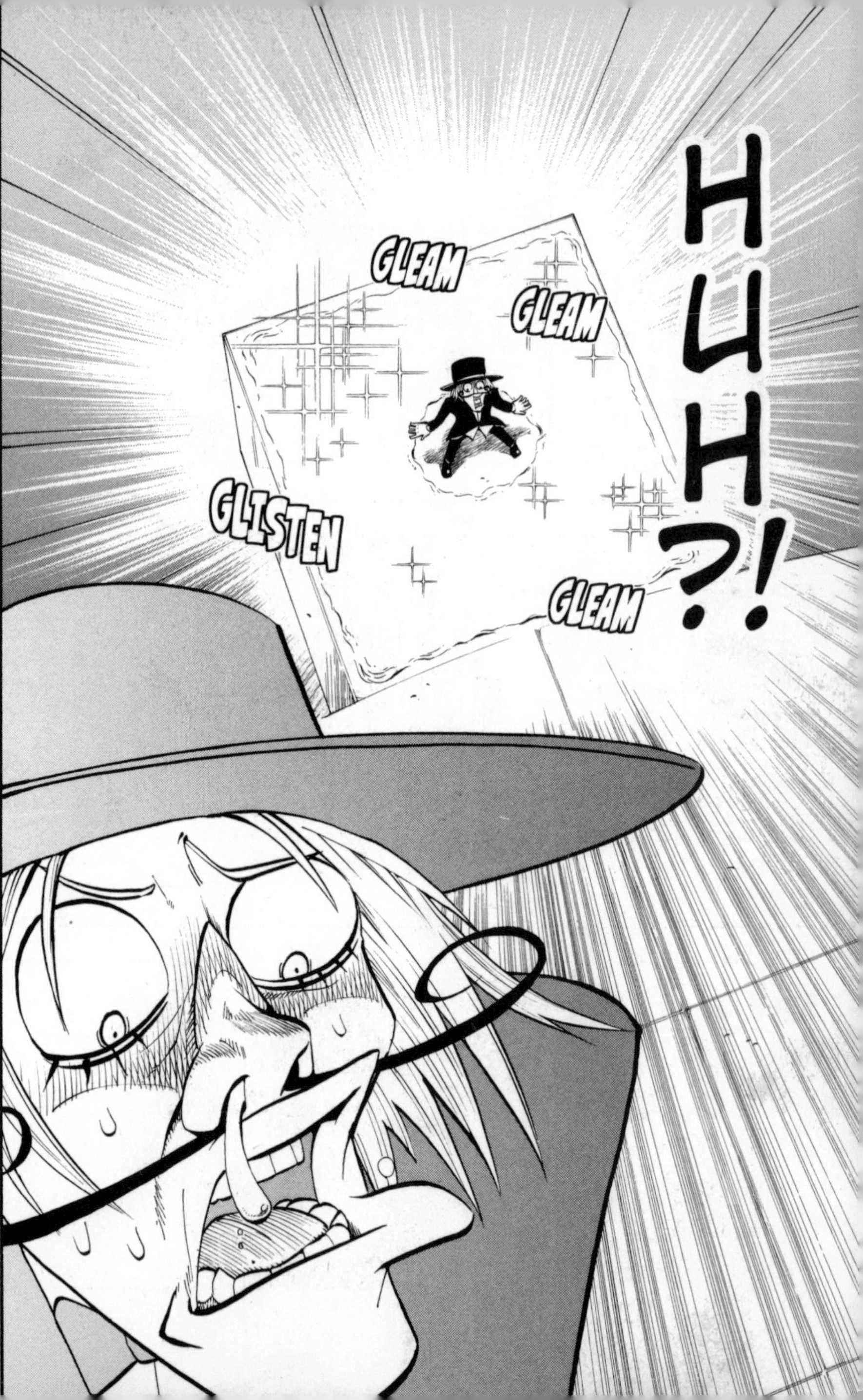
HUH?!
GLEAM
GLEAM
GLISTEN
GLEAM

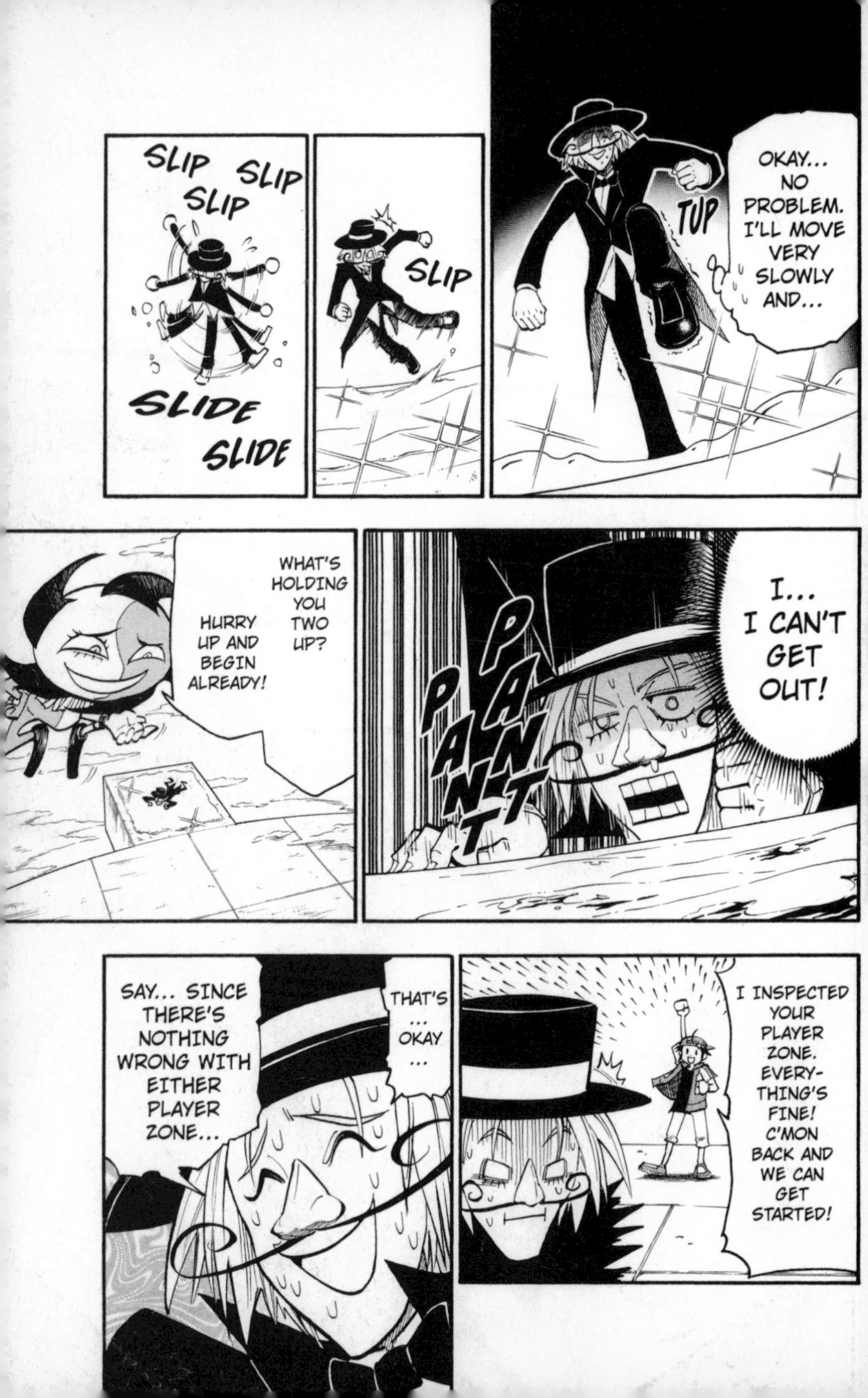
OKAY... NO PROBLEM. I'LL MOVE VERY SLOWLY AND...
TUP
SLIP
SLIP SLIP
SLIP
SLIDE
SLIDE
I... I CAN'T GET OUT!
PANT PANT
WHAT'S HOLDING YOU TWO UP?
HURRY UP AND BEGIN ALREADY!
I INSPECTED YOUR PLAYER ZONE. EVERY-THING'S FINE! C'MON BACK AND WE CAN GET STARTED!
THAT'S ... OKAY ...
SAY... SINCE THERE'S NOTHING WRONG WITH EITHER PLAYER ZONE...

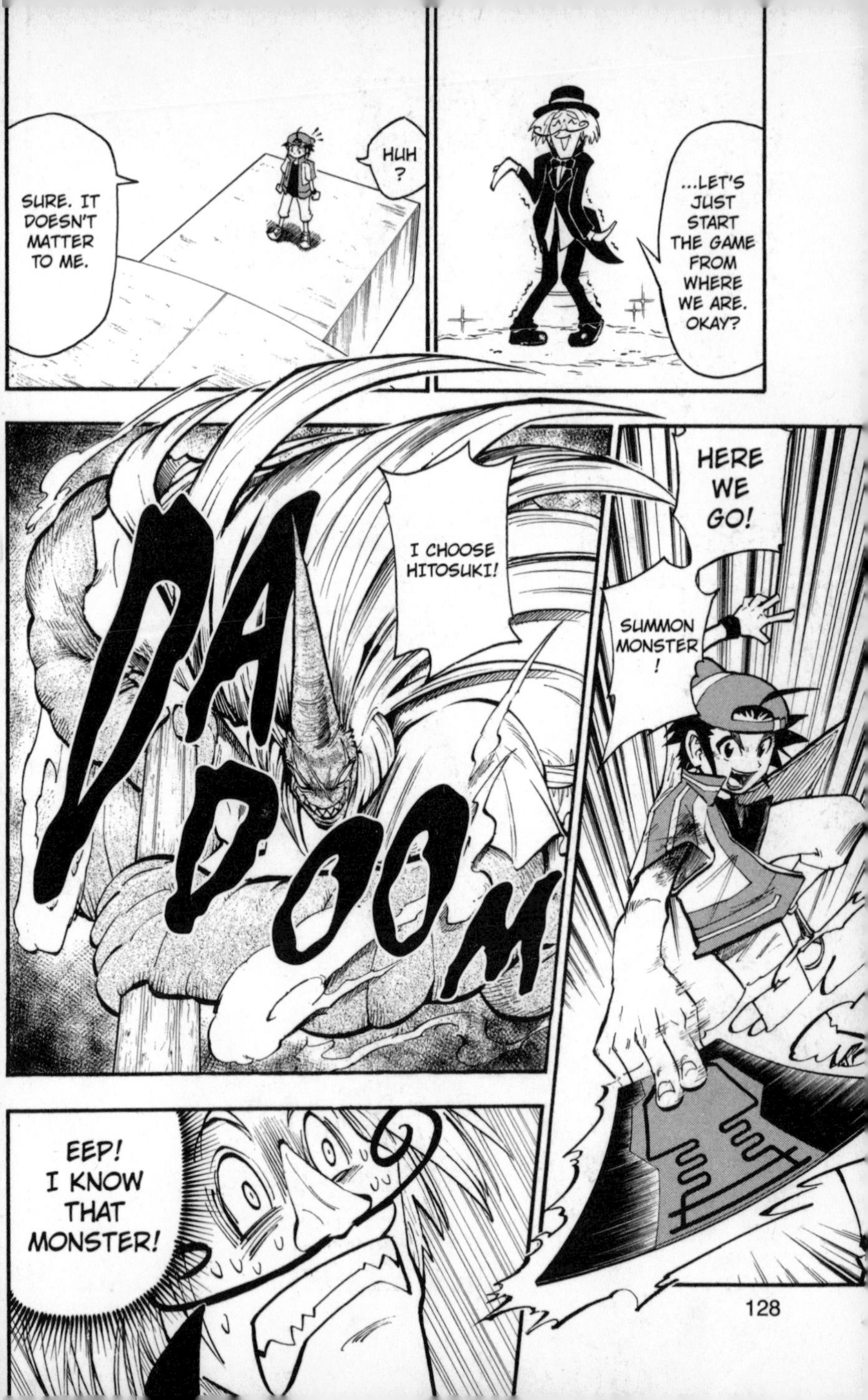
...LET'S JUST START THE GAME FROM WHERE WE ARE. OKAY?
HUH ?
SURE. IT DOESN'T MATTER TO ME.
HERE WE GO!
SUMMON MONSTER !
I CHOOSE HITOSUKI!
DA DOOM
EEP! I KNOW THAT MONSTER!

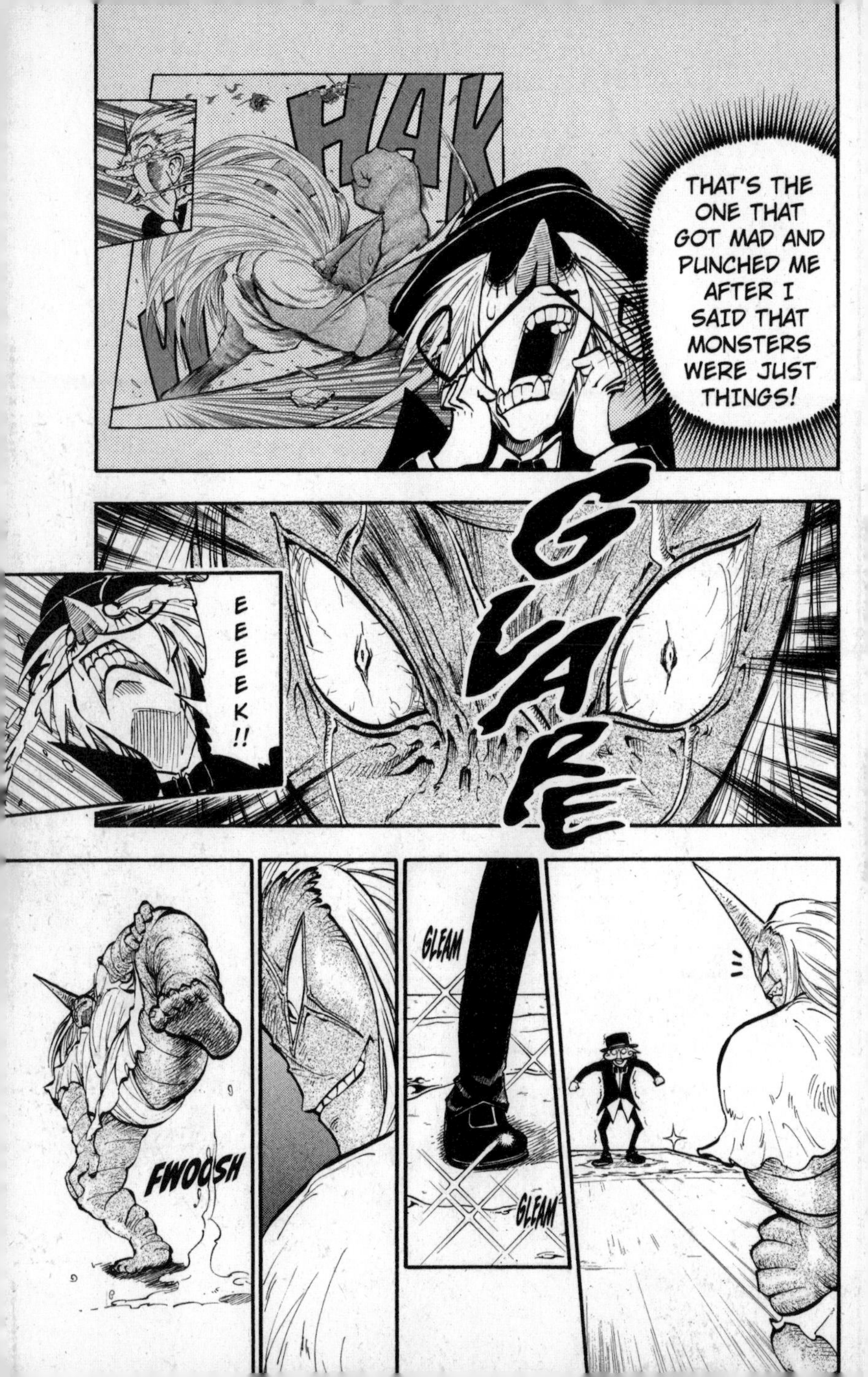
THAT'S THE ONE THAT GOT MAD AND PUNCHED ME AFTER I SAID THAT MONSTERS WERE JUST THINGS!
HAK
GLARE
EEEEEK!!
GLEAM
GLEAM
FWOOSH

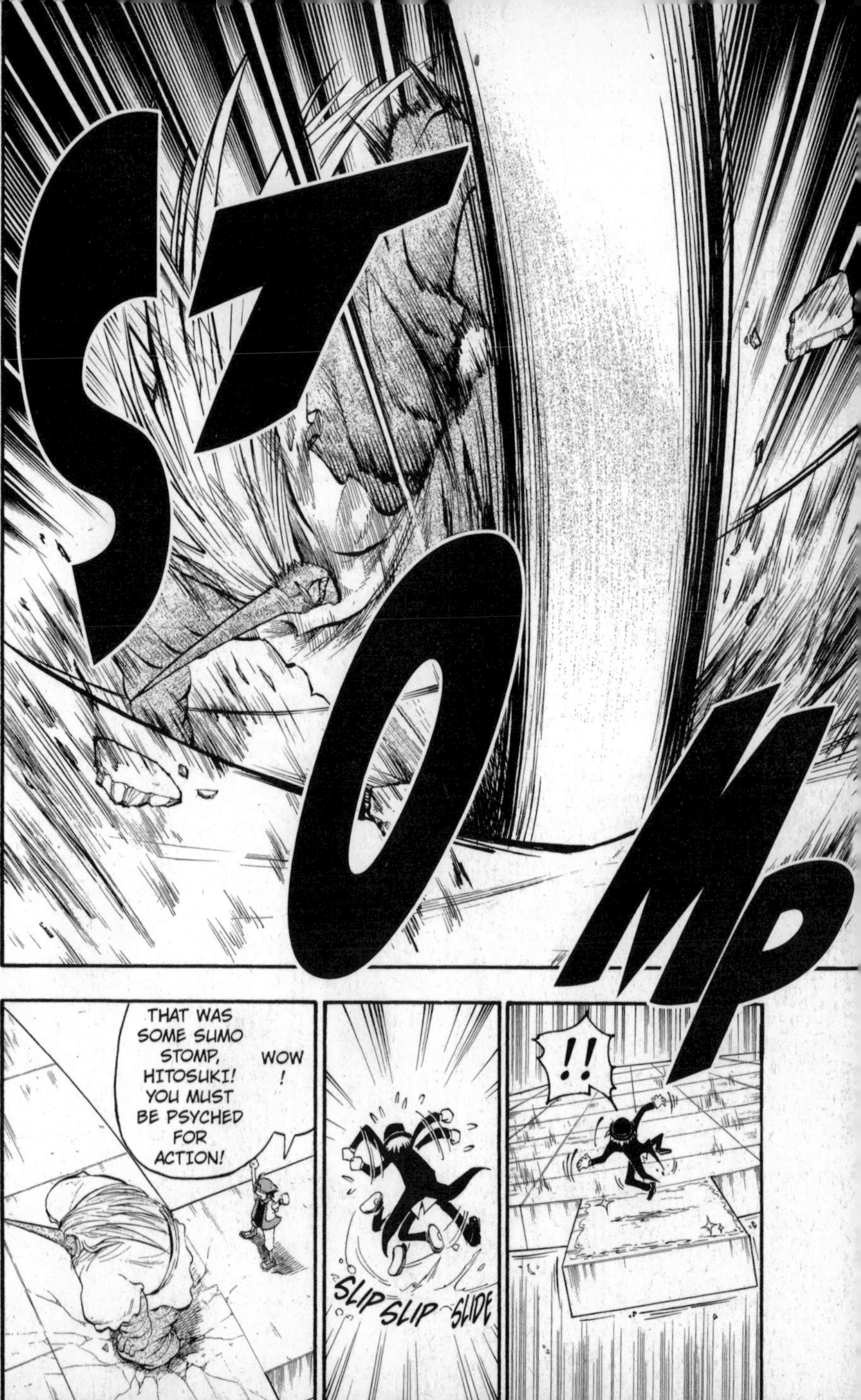
STOMP
!!
SLIP SLIP SLIDE
WOW!
THAT WAS SOME SUMO STOMP, HITOSUKI! YOU MUST BE PSYCHED FOR ACTION!

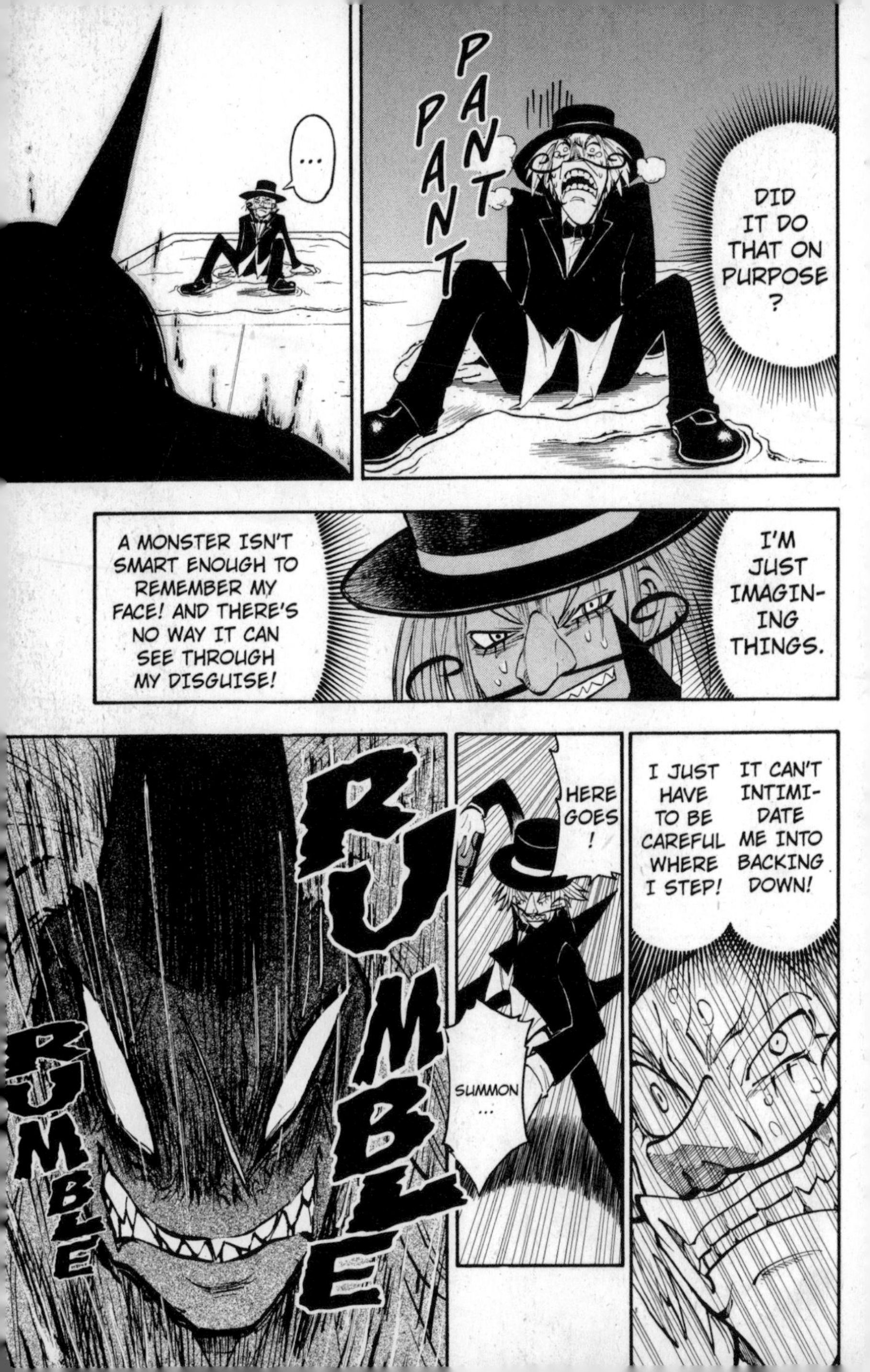
PANT PANT
DID IT DO THAT ON PURPOSE?
...
I'M JUST IMAGINING THINGS.
A MONSTER ISN'T SMART ENOUGH TO REMEMBER MY FACE! AND THERE'S NO WAY IT CAN SEE THROUGH MY DISGUISE!
IT CAN'T INTIMIDATE ME INTO BACKING DOWN!
I JUST HAVE TO BE CAREFUL WHERE I STEP!
HERE GOES!
SUMMON...
RUMBLE
RUMBLE

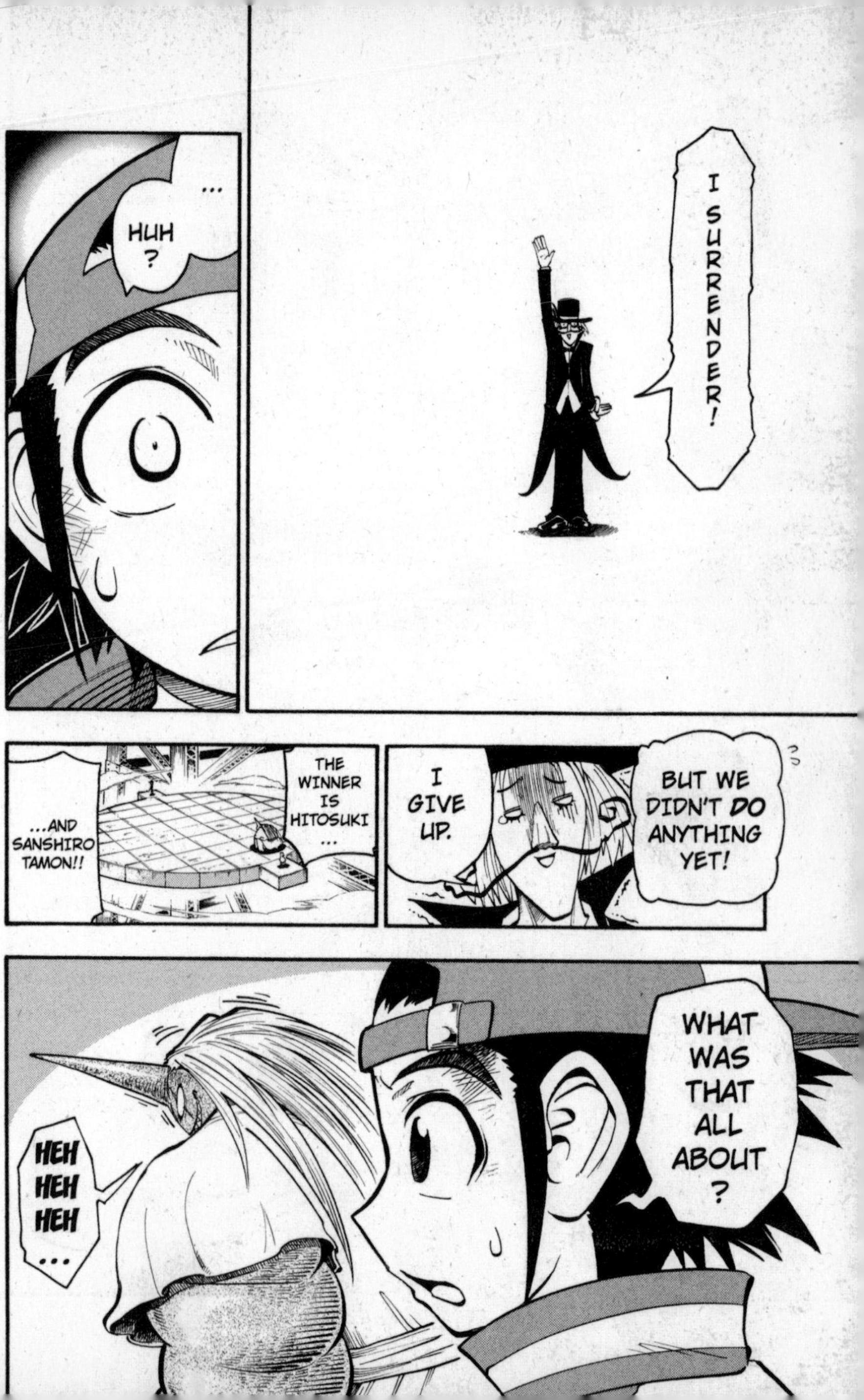
I SURRENDER!
...
HUH?
BUT WE DIDN'T *DO* ANYTHING YET!
I GIVE UP.
THE WINNER IS HITOSUKI...
...AND SANSHIRO TAMON!!
WHAT WAS THAT ALL ABOUT?
HEH HEH HEH...

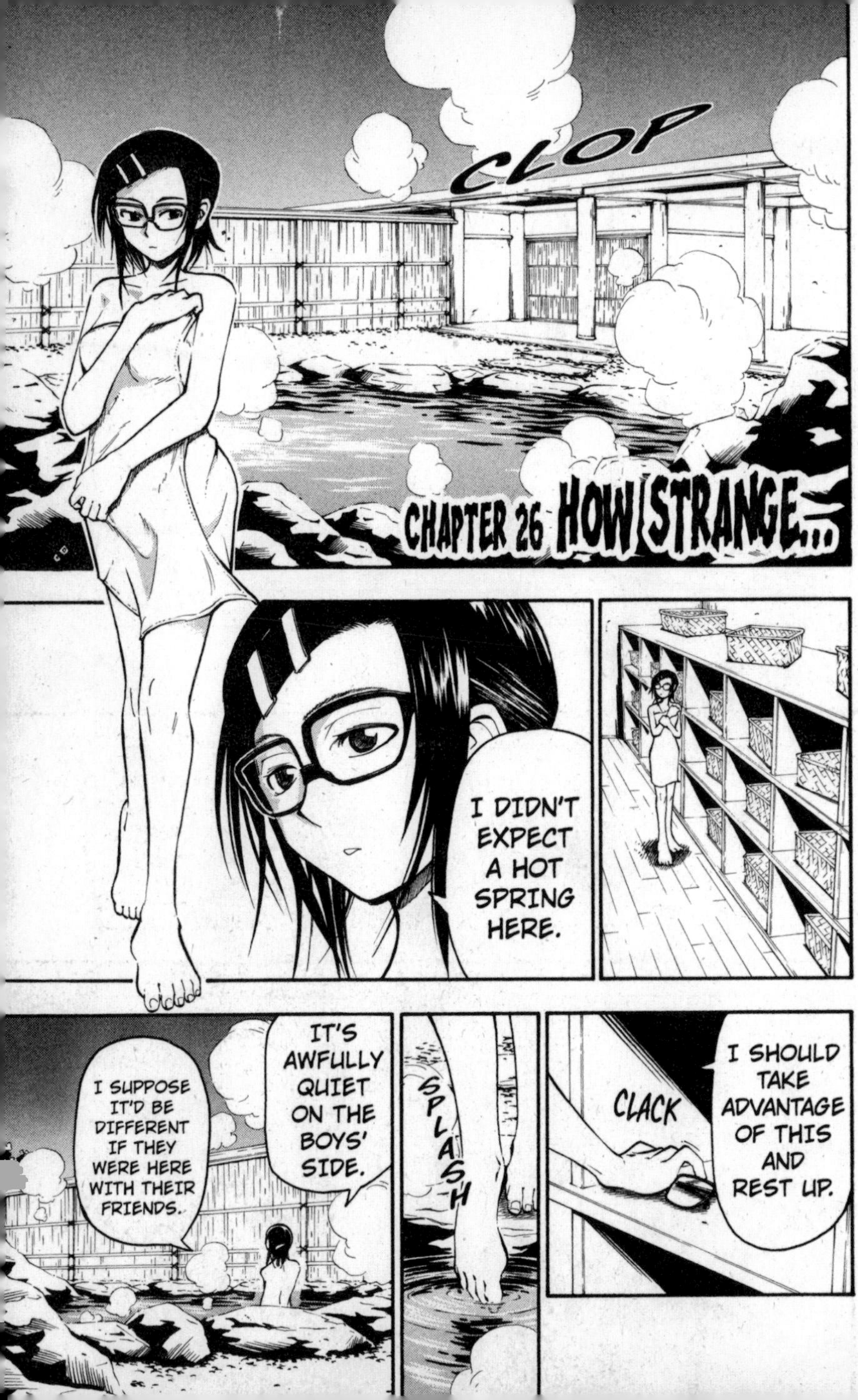
CLOP
CHAPTER 26 HOW STRANGE...
I DIDN'T EXPECT A HOT SPRING HERE.
I SHOULD TAKE ADVANTAGE OF THIS AND REST UP.
CLACK
SPLASH
IT'S AWFULLY QUIET ON THE BOYS' SIDE.
I SUPPOSE IT'D BE DIFFERENT IF THEY WERE HERE WITH THEIR FRIENDS.

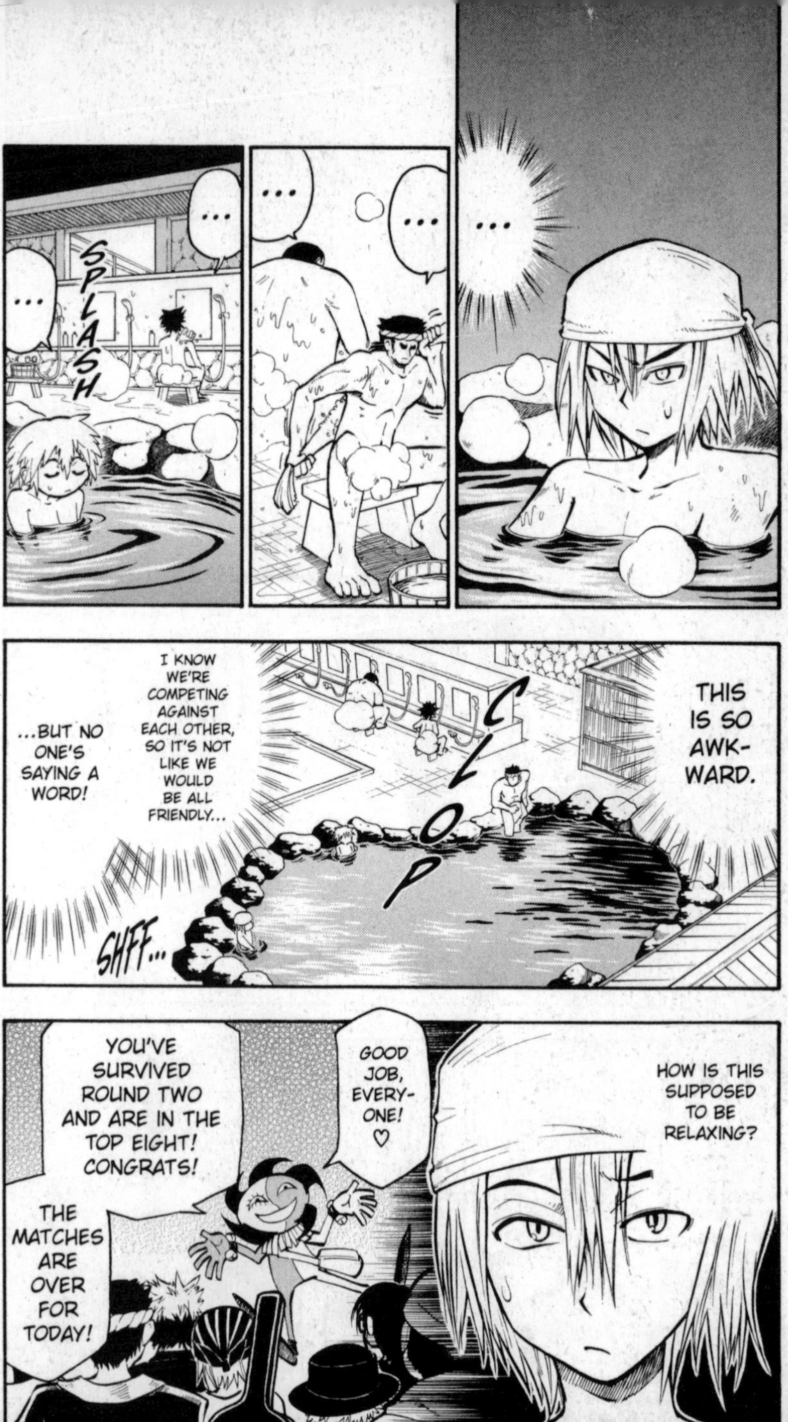
...
...
...
...
SPLASH
...
THIS IS SO AWKWARD.
CLOP
I KNOW WE'RE COMPETING AGAINST EACH OTHER, SO IT'S NOT LIKE WE WOULD BE ALL FRIENDLY...
...BUT NO ONE'S SAYING A WORD!
SHFF...
HOW IS THIS SUPPOSED TO BE RELAXING?
GOOD JOB, EVERYONE! ♡
YOU'VE SURVIVED ROUND TWO AND ARE IN THE TOP EIGHT! CONGRATS!
THE MATCHES ARE OVER FOR TODAY!

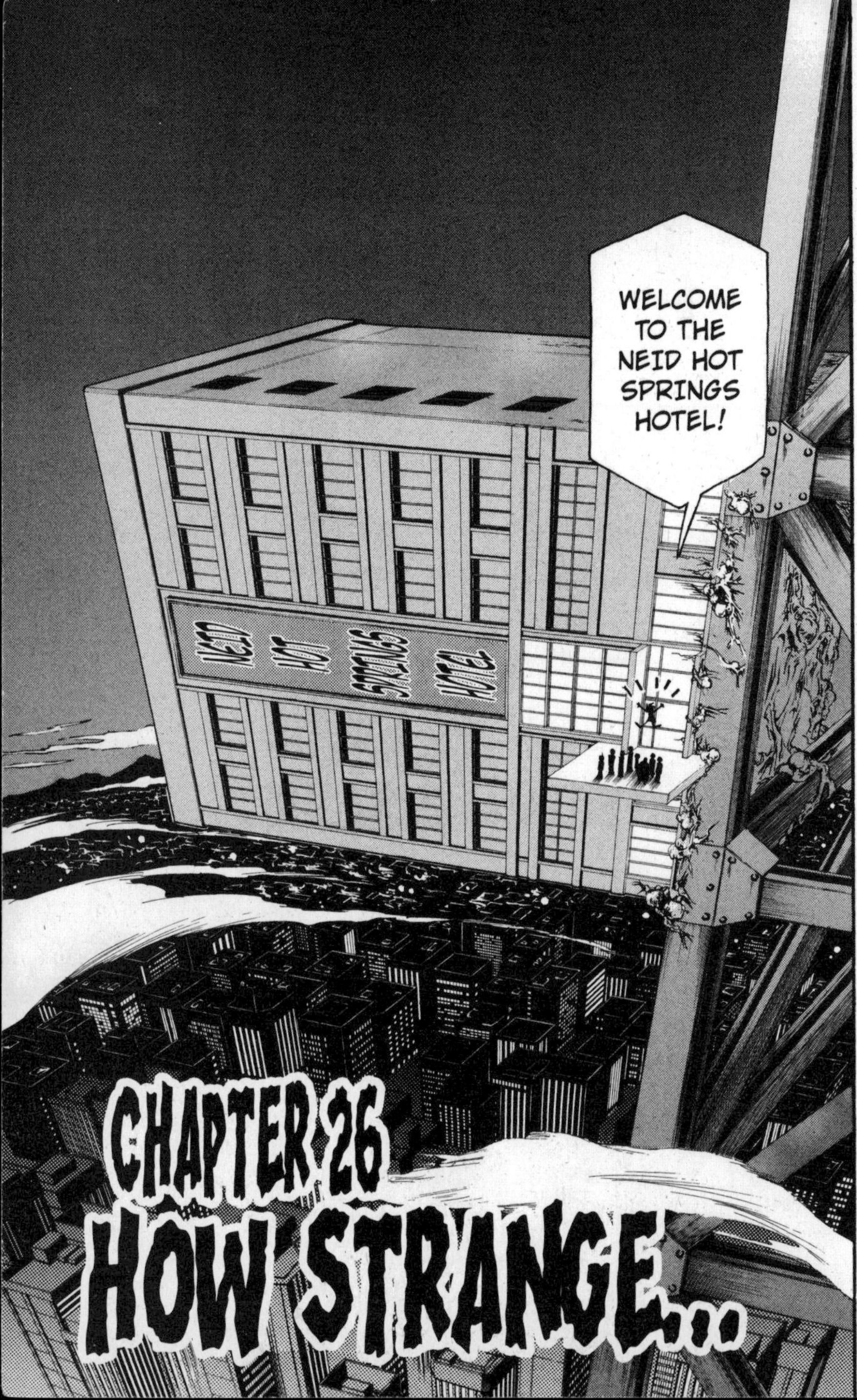
WELCOME TO THE NEID HOT SPRINGS HOTEL!
CHAPTER 26
HOW STRANGE...

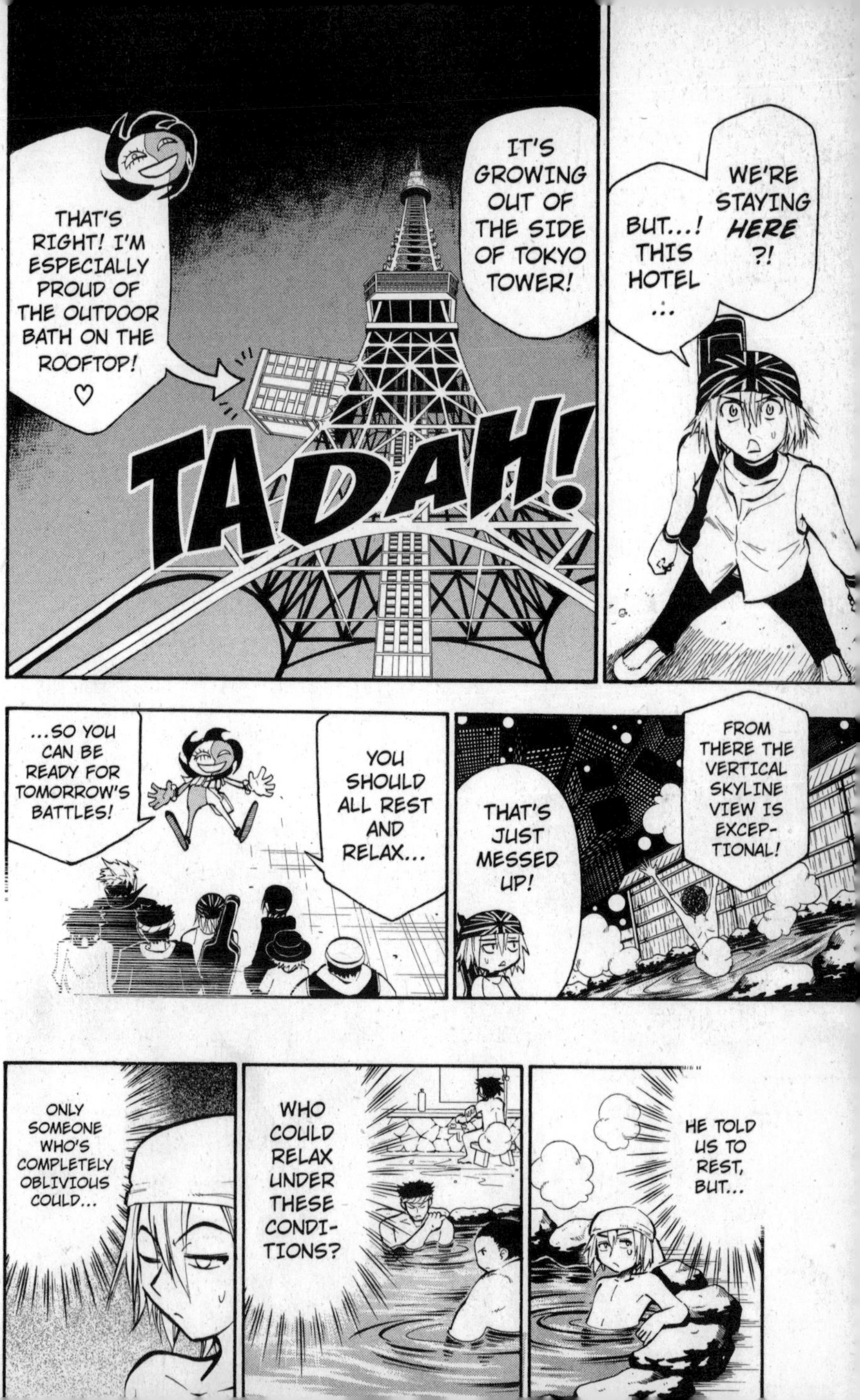
WE'RE STAYING HERE?!
BUT...! THIS HOTEL...
IT'S GROWING OUT OF THE SIDE OF TOKYO TOWER!
THAT'S RIGHT! I'M ESPECIALLY PROUD OF THE OUTDOOR BATH ON THE ROOFTOP! ♡
TADAH!
FROM THERE THE VERTICAL SKYLINE VIEW IS EXCEP-TIONAL!
THAT'S JUST MESSED UP!
YOU SHOULD ALL REST AND RELAX...
...SO YOU CAN BE READY FOR TOMORROW'S BATTLES!
HE TOLD US TO REST, BUT...
WHO COULD RELAX UNDER THESE CONDI-TIONS?
ONLY SOMEONE WHO'S COMPLETELY OBLIVIOUS COULD...

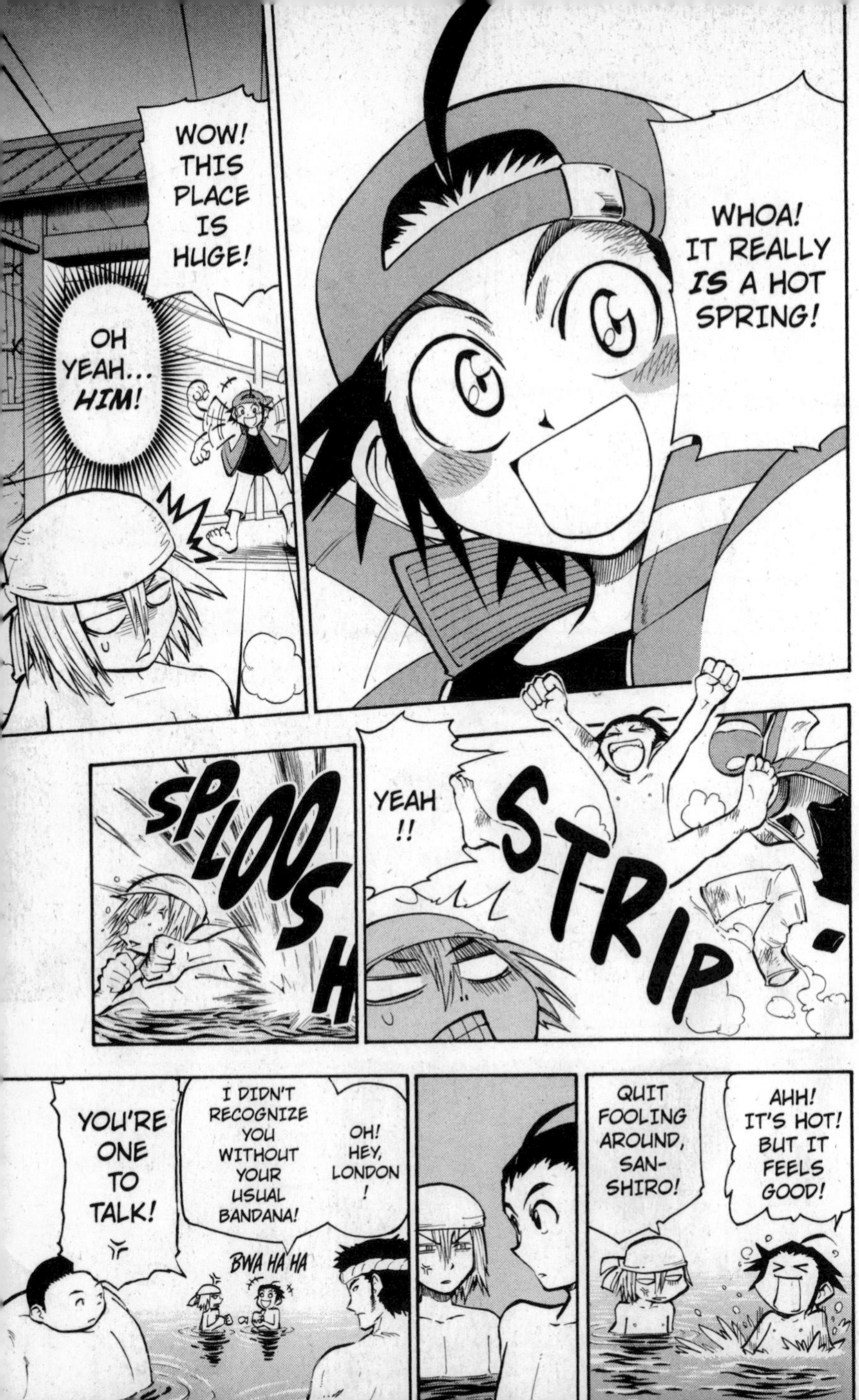
WHOA! IT REALLY IS A HOT SPRING!
WOW! THIS PLACE IS HUGE!
OH YEAH... HIM!
YEAH !!
STRIP
SPLOOSH
AHH! IT'S HOT! BUT IT FEELS GOOD!
QUIT FOOLING AROUND, SAN-SHIRO!
OH! HEY, LONDON!
I DIDN'T RECOGNIZE YOU WITHOUT YOUR USUAL BANDANA!
BWA HA HA
YOU'RE ONE TO TALK!

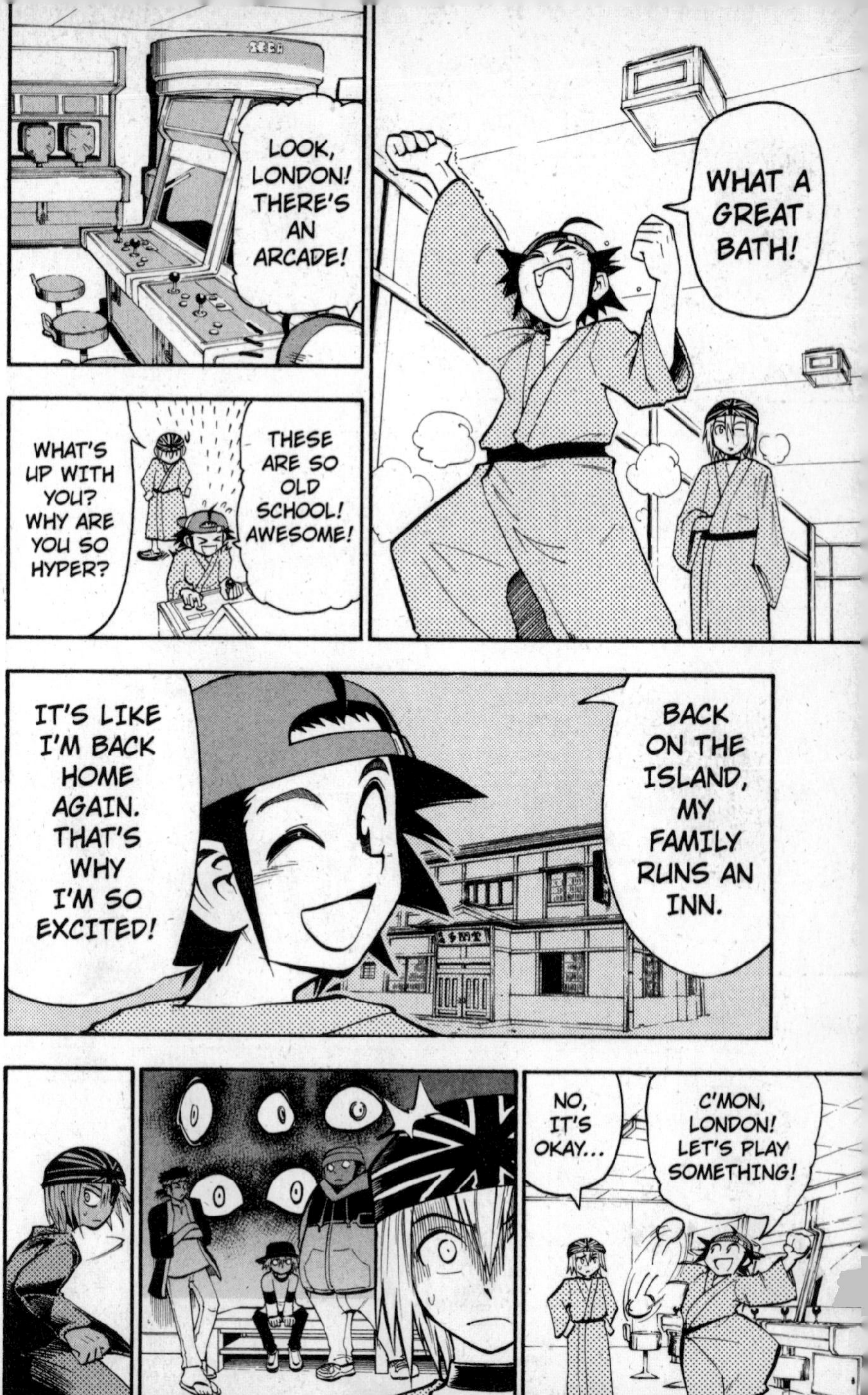
WHAT A GREAT BATH!
LOOK, LONDON! THERE'S AN ARCADE!
THESE ARE SO OLD SCHOOL! AWESOME!
WHAT'S UP WITH YOU? WHY ARE YOU SO HYPER?
BACK ON THE ISLAND, MY FAMILY RUNS AN INN.
IT'S LIKE I'M BACK HOME AGAIN. THAT'S WHY I'M SO EXCITED!
C'MON, LONDON! LET'S PLAY SOMETHING!
NO, IT'S OKAY...

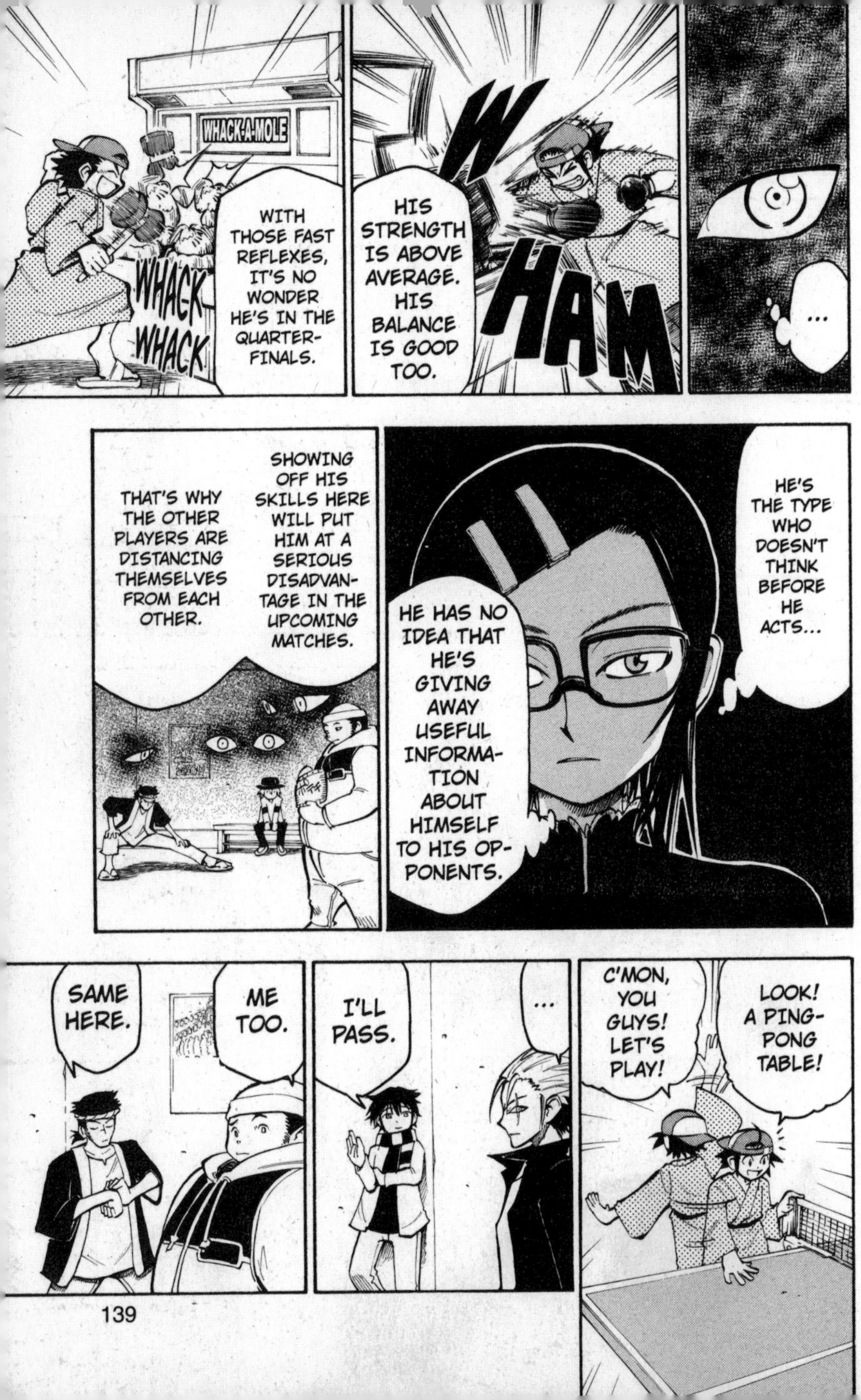
...
W
HIS STRENGTH IS ABOVE AVERAGE. HIS BALANCE IS GOOD TOO.
HAM
WITH THOSE FAST REFLEXES, IT'S NO WONDER HE'S IN THE QUARTER-FINALS.
WHACK-A-MOLE
WHACK WHACK
HE'S THE TYPE WHO DOESN'T THINK BEFORE HE ACTS...
HE HAS NO IDEA THAT HE'S GIVING AWAY USEFUL INFORMATION ABOUT HIMSELF TO HIS OPPONENTS.
SHOWING OFF HIS SKILLS HERE WILL PUT HIM AT A SERIOUS DISADVANTAGE IN THE UPCOMING MATCHES.
THAT'S WHY THE OTHER PLAYERS ARE DISTANCING THEMSELVES FROM EACH OTHER.
LOOK! A PING-PONG TABLE!
C'MON, YOU GUYS! LET'S PLAY!
...
I'LL PASS.
ME TOO.
SAME HERE.

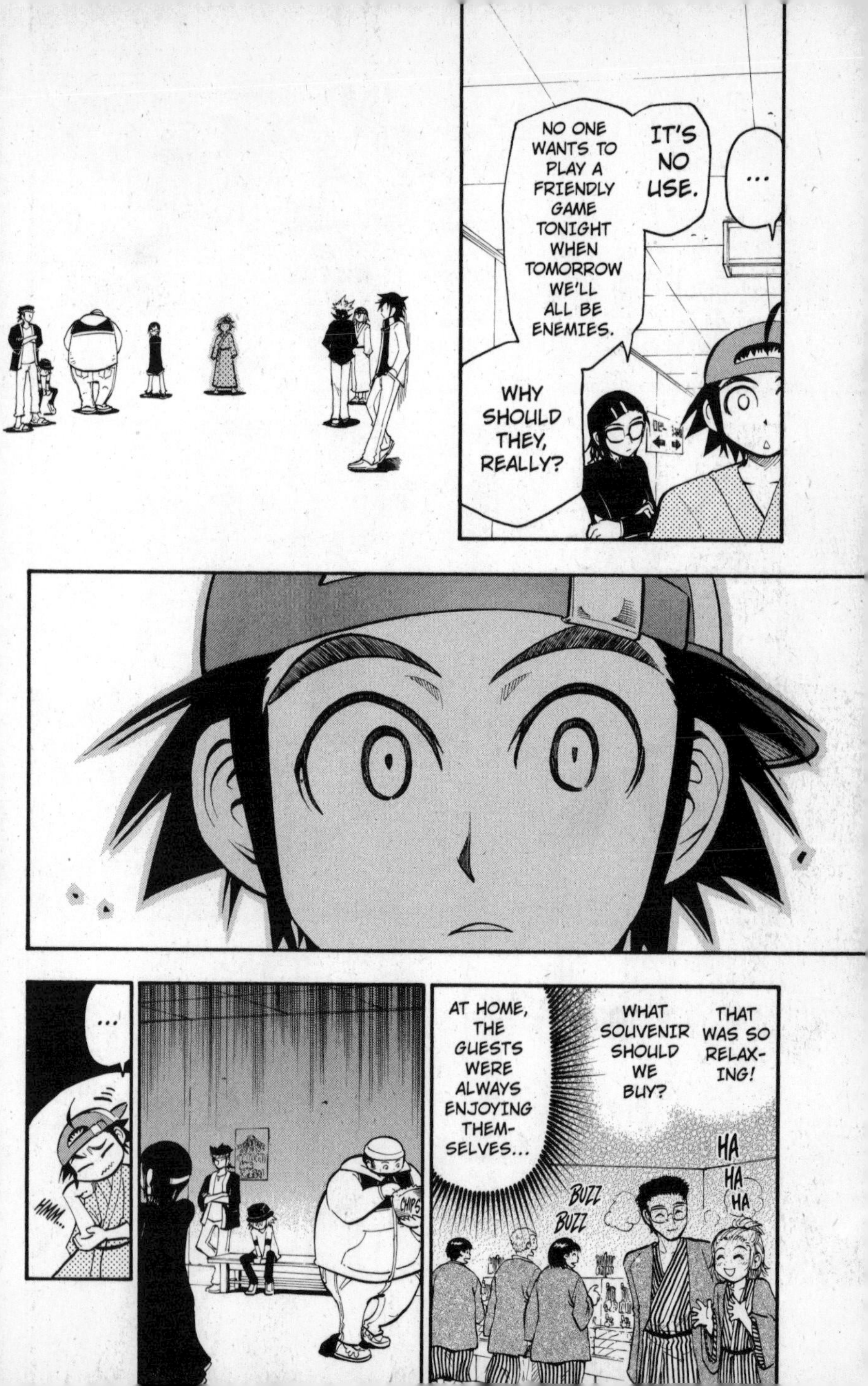
...
IT'S NO USE.
NO ONE WANTS TO PLAY A FRIENDLY GAME TONIGHT WHEN TOMORROW WE'LL ALL BE ENEMIES.
WHY SHOULD THEY, REALLY?
THAT WAS SO RELAX-ING!
WHAT SOUVENIR SHOULD WE BUY?
AT HOME, THE GUESTS WERE ALWAYS ENJOYING THEM-SELVES...
HA HA HA
BUZZ BUZZ
CHIPS
...
HMM...

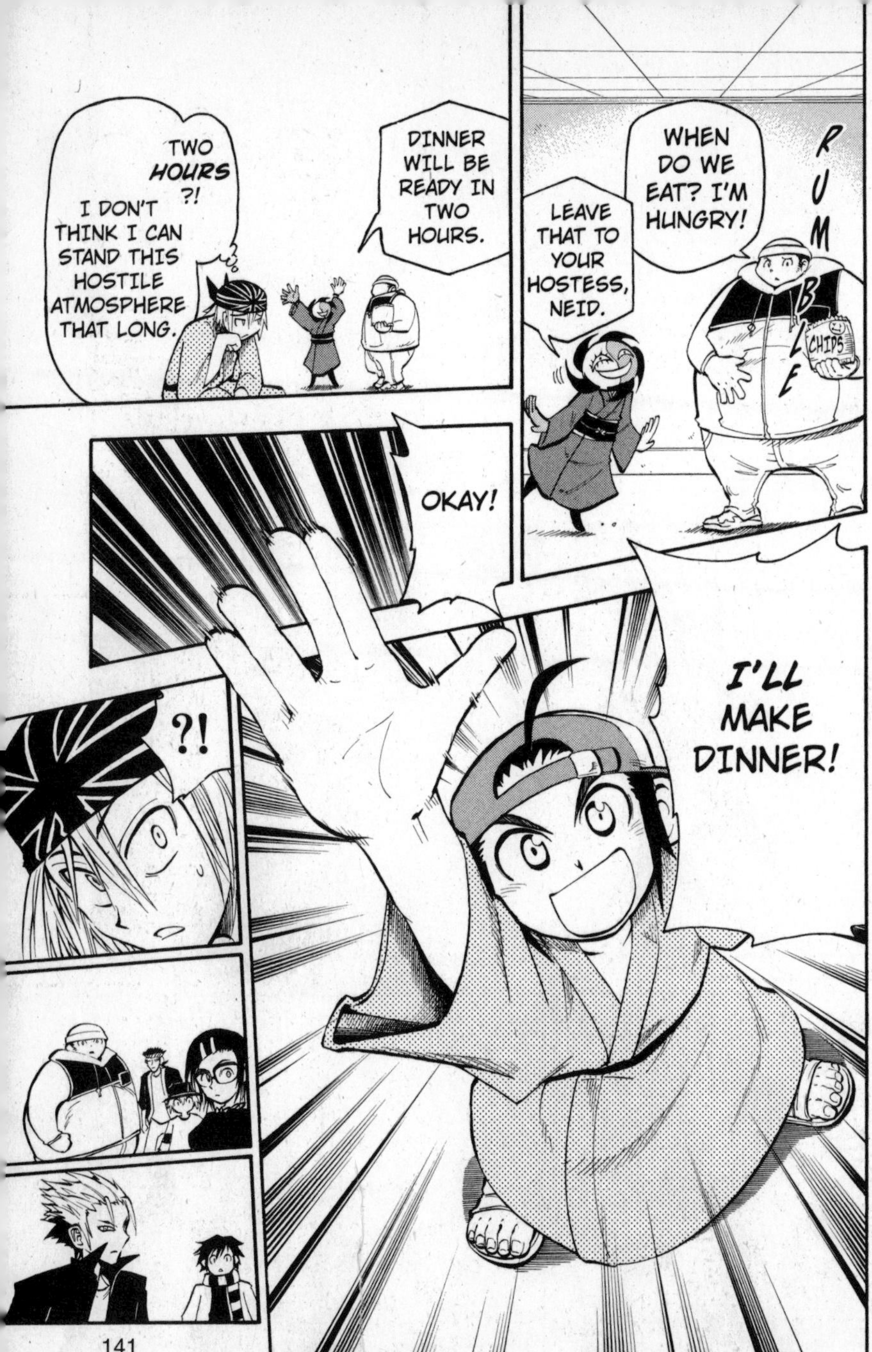
WHEN DO WE EAT? I'M HUNGRY!
RUMBLE
CHIPS
LEAVE THAT TO YOUR HOSTESS, NEID.
DINNER WILL BE READY IN TWO HOURS.
TWO HOURS?!
I DON'T THINK I CAN STAND THIS HOSTILE ATMOSPHERE THAT LONG.
OKAY!
I'LL MAKE DINNER!
?!

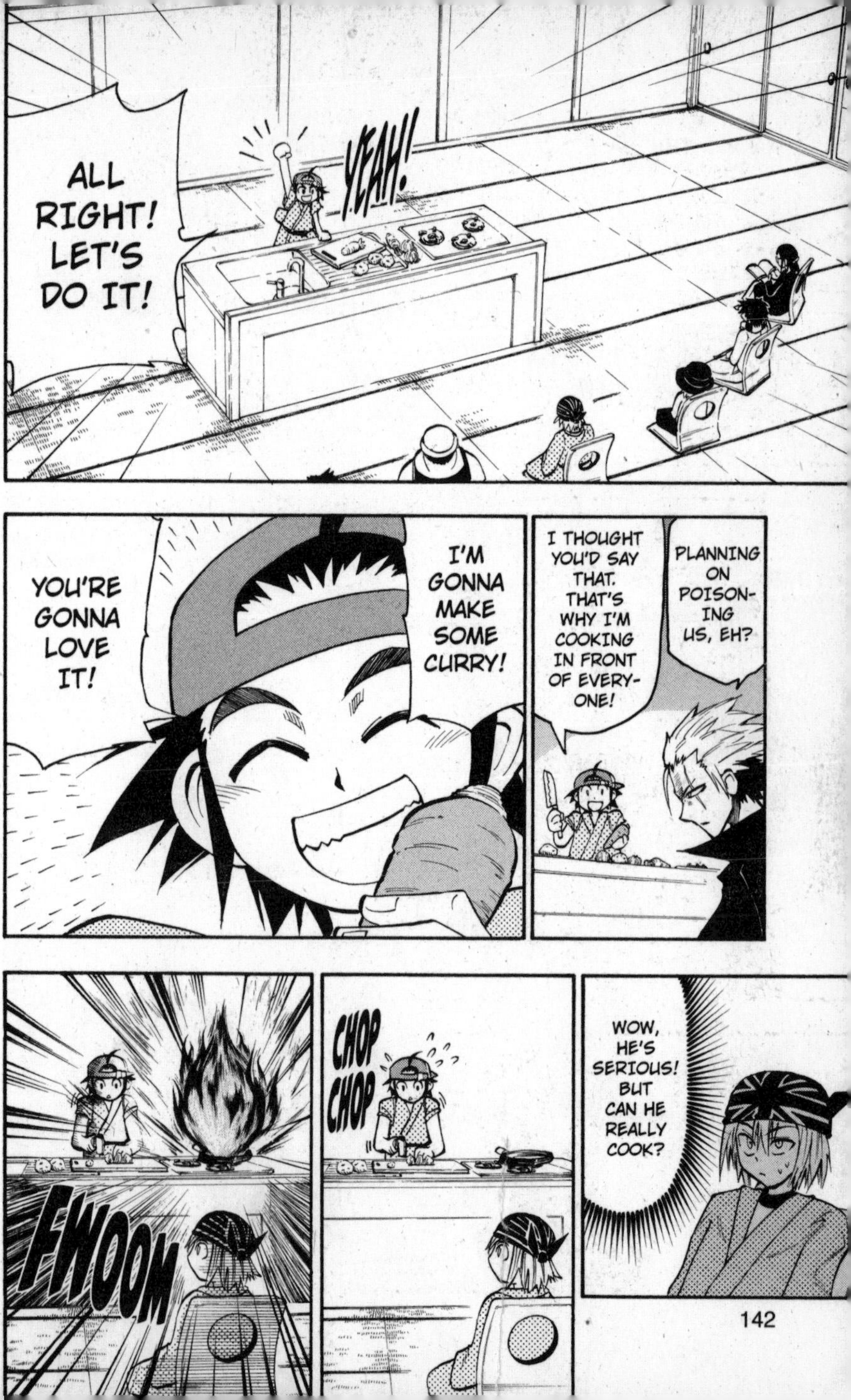
ALL RIGHT! LET'S DO IT!
YEAH!
PLANNING ON POISON-ING US, EH?
I THOUGHT YOU'D SAY THAT. THAT'S WHY I'M COOKING IN FRONT OF EVERY-ONE!
I'M GONNA MAKE SOME CURRY!
YOU'RE GONNA LOVE IT!
WOW, HE'S SERIOUS! BUT CAN HE REALLY COOK?
CHOP CHOP
FWOOM

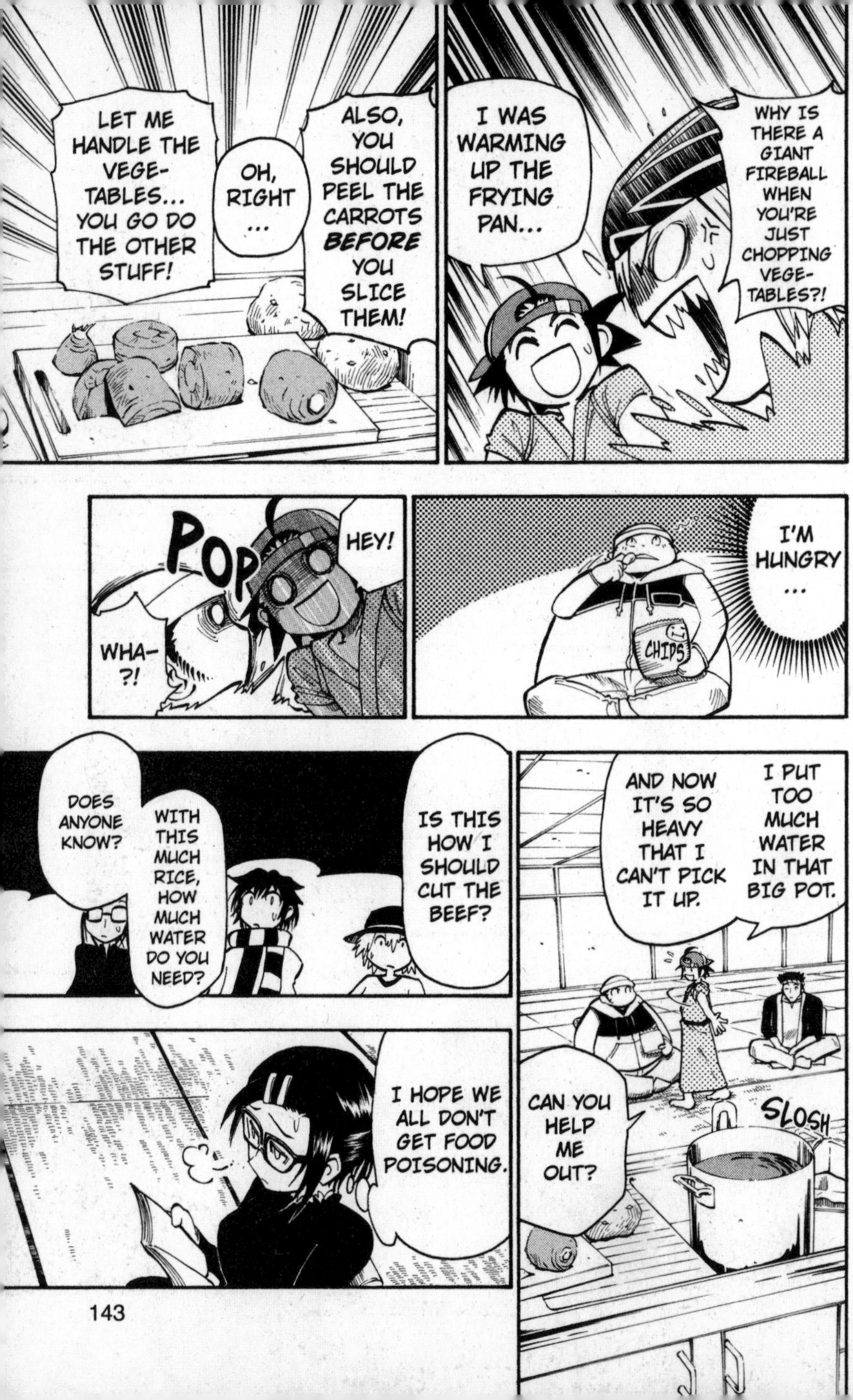
WHY IS THERE A GIANT FIREBALL WHEN YOU'RE JUST CHOPPING VEGE-TABLES?!
I WAS WARMING UP THE FRYING PAN...
ALSO, YOU SHOULD PEEL THE CARROTS BEFORE YOU SLICE THEM!
OH, RIGHT ...
LET ME HANDLE THE VEGE-TABLES... YOU GO DO THE OTHER STUFF!
I'M HUNGRY ...
CHIPS
HEY!
POP
WHA-?!
I PUT TOO MUCH WATER IN THAT BIG POT.
AND NOW IT'S SO HEAVY THAT I CAN'T PICK IT UP.
CAN YOU HELP ME OUT?
SLOSH
IS THIS HOW I SHOULD CUT THE BEEF?
WITH THIS MUCH RICE, HOW MUCH WATER DO YOU NEED?
DOES ANYONE KNOW?
I HOPE WE ALL DON'T GET FOOD POISONING.

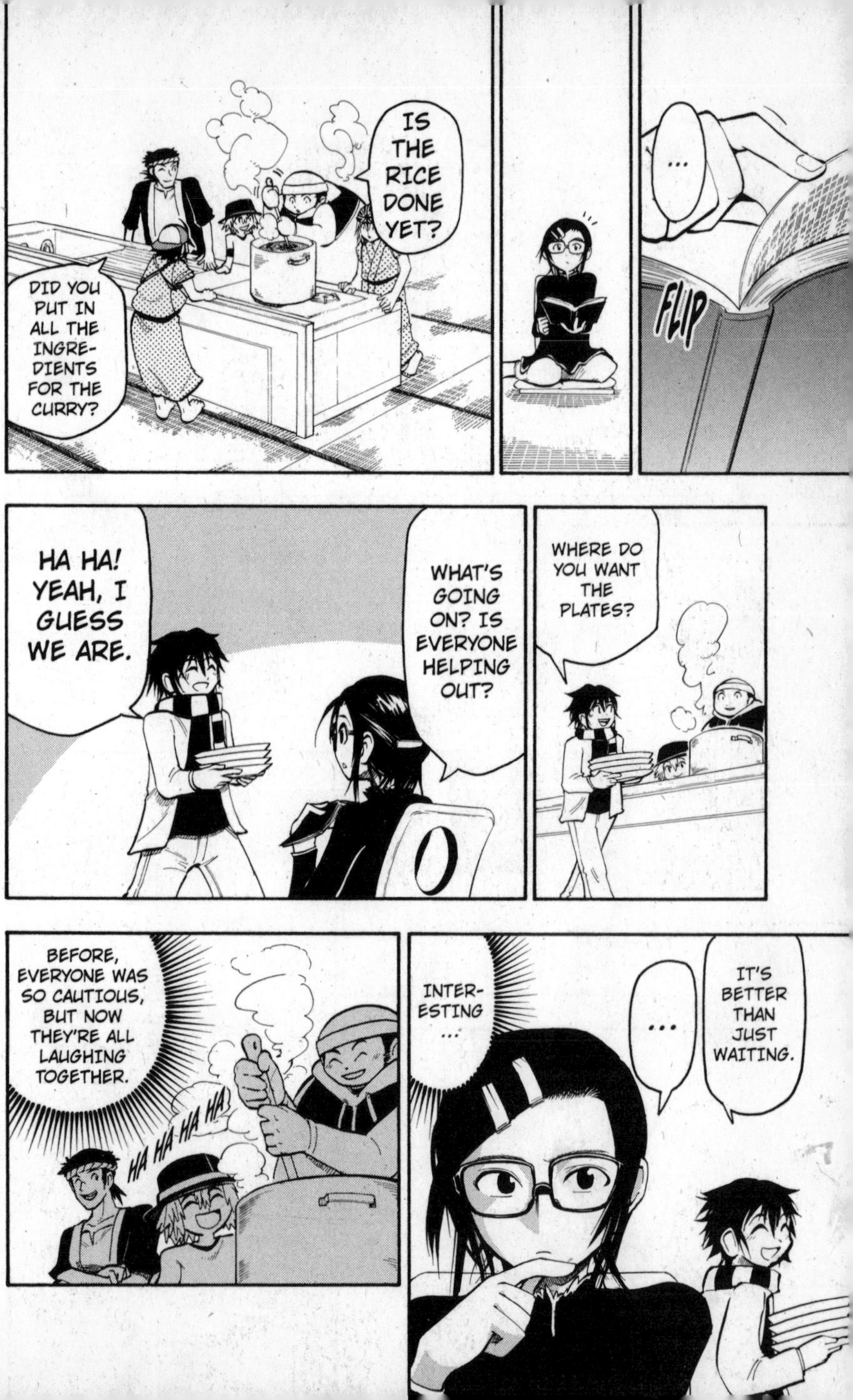
...
FLIP
IS THE RICE DONE YET?
DID YOU PUT IN ALL THE INGREDIENTS FOR THE CURRY?
WHERE DO YOU WANT THE PLATES?
WHAT'S GOING ON? IS EVERYONE HELPING OUT?
HA HA! YEAH, I GUESS WE ARE.
IT'S BETTER THAN JUST WAITING.
...
INTERESTING...
BEFORE, EVERYONE WAS SO CAUTIOUS, BUT NOW THEY'RE ALL LAUGHING TOGETHER.
HA HA HA HA

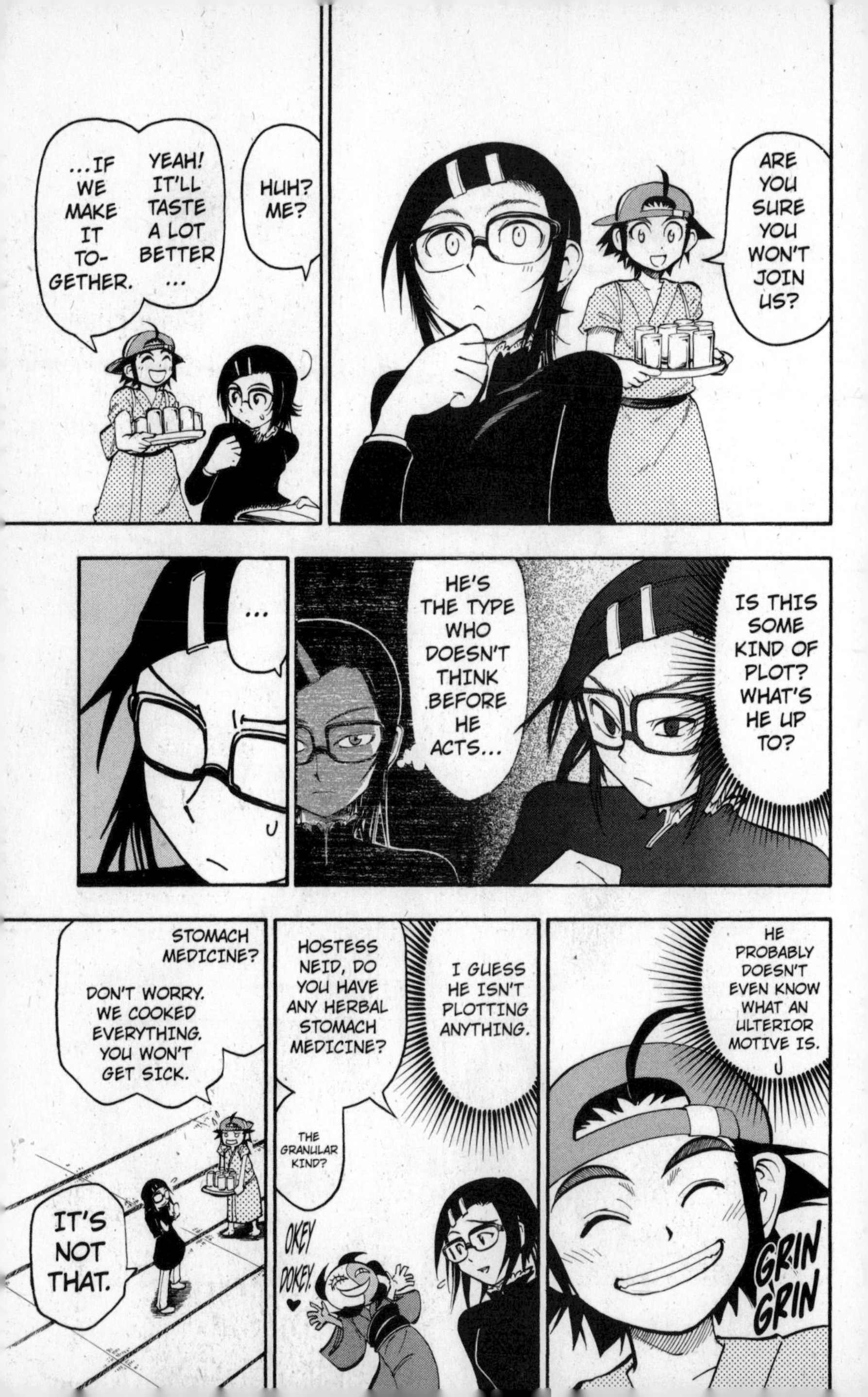
ARE YOU SURE YOU WON'T JOIN US?
HUH? ME?
YEAH! IT'LL TASTE A LOT BETTER ...
...IF WE MAKE IT TO-GETHER.
IS THIS SOME KIND OF PLOT? WHAT'S HE UP TO?
HE'S THE TYPE WHO DOESN'T THINK BEFORE HE ACTS...
...
HE PROBABLY DOESN'T EVEN KNOW WHAT AN ULTERIOR MOTIVE IS.
GRIN GRIN
I GUESS HE ISN'T PLOTTING ANYTHING.
HOSTESS NEID, DO YOU HAVE ANY HERBAL STOMACH MEDICINE?
THE GRANULAR KIND?
OKEY DOKEY.
STOMACH MEDICINE?
DON'T WORRY. WE COOKED EVERYTHING. YOU WON'T GET SICK.
IT'S NOT THAT.

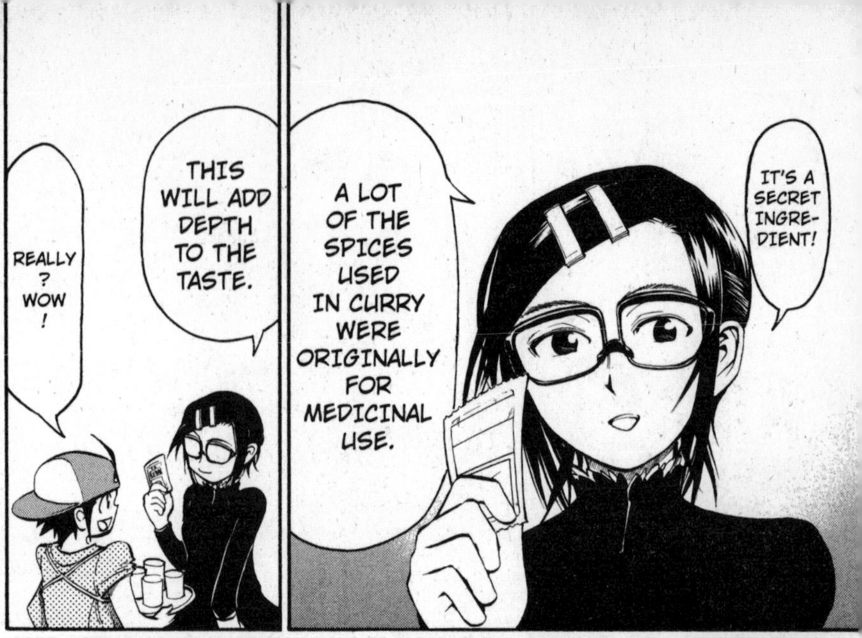
IT'S A SECRET INGRE-DIENT!
A LOT OF THE SPICES USED IN CURRY WERE ORIGINALLY FOR MEDICINAL USE.
THIS WILL ADD DEPTH TO THE TASTE.
REALLY? WOW!

SOME MEDICINES WILL ACTUALLY MAKE IT TASTE WORSE. DON'T TRY THIS AT HOME.

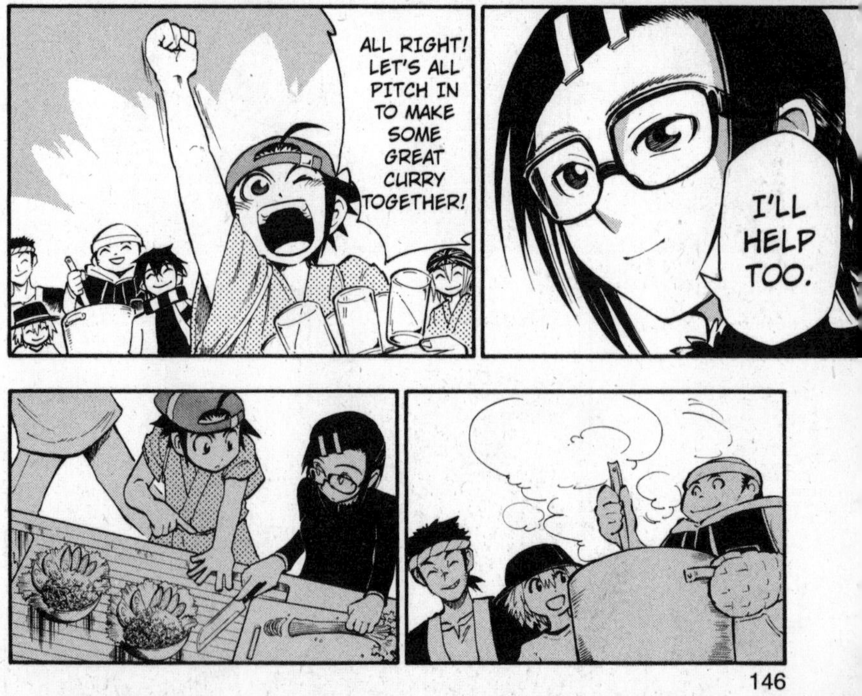
I'LL HELP TOO.
ALL RIGHT! LET'S ALL PITCH IN TO MAKE SOME GREAT CURRY TOGETHER!

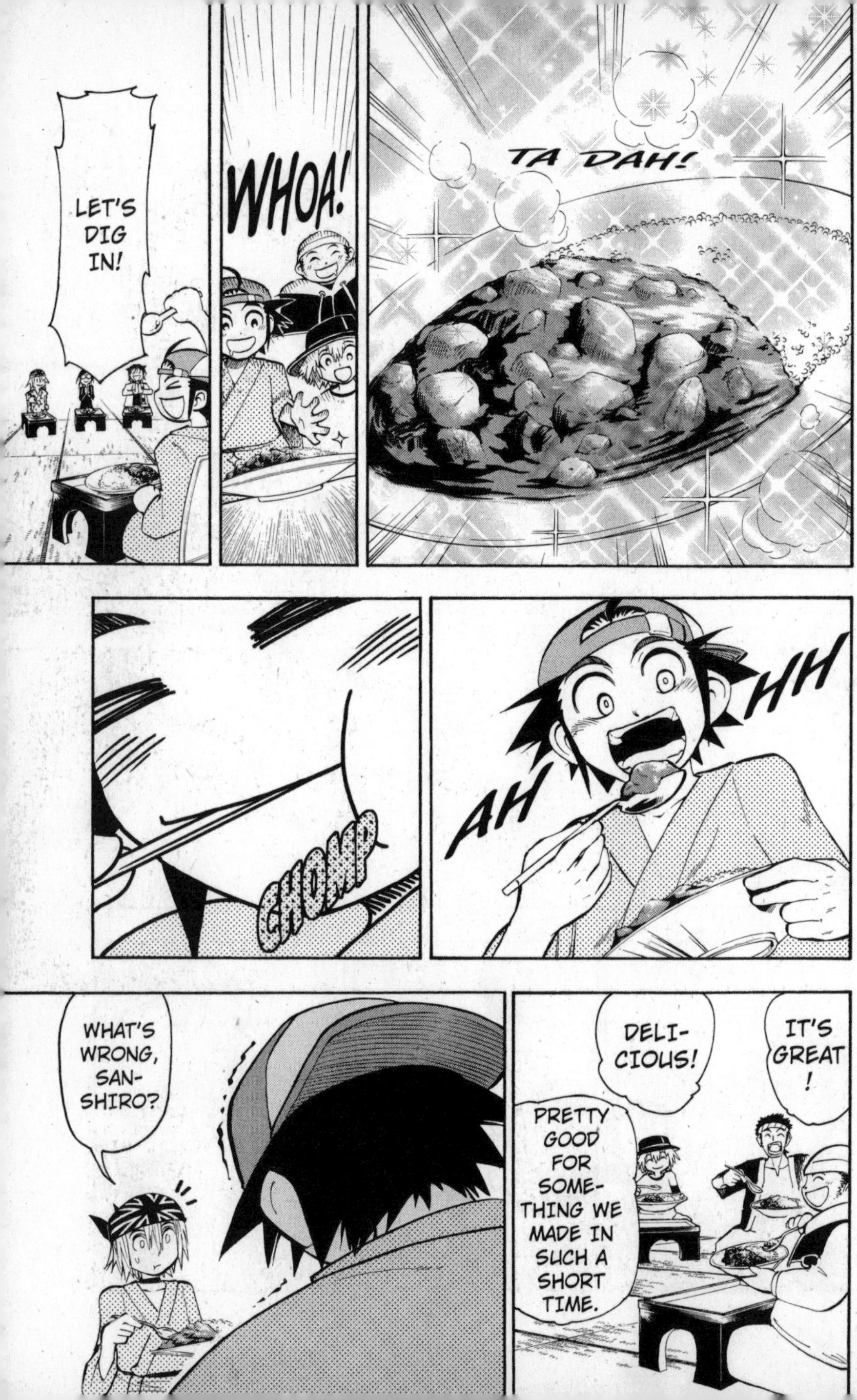
TA DAH!
WHOA!
LET'S DIG IN!
AH HH
CHOMP
IT'S GREAT!
DELI-CIOUS!
PRETTY GOOD FOR SOME-THING WE MADE IN SUCH A SHORT TIME.
WHAT'S WRONG, SAN-SHIRO?

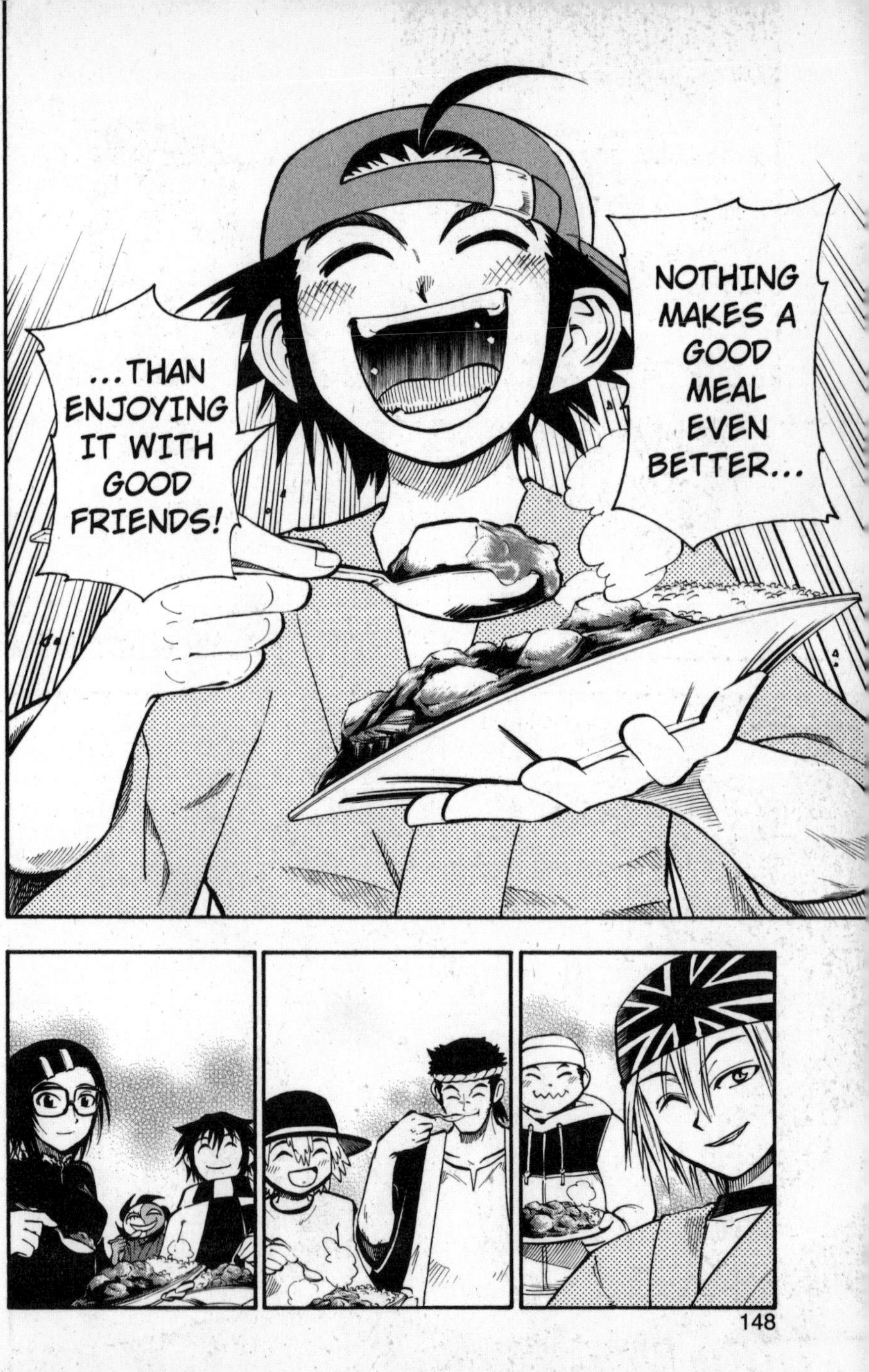
NOTHING MAKES A GOOD MEAL EVEN BETTER...
...THAN ENJOYING IT WITH GOOD FRIENDS!

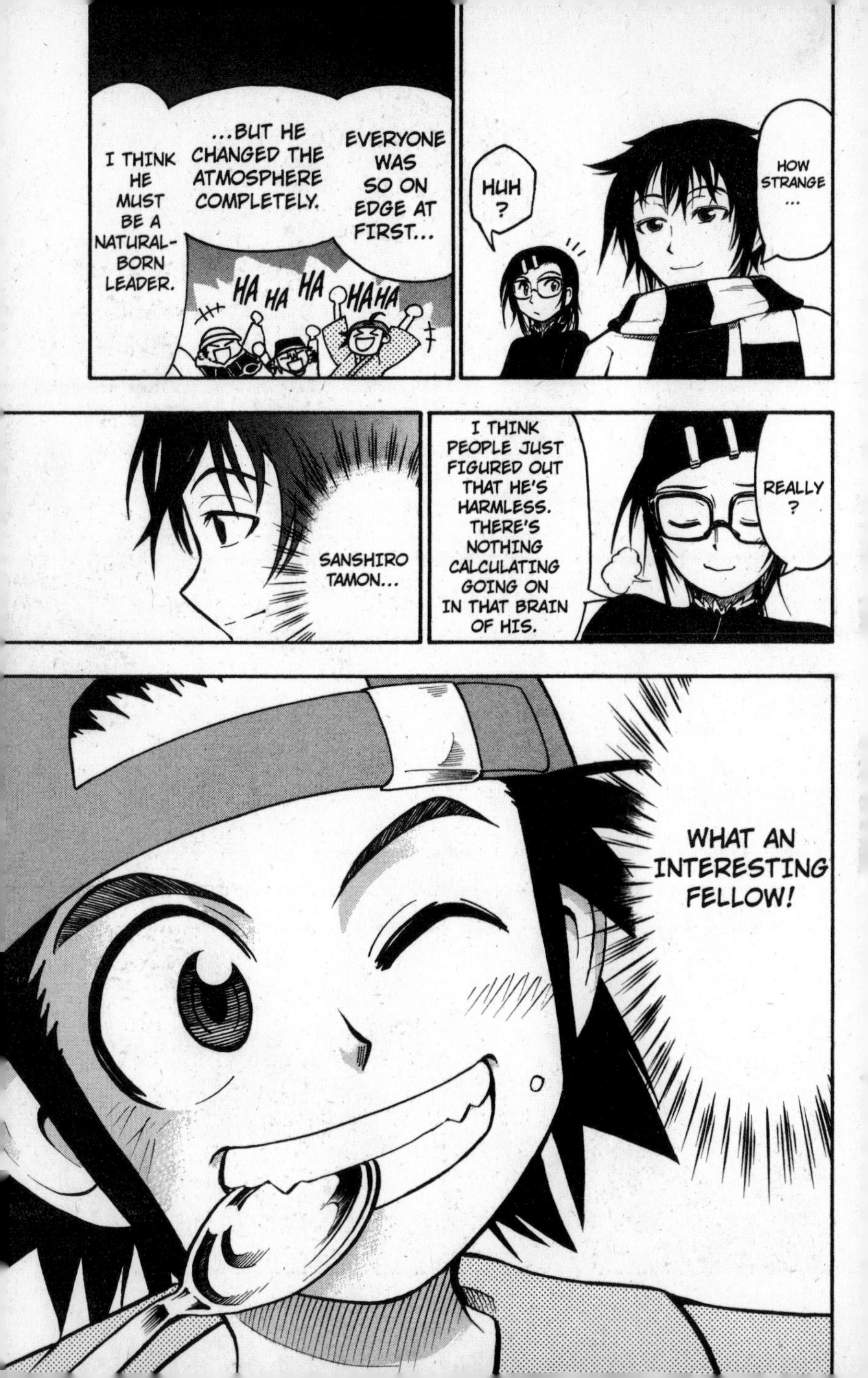
HOW STRANGE...
HUH?
EVERYONE WAS SO ON EDGE AT FIRST...
...BUT HE CHANGED THE ATMOSPHERE COMPLETELY.
I THINK HE MUST BE A NATURAL-BORN LEADER.
HA HA HA HAHA
REALLY?
I THINK PEOPLE JUST FIGURED OUT THAT HE'S HARMLESS. THERE'S NOTHING CALCULATING GOING ON IN THAT BRAIN OF HIS.
SANSHIRO TAMON...
WHAT AN INTERESTING FELLOW!

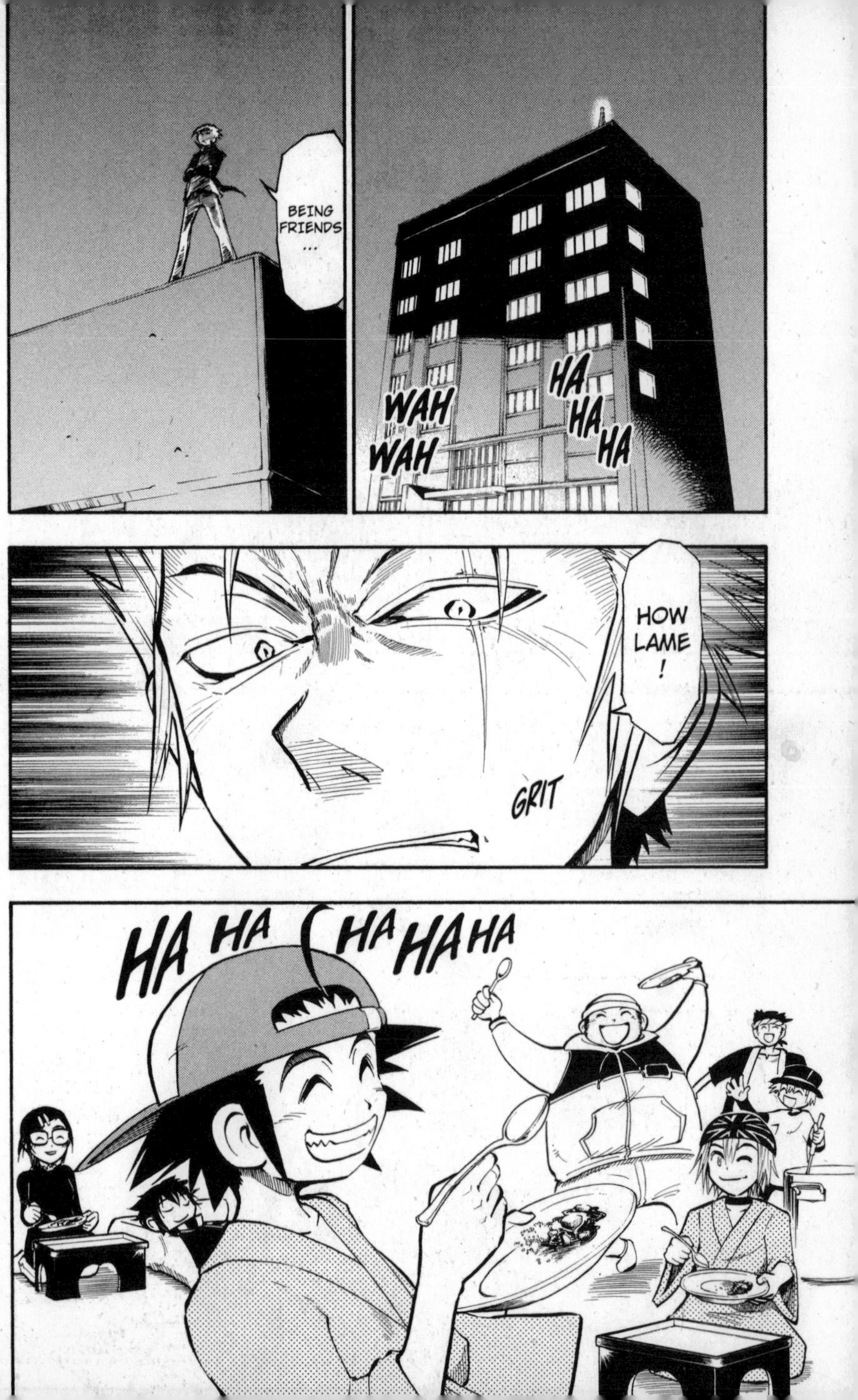
HA HA HA
WAH WAH
BEING FRIENDS ...
HOW LAME!
GRIT
HA HA HA HA HA HA

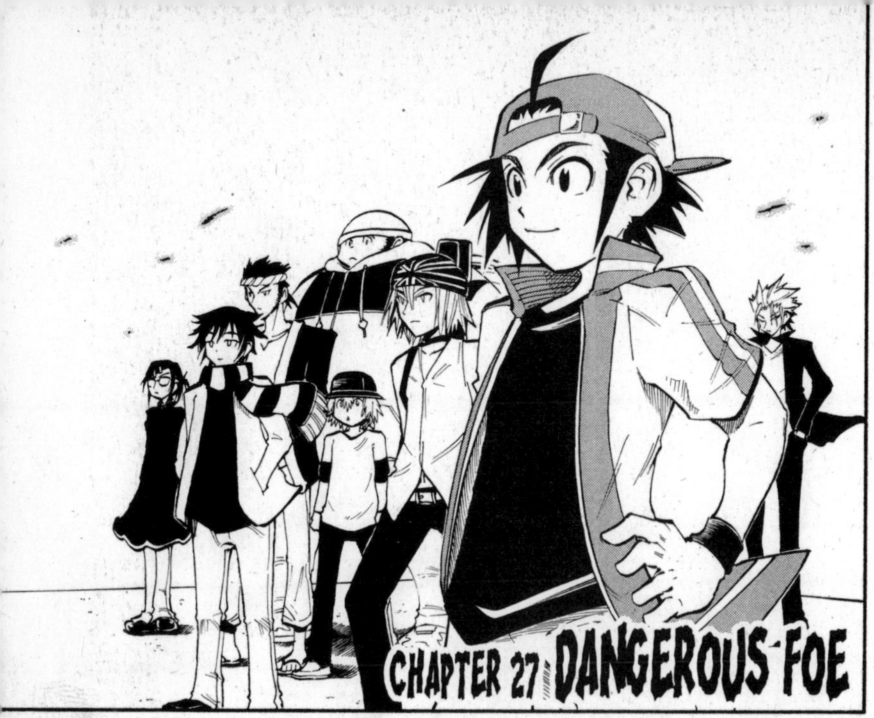
CHAPTER 27: DANGEROUS FOE

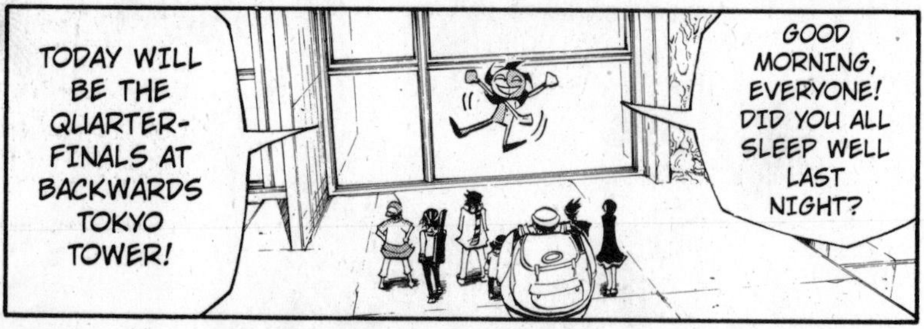
GOOD MORNING, EVERYONE! DID YOU ALL SLEEP WELL LAST NIGHT?
TODAY WILL BE THE QUARTER-FINALS AT BACKWARDS TOKYO TOWER!

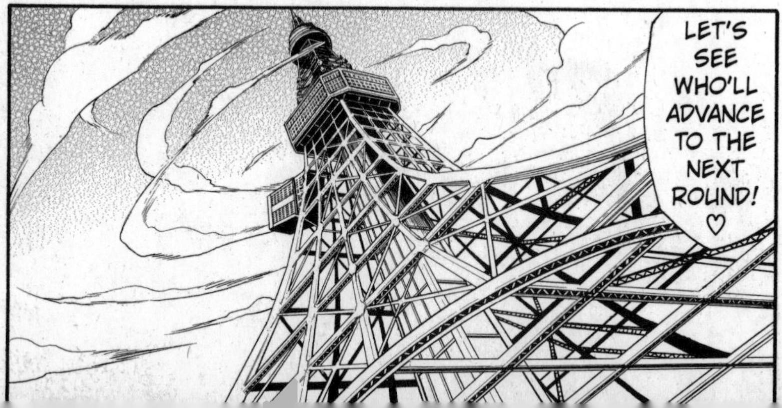
LET'S SEE WHO'LL ADVANCE TO THE NEXT ROUND! ♡

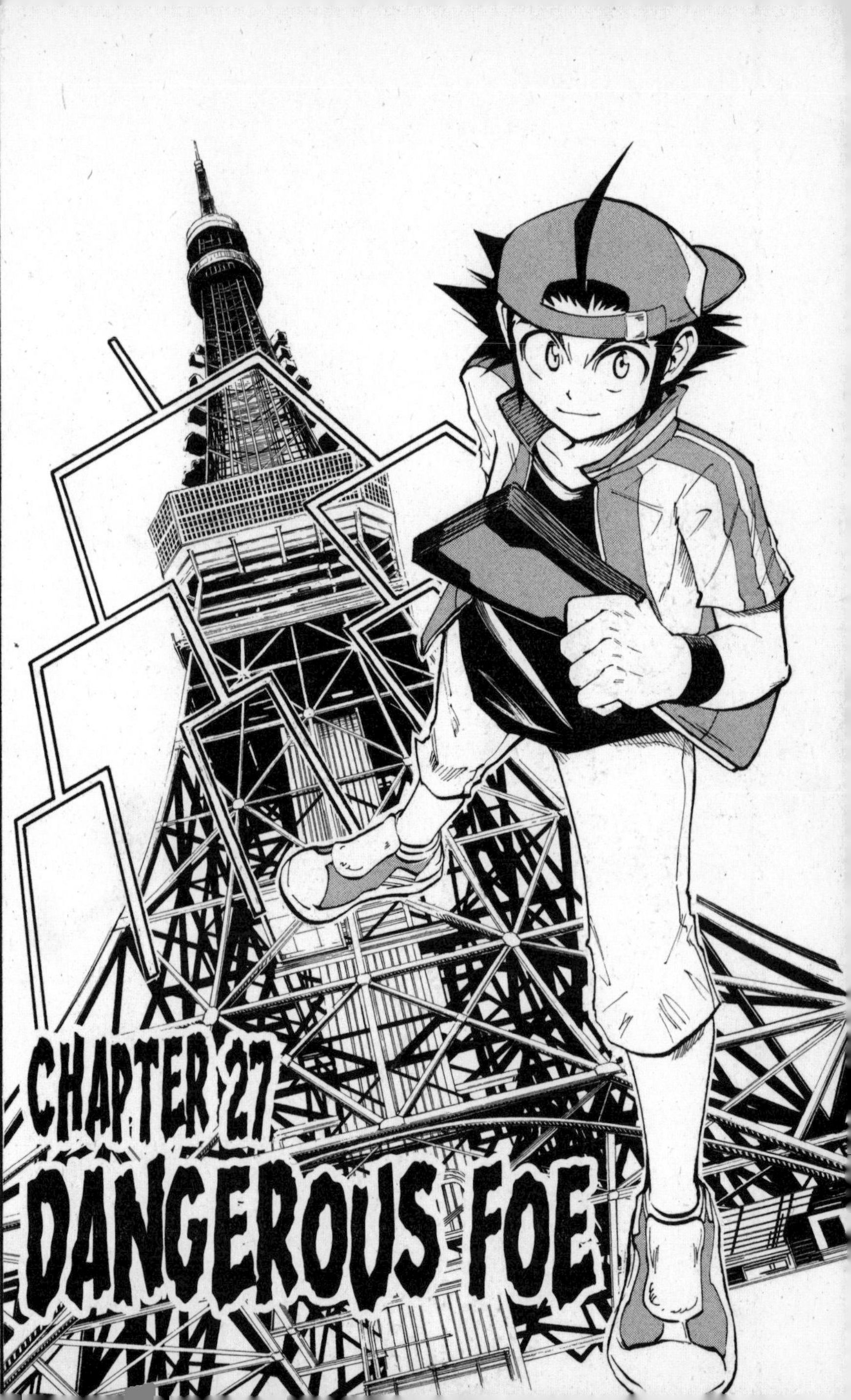
CHAPTER 27
DANGEROUS FOE

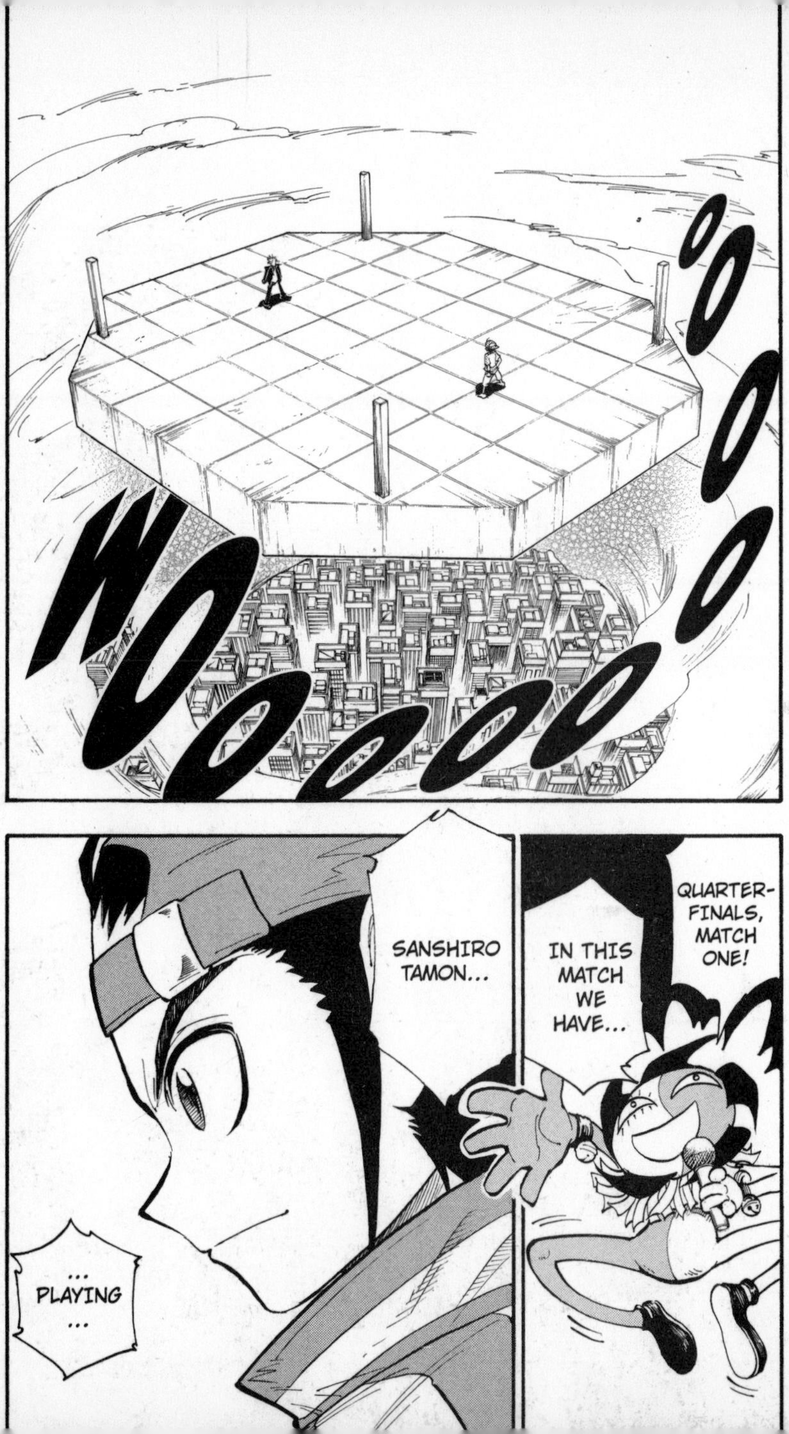
WOOOOOOOOOOOO
QUARTER-FINALS, MATCH ONE!
IN THIS MATCH WE HAVE...
SANSHIRO TAMON...
...PLAYING...

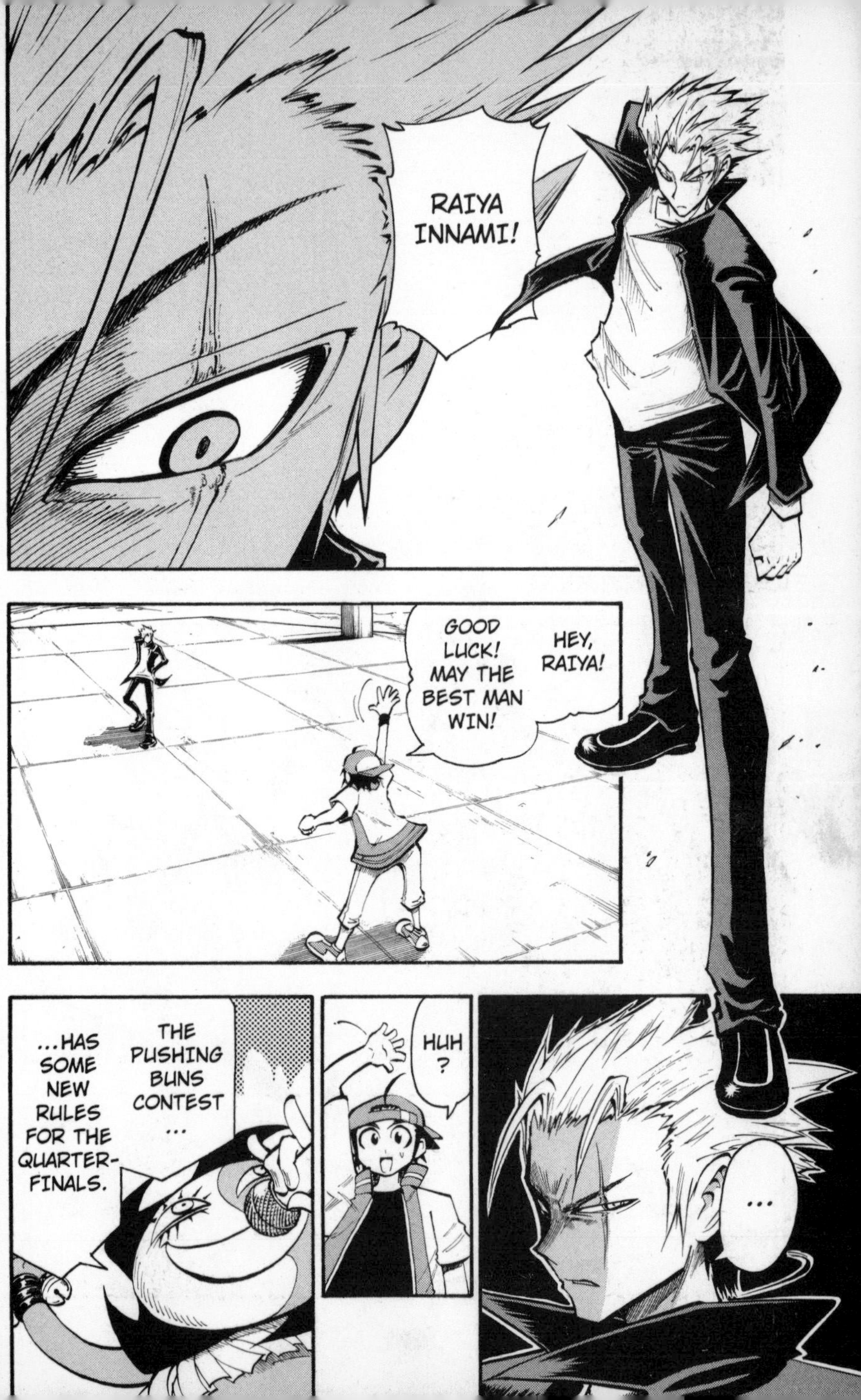
RAIYA INNAMI!
HEY, RAIYA!
GOOD LUCK! MAY THE BEST MAN WIN!
...
HUH ?
THE PUSHING BUNS CONTEST ...
...HAS SOME NEW RULES FOR THE QUARTER-FINALS.

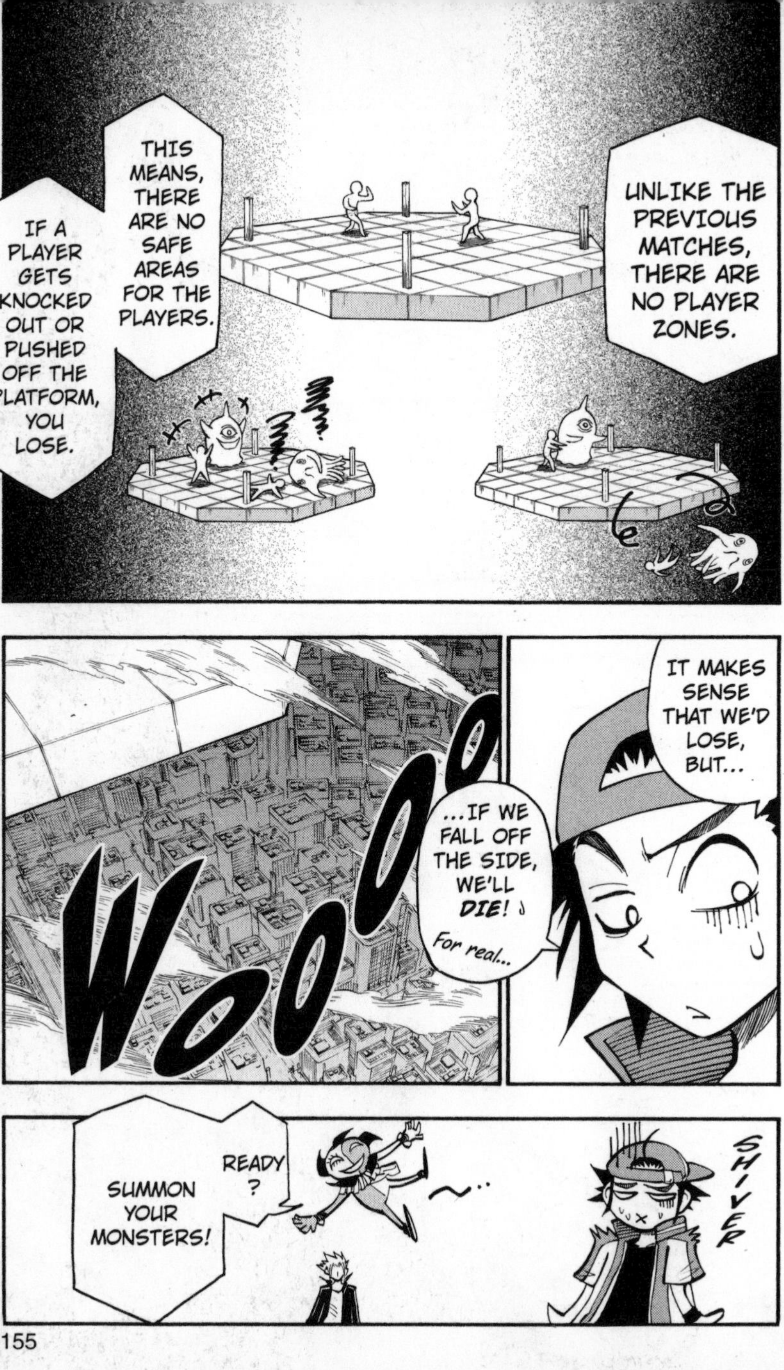
UNLIKE THE PREVIOUS MATCHES, THERE ARE NO PLAYER ZONES.
THIS MEANS, THERE ARE NO SAFE AREAS FOR THE PLAYERS.
IF A PLAYER GETS KNOCKED OUT OR PUSHED OFF THE PLATFORM, YOU LOSE.
IT MAKES SENSE THAT WE'D LOSE, BUT...
...IF WE FALL OFF THE SIDE, WE'LL DIE! ♪
For real...
WOOOOO
SHIVER
~..
READY?
SUMMON YOUR MONSTERS!

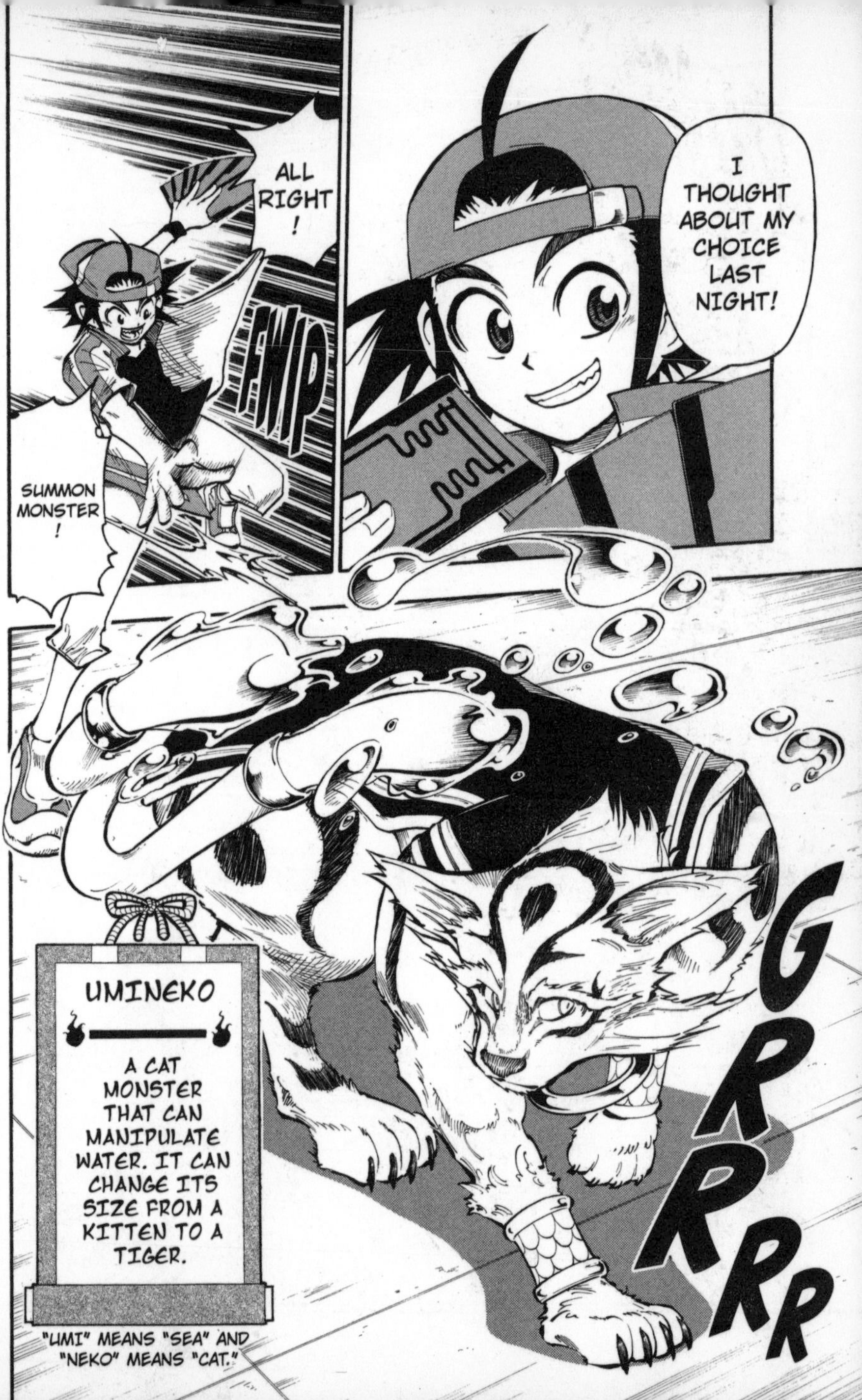
I THOUGHT ABOUT MY CHOICE LAST NIGHT!
ALL RIGHT!
FWIP
SUMMON MONSTER!
UMINEKO
A CAT MONSTER THAT CAN MANIPULATE WATER. IT CAN CHANGE ITS SIZE FROM A KITTEN TO A TIGER.
GRRRR
"UMI" MEANS "SEA" AND "NEKO" MEANS "CAT."

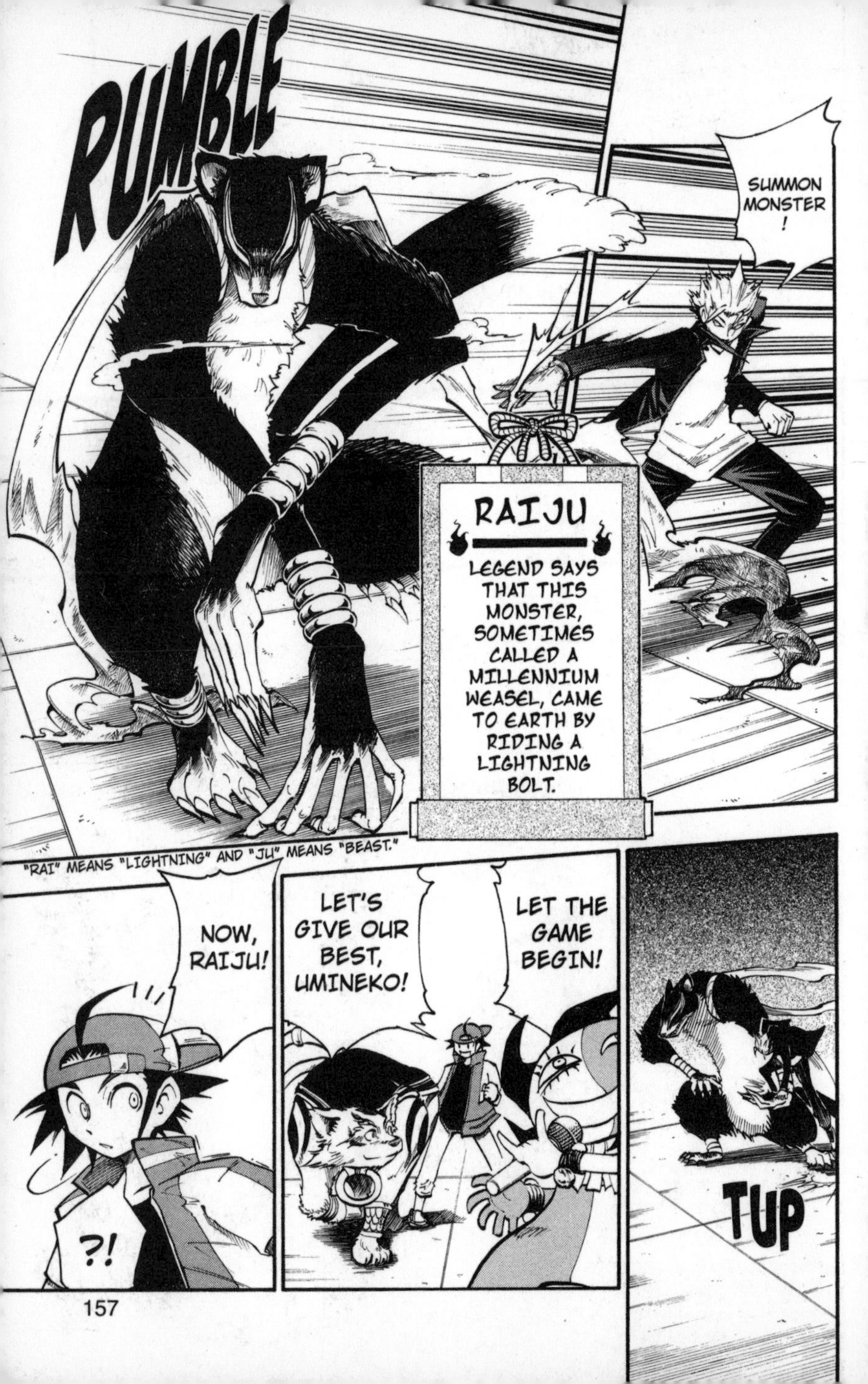
SUMMON MONSTER!
RUMBLE
RAIJU
LEGEND SAYS THAT THIS MONSTER, SOMETIMES CALLED A MILLENNIUM WEASEL, CAME TO EARTH BY RIDING A LIGHTNING BOLT.
TUP
LET THE GAME BEGIN!
LET'S GIVE OUR BEST, UMINEKO!
NOW, RAIJU!
?!

"RAI" MEANS "LIGHTNING" AND "JU" MEANS "BEAST."

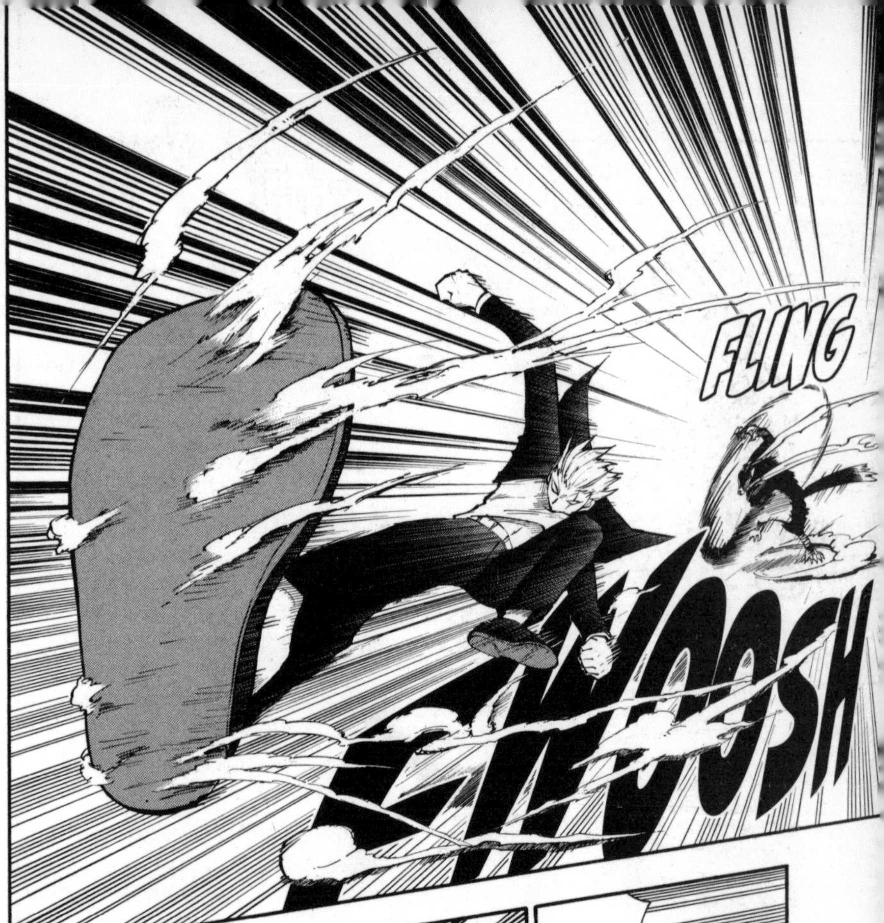
FLING

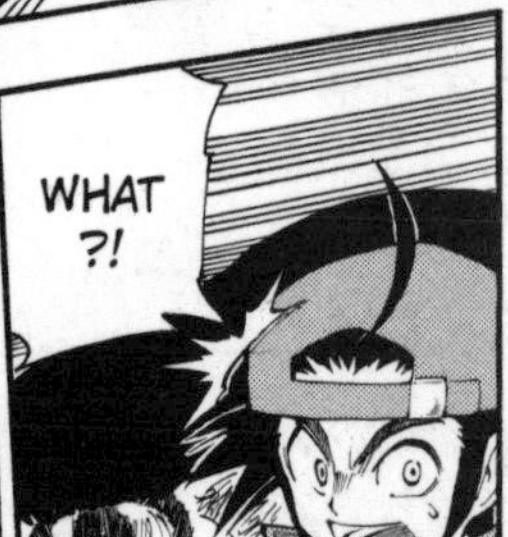
WHAT ?!

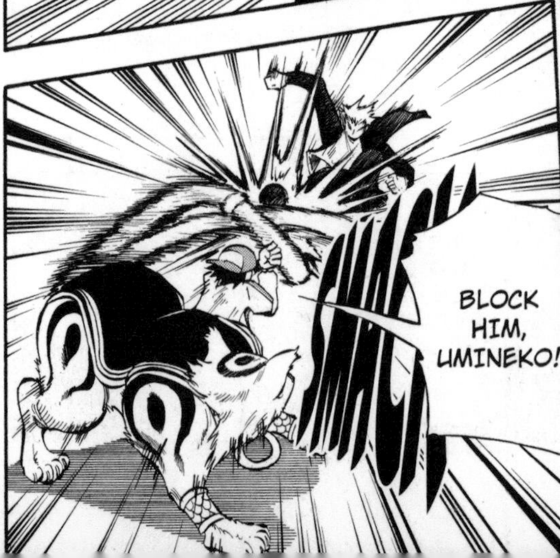
BLOCK HIM, UMINEKO!

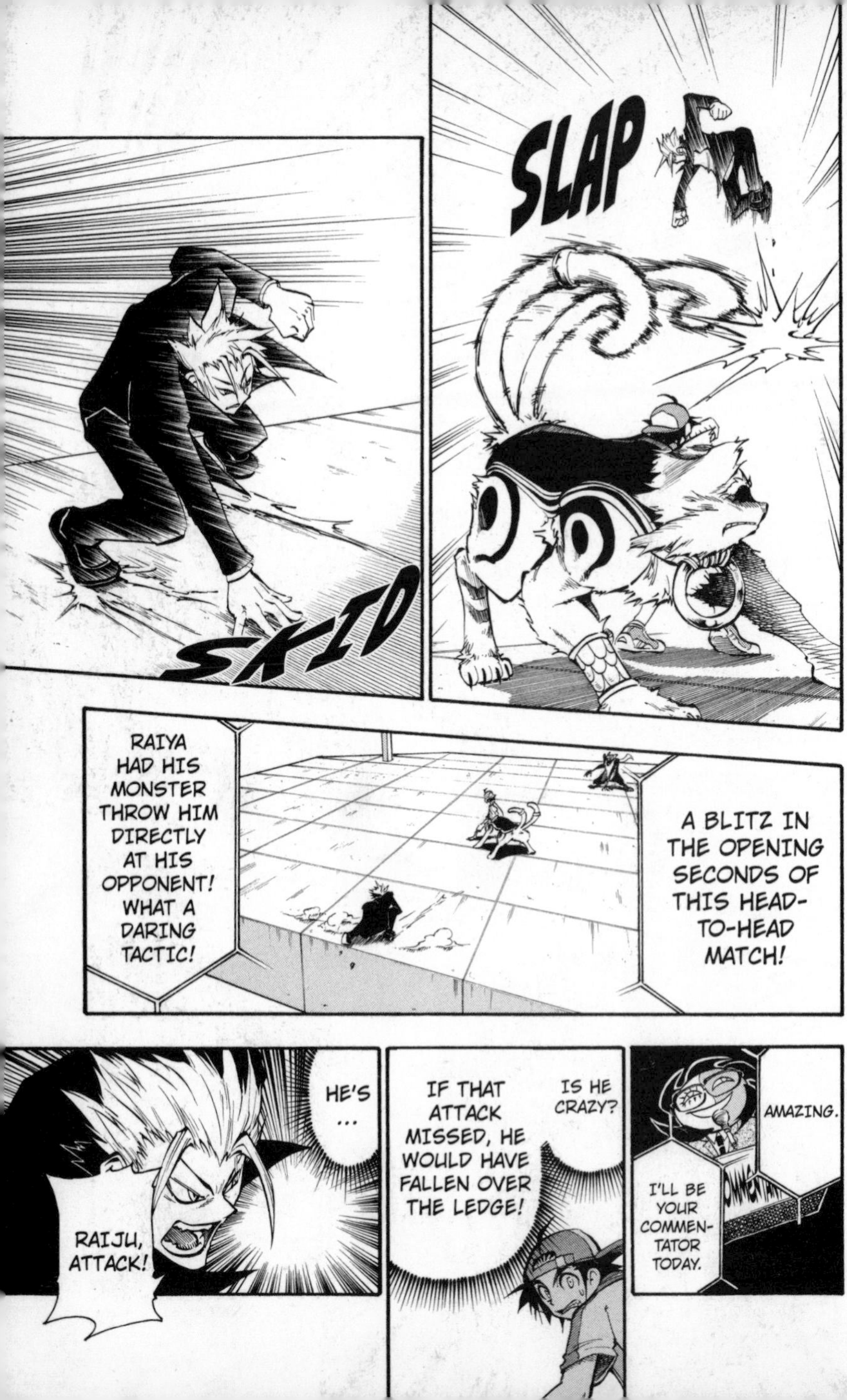

SLAP
SKID
A BLITZ IN THE OPENING SECONDS OF THIS HEAD-TO-HEAD MATCH!
RAIYA HAD HIS MONSTER THROW HIM DIRECTLY AT HIS OPPONENT! WHAT A DARING TACTIC!
AMAZING.
I'LL BE YOUR COMMENTATOR TODAY.
IS HE CRAZY?
IF THAT ATTACK MISSED, HE WOULD HAVE FALLEN OVER THE LEDGE!
HE'S ...
RAIJU, ATTACK!

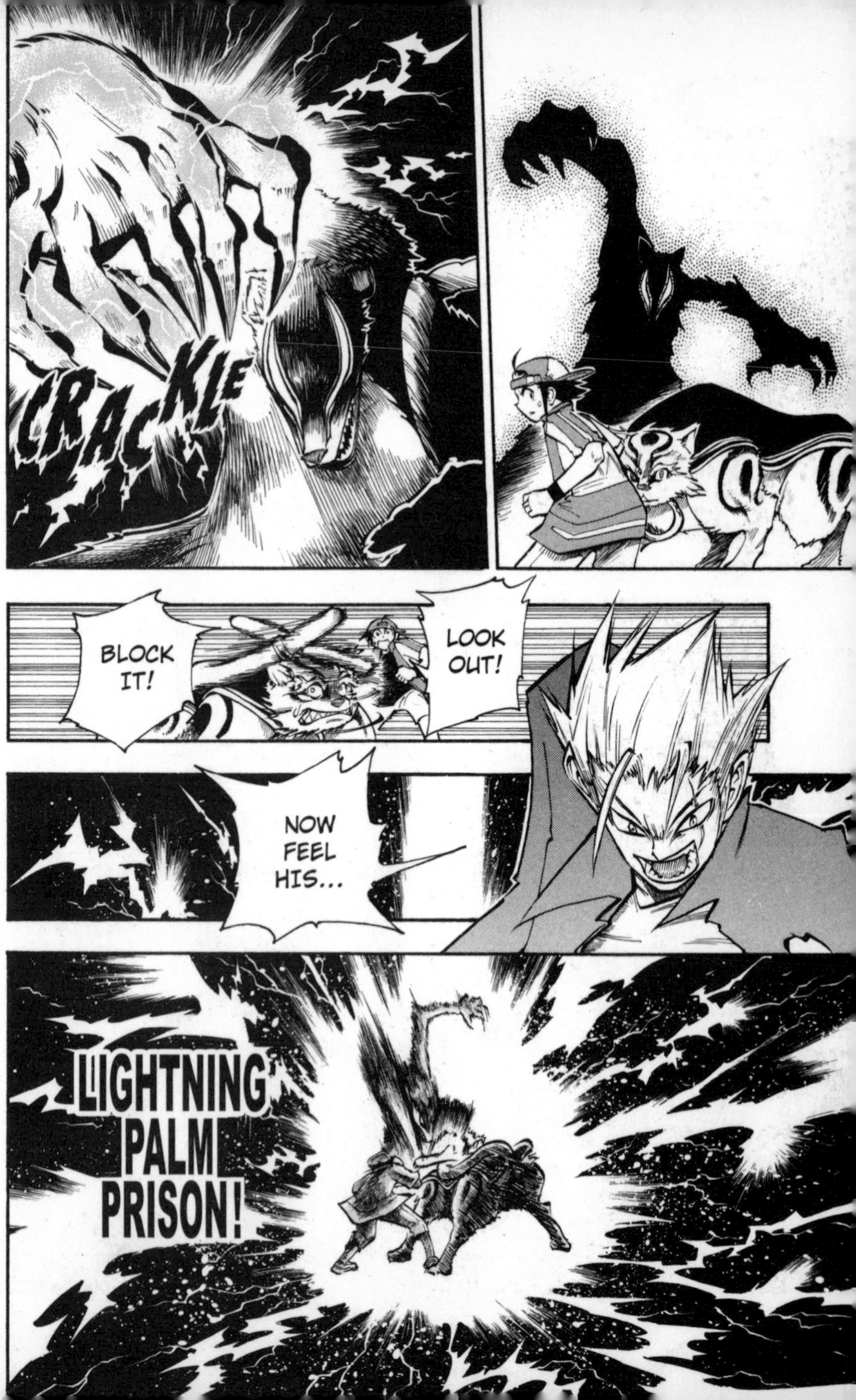
CRACKLE
LOOK OUT!
BLOCK IT!
NOW FEEL HIS...
LIGHTNING PALM PRISON!

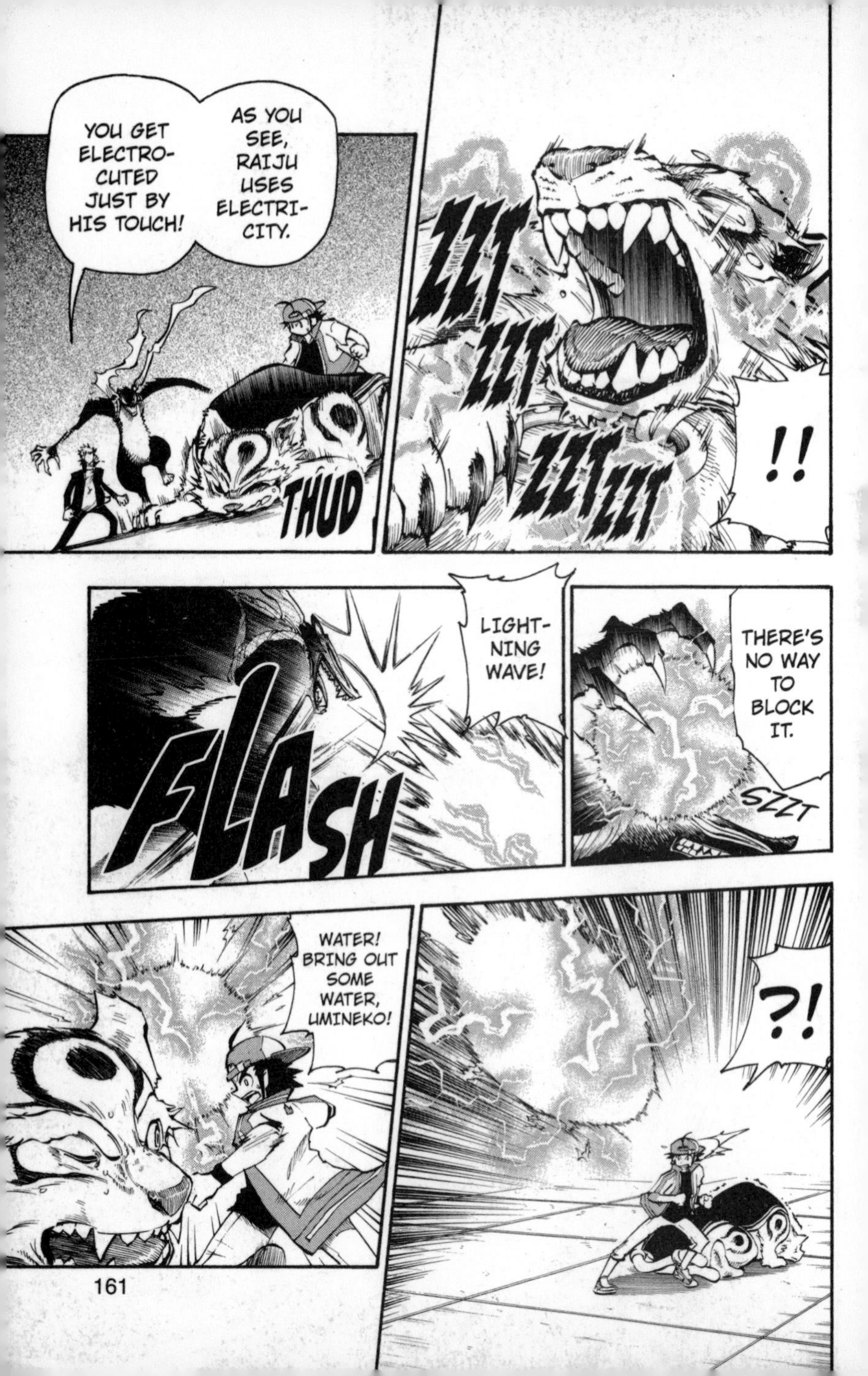
ZZZT
ZZZT
ZZZTZZZT
!!
AS YOU SEE, RAIJU USES ELECTRICITY.
YOU GET ELECTROCUTED JUST BY HIS TOUCH!
THUD
THERE'S NO WAY TO BLOCK IT.
SZZT
LIGHTNING WAVE!
FLASH
?!
WATER! BRING OUT SOME WATER, UMINEKO!

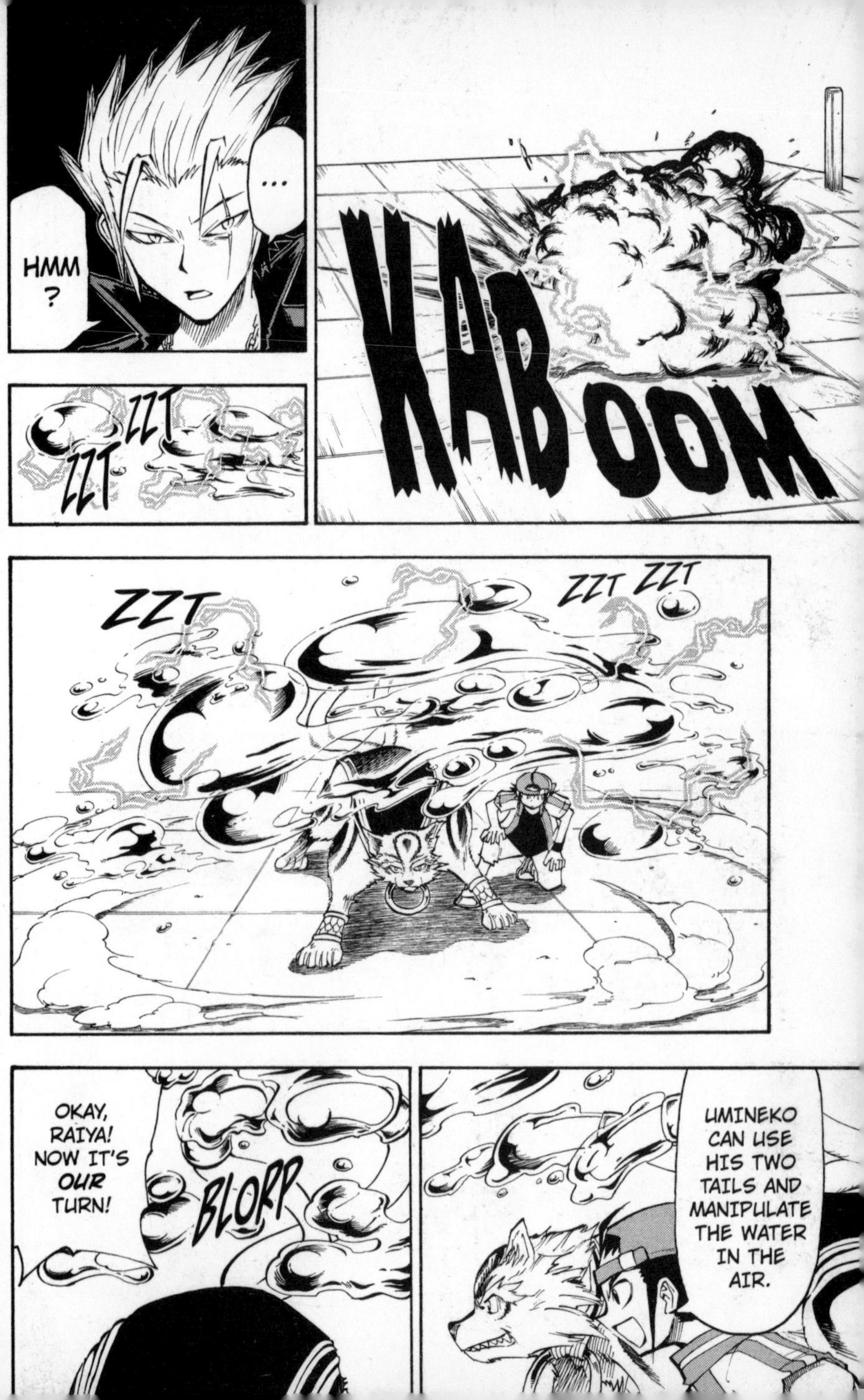
KABOOM
...
HMM ?
ZZT ZZT
ZZT ZZT
ZZT
UMINEKO CAN USE HIS TWO TAILS AND MANIPULATE THE WATER IN THE AIR.
OKAY, RAIYA! NOW IT'S ***OUR*** TURN!
BLORP

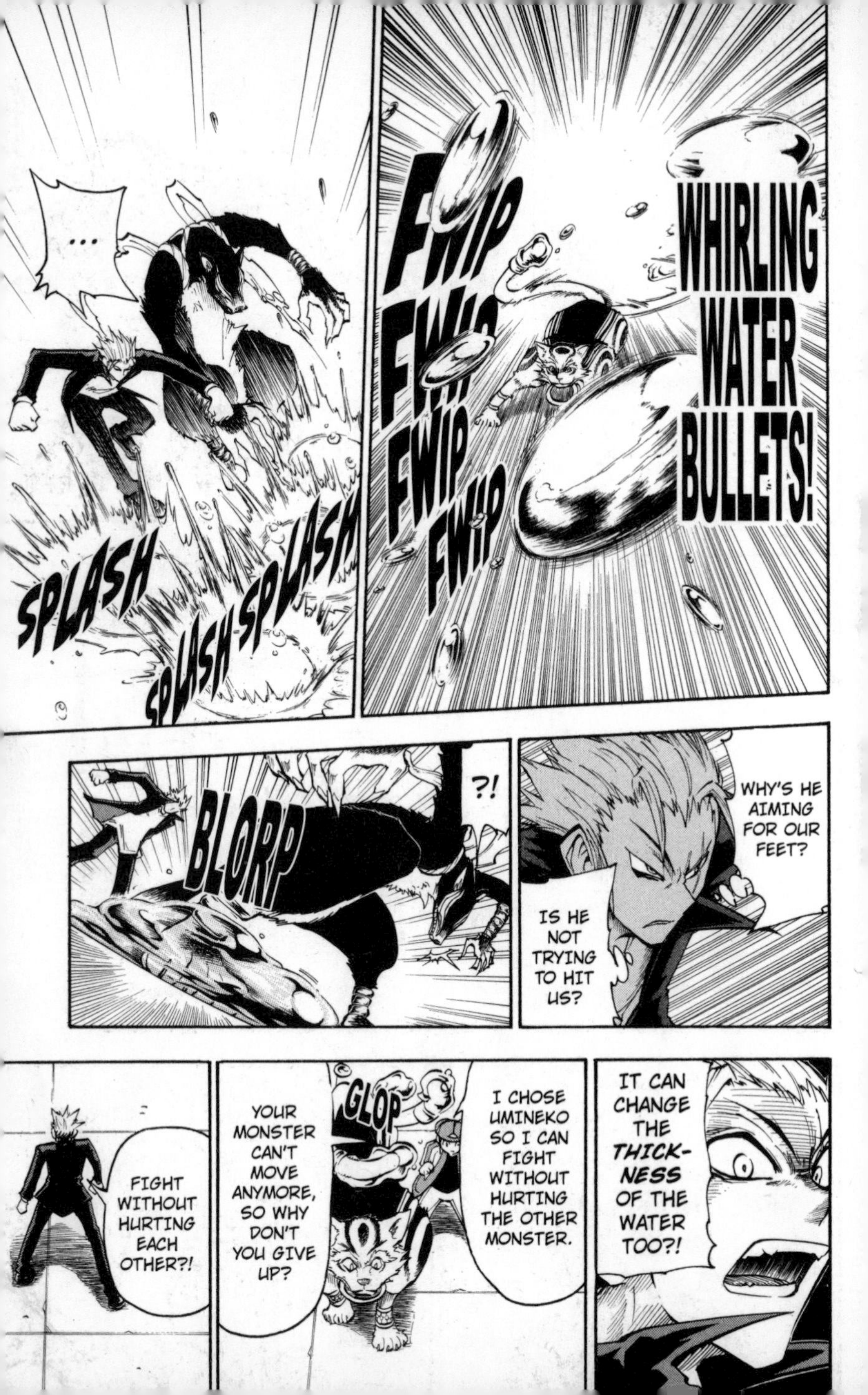
WHIRLING WATER BULLETS!
FWIP
FWIP
FWIP
FWIP
...
SPLASH
SPLASH SPLASH
WHY'S HE AIMING FOR OUR FEET?
IS HE NOT TRYING TO HIT US?
?!
BLORP
IT CAN CHANGE THE *THICKNESS* OF THE WATER TOO?!
I CHOSE UMINEKO SO I CAN FIGHT WITHOUT HURTING THE OTHER MONSTER.
GLOP
YOUR MONSTER CAN'T MOVE ANYMORE, SO WHY DON'T YOU GIVE UP?
FIGHT WITHOUT HURTING EACH OTHER?!

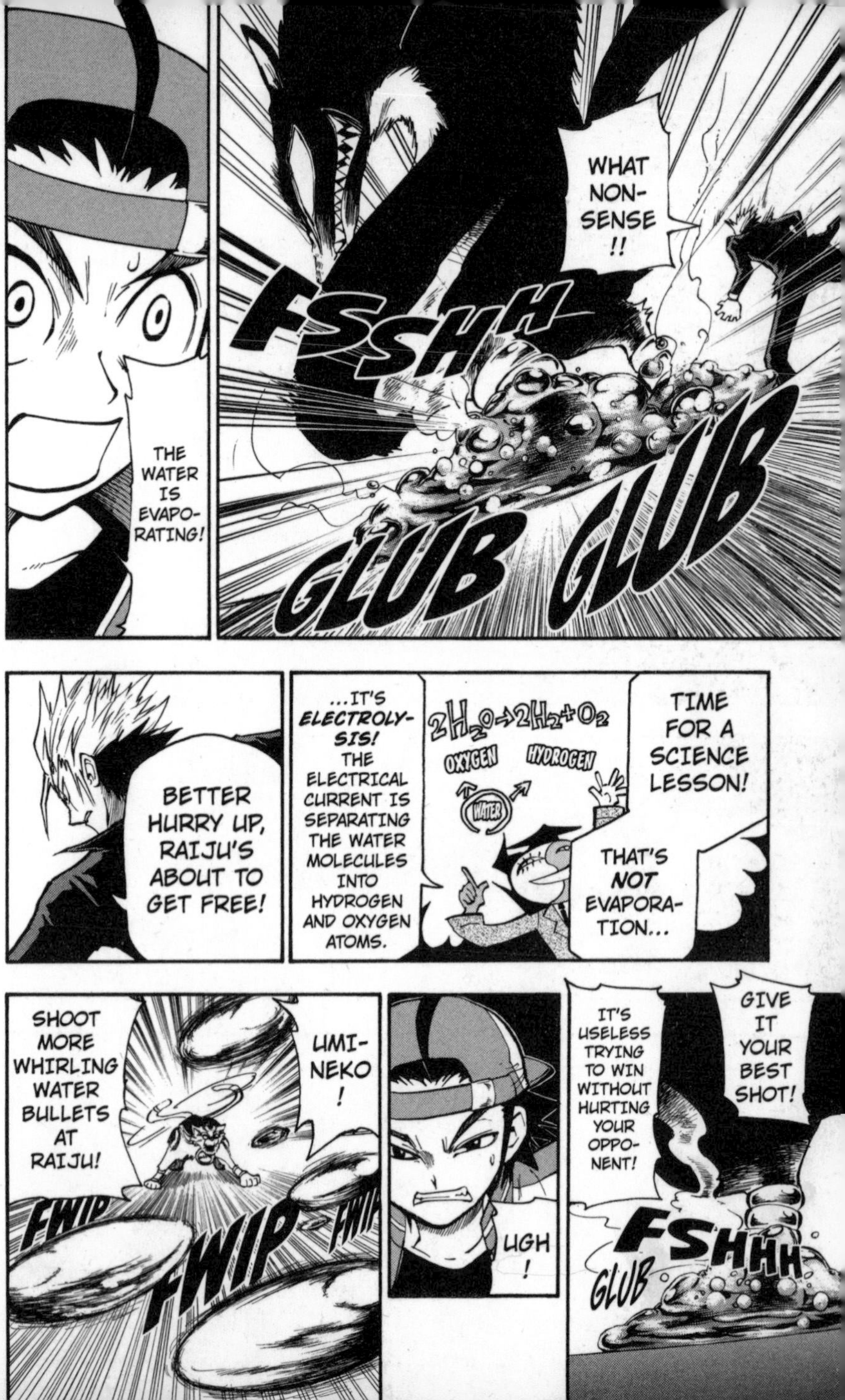
WHAT NON-SENSE!!
FSSHH
GLUB GLUB
THE WATER IS EVAPORATING!
TIME FOR A SCIENCE LESSON!
2H2O→2H2+O2
OXYGEN
HYDROGEN
WATER
THAT'S NOT EVAPORATION...
...IT'S ELECTROLYSIS! THE ELECTRICAL CURRENT IS SEPARATING THE WATER MOLECULES INTO HYDROGEN AND OXYGEN ATOMS.
BETTER HURRY UP, RAIJU'S ABOUT TO GET FREE!
GIVE IT YOUR BEST SHOT!
IT'S USELESS TRYING TO WIN WITHOUT HURTING YOUR OPPO-NENT!
FSHHH
GLUB
UGH!
UMI-NEKO!
SHOOT MORE WHIRLING WATER BULLETS AT RAIJU!
FWIP
FWIP
FWIP

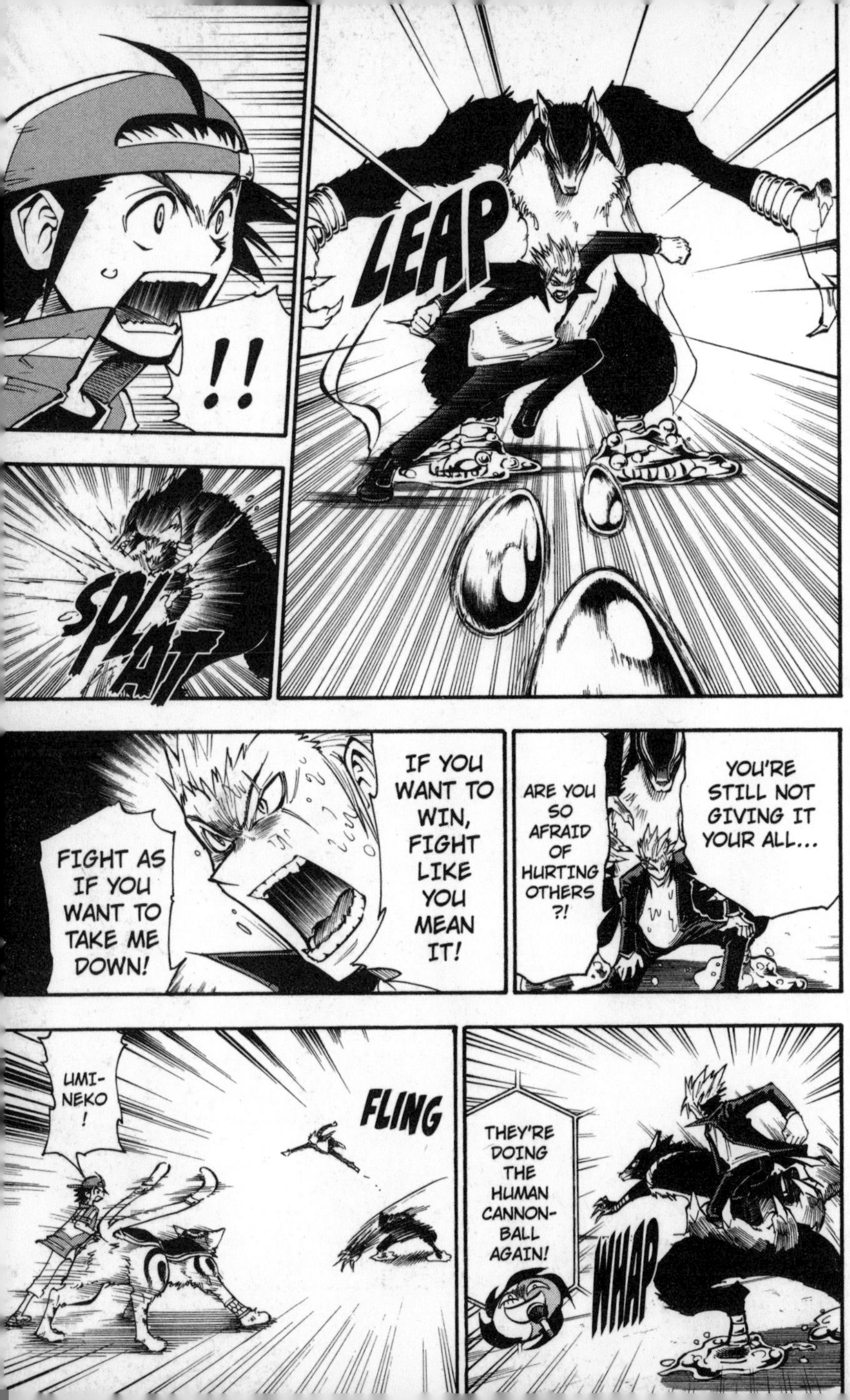
LEAP
!!
SPLAT
YOU'RE STILL NOT GIVING IT YOUR ALL...
ARE YOU SO AFRAID OF HURTING OTHERS?!
IF YOU WANT TO WIN, FIGHT LIKE YOU MEAN IT!
FIGHT AS IF YOU WANT TO TAKE ME DOWN!
THEY'RE DOING THE HUMAN CANNON-BALL AGAIN!
WHAP
UMI-NEKO!
FLING

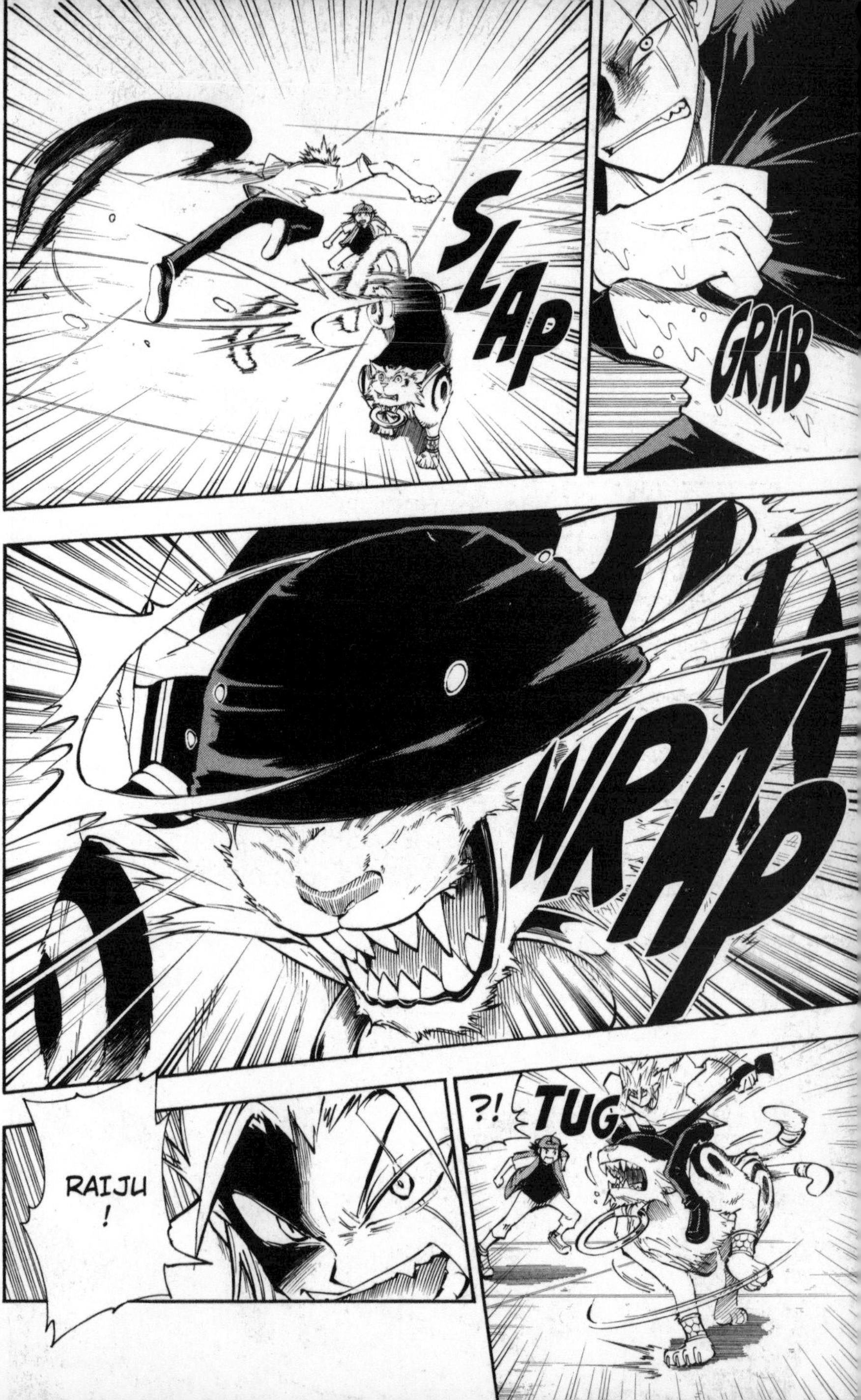
GRAB
SLAP
WHAP
?!
TUG
RAIJU!

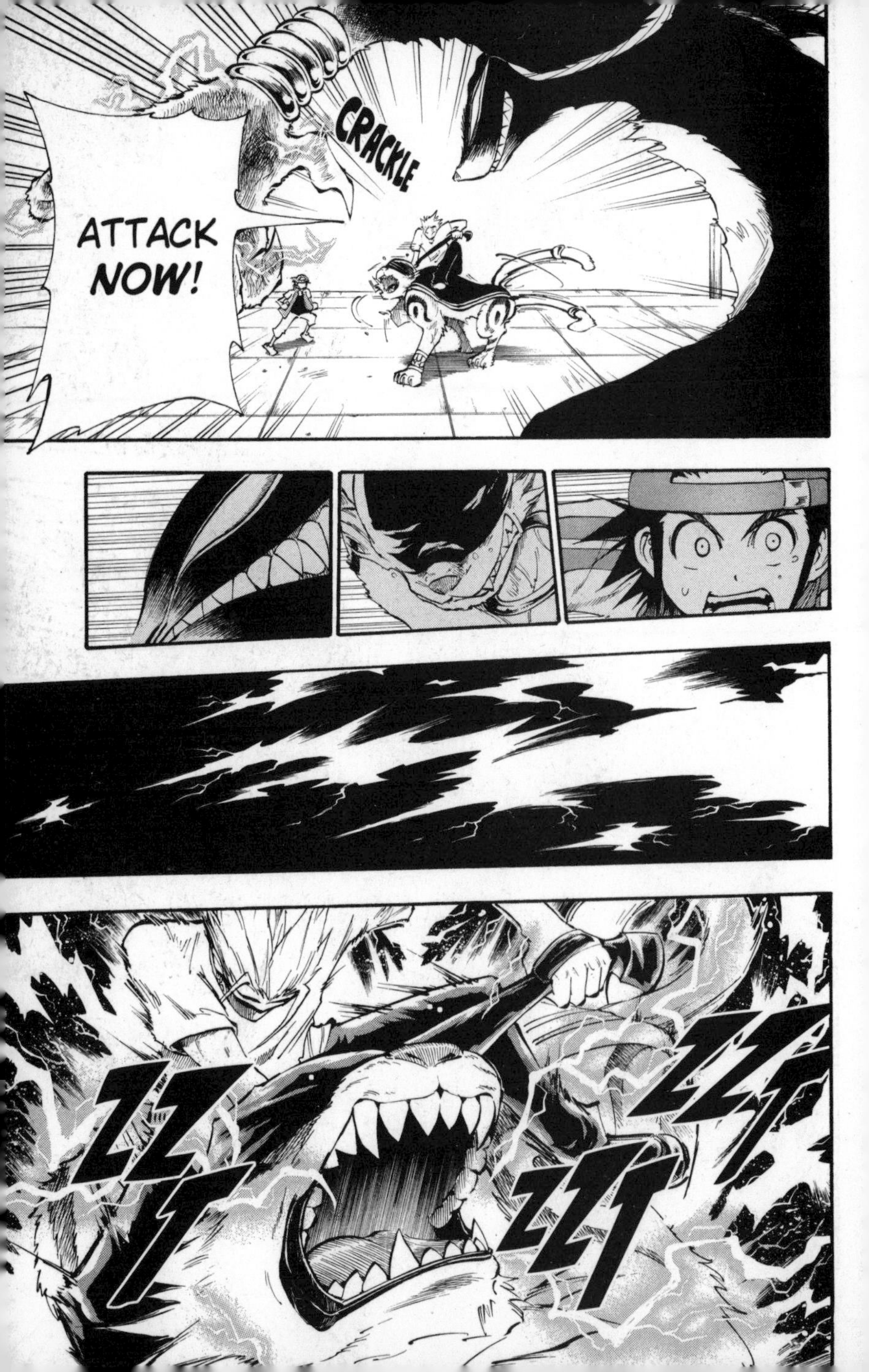
CRACKLE
ATTACK NOW!
ZZT
ZZT
ZZT

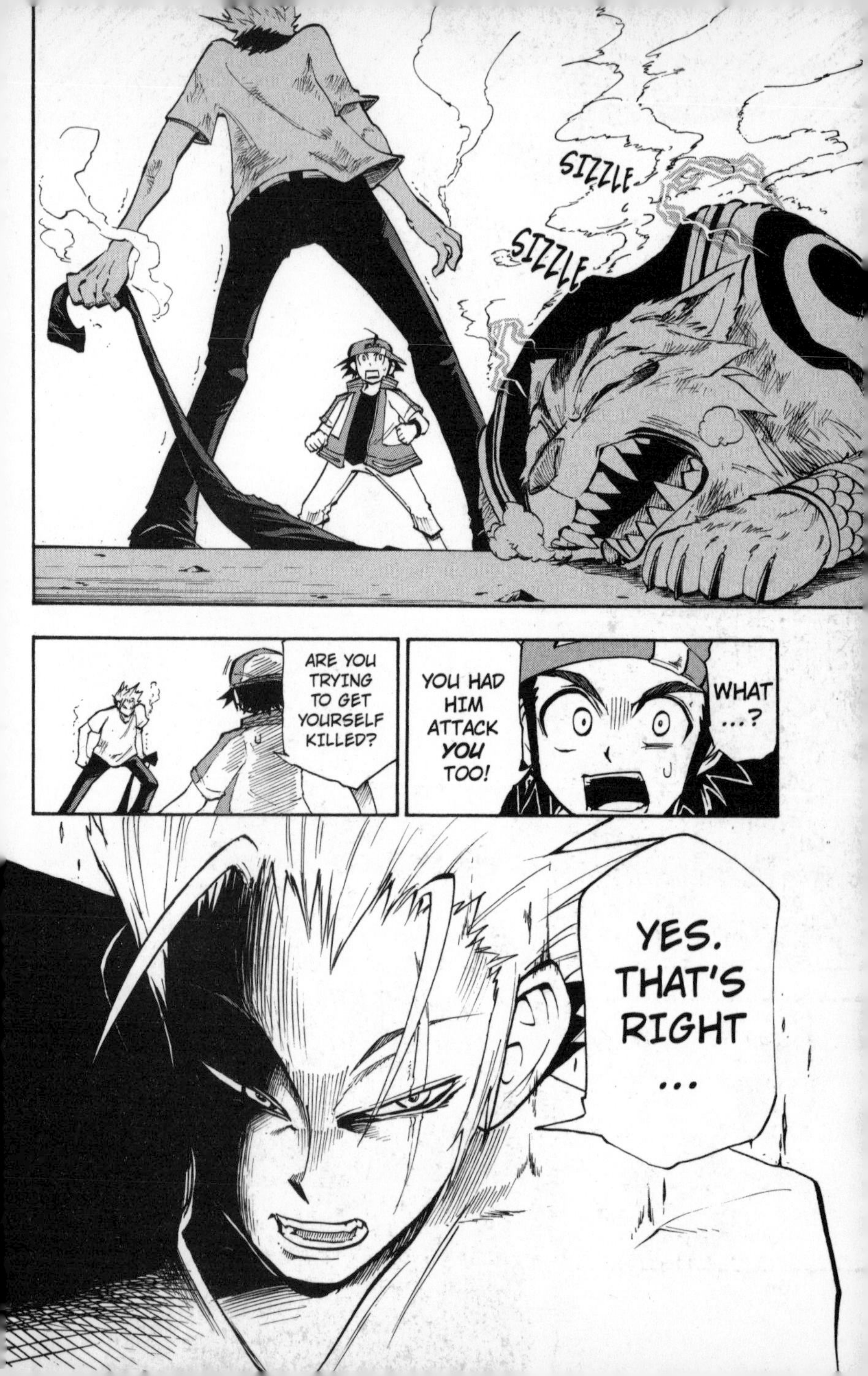
SIZZLE
SIZZLE
WHAT ...?
YOU HAD HIM ATTACK YOU TOO!
ARE YOU TRYING TO GET YOURSELF KILLED?
YES. THAT'S RIGHT ...

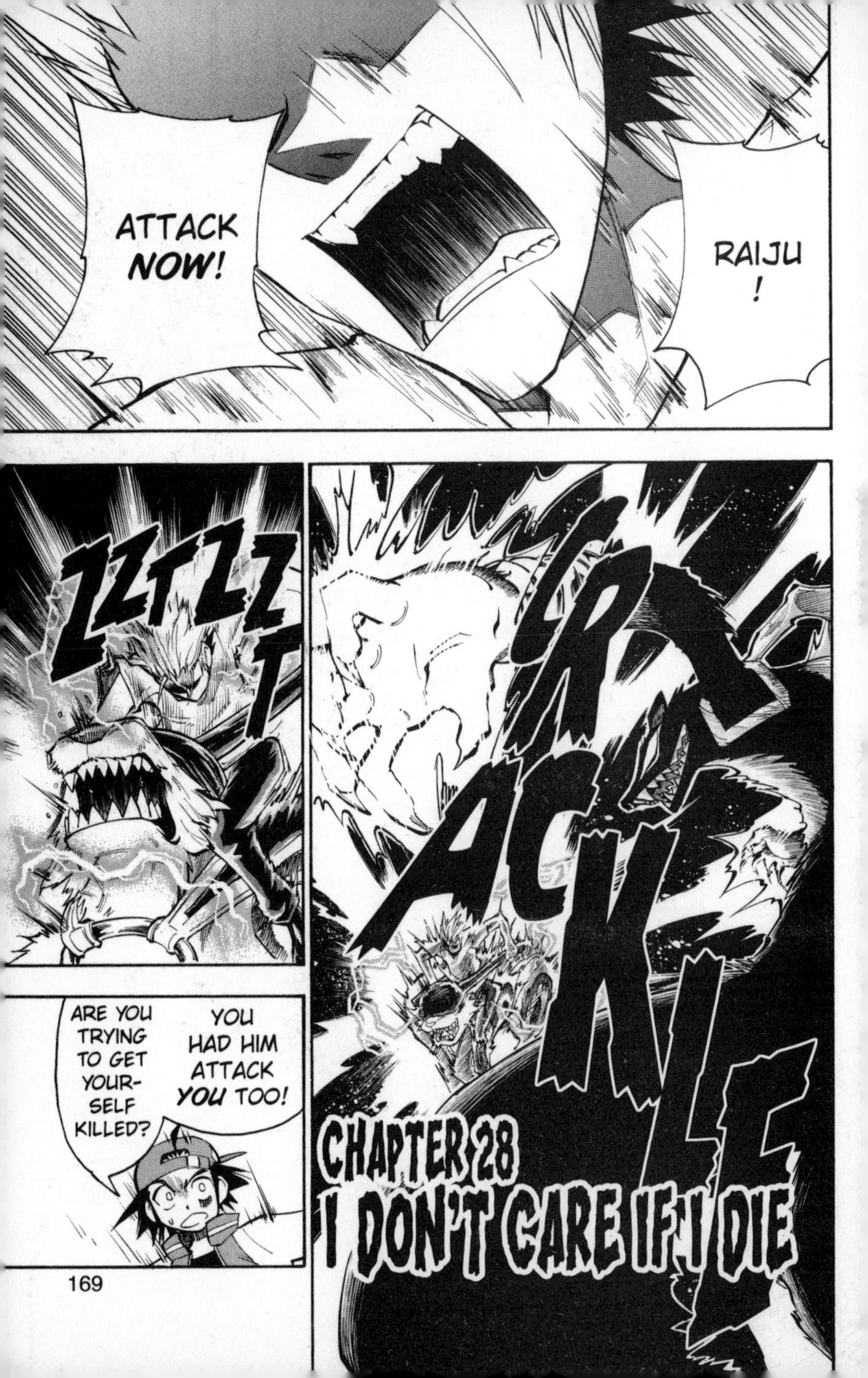
RAIJU !
ATTACK NOW!
CRACKLE
CHAPTER 28
I DON'T CARE IF I DIE
ZZZZT
YOU HAD HIM ATTACK YOU TOO!
ARE YOU TRYING TO GET YOUR-SELF KILLED?

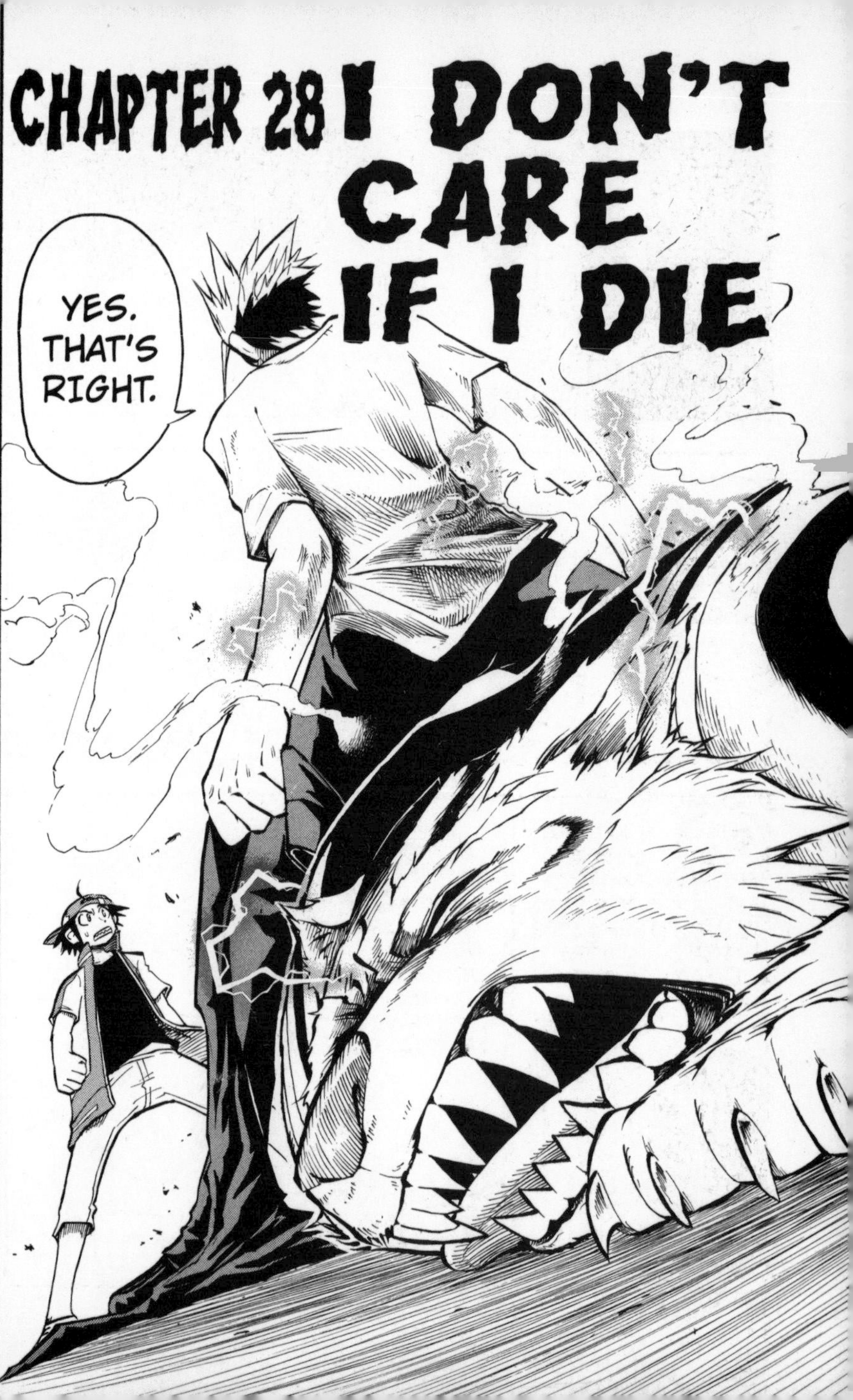
CHAPTER 28 I DON'T CARE IF I DIE
YES. THAT'S RIGHT.

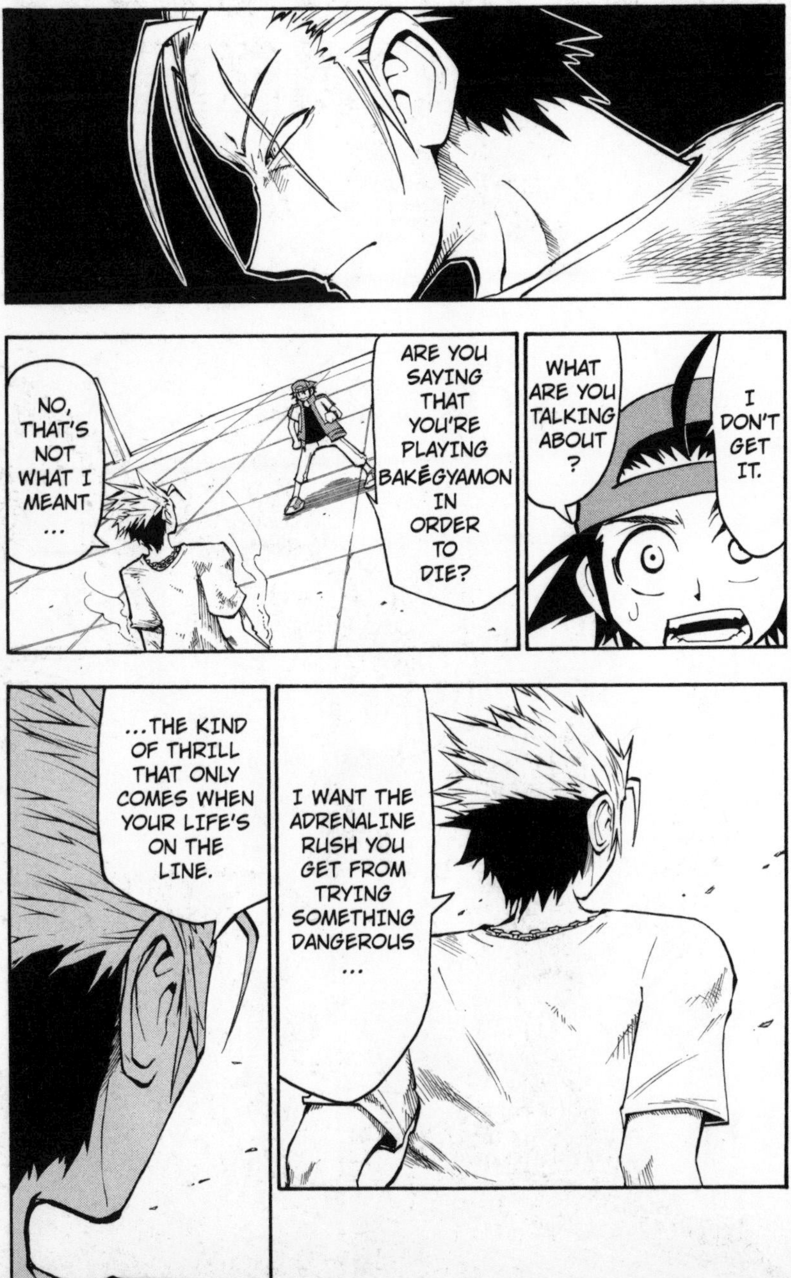
I DON'T GET IT.
WHAT ARE YOU TALKING ABOUT?
ARE YOU SAYING THAT YOU'RE PLAYING BAKĒGYAMON IN ORDER TO DIE?
NO, THAT'S NOT WHAT I MEANT...
I WANT THE ADRENALINE RUSH YOU GET FROM TRYING SOMETHING DANGEROUS...
...THE KIND OF THRILL THAT ONLY COMES WHEN YOUR LIFE'S ON THE LINE.

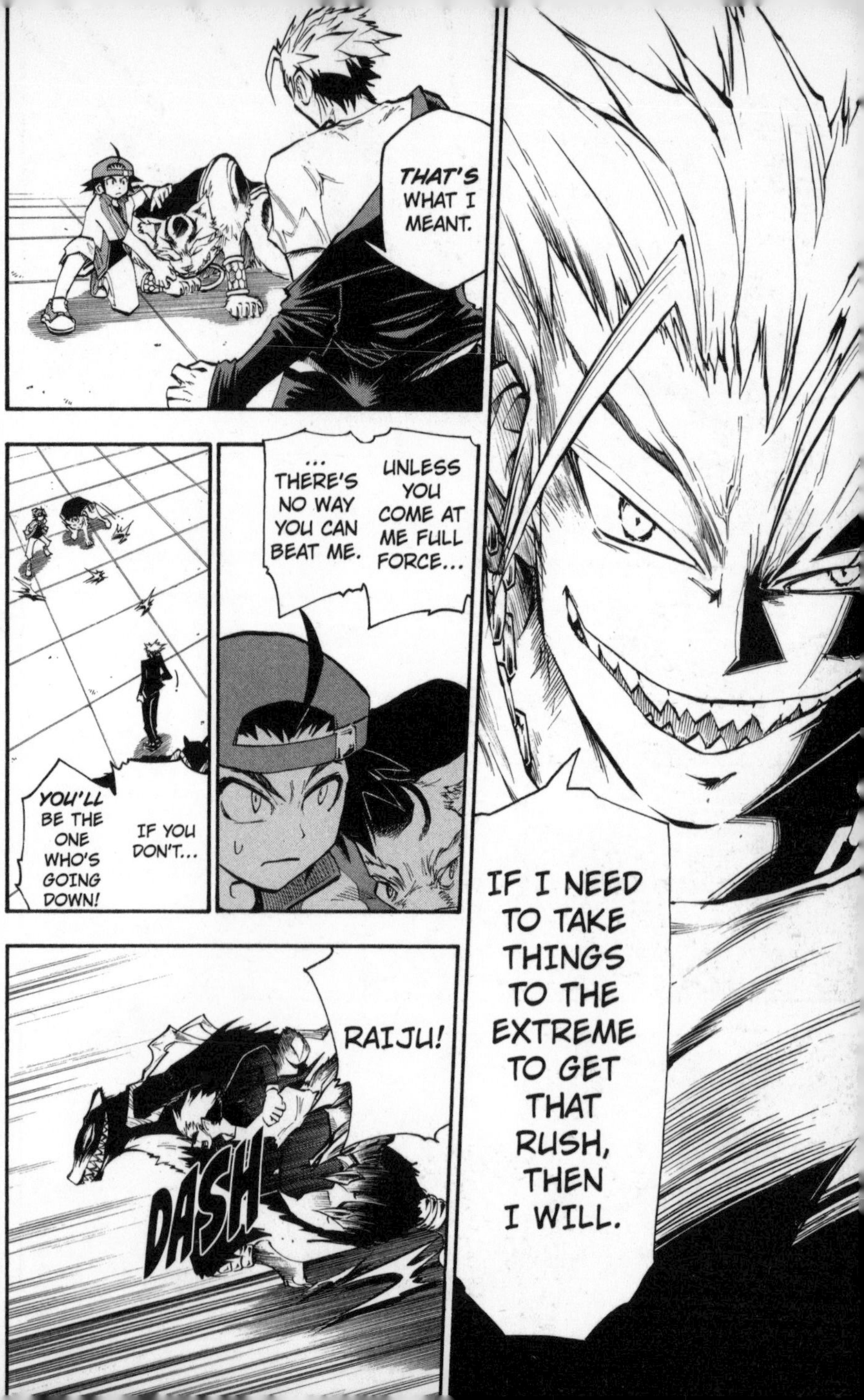
IF I NEED TO TAKE THINGS TO THE EXTREME TO GET THAT RUSH, THEN I WILL.
THAT'S WHAT I MEANT.
UNLESS YOU COME AT ME FULL FORCE...
... THERE'S NO WAY YOU CAN BEAT ME.
IF YOU DON'T...
YOU'LL BE THE ONE WHO'S GOING DOWN!
RAIJU!
DASH

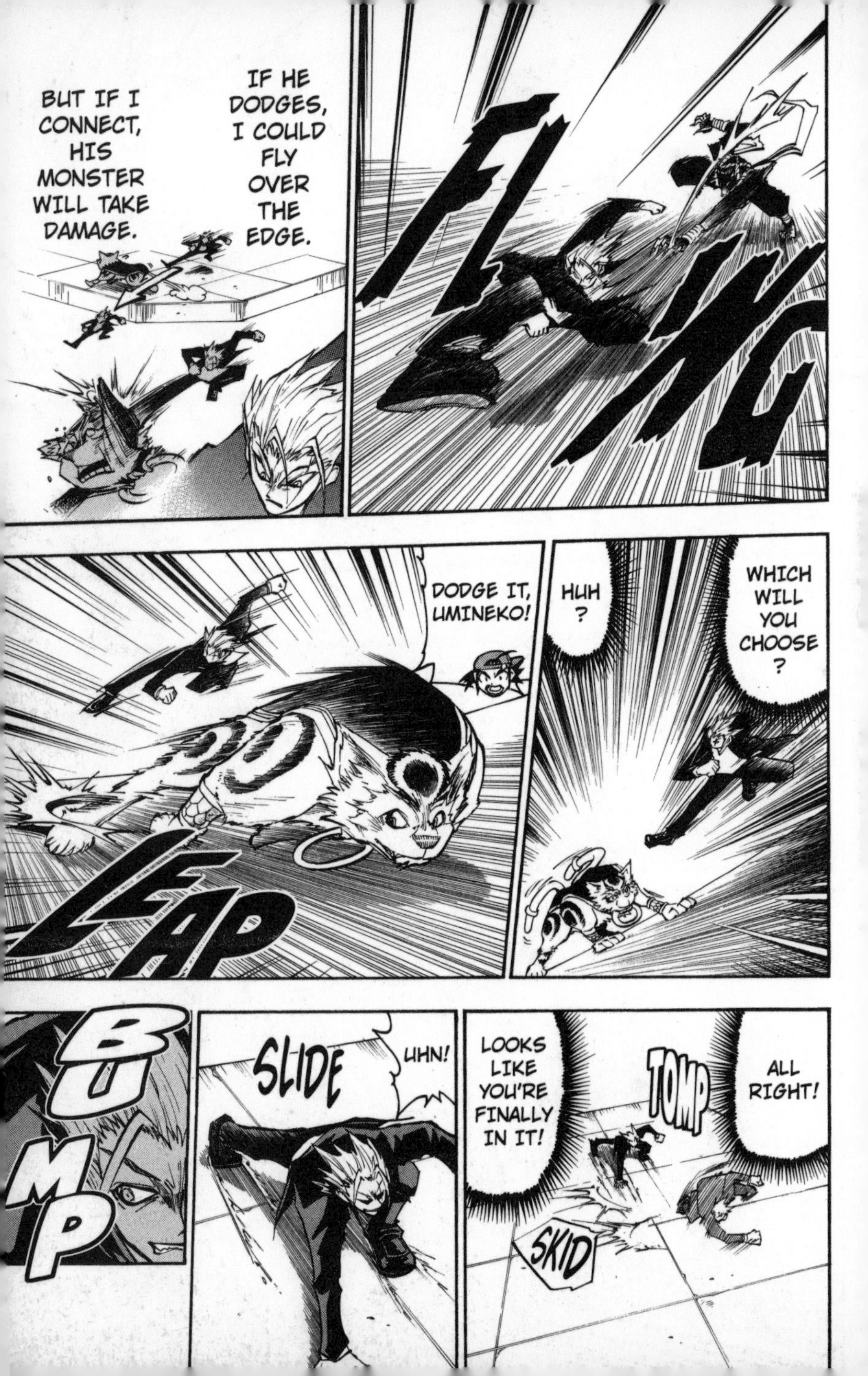
FLING
IF HE DODGES, I COULD FLY OVER THE EDGE.
BUT IF I CONNECT, HIS MONSTER WILL TAKE DAMAGE.
WHICH WILL YOU CHOOSE?
HUH?
DODGE IT, UMINEKO!
LEAP
ALL RIGHT!
TOMP
LOOKS LIKE YOU'RE FINALLY IN IT!
SKID
UHN!
SLIDE
BUMP

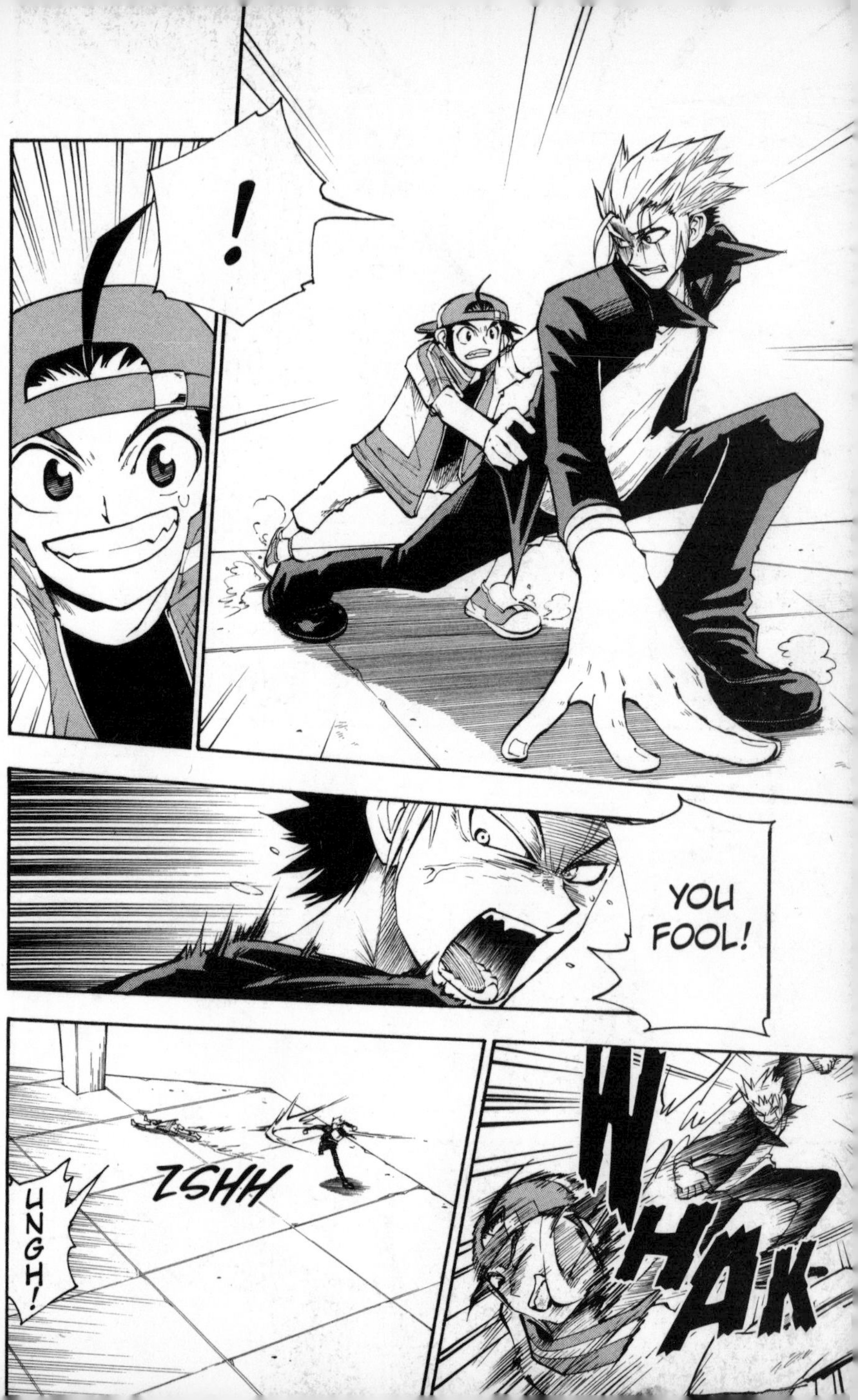
!
YOU FOOL!
WHAK
ZSHH
UNGH!

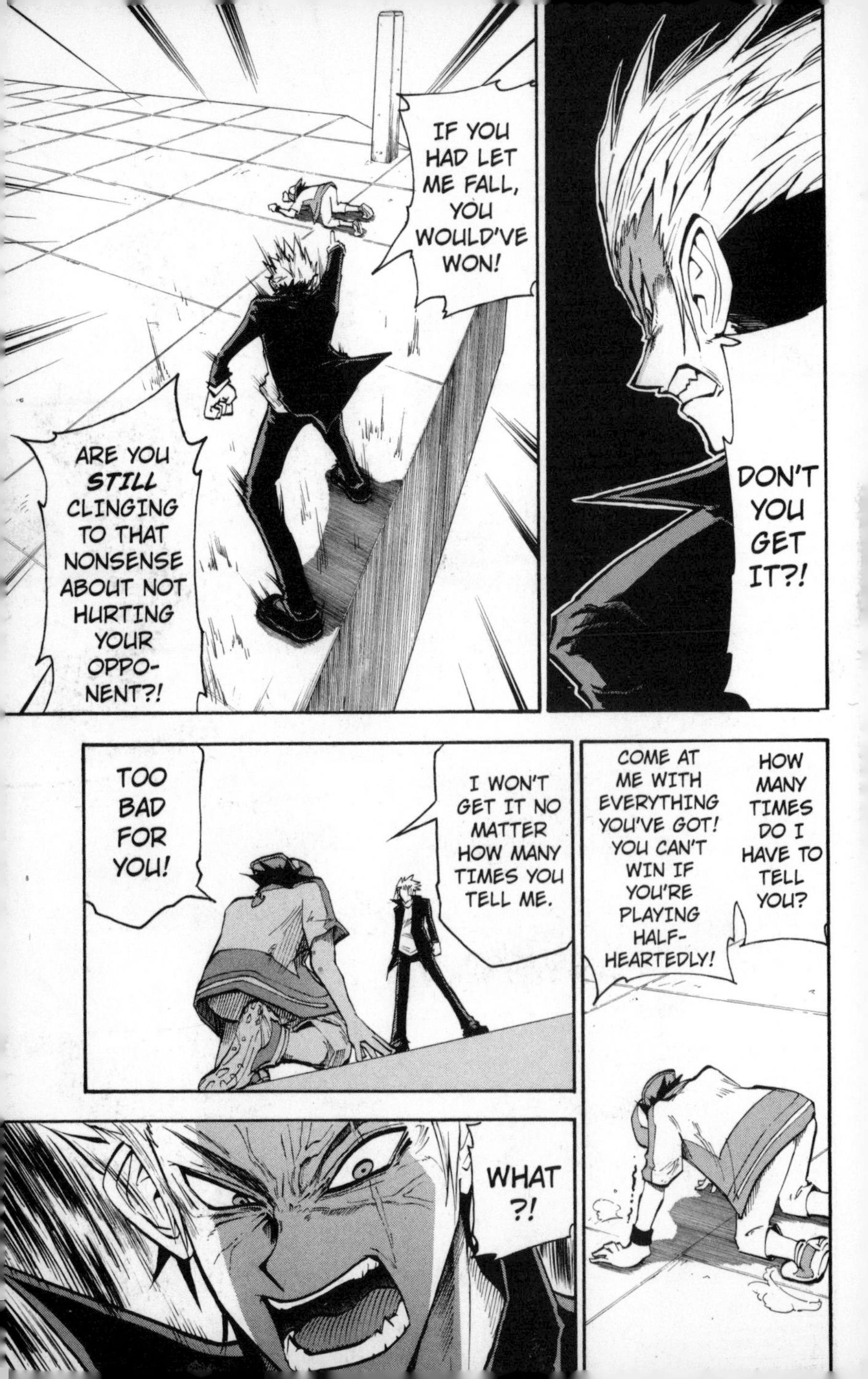
DON'T YOU GET IT?!
IF YOU HAD LET ME FALL, YOU WOULD'VE WON!
ARE YOU *STILL* CLINGING TO THAT NONSENSE ABOUT NOT HURTING YOUR OPPO-NENT?!
HOW MANY TIMES DO I HAVE TO TELL YOU?
COME AT ME WITH EVERYTHING YOU'VE GOT! YOU CAN'T WIN IF YOU'RE PLAYING HALF-HEARTEDLY!
I WON'T GET IT NO MATTER HOW MANY TIMES YOU TELL ME.
TOO BAD FOR YOU!
WHAT ?!

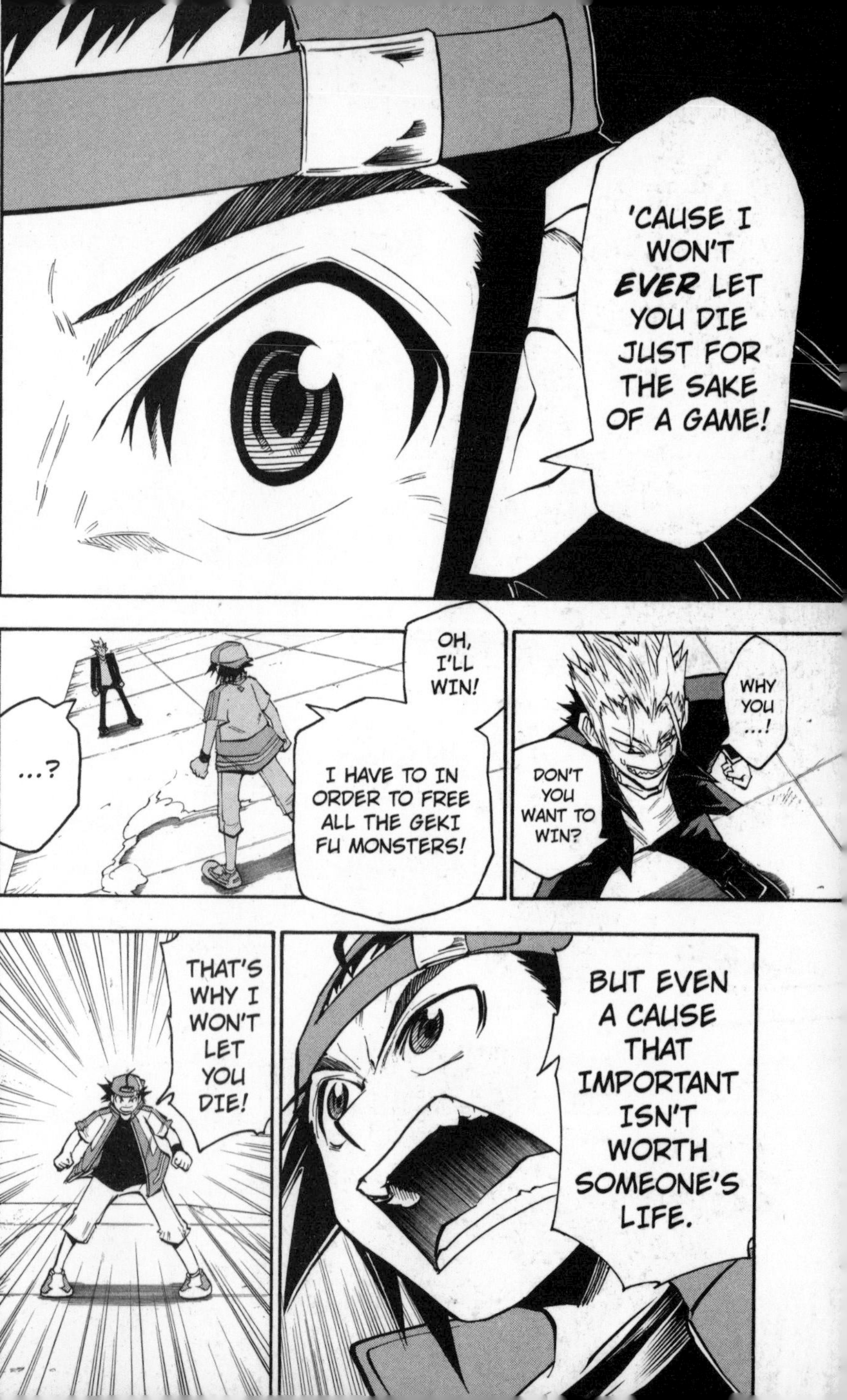
'CAUSE I WON'T **EVER** LET YOU DIE JUST FOR THE SAKE OF A GAME!
WHY YOU ...!
DON'T YOU WANT TO WIN?
OH, I'LL WIN!
I HAVE TO IN ORDER TO FREE ALL THE GEKI FU MONSTERS!
...?
BUT EVEN A CAUSE THAT IMPORTANT ISN'T WORTH SOMEONE'S LIFE.
THAT'S WHY I WON'T LET YOU DIE!

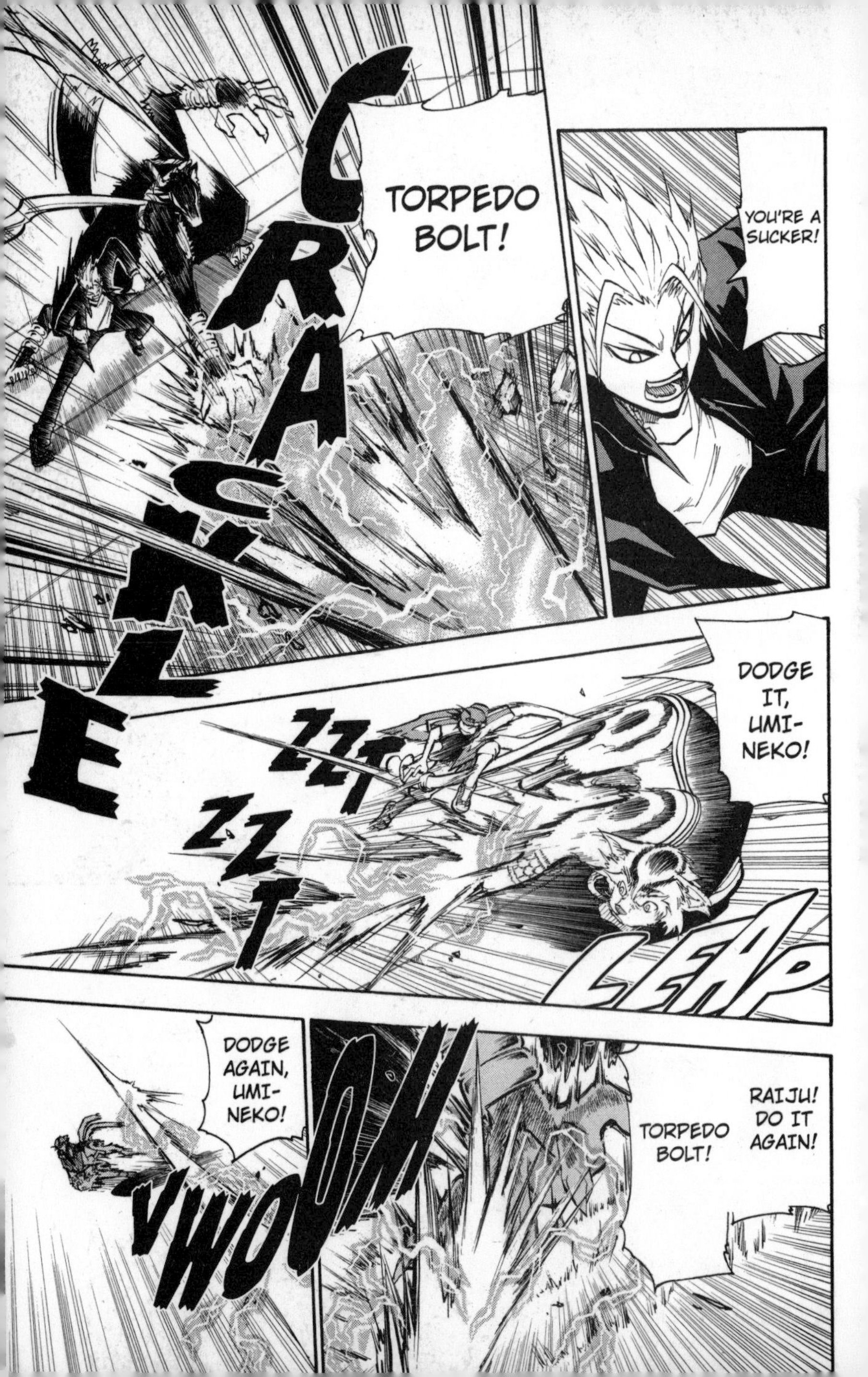
YOU'RE A SUCKER!
TORPEDO BOLT!
CRACKLE
DODGE IT, UMI-NEKO!
ZZZT
ZZT
LEAP
RAIJU! DO IT AGAIN!
TORPEDO BOLT!
DODGE AGAIN, UMI-NEKO!
VWOOM

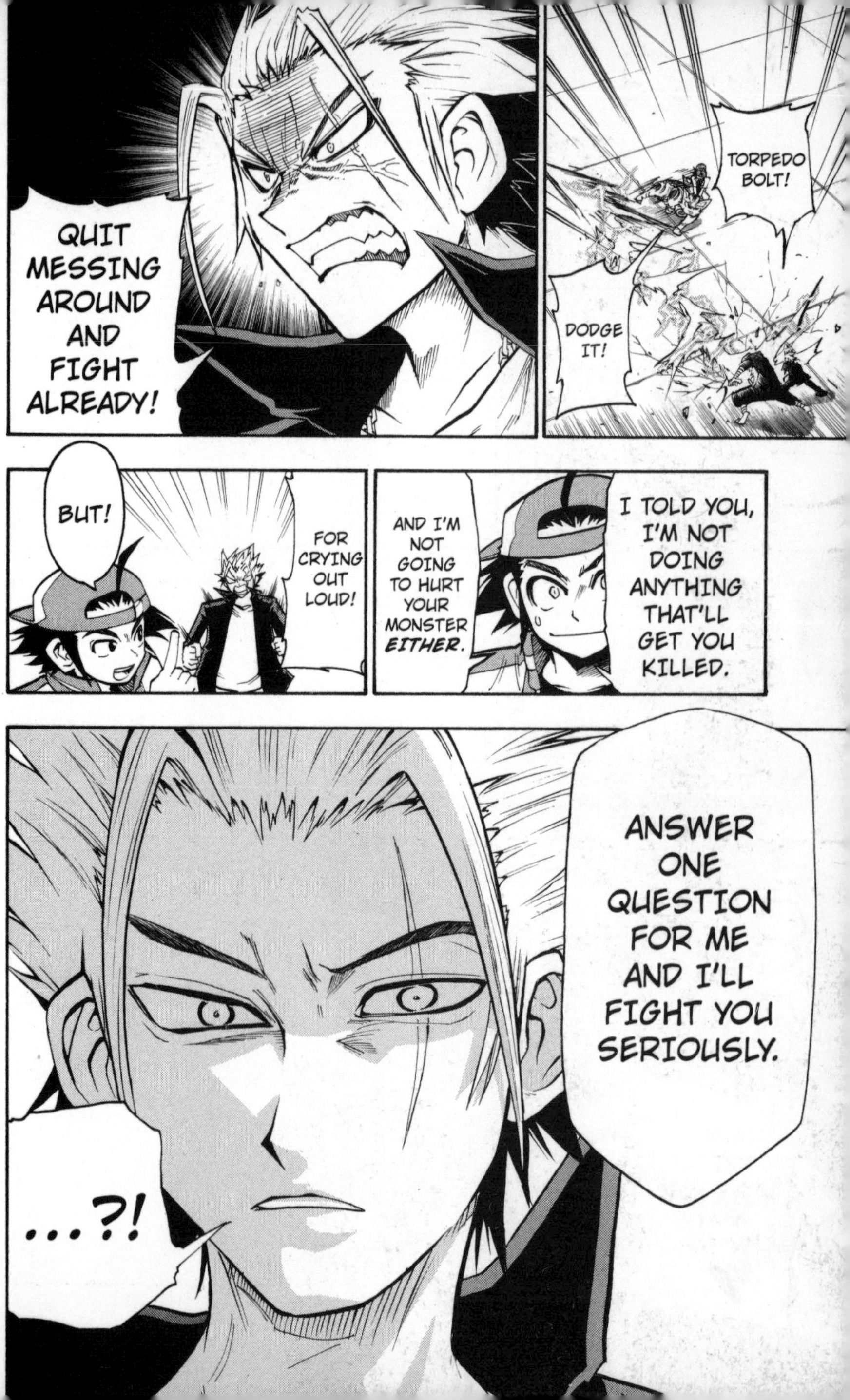
TORPEDO BOLT!
DODGE IT!
QUIT MESSING AROUND AND FIGHT ALREADY!
I TOLD YOU, I'M NOT DOING ANYTHING THAT'LL GET YOU KILLED.
AND I'M NOT GOING TO HURT YOUR MONSTER *EITHER*.
FOR CRYING OUT LOUD!
BUT!
ANSWER ONE QUESTION FOR ME AND I'LL FIGHT YOU SERIOUSLY.
...?!

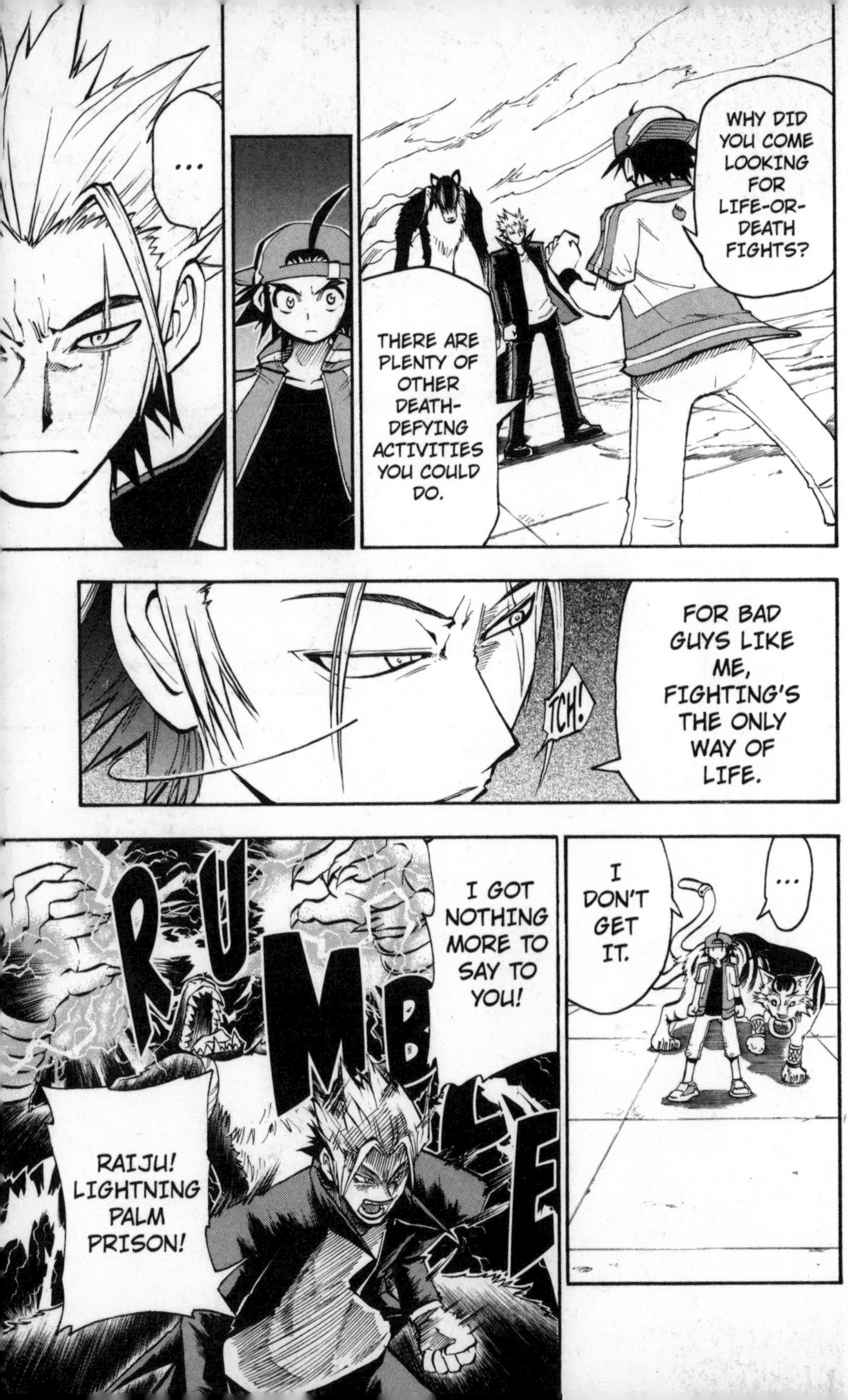
WHY DID YOU COME LOOKING FOR LIFE-OR-DEATH FIGHTS?
THERE ARE PLENTY OF OTHER DEATH-DEFYING ACTIVITIES YOU COULD DO.
...
FOR BAD GUYS LIKE ME, FIGHTING'S THE ONLY WAY OF LIFE.
TCH!
...
I DON'T GET IT.
I GOT NOTHING MORE TO SAY TO YOU!
RUMBLE
RAIJU! LIGHTNING PALM PRISON!

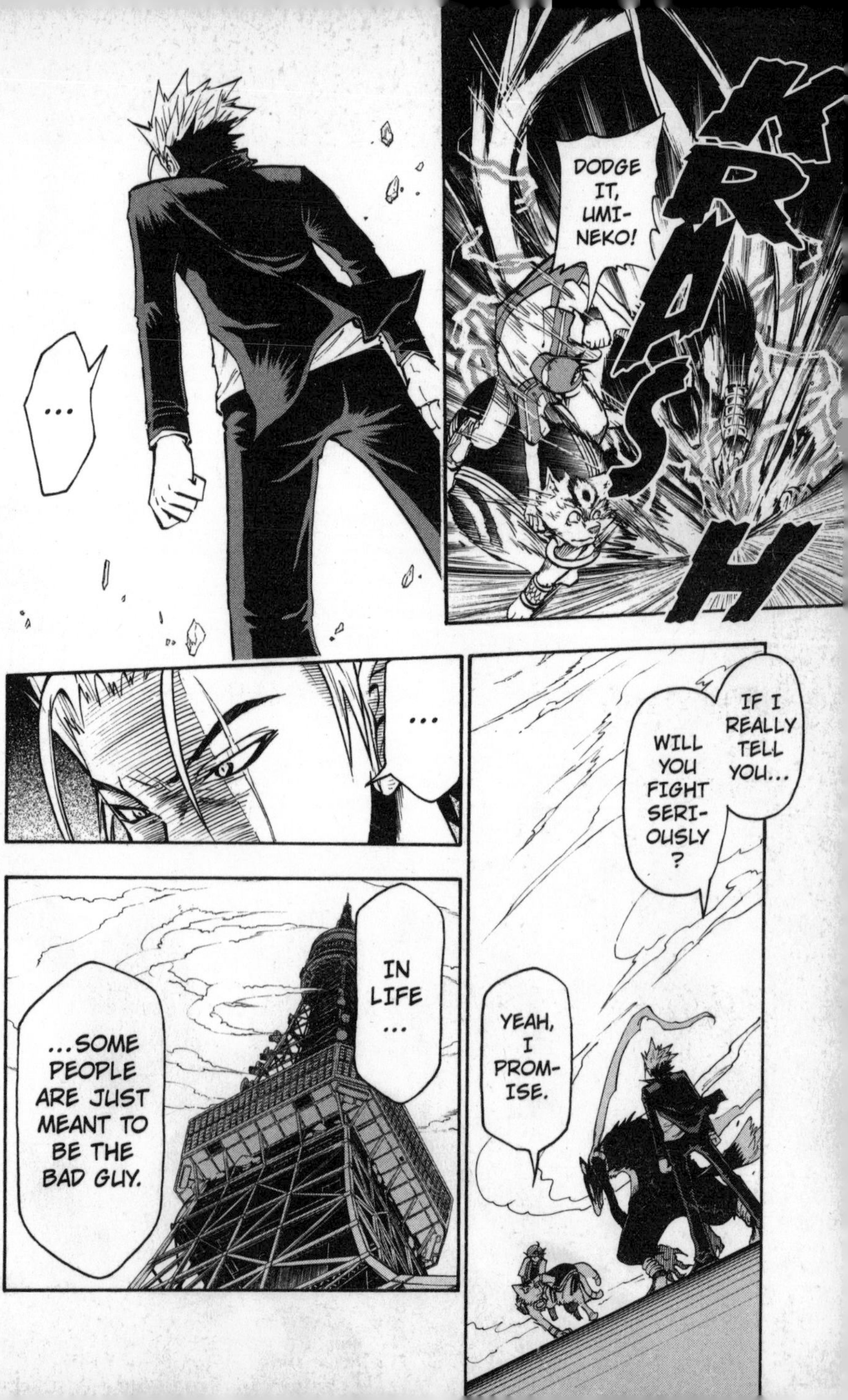
DODGE IT, UMI-NEKO!
KRASH
...
IF I REALLY TELL YOU...
WILL YOU FIGHT SERIOUSLY?
YEAH, I PROMISE.
...
IN LIFE...
...SOME PEOPLE ARE JUST MEANT TO BE THE BAD GUY.

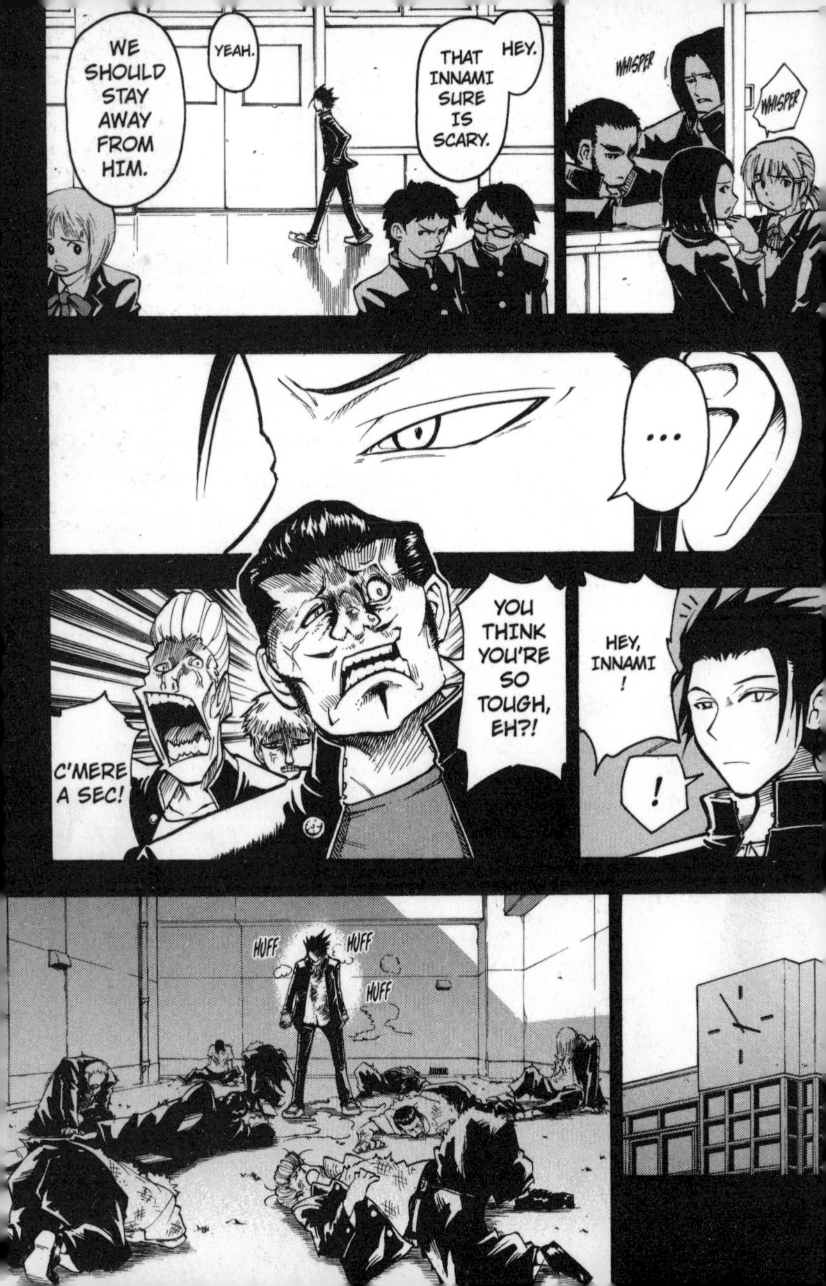
WHISPER
WHISPER
HEY.
THAT INNAMI SURE IS SCARY.
YEAH.
WE SHOULD STAY AWAY FROM HIM.
...
HEY, INNAMI!
!
YOU THINK YOU'RE SO TOUGH, EH?!
C'MERE A SEC!
HUFF
HUFF
HUFF

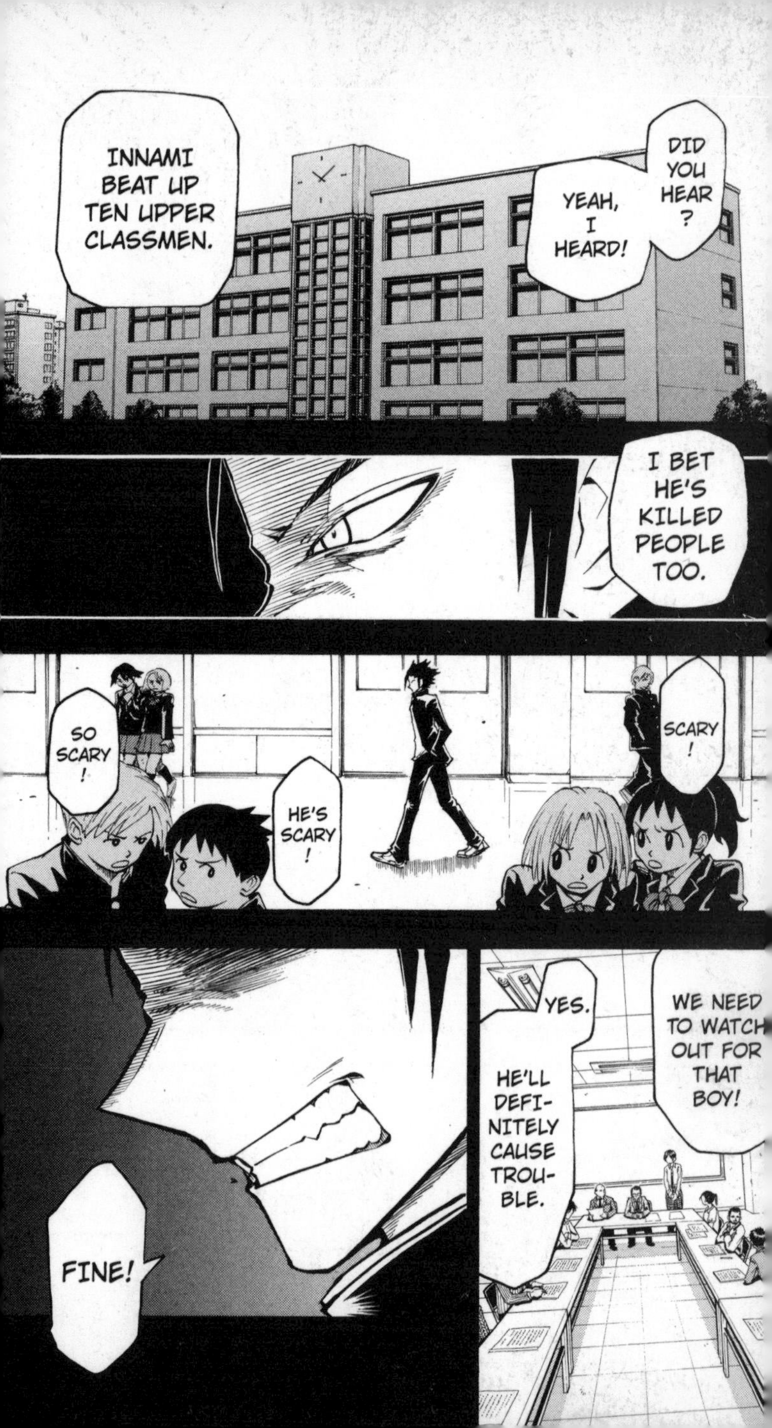
DID YOU HEAR?
YEAH, I HEARD!
INNAMI BEAT UP TEN UPPER CLASSMEN.
I BET HE'S KILLED PEOPLE TOO.
SCARY!
HE'S SCARY!
SO SCARY!
WE NEED TO WATCH OUT FOR THAT BOY!
YES.
HE'LL DEFI-NITELY CAUSE TROU-BLE.
FINE!

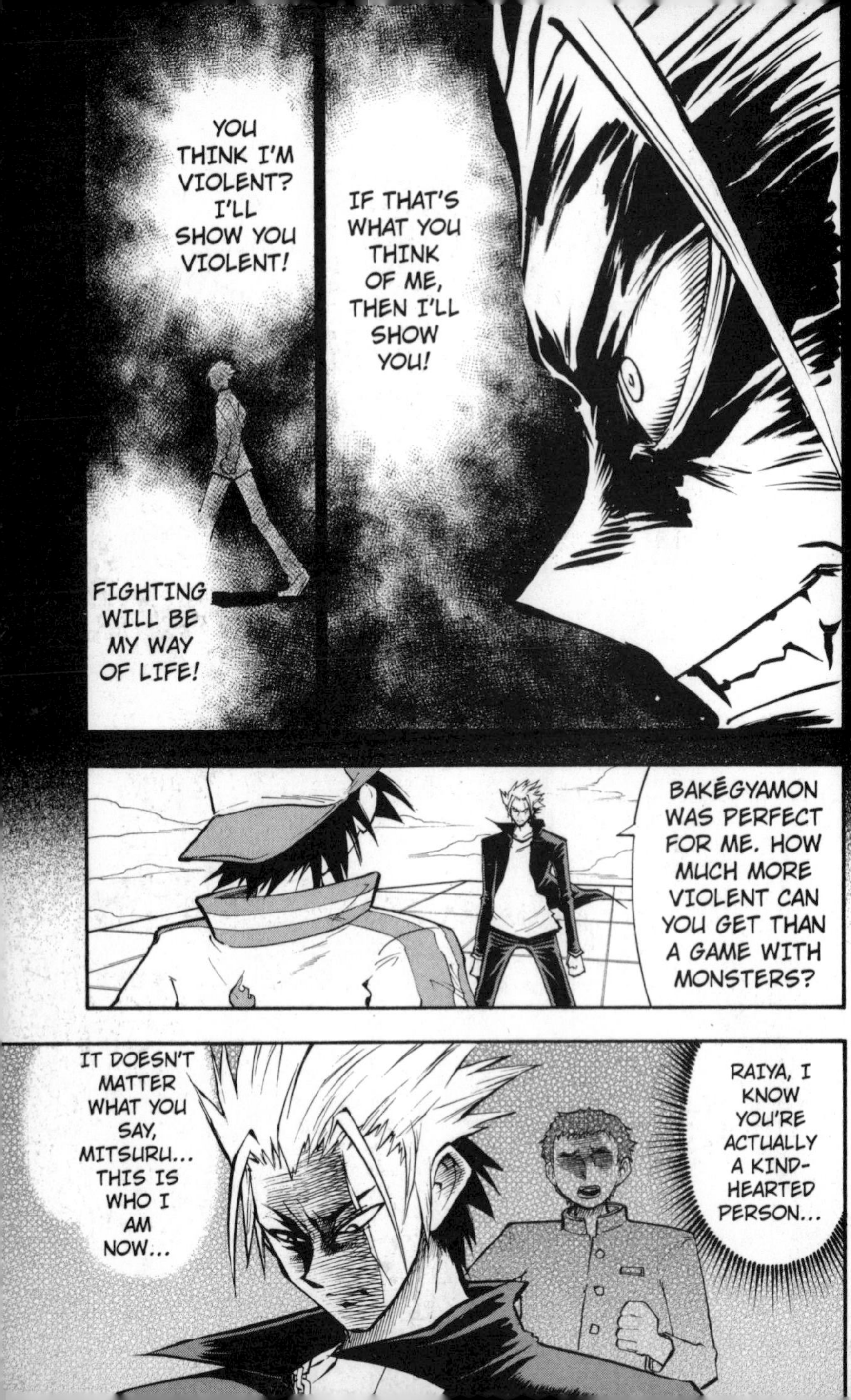
IF THAT'S WHAT YOU THINK OF ME, THEN I'LL SHOW YOU!
YOU THINK I'M VIOLENT? I'LL SHOW YOU VIOLENT!
FIGHTING WILL BE MY WAY OF LIFE!
BAKÉGYAMON WAS PERFECT FOR ME. HOW MUCH MORE VIOLENT CAN YOU GET THAN A GAME WITH MONSTERS?
RAIYA, I KNOW YOU'RE ACTUALLY A KIND-HEARTED PERSON...
IT DOESN'T MATTER WHAT YOU SAY, MITSURU... THIS IS WHO I AM NOW...

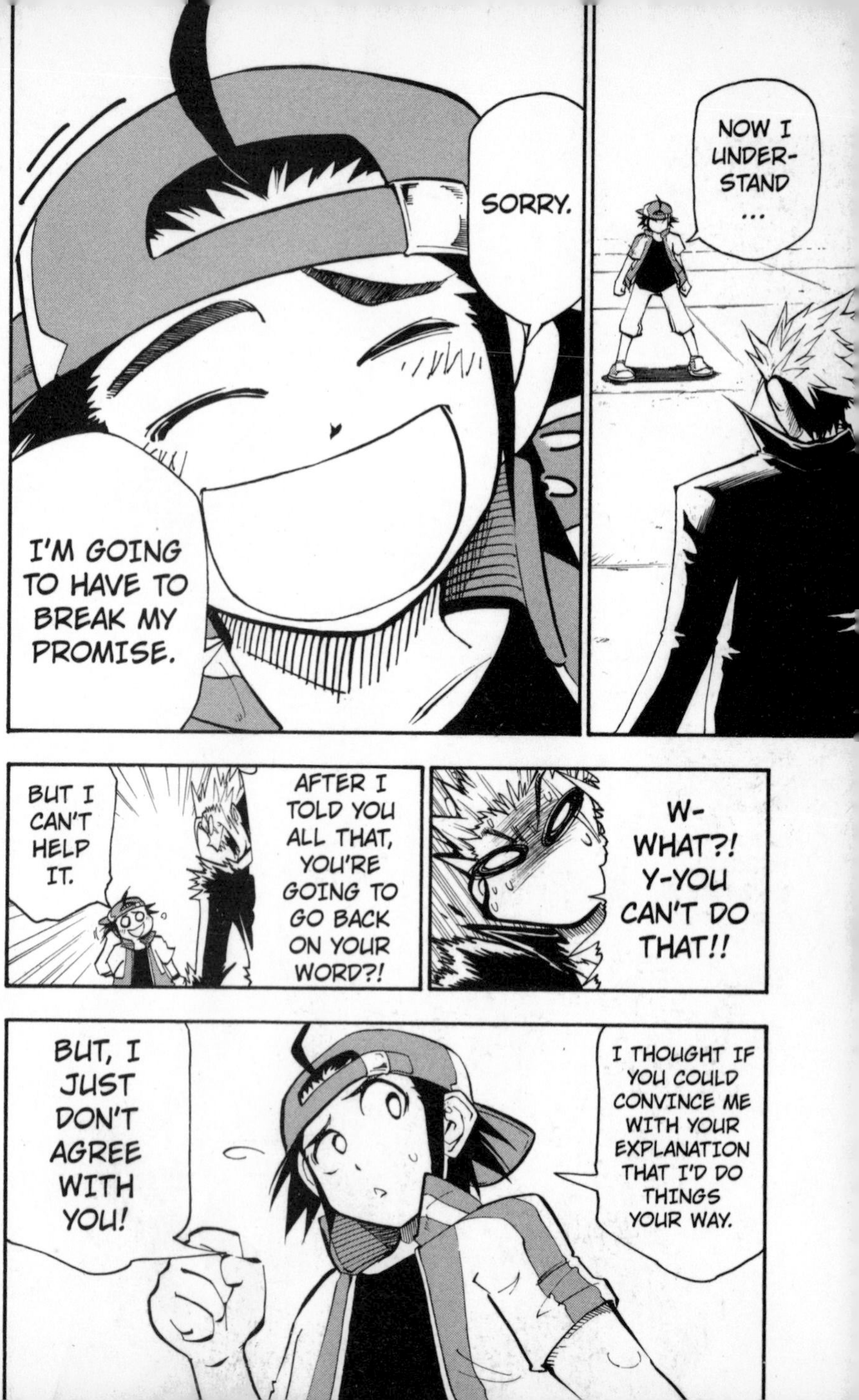
NOW I UNDER-STAND ...
SORRY.
I'M GOING TO HAVE TO BREAK MY PROMISE.
W-WHAT?! Y-YOU CAN'T DO THAT!!
AFTER I TOLD YOU ALL THAT, YOU'RE GOING TO GO BACK ON YOUR WORD?!
BUT I CAN'T HELP IT.
I THOUGHT IF YOU COULD CONVINCE ME WITH YOUR EXPLANATION THAT I'D DO THINGS YOUR WAY.
BUT, I JUST DON'T AGREE WITH YOU!

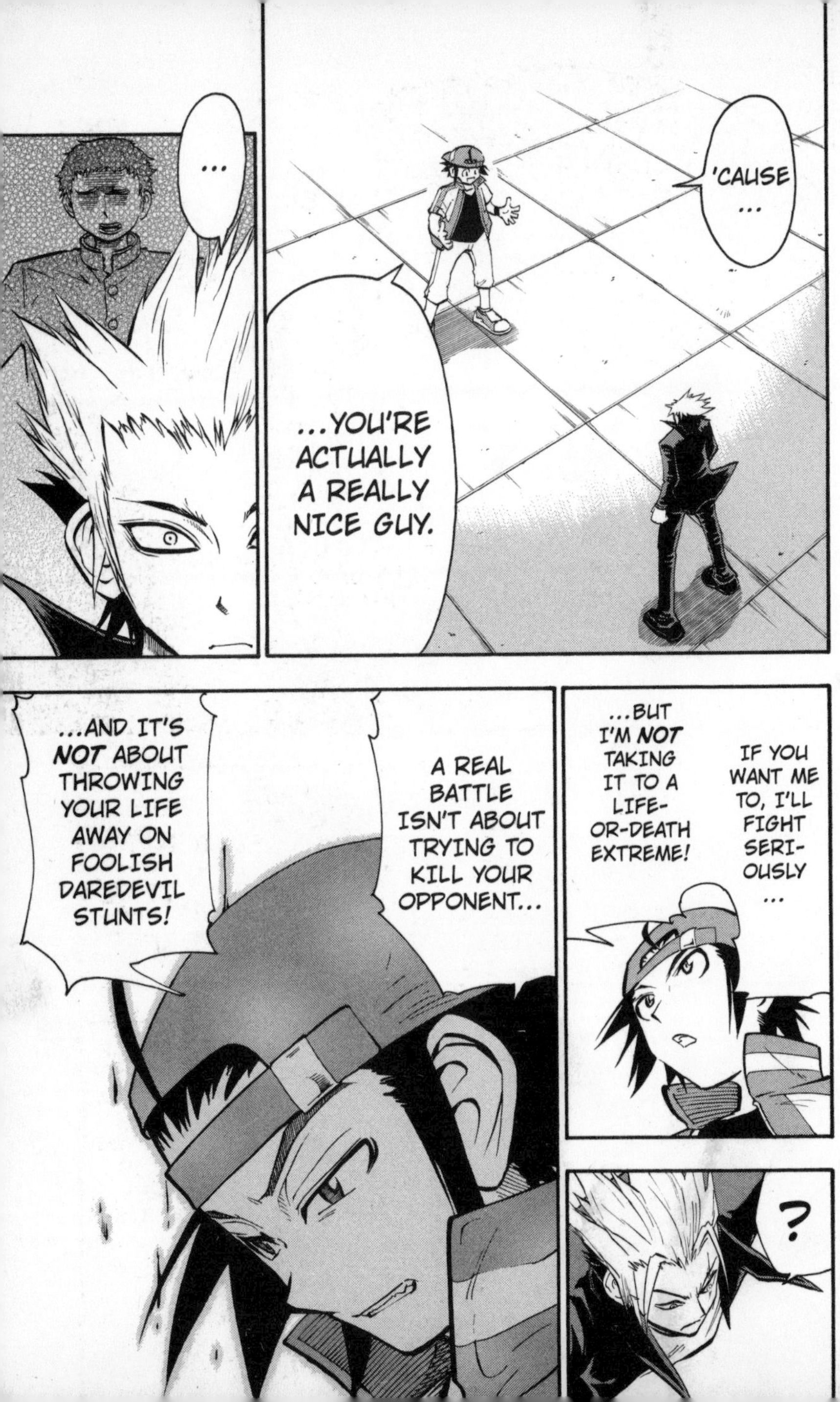

'CAUSE...
...YOU'RE ACTUALLY A REALLY NICE GUY.
...
IF YOU WANT ME TO, I'LL FIGHT SERIOUSLY...
...BUT I'M *NOT* TAKING IT TO A LIFE-OR-DEATH EXTREME!
?
A REAL BATTLE ISN'T ABOUT TRYING TO KILL YOUR OPPONENT...
...AND IT'S *NOT* ABOUT THROWING YOUR LIFE AWAY ON FOOLISH DAREDEVIL STUNTS!

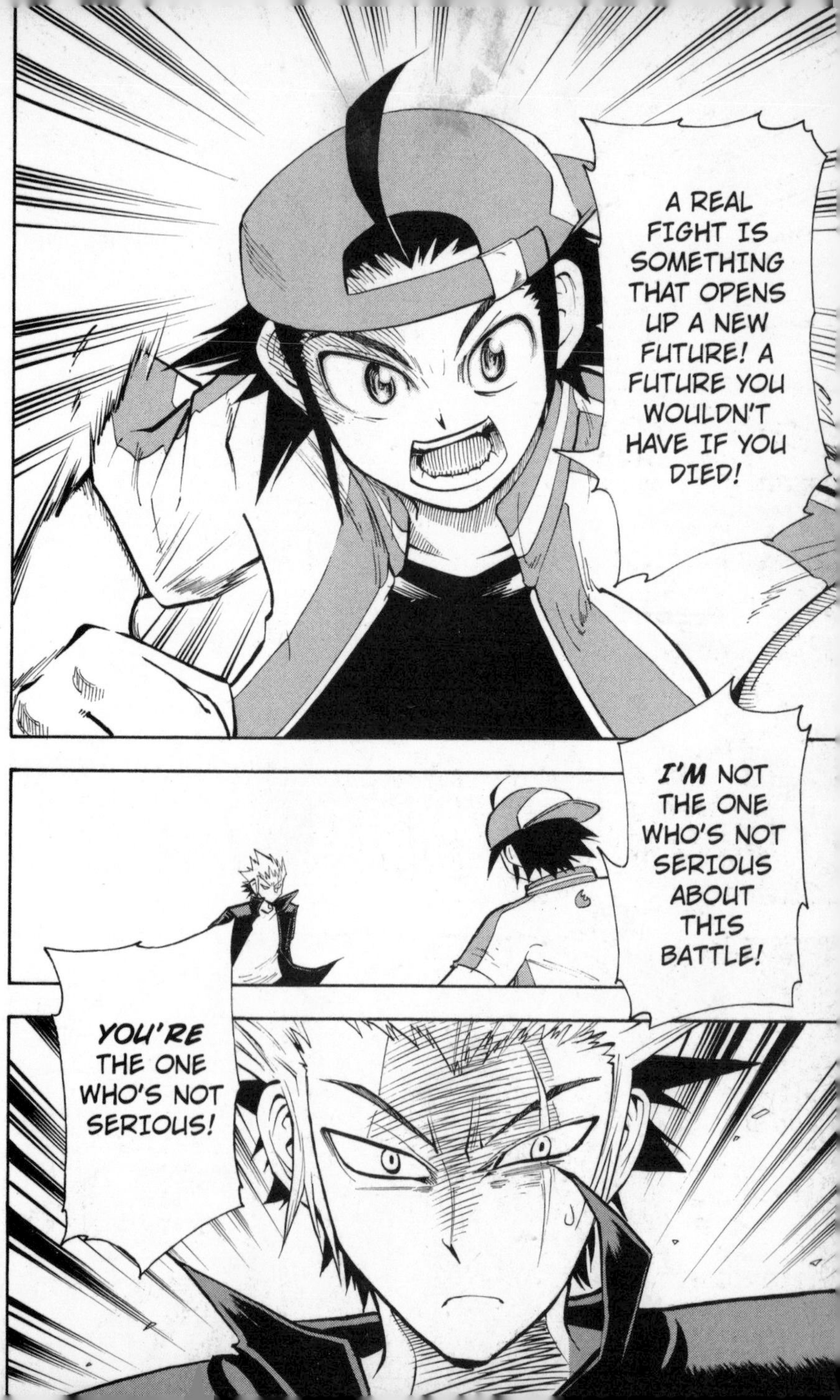
A REAL FIGHT IS SOMETHING THAT OPENS UP A NEW FUTURE! A FUTURE YOU WOULDN'T HAVE IF YOU DIED!
I'M NOT THE ONE WHO'S NOT SERIOUS ABOUT THIS BATTLE!
YOU'RE THE ONE WHO'S NOT SERIOUS!

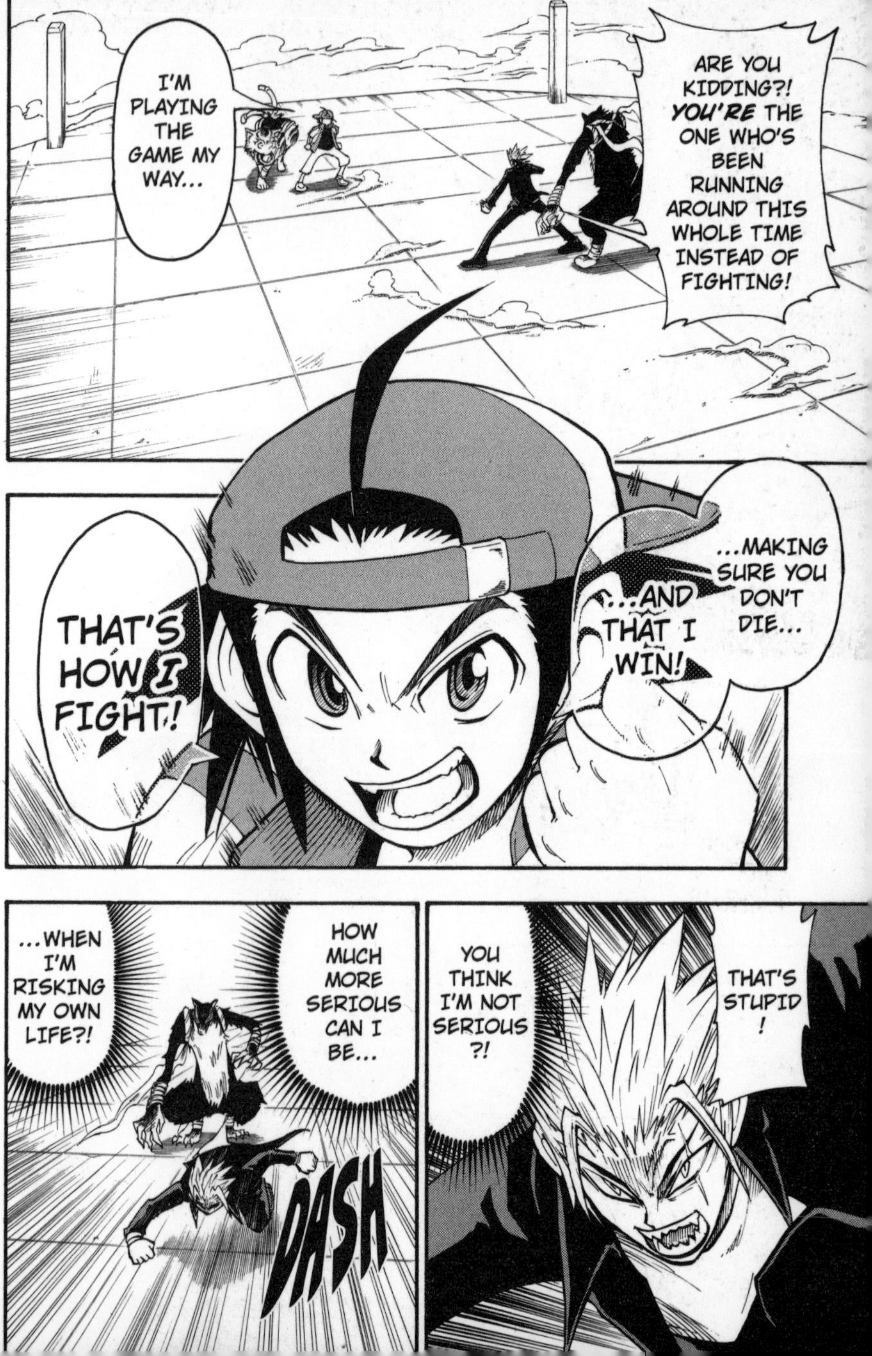
ARE YOU KIDDING?! *YOU'RE* THE ONE WHO'S BEEN RUNNING AROUND THIS WHOLE TIME INSTEAD OF FIGHTING!
I'M PLAYING THE GAME MY WAY...
...MAKING SURE YOU DON'T DIE...
...AND THAT I WIN!
THAT'S HOW *I* FIGHT!
THAT'S STUPID!
YOU THINK I'M NOT SERIOUS?!
HOW MUCH MORE SERIOUS CAN I BE...
...WHEN I'M RISKING MY OWN LIFE?!
DASH

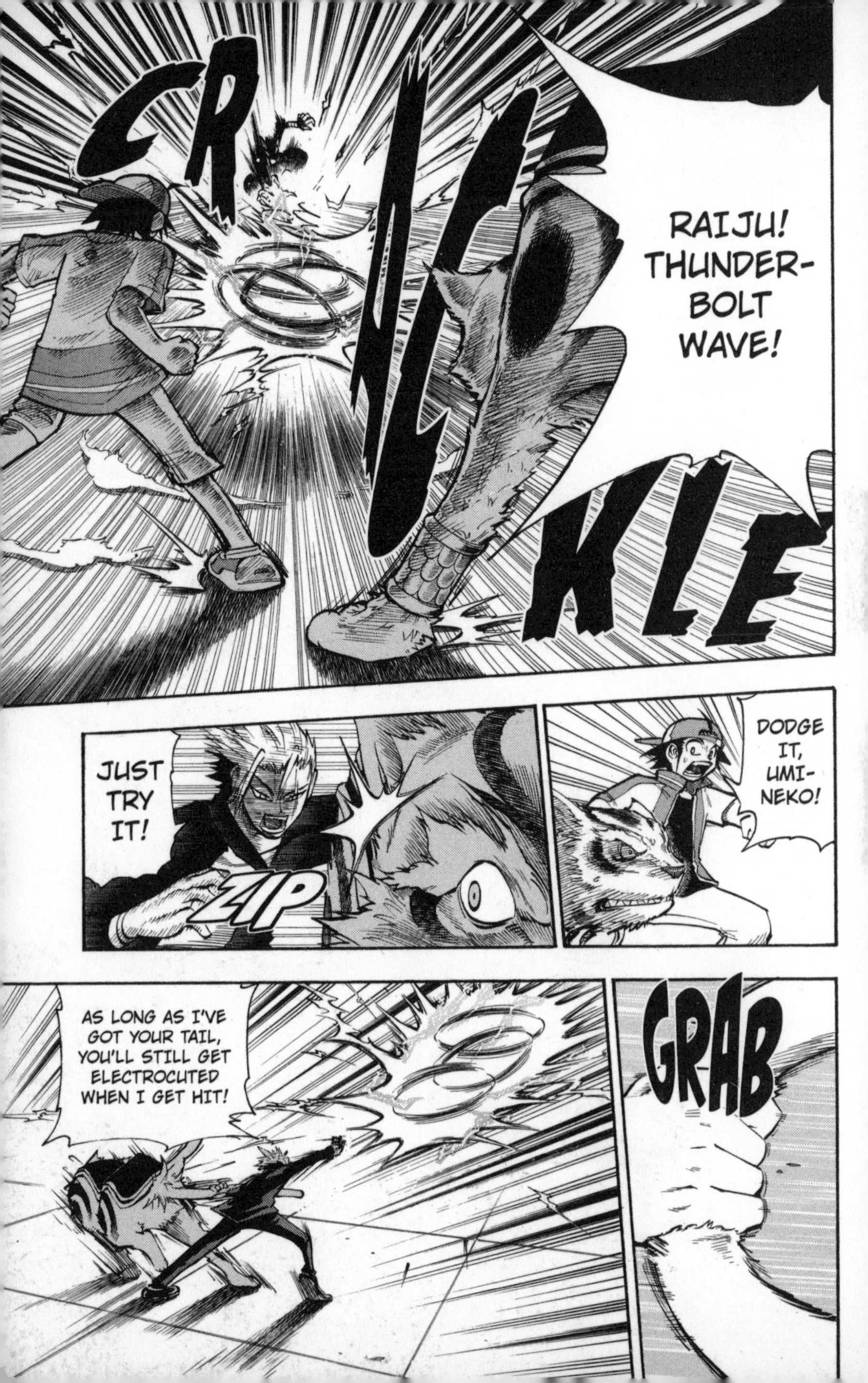
CRACKLE
RAIJU! THUNDER-BOLT WAVE!
DODGE IT, UMI-NEKO!
JUST TRY IT!
ZIP
GRAB
AS LONG AS I'VE GOT YOUR TAIL, YOU'LL STILL GET ELECTROCUTED WHEN I GET HIT!

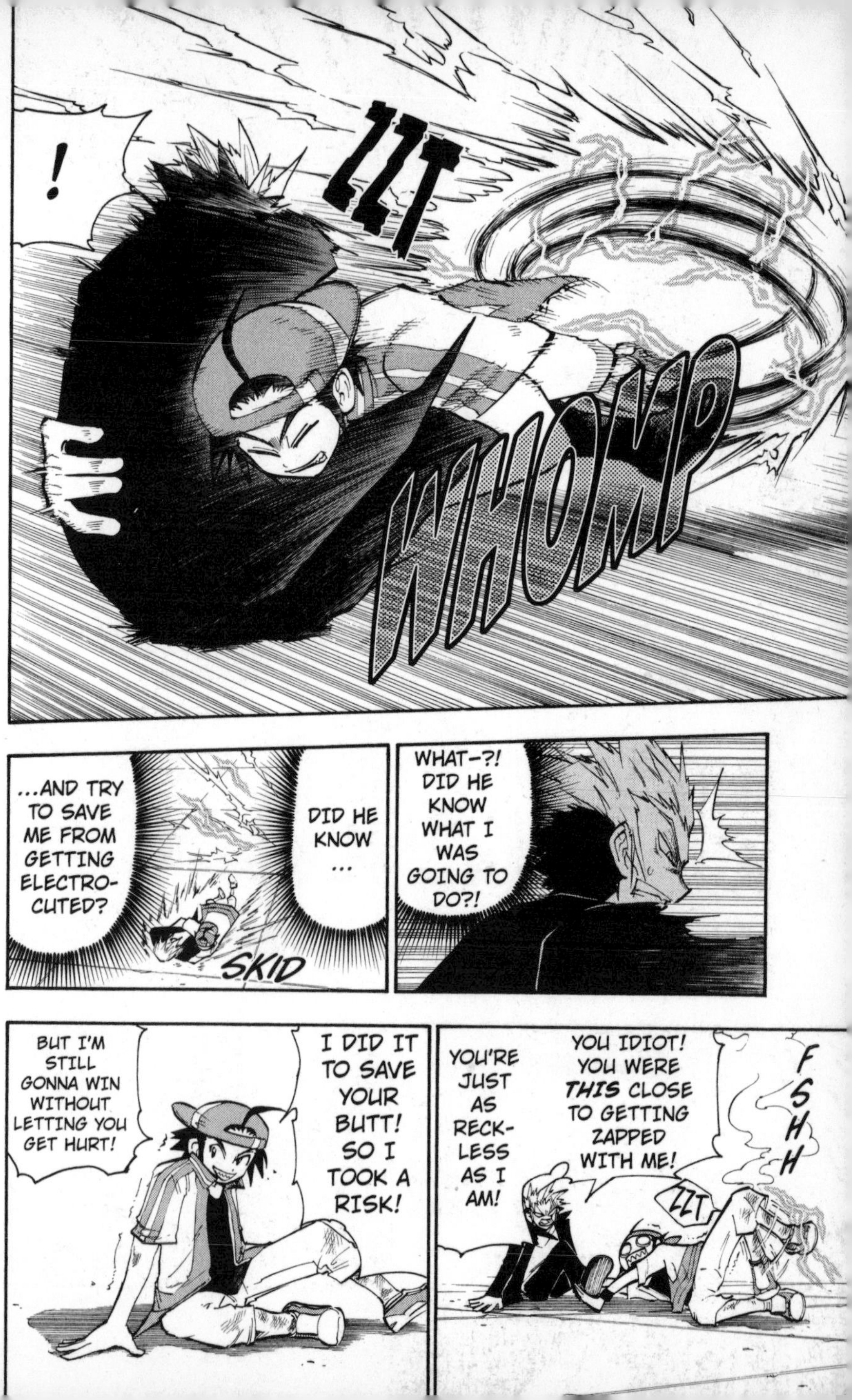
ZZT
WHOMP
!
WHAT–?! DID HE KNOW WHAT I WAS GOING TO DO?!
DID HE KNOW ...
...AND TRY TO SAVE ME FROM GETTING ELECTROCUTED?
SKID
FSHH
YOU IDIOT! YOU WERE *THIS* CLOSE TO GETTING ZAPPED WITH ME!
YOU'RE JUST AS RECKLESS AS I AM!
ZZT
I DID IT TO SAVE YOUR BUTT! SO I TOOK A RISK!
BUT I'M STILL GONNA WIN WITHOUT LETTING YOU GET HURT!

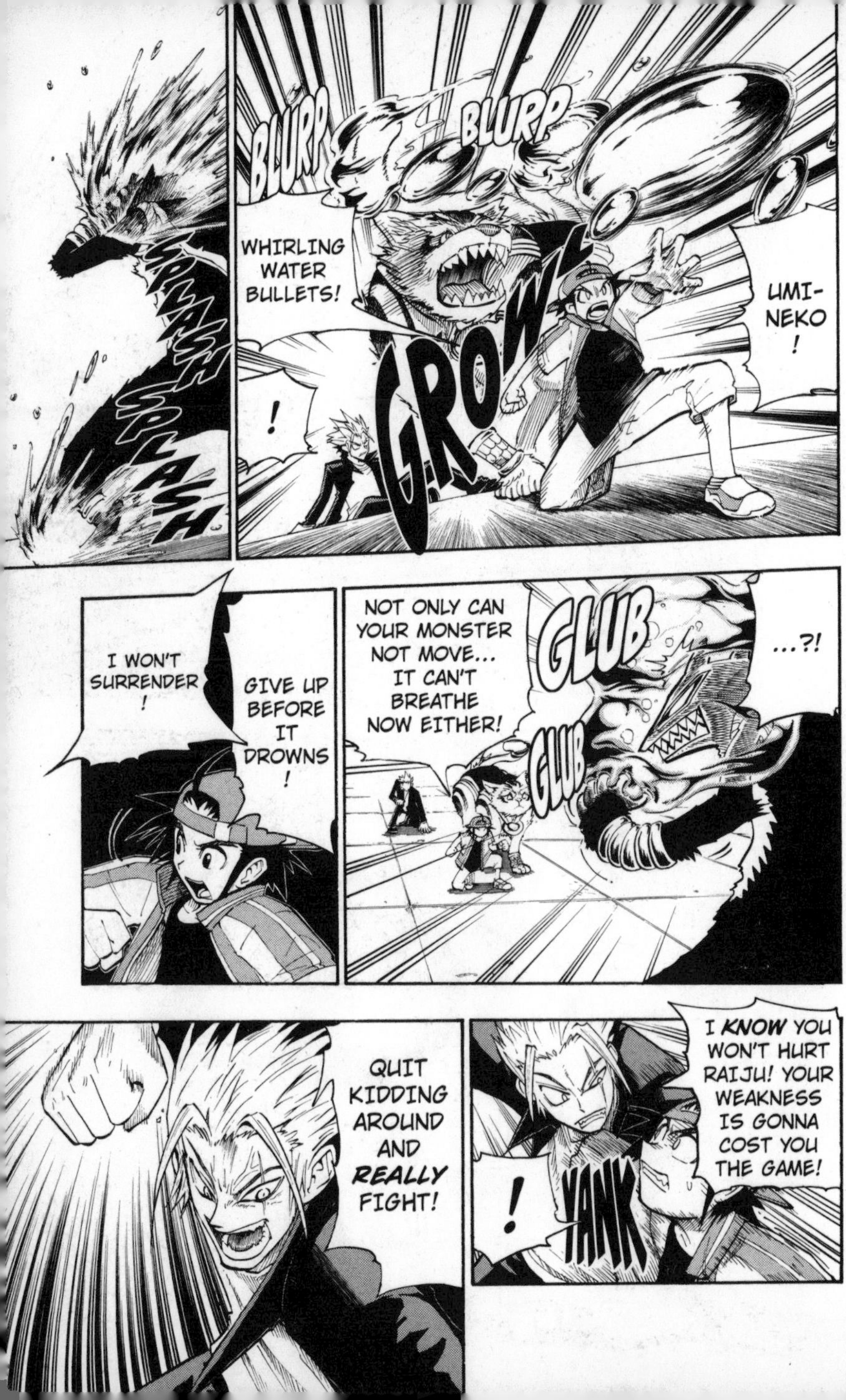
BLURP
BLURP
UMI-NEKO!
WHIRLING WATER BULLETS!
GROWL
!
SPLASH
SPLASH
...?!
GLUB
GLUB
NOT ONLY CAN YOUR MONSTER NOT MOVE... IT CAN'T BREATHE NOW EITHER!
GIVE UP BEFORE IT DROWNS!
I WON'T SURRENDER!
I ***KNOW*** YOU WON'T HURT RAIJU! YOUR WEAKNESS IS GONNA COST YOU THE GAME!
YANK
!
QUIT KIDDING AROUND AND ***REALLY*** FIGHT!

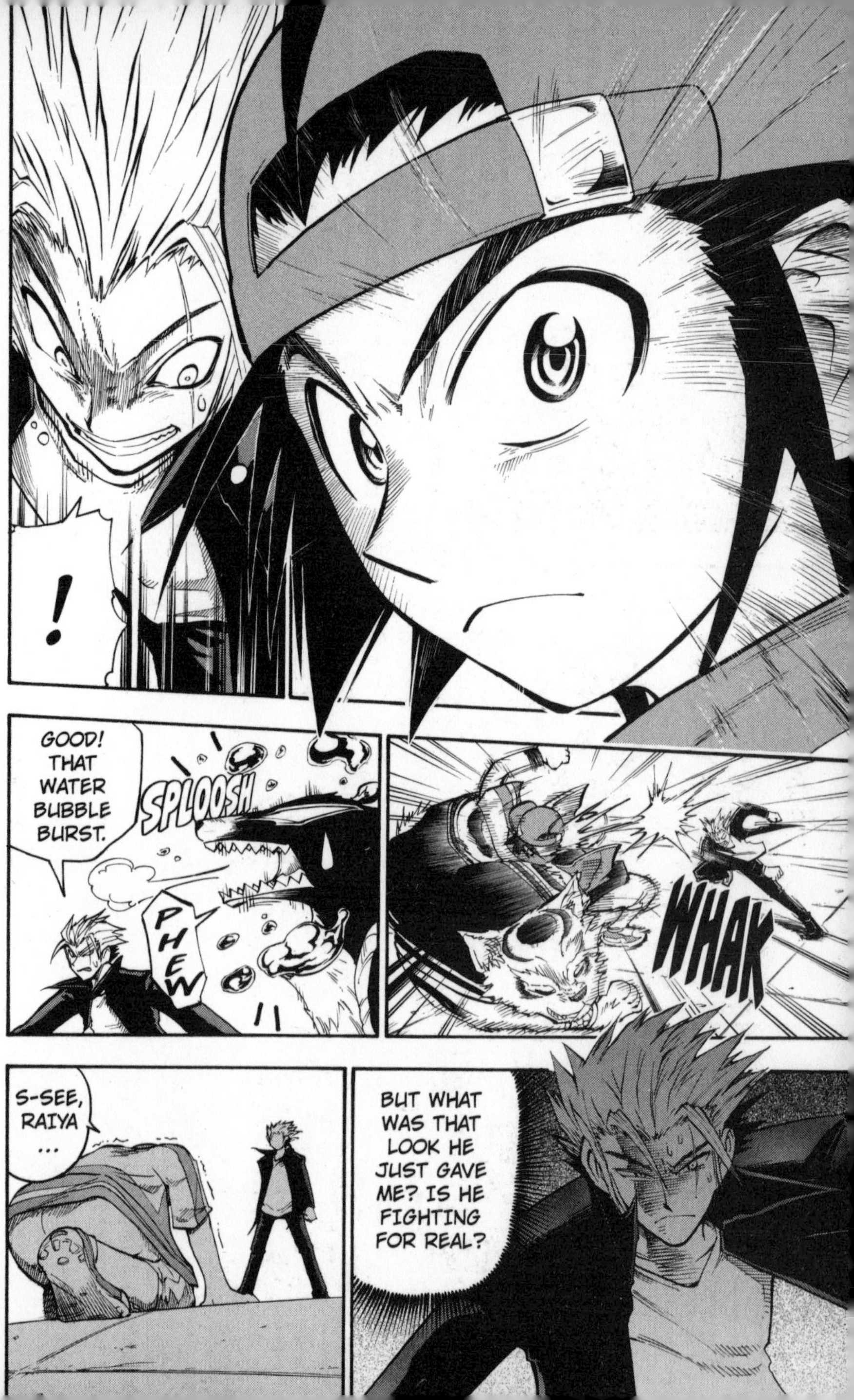
!
WHAK
GOOD! THAT WATER BUBBLE BURST.
SPLOOSH
PHEW
BUT WHAT WAS THAT LOOK HE JUST GAVE ME? IS HE FIGHTING FOR REAL?
S-SEE, RAIYA ...

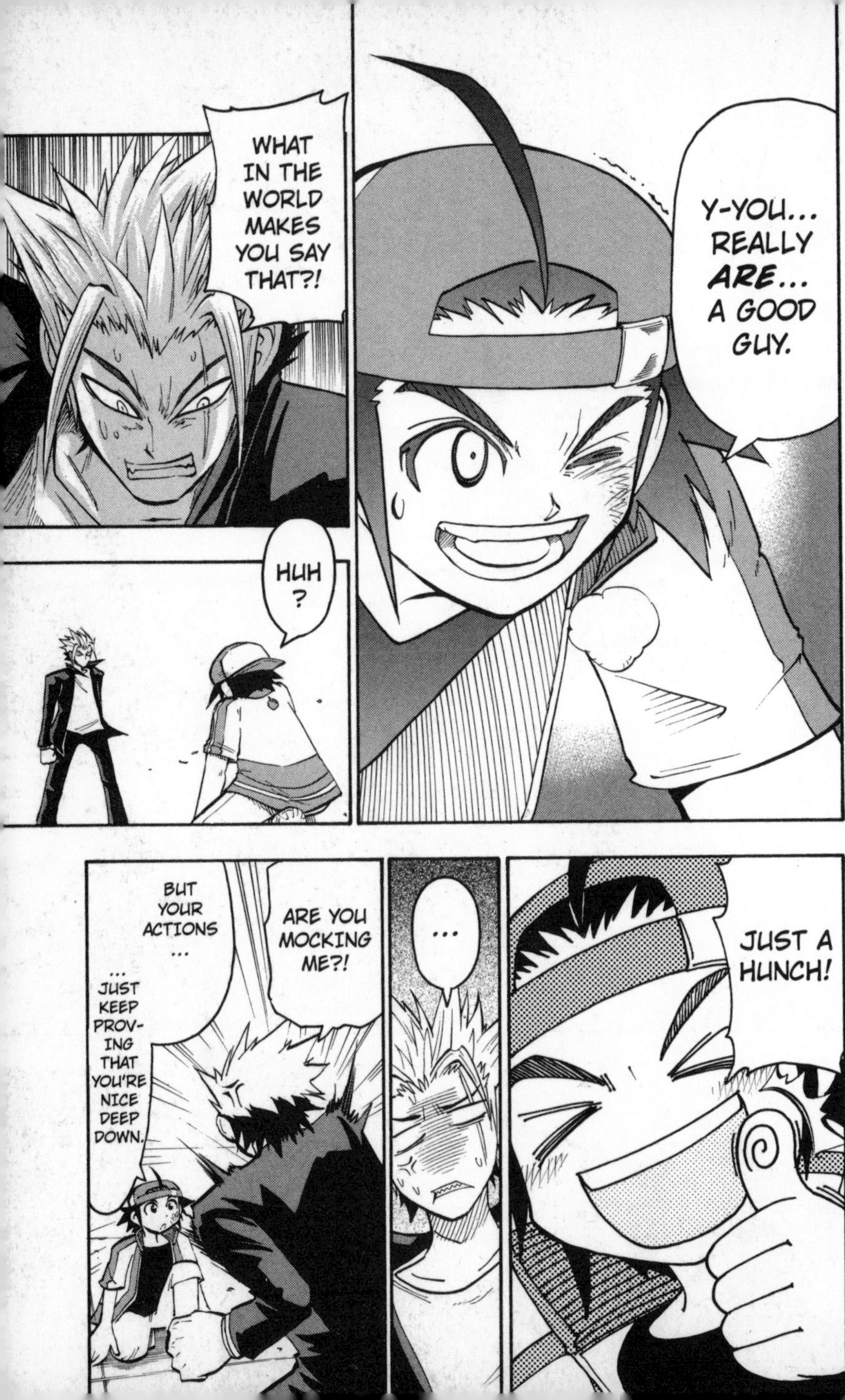
Y-YOU... REALLY ARE... A GOOD GUY.
WHAT IN THE WORLD MAKES YOU SAY THAT?!
HUH?
JUST A HUNCH!
...
ARE YOU MOCKING ME?!
BUT YOUR ACTIONS ...
... JUST KEEP PROVING THAT YOU'RE NICE DEEP DOWN.

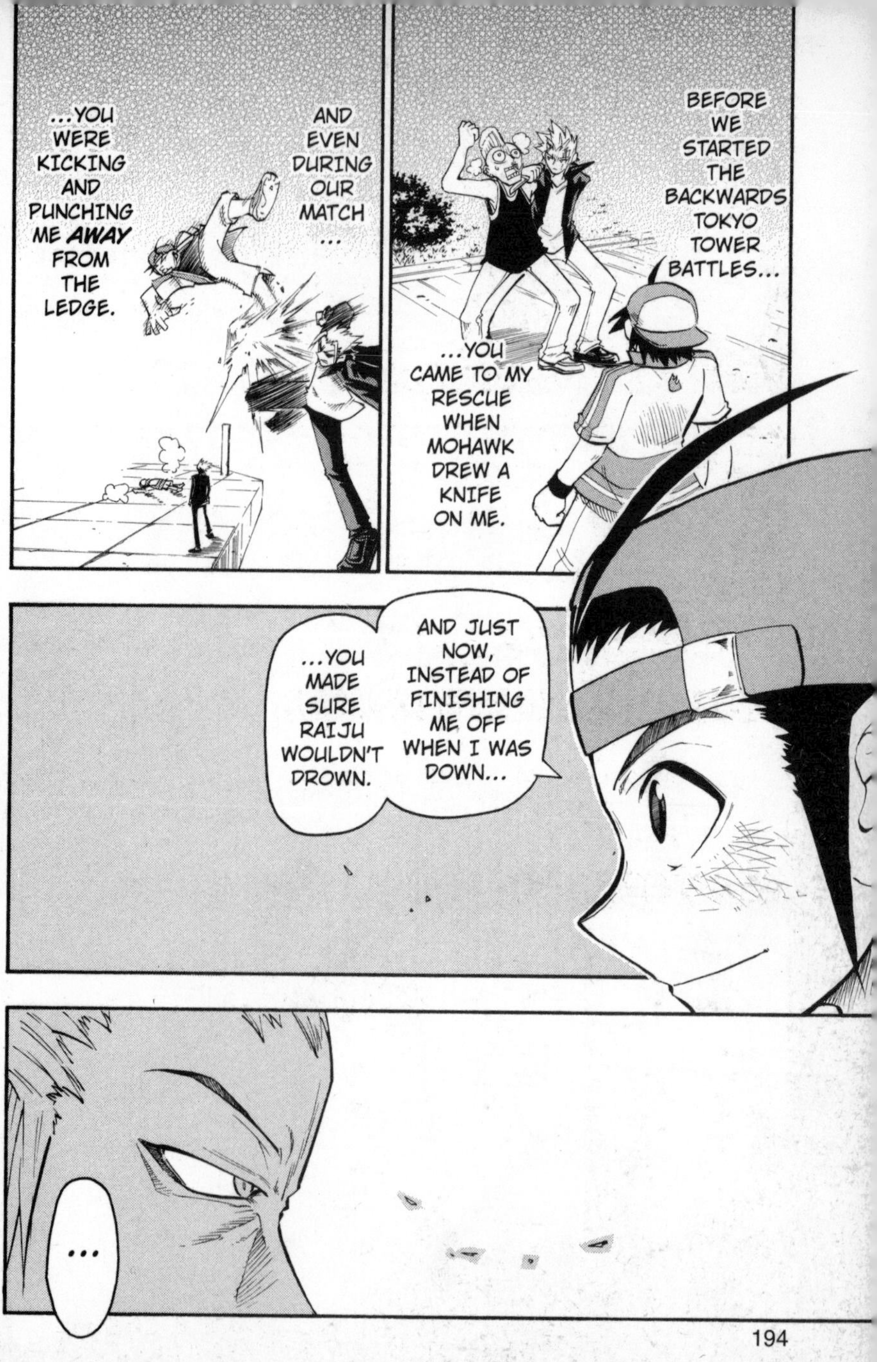
BEFORE WE STARTED THE BACKWARDS TOKYO TOWER BATTLES...
...YOU CAME TO MY RESCUE WHEN MOHAWK DREW A KNIFE ON ME.
AND EVEN DURING OUR MATCH ...
...YOU WERE KICKING AND PUNCHING ME *AWAY* FROM THE LEDGE.
AND JUST NOW, INSTEAD OF FINISHING ME OFF WHEN I WAS DOWN...
...YOU MADE SURE RAIJU WOULDN'T DROWN.
...

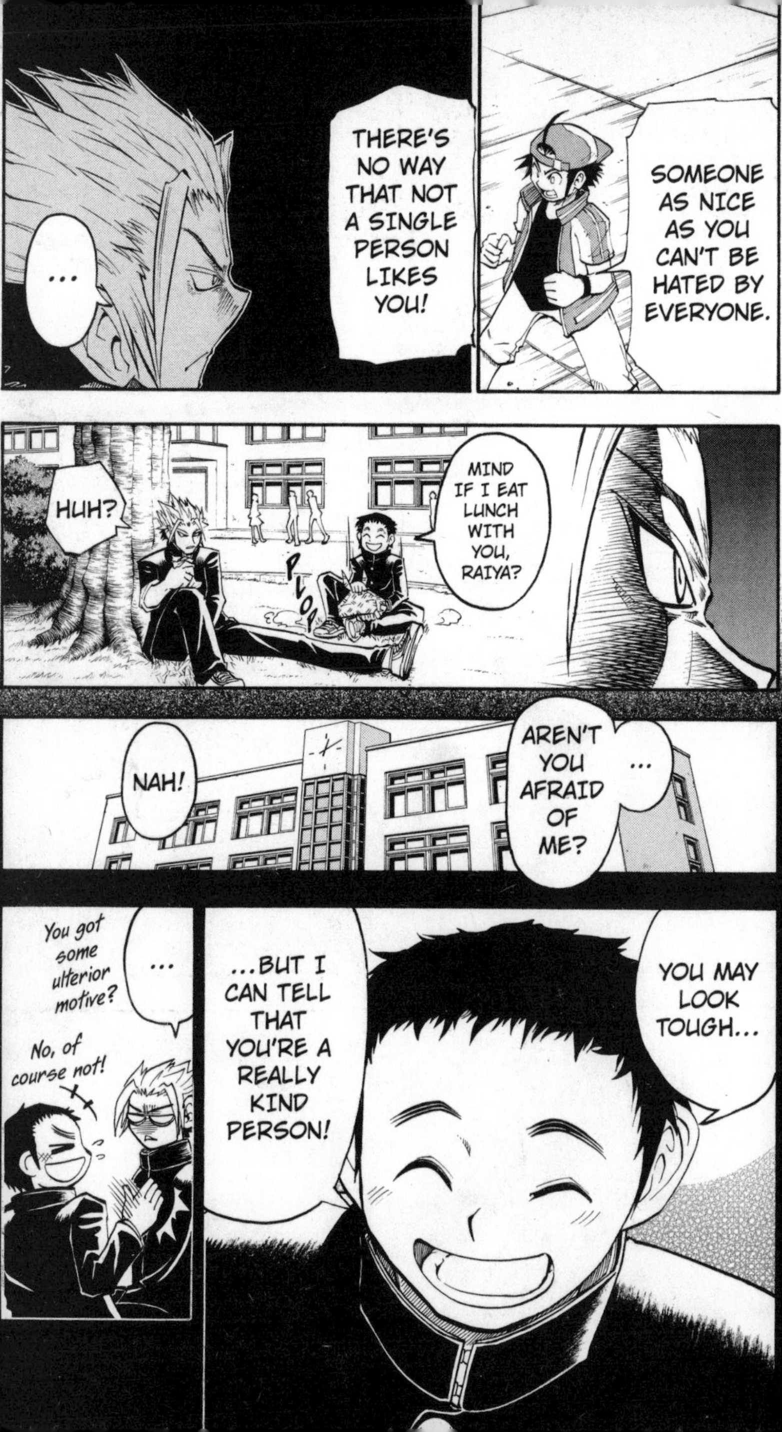
SOMEONE AS NICE AS YOU CAN'T BE HATED BY EVERYONE.
THERE'S NO WAY THAT NOT A SINGLE PERSON LIKES YOU!
...
MIND IF I EAT LUNCH WITH YOU, RAIYA?
PLOP
HUH?
...
AREN'T YOU AFRAID OF ME?
NAH!
YOU MAY LOOK TOUGH...
...BUT I CAN TELL THAT YOU'RE A REALLY KIND PERSON!
...
You got some ulterior motive?
No, of course not!

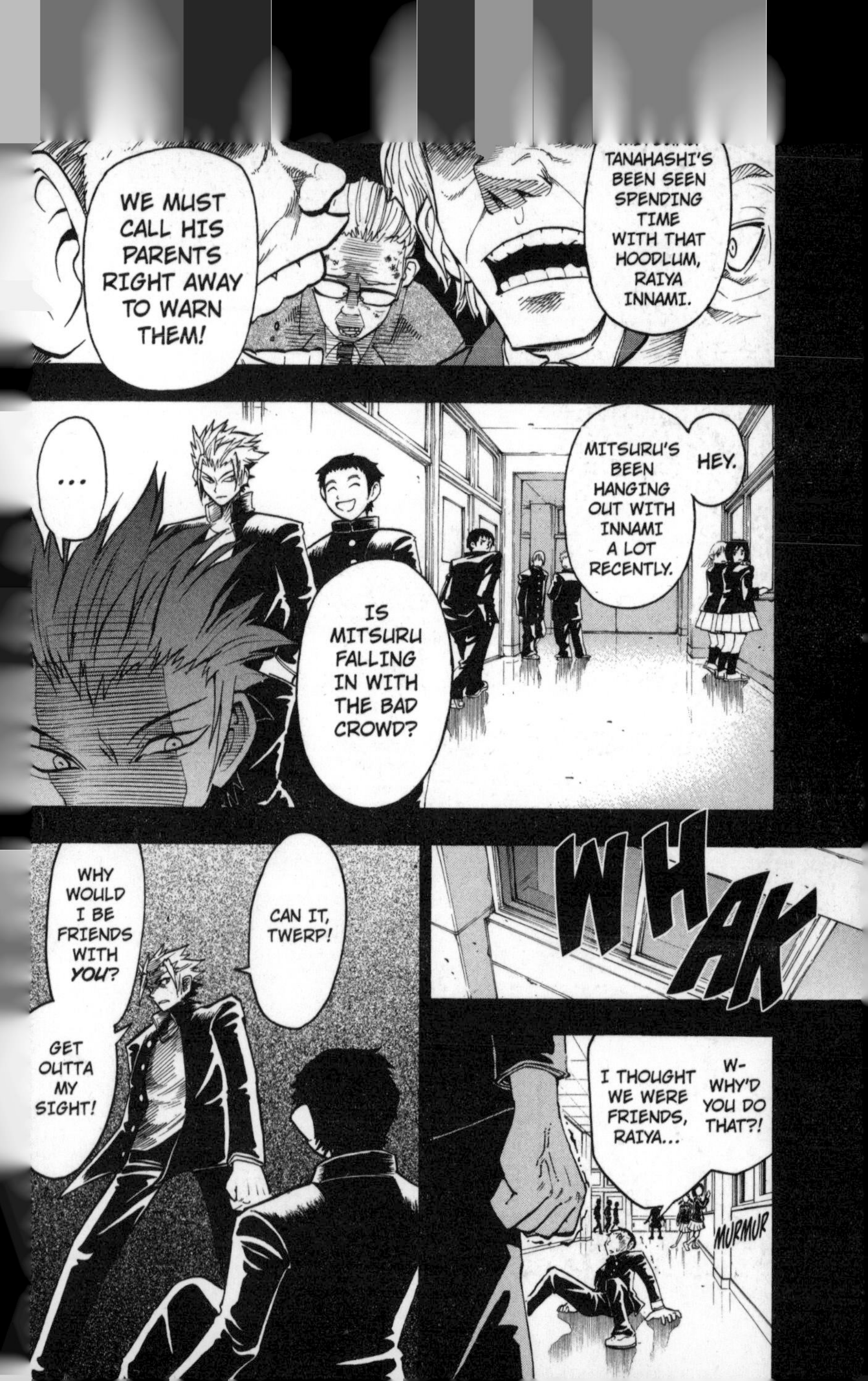
TANAHASHI'S BEEN SEEN SPENDING TIME WITH THAT HOODLUM, RAIYA INNAMI.
WE MUST CALL HIS PARENTS RIGHT AWAY TO WARN THEM!
HEY.
MITSURU'S BEEN HANGING OUT WITH INNAMI A LOT RECENTLY.
IS MITSURU FALLING IN WITH THE BAD CROWD?
...
WHAK
W- WHY'D YOU DO THAT?!
I THOUGHT WE WERE FRIENDS, RAIYA...
MURMUR
CAN IT, TWERP!
WHY WOULD I BE FRIENDS WITH *YOU*?
GET OUTTA MY SIGHT!

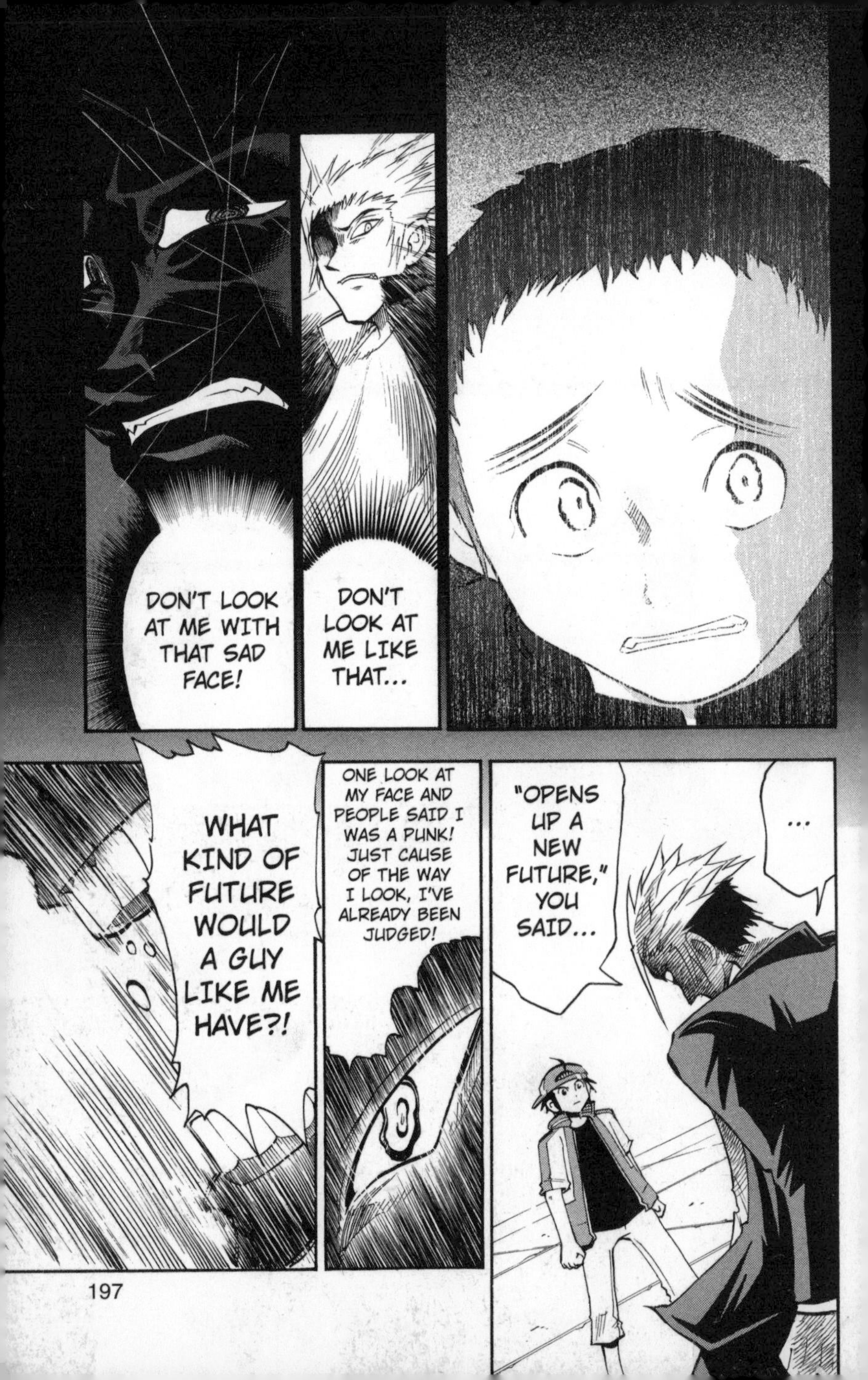
DON'T LOOK AT ME LIKE THAT...
DON'T LOOK AT ME WITH THAT SAD FACE!
...
"OPENS UP A NEW FUTURE," YOU SAID...
ONE LOOK AT MY FACE AND PEOPLE SAID I WAS A PUNK! JUST CAUSE OF THE WAY I LOOK, I'VE ALREADY BEEN JUDGED!
WHAT KIND OF FUTURE WOULD A GUY LIKE ME HAVE?!

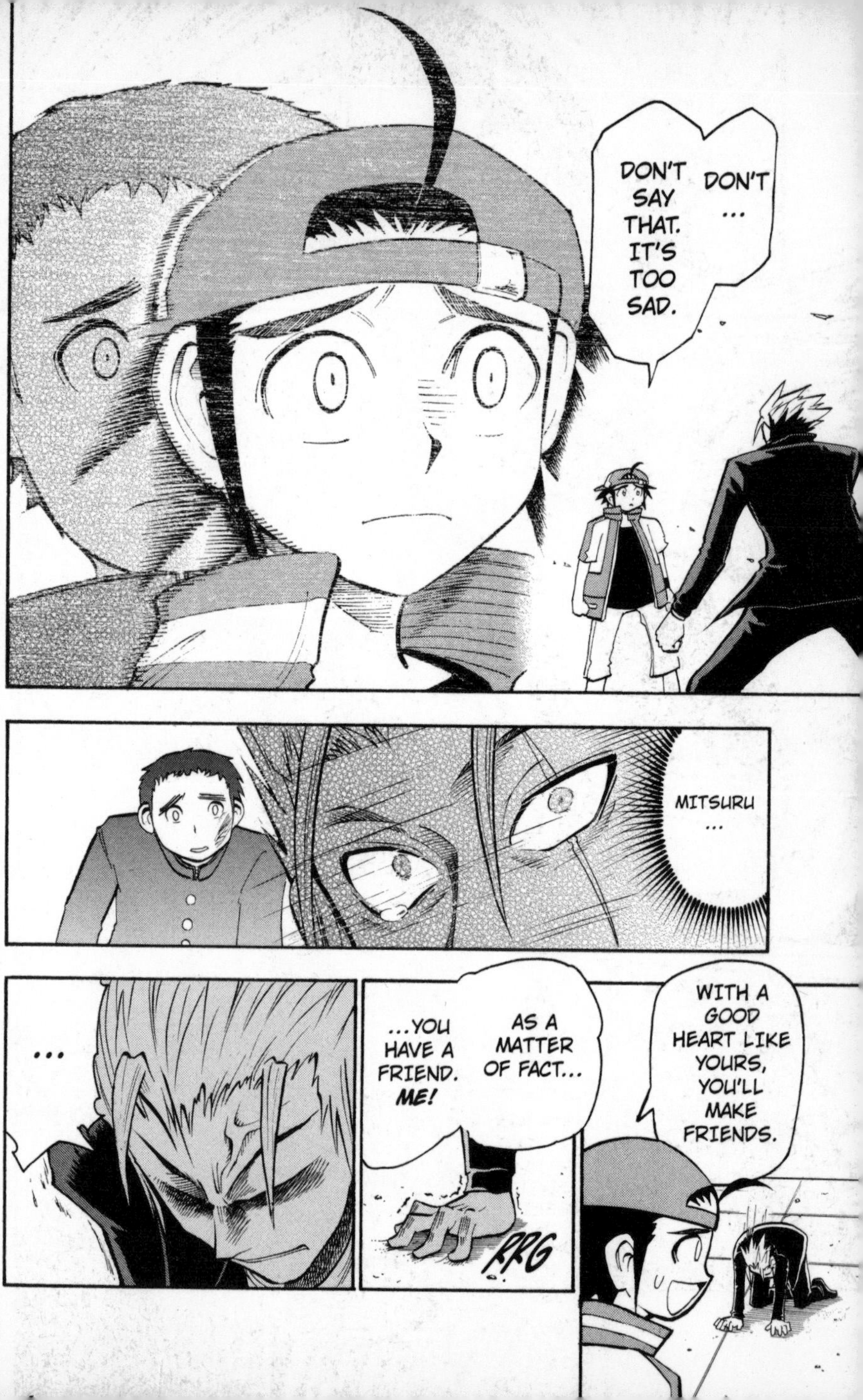
DON'T ...
DON'T SAY THAT. IT'S TOO SAD.
MITSURU ...
WITH A GOOD HEART LIKE YOURS, YOU'LL MAKE FRIENDS.
AS A MATTER OF FACT...
...YOU HAVE A FRIEND. ME!
RRG
...

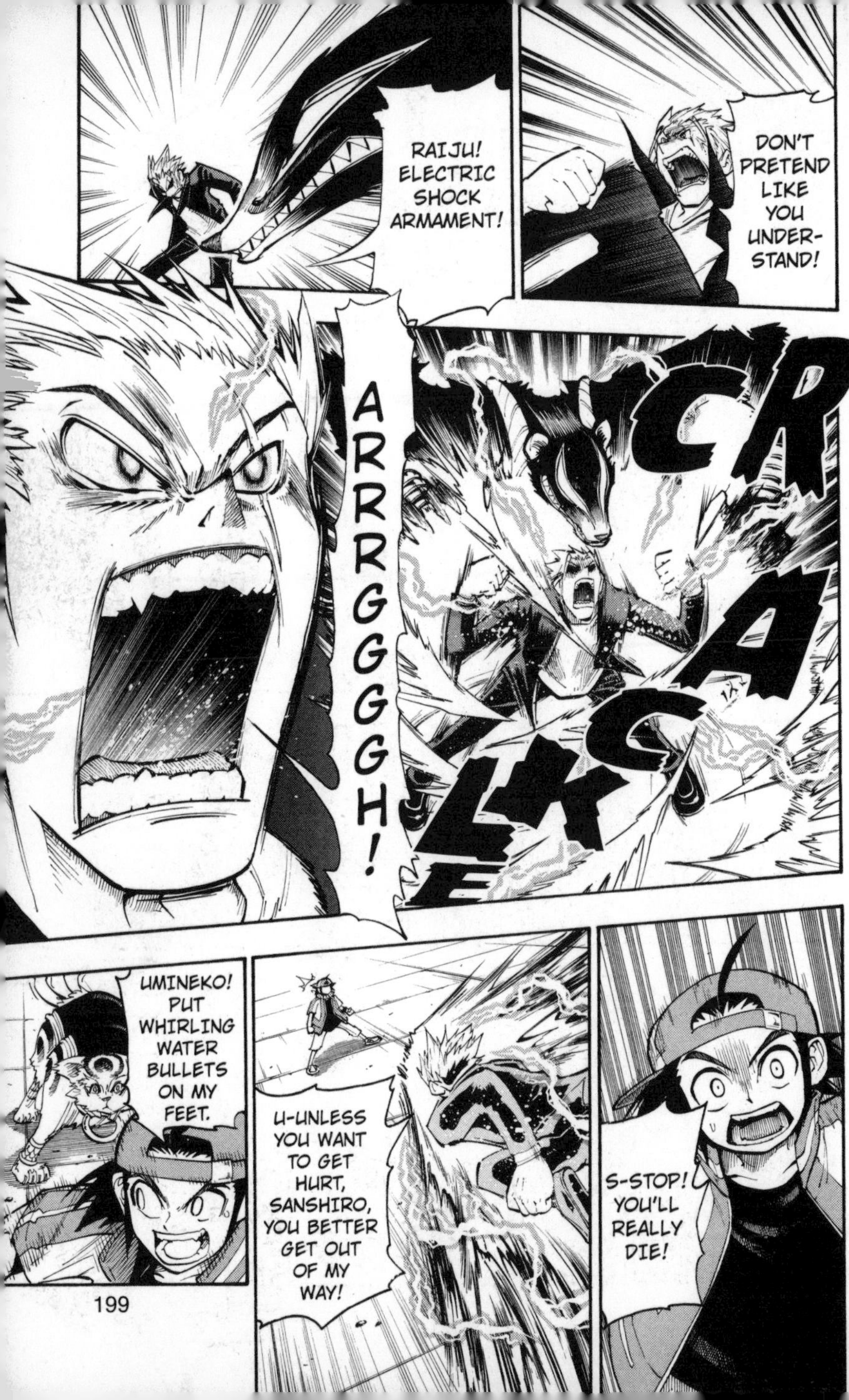
DON'T PRETEND LIKE YOU UNDER-STAND!
RAIJU! ELECTRIC SHOCK ARMAMENT!
CRACKLE
ARRRRGGGGGH!
S-STOP! YOU'LL REALLY DIE!
U-UNLESS YOU WANT TO GET HURT, SANSHIRO, YOU BETTER GET OUT OF MY WAY!
UMINEKO! PUT WHIRLING WATER BULLETS ON MY FEET.

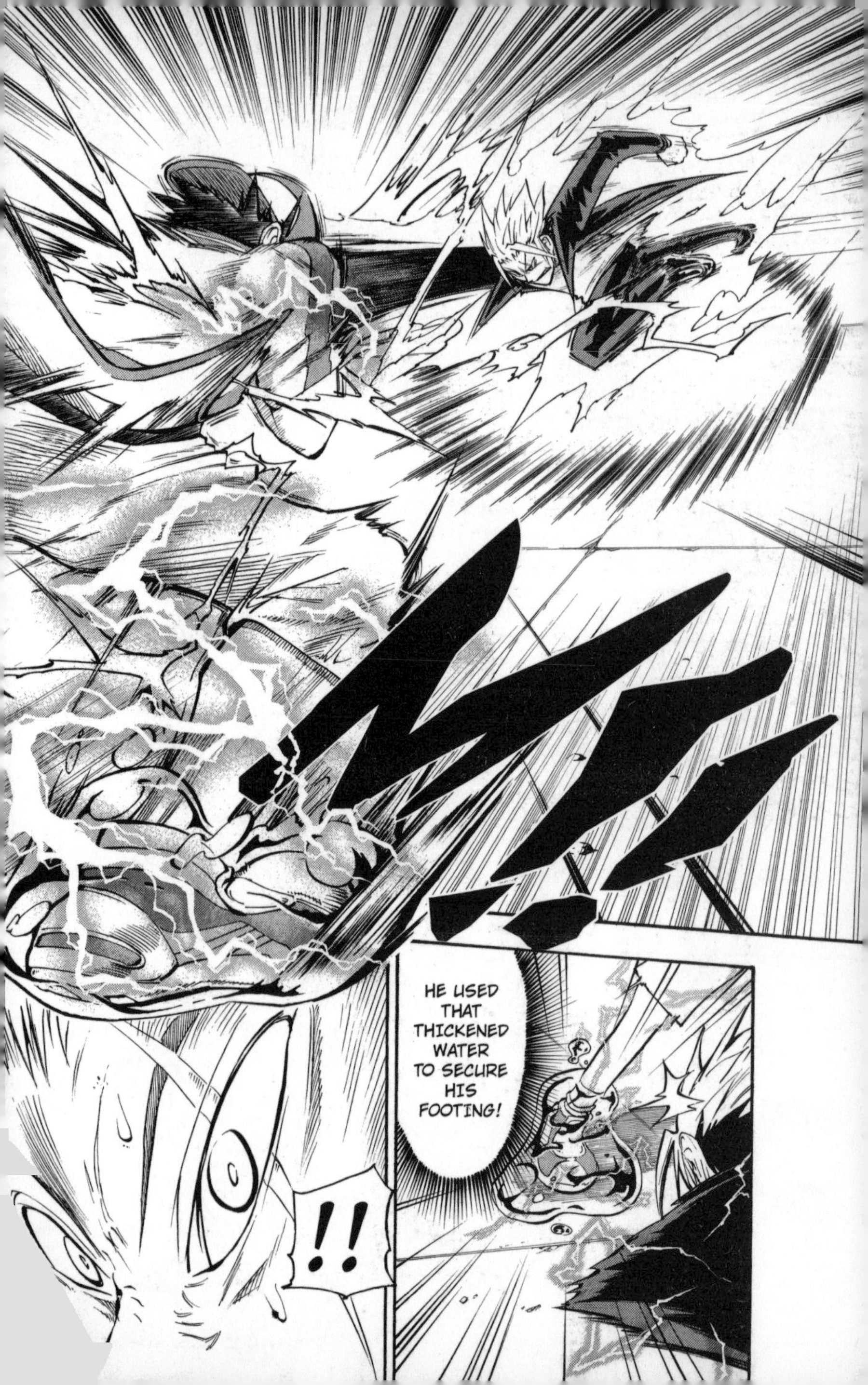
HE USED THAT THICKENED WATER TO SECURE HIS FOOTING!
!!

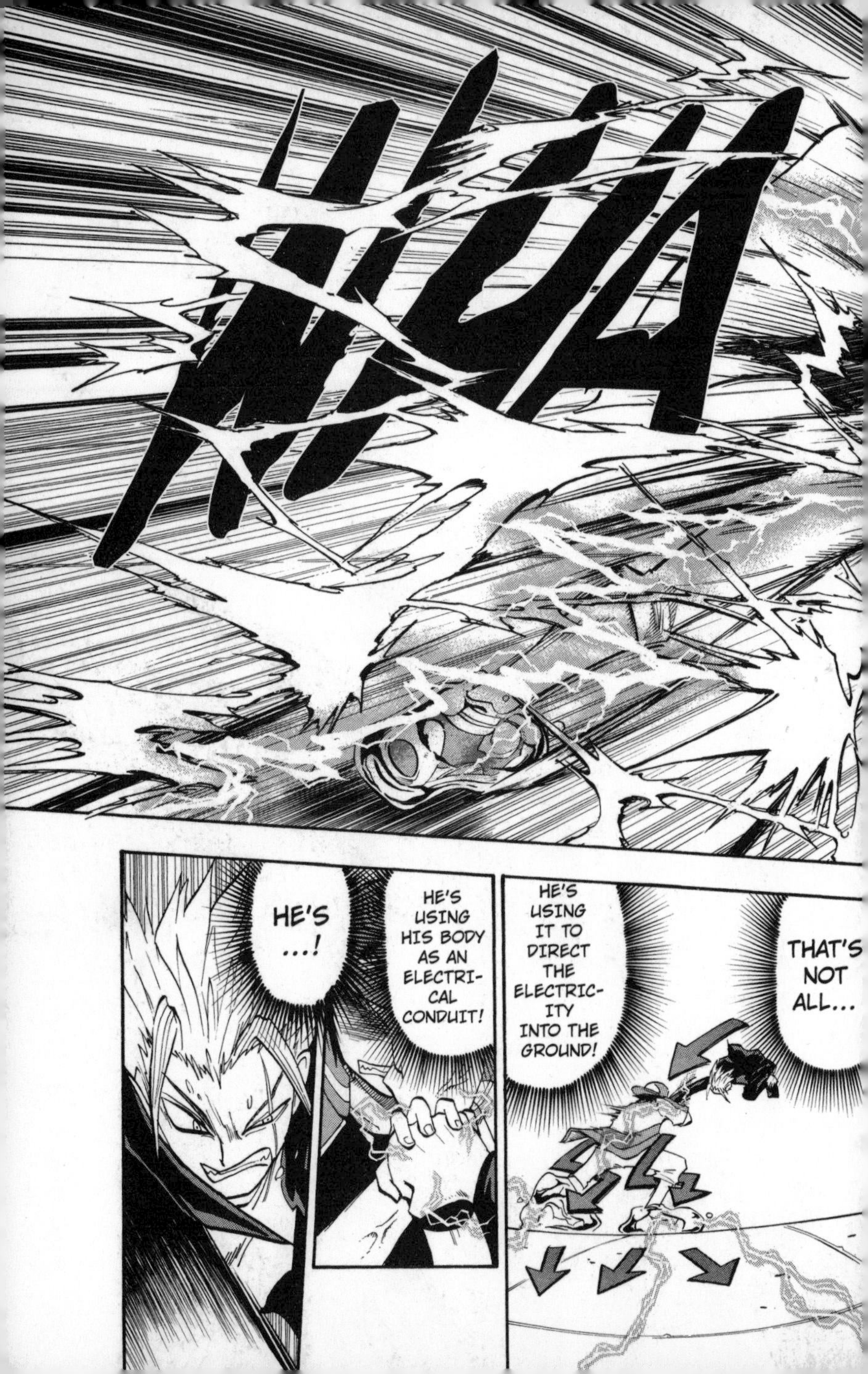
THAT'S NOT ALL...
HE'S USING IT TO DIRECT THE ELECTRIC-ITY INTO THE GROUND!
HE'S USING HIS BODY AS AN ELECTRI-CAL CONDUIT!
HE'S ...!

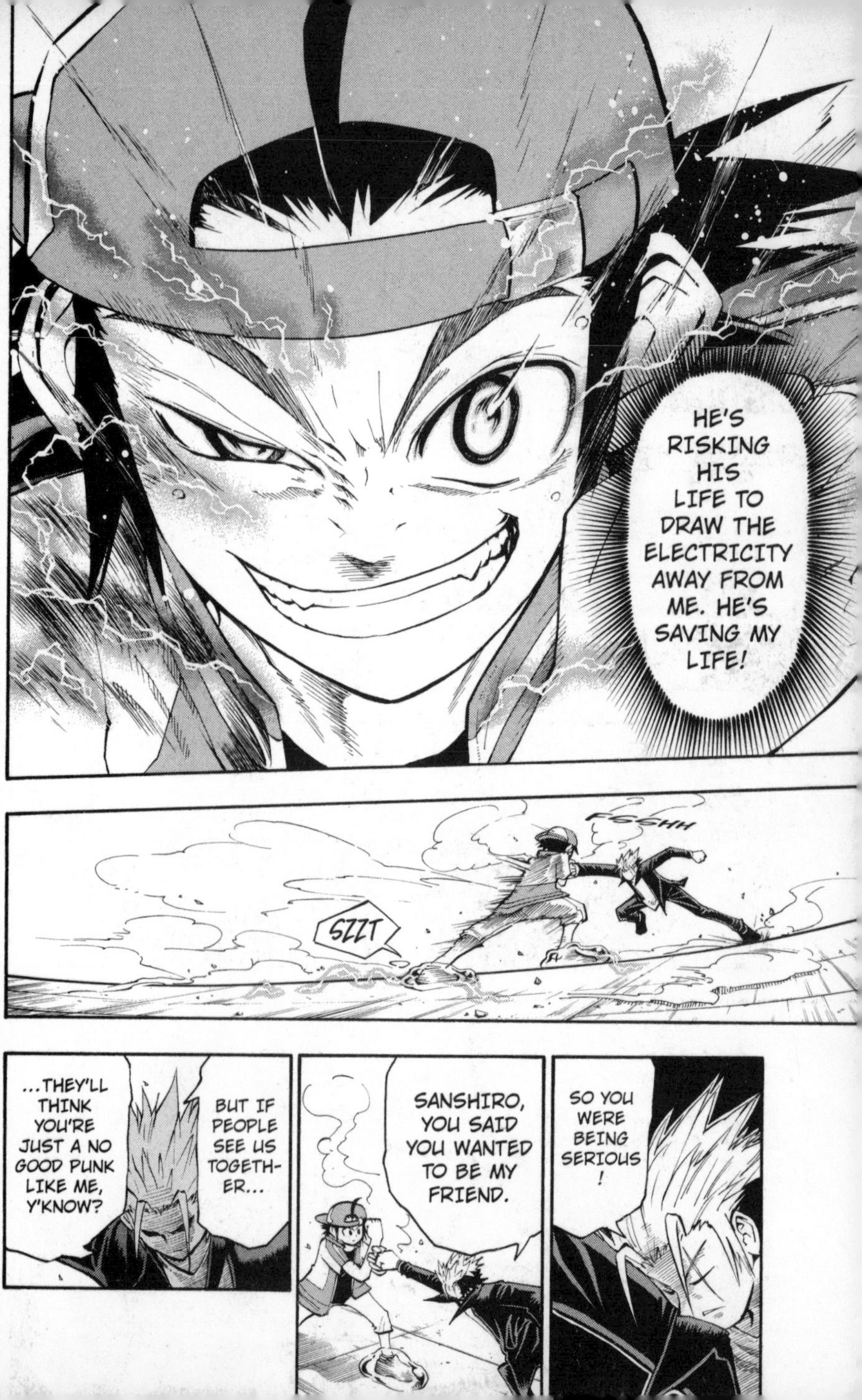
HE'S RISKING HIS LIFE TO DRAW THE ELECTRICITY AWAY FROM ME. HE'S SAVING MY LIFE!
FSSHH
SZZT
SO YOU WERE BEING SERIOUS!
SANSHIRO, YOU SAID YOU WANTED TO BE MY FRIEND.
BUT IF PEOPLE SEE US TOGETH-ER...
...THEY'LL THINK YOU'RE JUST A NO GOOD PUNK LIKE ME, Y'KNOW?

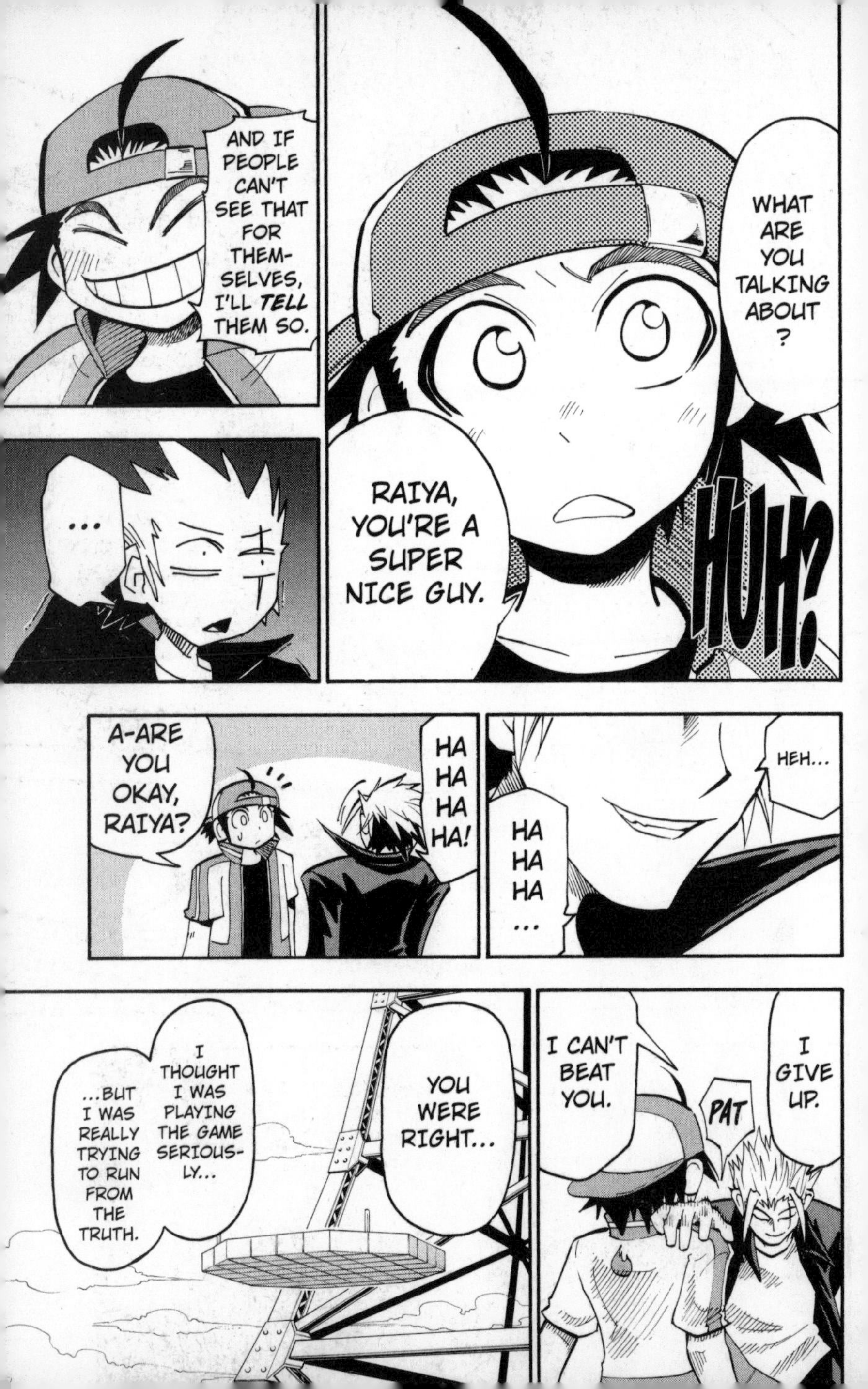
WHAT ARE YOU TALKING ABOUT?
HUH!?
RAIYA, YOU'RE A SUPER NICE GUY.
AND IF PEOPLE CAN'T SEE THAT FOR THEMSELVES, I'LL *TELL* THEM SO.
...
HEH...
HA HA HA ...
HA HA HA HA!
A-ARE YOU OKAY, RAIYA?
I GIVE UP.
PAT
I CAN'T BEAT YOU.
YOU WERE RIGHT...
I THOUGHT I WAS PLAYING THE GAME SERIOUSLY...
...BUT I WAS REALLY TRYING TO RUN FROM THE TRUTH.

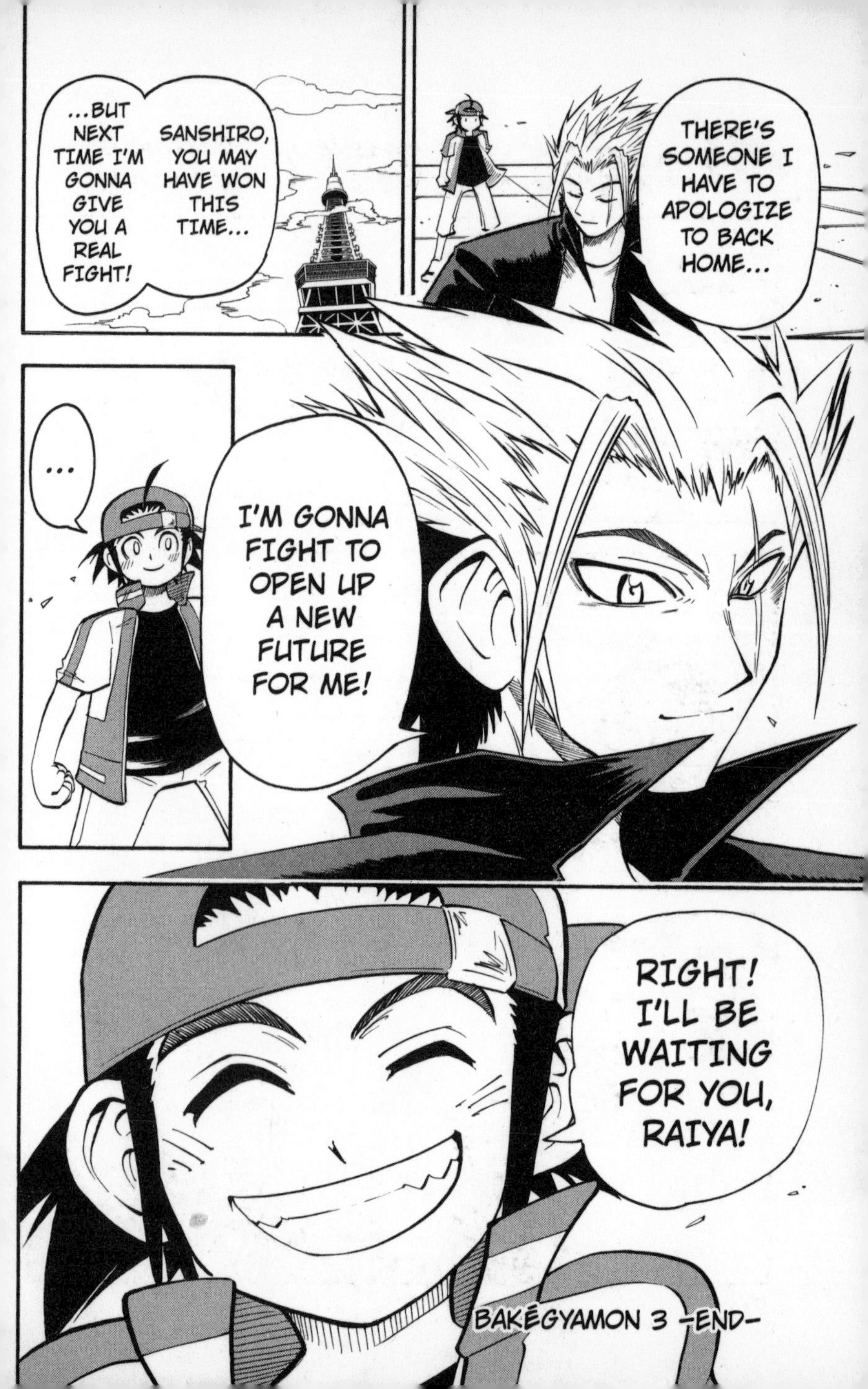
THERE'S SOMEONE I HAVE TO APOLOGIZE TO BACK HOME...
SANSHIRO, YOU MAY HAVE WON THIS TIME...
...BUT NEXT TIME I'M GONNA GIVE YOU A REAL FIGHT!
I'M GONNA FIGHT TO OPEN UP A NEW FUTURE FOR ME!
...
RIGHT! I'LL BE WAITING FOR YOU, RAIYA!
BAKĒGYAMON 3 -END-

BAKÉGYAMON DIARY 2 THE COMING OF THE ASSISTANT

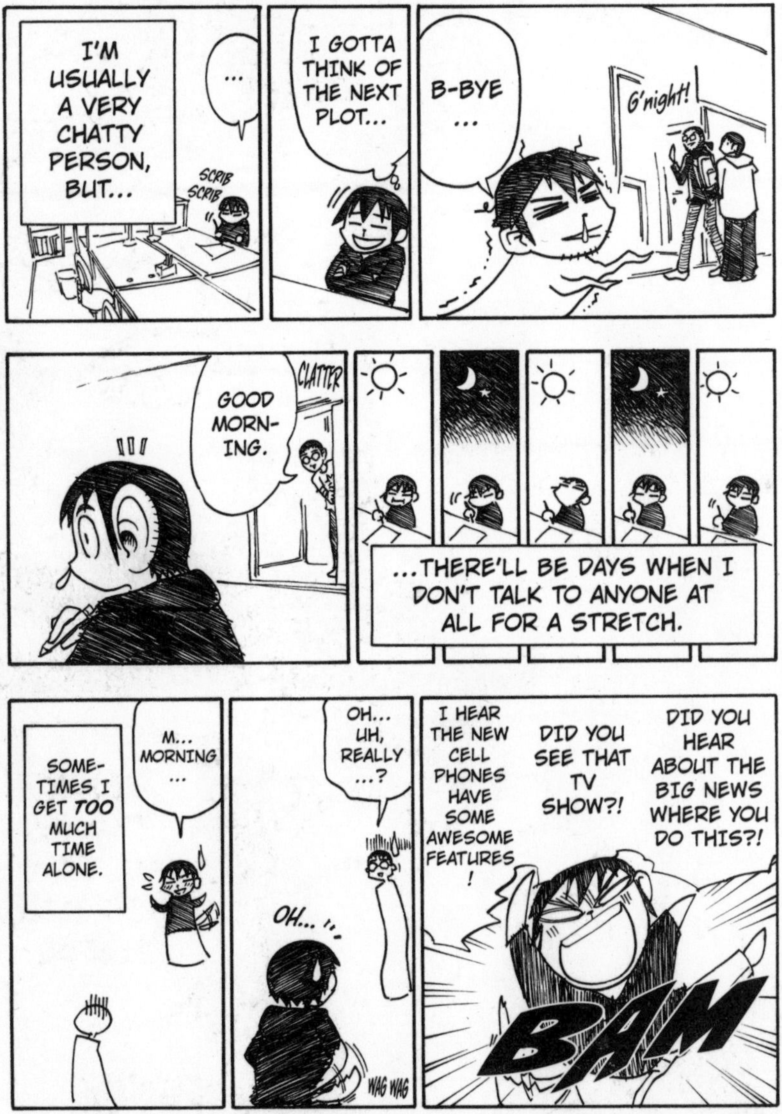
B-BYE ...
G'night!
I GOTTA THINK OF THE NEXT PLOT...
I'M USUALLY A VERY CHATTY PERSON, BUT...
...
SCRIB SCRIB
...THERE'LL BE DAYS WHEN I DON'T TALK TO ANYONE AT ALL FOR A STRETCH.
CLATTER
GOOD MORNING.
!!!
DID YOU HEAR ABOUT THE BIG NEWS WHERE YOU DO THIS?!
DID YOU SEE THAT TV SHOW?!
I HEAR THE NEW CELL PHONES HAVE SOME AWESOME FEATURES!
BAM
OH... UH, REALLY ...?
OH...
WAG WAG
M... MORNING ...
SOMETIMES I GET *TOO* MUCH TIME ALONE.

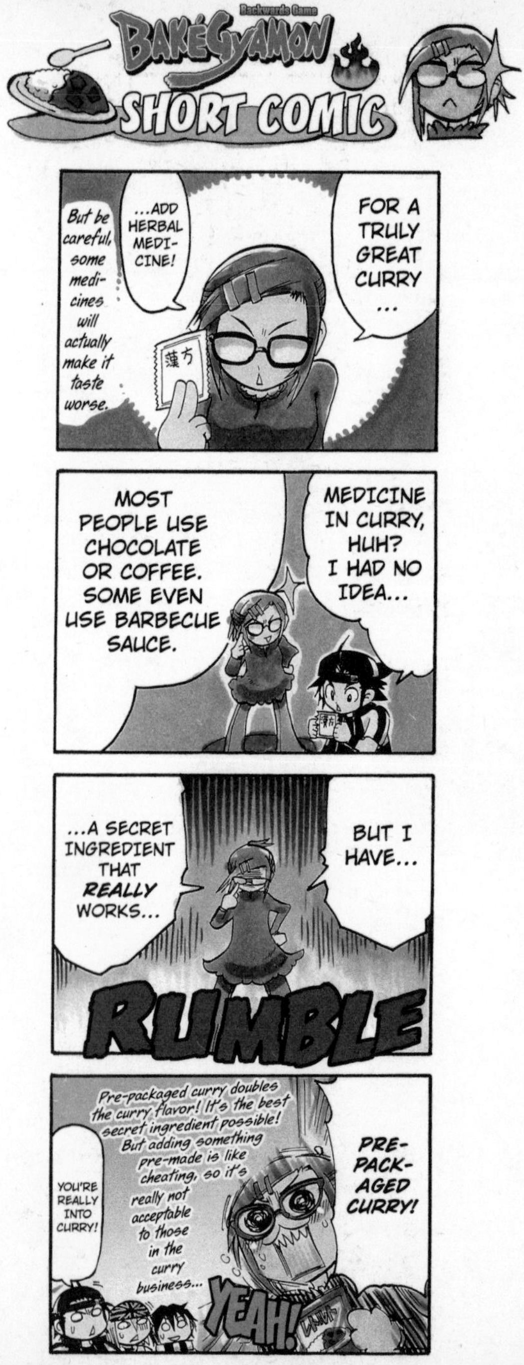
Backwards Game
BAKÉGYAMON
SHORT COMIC
FOR A TRULY GREAT CURRY...
...ADD HERBAL MEDICINE!
漢方
But be careful, some medicines will actually make it taste worse.
MEDICINE IN CURRY, HUH? I HAD NO IDEA...
MOST PEOPLE USE CHOCOLATE OR COFFEE. SOME EVEN USE BARBECUE SAUCE.
BUT I HAVE...
...A SECRET INGREDIENT THAT REALLY WORKS...
RUMBLE
PRE-PACKAGED CURRY!
Pre-packaged curry doubles the curry flavor! It's the best secret ingredient possible! But adding something pre-made is like cheating, so it's really not acceptable to those in the curry business...
YEAH!
YOU'RE REALLY INTO CURRY!

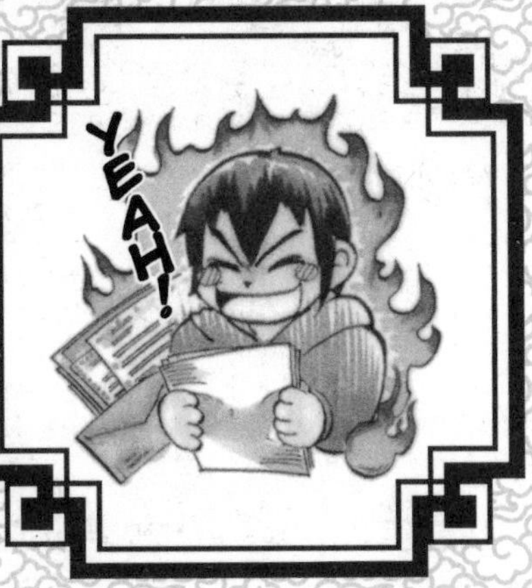
YEAH!

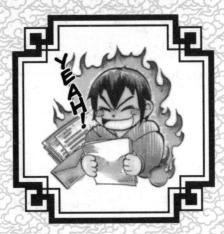

Thank you for all the fan letters! I get so excited reading them over and over again—it really gets me going!

-Mitsuhisa Tamura, 2007

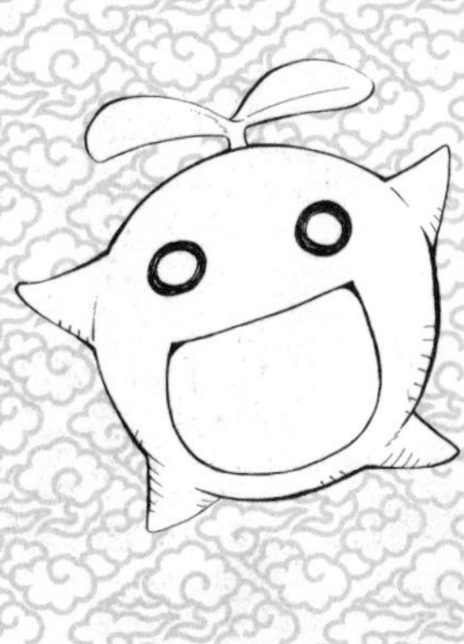

Mitsuhisa Tamura debuted in 2004 with "Comical Magical," a one-shot manga in *Shonen Sunday R*. *BakéGyamon* is his first serialized manga. His favorite foods are cutlet curry and chocolate snacks.

BakéGyamon Vol. 3
Backwards Game

The VIZ Kids Manga Edition

STORY AND ART BY MITSUHISA TAMURA
Original Concept by Kazuhiro Fujita

Translation/Labaaman, HC Language Solutions, Inc.
English Adaptation/Stan!
Touch-up Art & Lettering/Primary Graphix
Design/Sean Lee
Editor/Yuki Murashige

Editor in Chief, Books/Alvin Lu
Editor in Chief, Magazines/Marc Weidenbaum
VP, Publishing Licensing/Rika Inouye
VP, Sales & Product Marketing/Gonzalo Ferreyra
VP, Creative/Linda Espinosa
Publisher/Hyoe Narita

BAKEGYAMON 3 by Mitsuhisa TAMURA, Kazuhiro FUJITA
© 2007 Mitsuhisa TAMURA, Kazuhiro FUJITA
All rights reserved. Original Japanese edition published in 2007
by Shogakukan Inc., Tokyo.
The stories, characters and incidents mentioned in this
publication are entirely fictional.

Printed in the U.S.A.

Published by VIZ Media, LLC
P.O. Box 77010
San Francisco, CA 94107

VIZ Kids Manga Edition
10 9 8 7 6 5 4 3 2 1
First printing, August 2009

PARENTAL ADVISORY
BAKÉGYAMON is rated
A and is suitable for
readers of all ages.
ratings.viz.com

www.viz.com

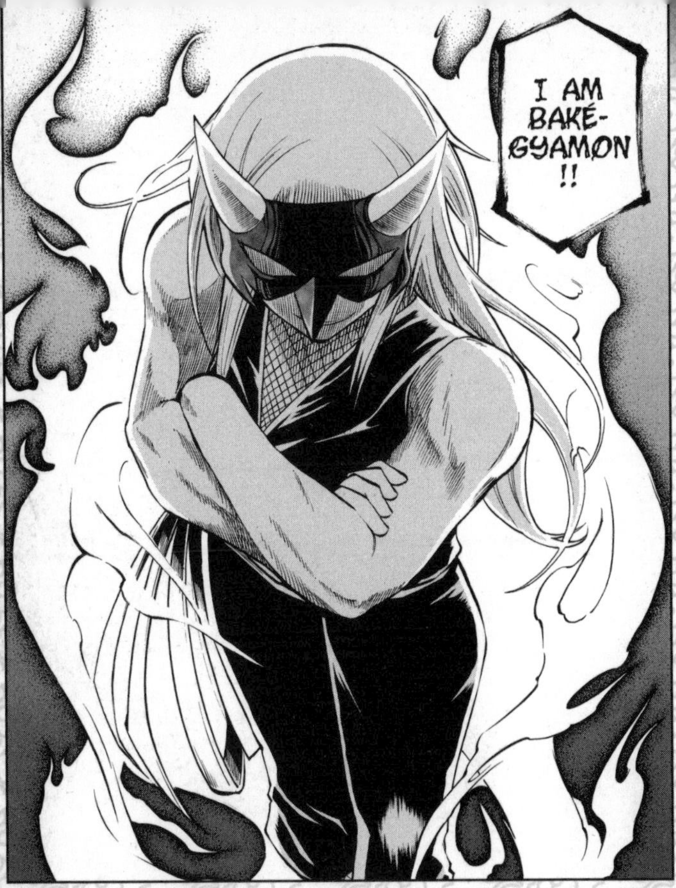
I AM BAKÉ-GYAMON !!

Coming Next Volume

Sanshiro makes it to the final four, but he's going up against some stiff competition! One challenge he'll have to face is the reigning BakéGyamon champion—an opponent so fierce he doesn't mind attacking the players too!!

Coming October 2009!

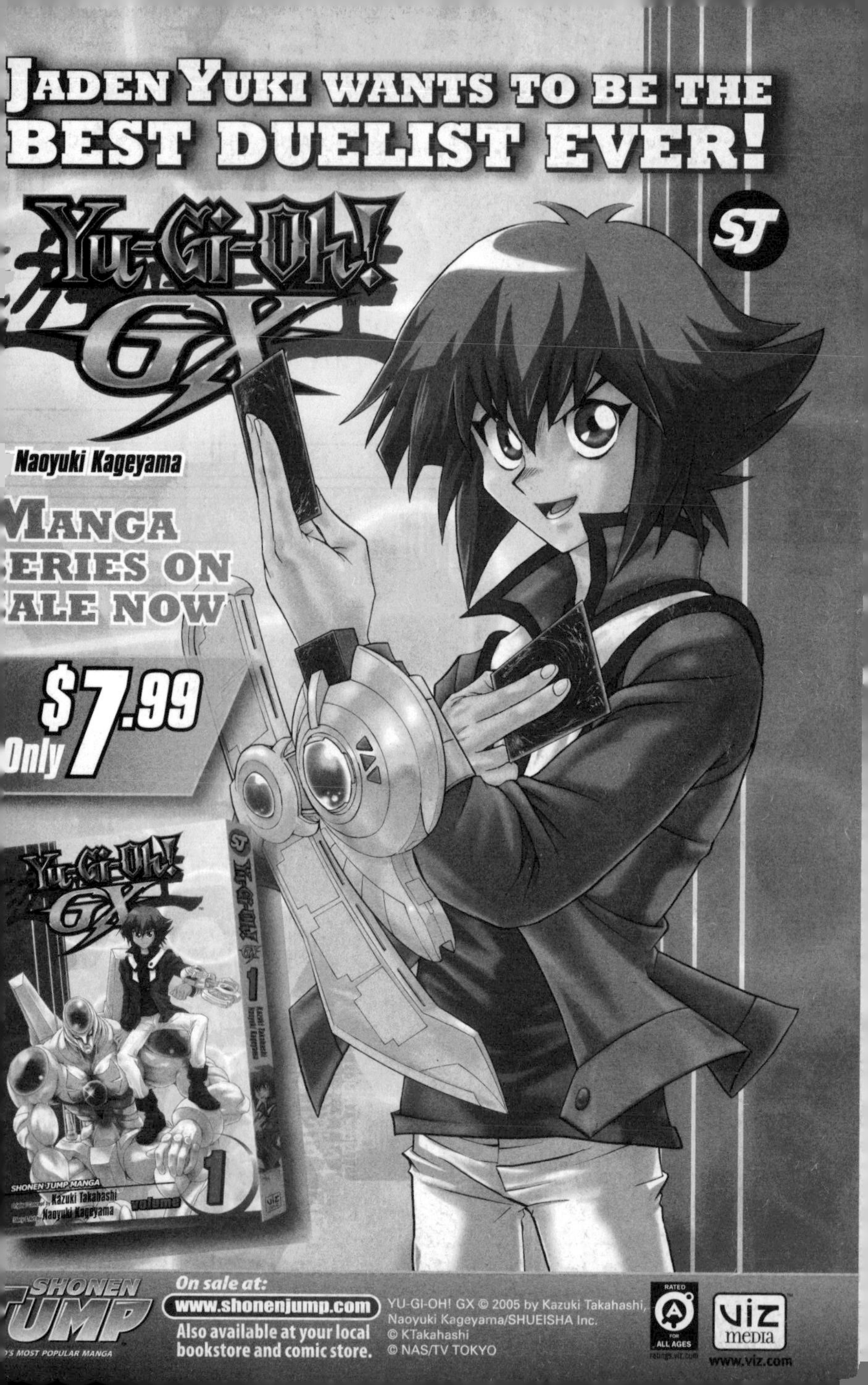
JADEN YUKI WANTS TO BE THE BEST DUELIST EVER!
SJ
YU-GI-OH! GX
Naoyuki Kageyama
MANGA
ERIES ON
ALE NOW
Only $7.99
YU-GI-OH! GX
SHONEN JUMP MANGA
Kazuki Takahashi
Naoyuki Kageyama
volume 1
SHONEN JUMP
'S MOST POPULAR MANGA
On sale at:
www.shonenjump.com
Also available at your local bookstore and comic store.
YU-GI-OH! GX © 2005 by Kazuki Takahashi, Naoyuki Kageyama/SHUEISHA Inc.
© KTakahashi
© NAS/TV TOKYO
RATED A FOR ALL AGES
viz media
www.viz.com

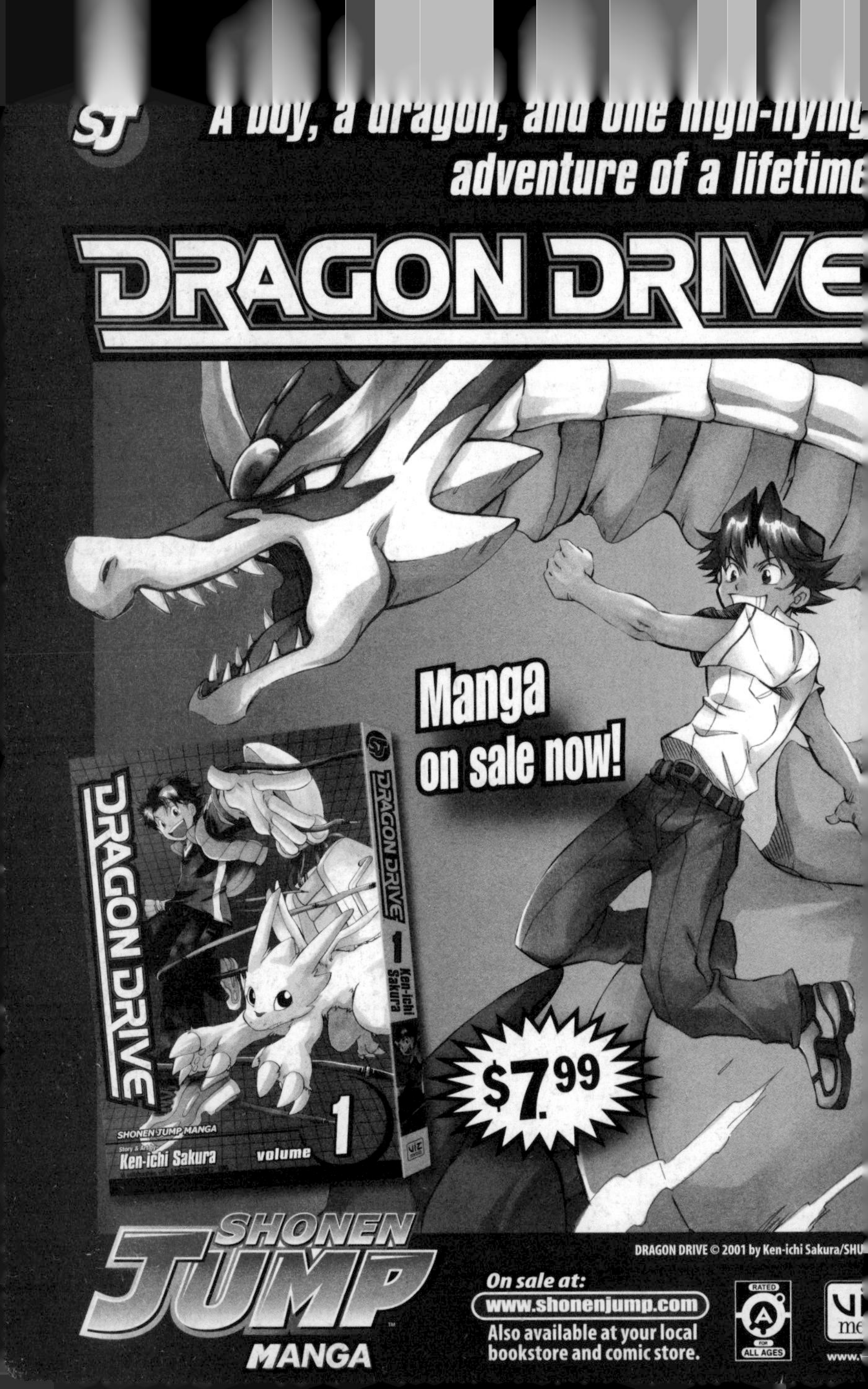
SJ
A boy, a dragon, and one high-flying
adventure of a lifetime
DRAGON DRIVE
Manga
on sale now!
DRAGON DRIVE
1
Ken-ichi Sakura
SHONEN JUMP MANGA
Story & Art by
Ken-ichi Sakura
volume 1
$7.99
SHONEN JUMP MANGA
DRAGON DRIVE © 2001 by Ken-ichi Sakura/SHU
On sale at:
www.shonenjump.com
Also available at your local
bookstore and comic store.
RATED
A
FOR
ALL AGES

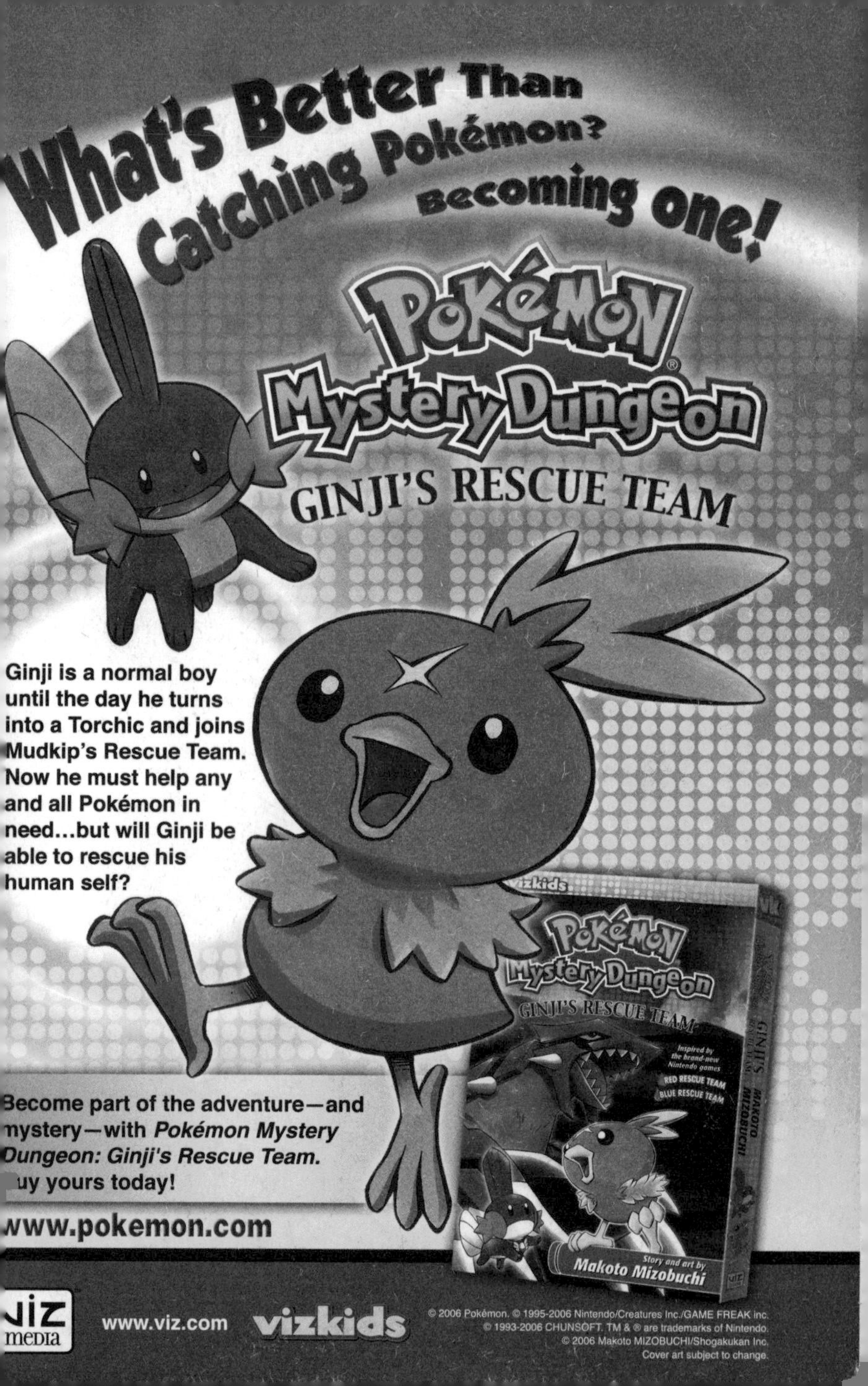
What's Better Than Catching Pokémon?
Becoming one!
Pokémon® Mystery Dungeon
GINJI'S RESCUE TEAM
Ginji is a normal boy until the day he turns into a Torchic and joins Mudkip's Rescue Team. Now he must help any and all Pokémon in need...but will Ginji be able to rescue his human self?
vizkids
Pokémon Mystery Dungeon
GINJI'S RESCUE TEAM
Inspired by the brand-new Nintendo games
RED RESCUE TEAM
BLUE RESCUE TEAM
Story and art by Makoto Mizobuchi
Become part of the adventure—and mystery—with *Pokémon Mystery Dungeon: Ginji's Rescue Team.*
uy yours today!
www.pokemon.com
viz media
www.viz.com
vizkids
© 2006 Pokémon. © 1995-2006 Nintendo/Creatures Inc./GAME FREAK inc.
© 1993-2006 CHUNSOFT. TM & ® are trademarks of Nintendo.
© 2006 Makoto MIZOBUCHI/Shogakukan Inc.
Cover art subject to change.

POKÉMON®
DIAMOND AND PEARL ADVENTURE!

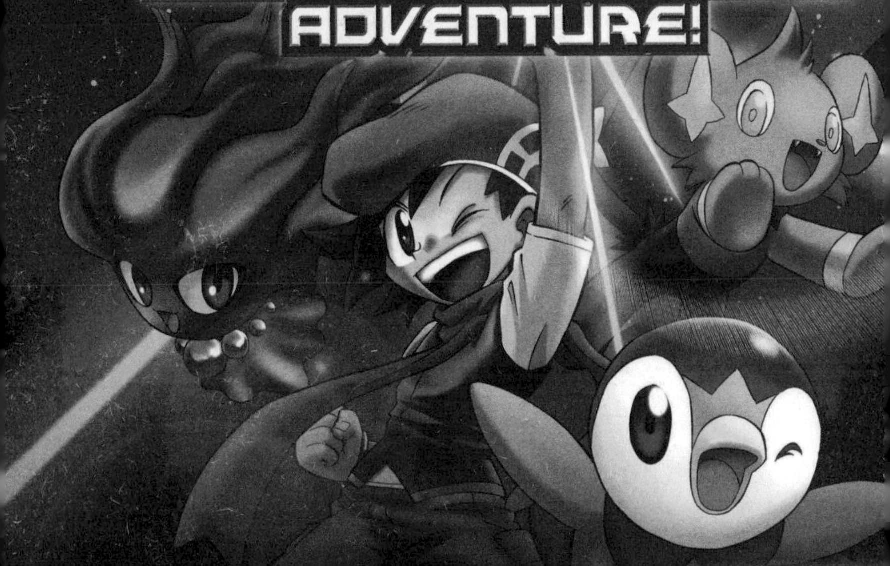

A BRAND NEW QUEST

Can a new trainer and his friends track down the legendary Pokémon Dialga before it's too late?

Find out in the *Pokémon Diamond and Pearl Adventure* manga—buy yours today!

On sale at store.viz.com
Also available at your local bookstore or comic store.

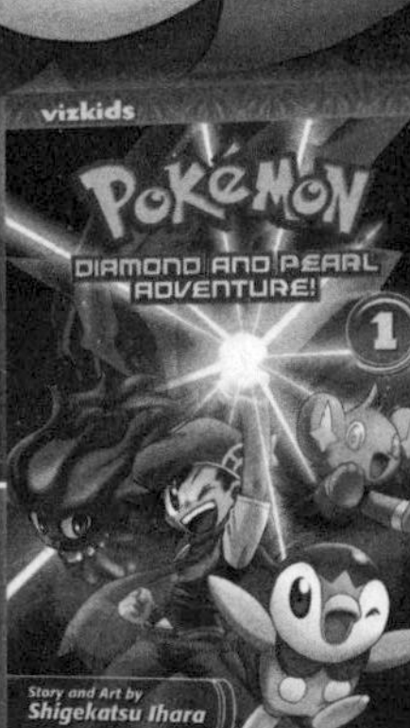
vizkids
POKÉMON
DIAMOND AND PEARL ADVENTURE!
1
Story and Art by
Shigekatsu Ihara

vizkids
www.vizkids.com

RATED A FOR ALL AGES
ratings.viz.com

www.vi

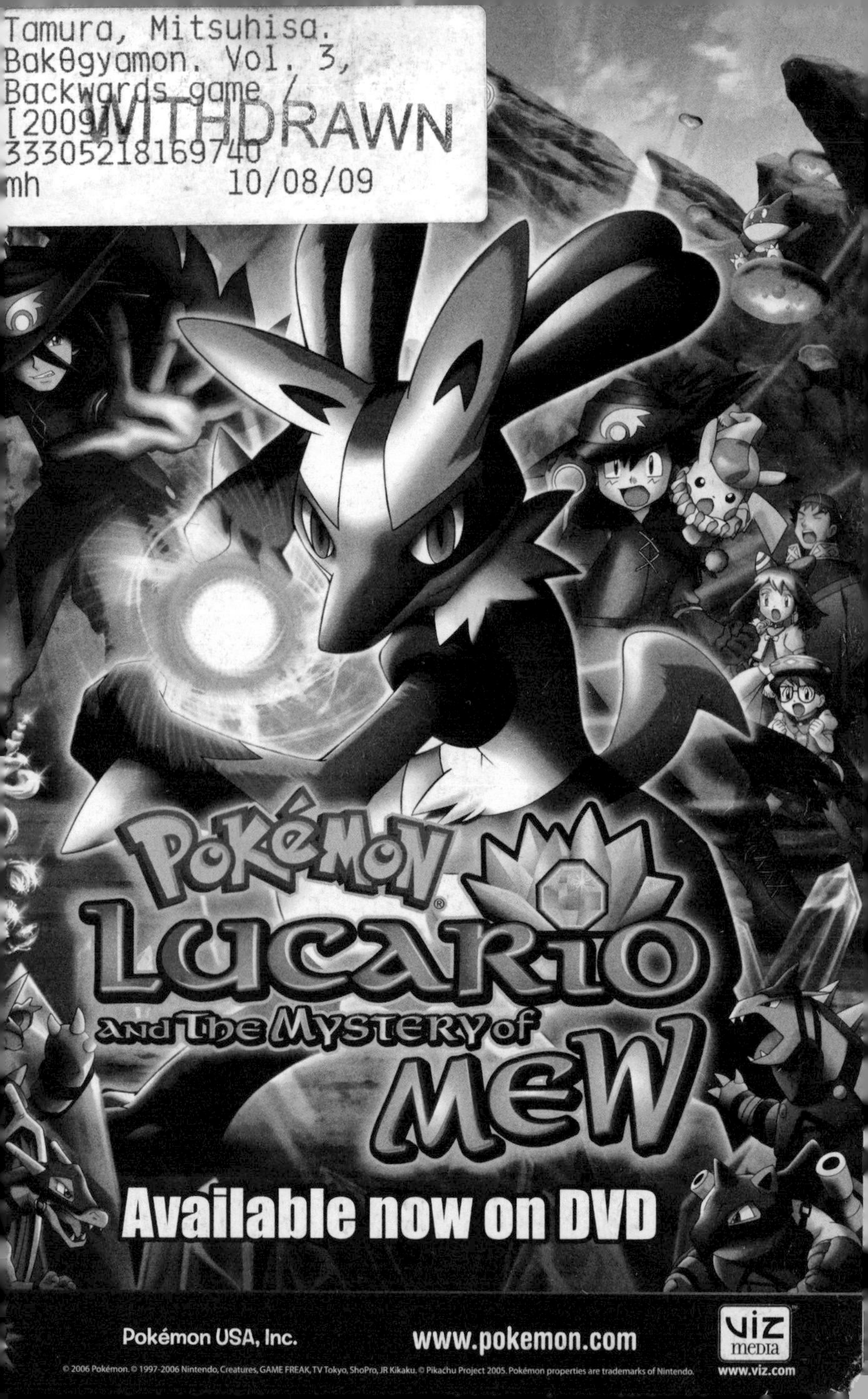
POKÉMON
LUCARIO
AND THE MYSTERY OF
MEW
Available now on DVD
Pokémon USA, Inc.
www.pokemon.com
VIZ media
© 2006 Pokémon. © 1997-2006 Nintendo, Creatures, GAME FREAK, TV Tokyo, ShoPro, JR Kikaku. © Pikachu Project 2005. Pokémon properties are trademarks of Nintendo.
www.viz.com

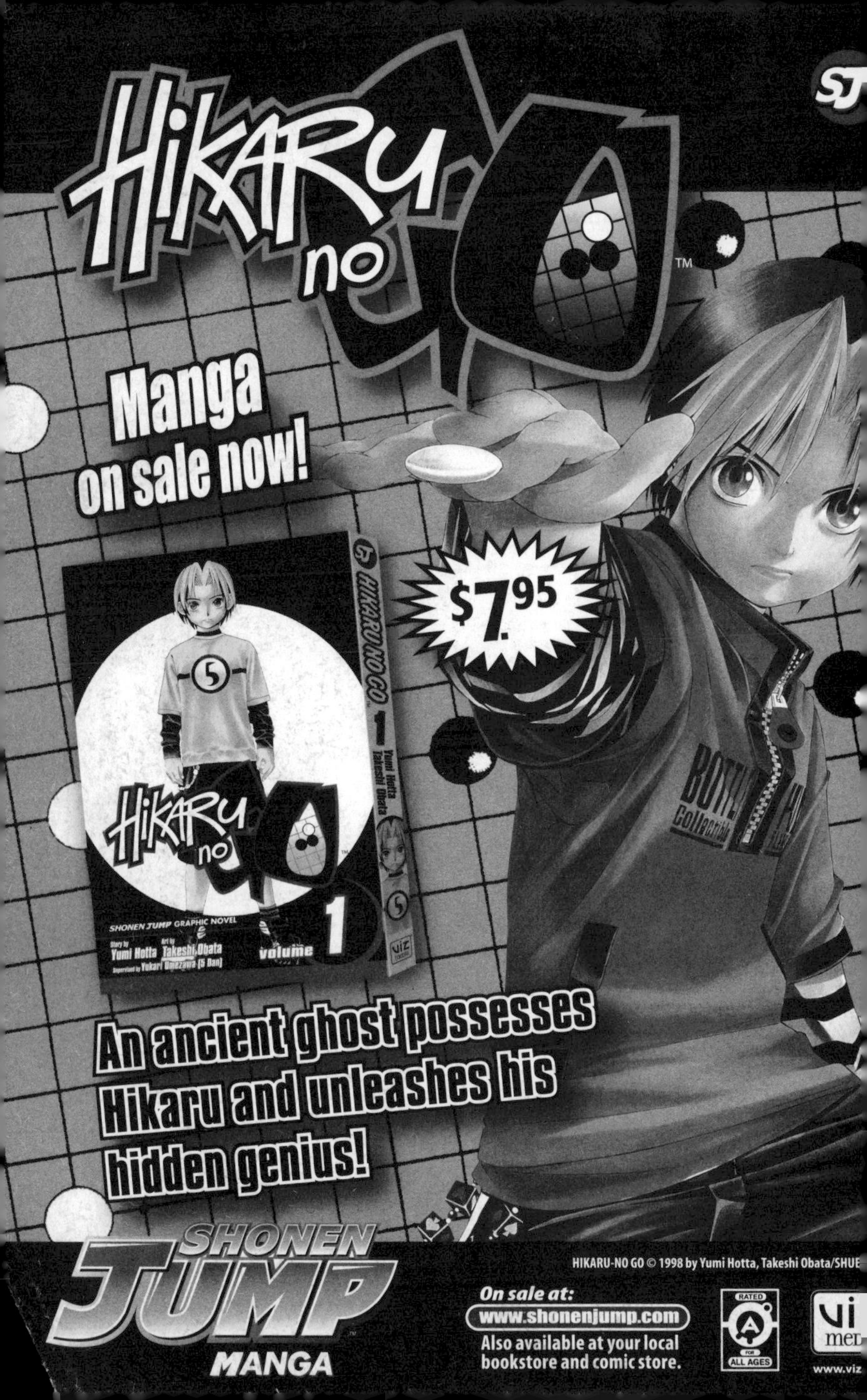
SJ
Hikaru no Go™
Manga on sale now!
$7.95
SJ HIKARU NO GO 1 Yumi Hotta Takeshi Obata
Hikaru no Go
SHONEN JUMP GRAPHIC NOVEL
Story by Yumi Hotta Art by Takeshi Obata
Supervised by Yukari Umezawa (5 Dan)
volume 1
An ancient ghost possesses Hikaru and unleashes his hidden genius!
SHONEN JUMP MANGA
HIKARU-NO GO © 1998 by Yumi Hotta, Takeshi Obata/SHUE
On sale at:
www.shonenjump.com
Also available at your local bookstore and comic store.
RATED A FOR ALL AGES
www.viz